A Themed Issue on Mathematical Inequalities, Analytic Combinatorics and Related Topics in Honor of Professor Feng Qi

A Themed Issue on Mathematical Inequalities, Analytic Combinatorics and Related Topics in Honor of Professor Feng Qi

Editors

Wei-Shih Du
Ravi P. Agarwal
Erdal Karapinar
Marko Kostić
Jian Cao

Basel • Beijing • Wuhan • Barcelona • Belgrade • Novi Sad • Cluj • Manchester

Editors

Wei-Shih Du
Department of Mathematics
National Kaohsiung Normal University
Kaohsiung
Taiwan

Ravi P. Agarwal
Department of Mathematics
Texas A&M University-Kingsville
Kingsville
United States

Erdal Karapinar
Department of Mathematics
Çankaya University
Ankara
Turkey

Marko Kostić
Faculty of Technical Sciences
University of Novi Sad
Novi Sad
Serbia

Jian Cao
School of Mathematics
Hangzhou Normal University
Hangzhou
China

Editorial Office
MDPI
St. Alban-Anlage 66
4052 Basel, Switzerland

This is a reprint of articles from the Special Issue published online in the open access journal *Axioms* (ISSN 2075-1680) (available at: www.mdpi.com/journal/axioms/special_issues/math_inequalities).

For citation purposes, cite each article independently as indicated on the article page online and as indicated below:

Lastname, A.A.; Lastname, B.B. Article Title. *Journal Name* **Year**, *Volume Number*, Page Range.

ISBN 978-3-0365-9001-1 (Hbk)
ISBN 978-3-0365-9000-4 (PDF)
doi.org/10.3390/books978-3-0365-9000-4

© 2023 by the authors. Articles in this book are Open Access and distributed under the Creative Commons Attribution (CC BY) license. The book as a whole is distributed by MDPI under the terms and conditions of the Creative Commons Attribution-NonCommercial-NoDerivs (CC BY-NC-ND) license.

Contents

About the Editors vii

Preface ix

Wei-Shih Du, Ravi Prakash Agarwal, Erdal Karapinar, Marko Kostić and Jian Cao
Preface to the Special Issue "A Themed Issue on Mathematical Inequalities, Analytic Combinatorics and Related Topics in Honor of Professor Feng Qi"
Reprinted from: *Axioms* **2023**, *12*, 846, doi:10.3390/axioms12090846 1

Ravi Prakash Agarwal, Erdal Karapinar, Marko Kostić, Jian Cao and Wei-Shih Du
A Brief Overview and Survey of the Scientific Work by Feng Qi
Reprinted from: *Axioms* **2022**, *11*, 385, doi:10.3390/axioms11080385 6

Wen-Hui Li, Peng Miao and Bai-Ni Guo
Bounds for the Neuman–Sándor Mean in Terms of the Arithmetic and Contra-Harmonic Means
Reprinted from: *Axioms* **2022**, *11*, 236, doi:10.3390/axioms11050236 33

Huan-Nan Shi and Wei-Shih Du
New Inequalities and Generalizations for Symmetric Means Induced by MajorizationTheory
Reprinted from: *Axioms* **2022**, *11*, 279, doi:10.3390/axioms11060279 45

Roberta Rui Zhou, Jean Yeh and Fuquan Ren
Context-Free Grammars for Several Triangular Arrays
Reprinted from: *Axioms* **2022**, *11*, 297, doi:10.3390/axioms11060297 53

Wen-Hui Li, Qi-Xia Shen and Bai-Ni Guo
Several Double Inequalities for Integer Powers of the Sinc and Sinhc Functions with Applications to the Neuman–Sándor Mean and the First Seiffert Mean
Reprinted from: *Axioms* **2022**, *11*, 304, doi:10.3390/axioms11070304 63

Jing-Yu Wang, Hong-Ping Yin, Wen-Long Sun and Bai-Ni Guo
Hermite–Hadamard's Integral Inequalities of (α, s)-GA- and (α, s, m)-GA-Convex Functions
Reprinted from: *Axioms* **2022**, *11*, 616, doi:10.3390/axioms11110616 75

Huan-Nan Shi, Dong-Sheng Wang and Chun-Ru Fu
Schur-Convexity of the Mean of Convex Functions for Two Variables
Reprinted from: *Axioms* **2022**, *11*, 681, doi:10.3390/axioms11120681 87

Najla Altwaijry, Silvestru Sever Dragomir and Kais Feki
Inequalities and Reverse Inequalities for the Joint A-Numerical Radius of Operators
Reprinted from: *Axioms* **2023**, *12*, 316, doi:10.3390/axioms12030316 95

Yangmin Zhong and Huaping Huang
Reinsurance Policy under Interest Force and Bankruptcy Prohibition
Reprinted from: *Axioms* **2023**, *12*, 378, doi:10.3390/axioms12040378 115

Maryam M. Abuelwafa, Ravi P. Agarwal, Safi S. Rabie and Samir H. Saker
Self-Improving Properties of Continuous and Discrete Muckenhoupt Weights: A Unified Approach
Reprinted from: *Axioms* **2023**, *12*, 505, doi:10.3390/axioms12060505 128

Zhen-Wei Li and Wen-Biao Gao
Inequalities for the Windowed Linear Canonical Transform of Complex Functions
Reprinted from: *Axioms* **2023**, *12*, 554, doi:10.3390/axioms12060554 150

Tao Zhang and Alatancang Chen
Some New Estimates of Hermite–Hadamard Inequality with Application
Reprinted from: *Axioms* **2023**, *12*, 688, doi:10.3390/axioms12070688 . . . . **160**

About the Editors

Wei-Shih Du

Wei-Shih Du is a Full Professor of Mathematics in the Department of Mathematics, National Kaohsiung Normal University, Kaohsiung 82444, Taiwan. His main research interests include nonlinear analysis and its applications, fixed point theory and its applications, variational principles and inequalities, iterative methods for nonlinear mappings, optimization theory, equilibrium problems, and fractional calculus theory.

Ravi P. Agarwal

Ravi Prakash Agarwal is a Full Professor of Mathematics in the Department of Mathematics, Texas A&M University—Kingsville, Kingsville, TX 78363-8202, USA. His main research interests include nonlinear analysis, differential and difference equations, fixed point theory, and general inequalities.

Erdal Karapinar

Erdal Karapinar is a Full Professor of Mathematics in the Department of Mathematics, Çankaya University, Etimesgut, Ankara 06790, Turkey. His main research interests include functional analysis, operator theory, linear topological invariants, fixed point theory, and best proximity.

Marko Kostić

Marko Kostić is a Full Professor of Mathematics in the Faculty of Technical Sciences, University of Novi Sad, Trg D. Obradovića 6, 21125 Novi Sad, Serbia. His main research interests include abstract Volterra integro-differential equations, abstract fractional differential equations, topological dynamics of linear operators, and abstract PDEs.

Jian Cao

Jian Cao is a Full Professor of Mathematics in the School of Mathematics, Hangzhou Normal University, Hangzhou 311121, China. His main research interests include mathematical inequalities and means, analytic combinatorics, q-series, q-difference equations, generating functions, and fractional q-calculus.

Preface

This Special Issue of Axioms pays tribute to Professor Feng Qi's significant contributions and provides some important recent advances in mathematics. It comprises original, creative, and high-quality research papers that inspire advances in mathematical inequalities, mathematical means, the theory of special functions, analytic combinatorics, the analytic number theory, optimization, the convex analysis of functions, the matrix theory, and their applications.

Our five Guest Editors have exerted our best efforts to ensure the success of this Special Issue, and we believe our efforts will be rewarded. Our Guest Editors organized a comprehensive review process for each submission based on the journal's policy, instructions, and guidelines. We received 35 submissions and, after a comprehensive peer-review process, only 12 high-quality articles were accepted for publication (the acceptance rate is over 34%). The accepted papers can be classified according to the following seven schemes:

(1) Mathematical inequalities and applications;
(2) Mathematical means and applications;
(3) Matrix theory;
(4) Convex analysis of functions;
(5) Special functions and applications;
(6) Combinatorial number theory;
(7) Optimization.

We hope that interested researchers and practitioners will be inspired by this Special Issue and find it valuable to their own research. This Special Issue has highlighted important issues and raised several new problems in these research areas. We would like to heartily thank the Editorial team and the reviewers of *Axioms*, particularly the Editor-in-Chief, Professor Humberto Bustince, and the Assistant Editor, Luna Shen, for their invaluable support and kind help throughout the editing process.

Wei-Shih Du, Ravi P. Agarwal, Erdal Karapinar, Marko Kostić, and Jian Cao
Editors

Editorial

Preface to the Special Issue "A Themed Issue on Mathematical Inequalities, Analytic Combinatorics and Related Topics in Honor of Professor Feng Qi"

Wei-Shih Du [1,*,†], Ravi Prakash Agarwal [2], Erdal Karapinar [3,4], Marko Kostić [5] and Jian Cao [6]

1. Department of Mathematics, National Kaohsiung Normal University, Kaohsiung 82444, Taiwan
2. Department of Mathematics, Texas A&M University-Kingsville, Kingsville, TX 78363-8202, USA; ravi.agarwal@tamuk.edu
3. Department of Mathematics, Çankaya University, Etimesgut, Ankara 06790, Turkey; erdalkarapinar@yahoo.com
4. Department of Medical Research, China Medical University Hospital, China Medical University, Taichung 40402, Taiwan
5. Faculty of Technical Sciences, University of Novi Sad, Trg D. Obradovića 6, 21125 Novi Sad, Serbia; marco.s@verat.net
6. School of Mathematics, Hangzhou Normal University, Hangzhou 311121, China; 21caojian@163.com
* Correspondence: wsdu@mail.nknu.edu.tw
† Lead Guest Editor.

This Special Issue of the journal *Axioms* pays tribute to Professor Feng Qi's significant contributions and provides some important recent advances in mathematics. It comprises original, creative, and high-quality research papers that inspire advances in mathematical inequalities, mathematical means, the theory of special functions, analytic combinatorics, the analytic number theory, optimization, the convex analysis of functions, the matrix theory, and their applications. For more detailed information, please visit the website https://www.mdpi.com/journal/axioms/special_issues/math_inequalities (accessed on 22 April 2022).

Professor Feng Qi

Professor Feng Qi earned his Ph.D. degree, supervised by Professor Sen-Lin Xu (born in December 1941, passed away on 2 October 2022 in Beijing), from the University of Science and Technology of China in 1999. He received his master's degree, supervised by Professor Yi-Pei Chen (passed away), from Xiamen University in 1989. He graduated with his bachelor's degree from Henan University in 1986.

He is now a full-time professor at Henan Polytechnic University and Tiangong University, as well as an adjunct professor at Hulunbuir University, China. Additionally, he was an adjunct professor at Henan Normal University, Henan University, and Inner Mongolia University for Nationalities in China, and Victoria University in Australia. In 2005, he was promoted as the Specially Appointed Professor of the Education Committee of Henan Province, China.

Professor Feng Qi won the Award of Science and Technology from the Inner Mongolia Autonomous Region in 2017 and received the Certificate of High-level Talent in Henan Province in 2020. He also won several other academic awards and scientific funds from Henan Province, Inner Mongolia Autonomous Region, and Shaanxi Province in China.

He was the first former Head of the Department of Applied Mathematics and Informatics (current School of Mathematics and Informatics) at Henan Polytechnic University.

He has published over 691 research papers (accessed on 9 August 2023), affiliated to eight universities (accessed on 9 August 2023) (Henan Polytechnic University, Hulunbuir University, Tiangong University (357), Inner Mongolia Minzu University (199), Henan University (13), Henan Normal University (11), University of Science and Technology of China (20), and University of Electronic Science and Technology of China (8)), in over 225 journals, conference proceedings, Special Issues, books, and collections. Since 2012, Professor Feng Qi and many teachers and graduates at Inner Mongolia Minzu University jointly published 127 papers (accessed on 9 August 2023), in which 72 papers were abstracted and indexed by the Web of Science Core Collection and five papers were abstracted and indexed by the Engineering Village. His Erdös number is 3 (accessed on 9 August 2023).

From 2014 to 2023, he was named as one of the Most (Highly) Cited Chinese Researchers by the Elsevier-Shanghai Ranking for nine consecutive years. Since 2002, there have been over 91 papers or preprints (accessed on 8 August 2023) with titles that contain one of the following names: "Feng Qi", "F. Qi", or "Qi". His name was mentioned by Mourad Ismail in [1]. Since 2006, over 40 papers or preprints (accessed on 8 August 2023) have been published by other mathematicians around the world, with titles containing the notions of "logarithmically completely (absolutely) monotonic function" or its analogs. These notions were created or invented by Professor Feng Qi and his coauthors in 2004 and 2009, respectively. Many works published by Professor Feng Qi and his coauthors have been collected in the famous databases "The On-Line Encyclopedia of Integer Sequences" (accessed on 9 August 2023) and "Wikipedia, The Free Encyclopedia" (accessed on 9 August 2023), in monographs and handbooks [2–9], and in a Chinese textbook published by Beijing Normal University Press in 2017 for middle school students.

Professor Feng Qi delivered academic speeches (invited, keynote, and plenary) at international academic conferences, was financially supported to attend international academic conferences, was invited to be a member of the Scientific Committee, the International Advisory Committee, the International Committee, the International Organizing Committee, the International Advisory Board, the International Scientific Committee, and the Scientific Program Committee of international academic conferences, and was invited and financially supported to be a visiting professor in Australia, Denmark, Hong Kong, India, North Macedonia, Pakistan, Romania, South Korea, Taiwan, Turkey, and the USA over 25 times. He also attended domestic academic conferences and was invited and financially supported to deliver speeches over 30 times.

He is serving on the editorial boards for over 21 international mathematical journals (accessed on 8 August 2023). Moreover, he was appointed to the editorial boards for over 43 international mathematical journals (accessed on 8 August 2023). He won the top reviewer in Mathematics powered by Publons (accessed on 8 August 2023) twice: the Top Peer Reviewer 2019 and the Certified Sentinel of Science Award Recipient 2016 (The Top 10 Per Cent of Reviewers).

Since 1990, he has taught many courses for hundreds of thousands of undergraduate and graduate students, some of which include the following:

Analytic Geometry	Linear Programming
Calculus	Mathematical Inequalities and Applications
Differential Geometry	Probability and Statistics
Equations of Mathematical Physics	Real Analysis
Functions of Single Complex Variable	Real and Complex Analysis
Higher Mathematics	Selected Topics of Modern Mathematics
Integral Transforms	Special Functions and Applications
Linear Algebra	Typesetting in Mathematics ($\mathcal{A}_{\mathcal{M}}\mathcal{S}$-LaTeX)

Along with teaching, he has also supervised two graduates (accessed on 8 August 2023) (Jian Cao and Da-Wei Niu) at Henan Polytechnic University and six graduates (accessed on 8 August 2023) (Xiao-Jing Zhang, Wen-Hui Li, Miao-Miao Zheng, Fang-Fang Liu, Xiao-Ting Shi, and Jing-Lin Wang) at Tiangong University.

Professor Feng Qi's main academic research interests (accessed on 9 August 2023) included, but were not limited to, the following:

Analytic Combinatorics	Differential Geometry
Analytic Number Theory	Integral Transforms
Approximation Theory	Logarithmically Complete Monotonicity
Asymptotic Analysis	Mathematical Inequalities and Applications
Classical Mathematical Analysis	Mathematical Means and Applications
Completely Monotonic Degrees	Theory of Convex Functions
Complex Functions of One Variable	Theory of Special Functions

Our five Guest Editors have done our best to ensure the success of this Special Issue, and we believe our efforts will be rewarded. Our Guest Editors organized a comprehensive review process for each submission basing on the journal's policy, instructions, and guidelines. We have received 35 submissions and, after a comprehensive peer review process, only 12 high-quality articles have been accepted for publication (the acceptance rate is over 34%). The list of published contributions is as follows:

i.   Abuelwafa, M. M.; Agarwal, R. P.; Rabie, S. S.; Saker, S. H. Self-improving properties of continuous and discrete Muckenhoupt weights: a unified approach. *Axioms* **2023**, *12*, 505. https://doi.org/10.3390/axioms12060505;

ii. Agarwal, R. P.; Karapinar, E.; Kostić, M.; Cao, J.; Du, W.-S. A brief overview and survey of the scientific work by Feng Qi. *Axioms* **2022**, *11*, 385. https://doi.org/10.3390/axioms11080385;

iii. Altwaijry, N.; Dragomir, S. S.; Feki, K. Inequalities and reverse inequalities for the joint A-numerical radius of operators. *Axioms* **2023**, *12*, 316. https://doi.org/10.3390/axioms12030316;

iv. Li, Z.-W.; Gao, W.-B. Inequalities for the windowed linear canonical transform of complex functions. *Axioms* **2023**, *12*, 554. https://doi.org/10.3390/axioms12060554;

v.   Li, W.-H.; Miao, P.; Guo, B.-N. Bounds for the Neuman–Sándor mean in terms of the arithmetic and contra-harmonic means. *Axioms* **2022**, *11*, 236. https://doi.org/10.3390/axioms11050236;

vi. Li, W.-H.; Shen, Q.-X.; Guo, B.-N. Several double inequalities for integer powers of the sinc and sinhc functions with applications to the Neuman–Sándor mean and the first Seiffert mean. *Axioms* **2022**, *11*, 304. https://doi.org/10.3390/axioms11070304;

vii. Shi, H.-N.; Du, W.-S. New Inequalities and generalizations for symmetric means induced by majorization theory. *Axioms* **2022**, *11*, 279. https://doi.org/10.3390/axioms11060279;

viii. Shi, H.-N.; Wang, D.-S.; Fu, C.-R. Schur-convexity of the mean of convex functions for two variables. *Axioms* **2022**, *11*, 681. https://doi.org/10.3390/axioms11120681;

ix. Wang, J.-Y.; Yin, H.-P.; Sun, W.-L.; Guo, B.-N. Hermite–Hadamard's integral inequalities of (α, s)-GA- and (α, s, m)-GA-convex functions. *Axioms* **2022**, *11*, 616. https://doi.org/10.3390/axioms11110616;

x. Zhang, T.; Chen, A. Some new estimates of Hermite–Hadamard inequality with application. *Axioms* **2023**, *12*, 688. https://doi.org/10.3390/axioms12070688;
xi. Zhong, Y.; Huang, H. Reinsurance policy under interest force and bankruptcy prohibition. *Axioms* **2023**, *12*, 378. https://doi.org/10.3390/axioms12040378;
xii. Zhou, R. R.; Yeh, J.; Ren, F. Context-free grammars for several triangular arrays. *Axioms* **2022**, *11*, 297. https://doi.org/10.3390/axioms11060297.

The 30 authors of these 12 papers are as follows:

Maryam M. Abuelwafa (see i)
Najla Altwaijry (see iii)
Alatancang Chen (see x)
Wei-Shih Du (see ii, vii)
Chun-Ru Fu (see viii)
Bai-Ni Guo (see v, vi, ix)
Erdal Karapinar (see ii)
Wen-Hui Li (see v, vi)
Peng Miao (see v)
Fuquan Ren (see xii)
Qi-Xia Shen (see vi)
Wen-Long Sun (see ix)
Jing-Yu Wang (see ix)
Hong-Ping Yin (see ix)
Yangmin Zhong (see xi)

Ravi Prakash Agarwal (see i, ii)
Jian Cao (see ii)
Silvestru Sever Dragomir (see iii)
Kais Feki (see iii)
Wen-Biao Gao (see iv)
Huaping Huang (see xi)
Marko Kostić (see ii)
Zhen-Wei Li (see iv)
Safi S. Rabie (see i)
Samir H. Saker (see i)
Huan-Nan Shi (see vii, viii)
Dong-Sheng Wang (see viii)
Jean Yeh (see xii)
Tao Zhang (see x)
Roberta Rui Zhou (see xii)

The accepted papers can be classified according to the following seven schemes:

(1) Mathematical inequalities and applications (see i, ii, iii, iv, v, vi, vii, viii, ix, x);
(2) Mathematical means and applications (see ii, v, vi, viii, ix, x);
(3) Matrix theory (see ii);
(4) Convex analysis of functions (see ii, viii, ix, x);
(5) Special functions and applications (see ii, v, vi);
(6) Combinatorial number theory (see ii, xii);
(7) Optimization (see ii, vii, xi).

As of 9 August 2023, two of these twelve papers have been cited, as shown in the following table.

Published contributions	Times cited from Crossref	Times cited from Scopus	Times cited from Web of Science
v	2	3	2
vi	1	1	1

We hope that interested researchers and practitioners will be inspired by this Special Issue and find it valuable to their own research. This Special Issue has highlighted important issues and raised several new problems in these research areas. We would like to heartily thank the editorial team and the reviewers of the journal *Axioms*, particularly the Editor-in-Chief, Professor Humberto Bustince, and the Assistant Editor, Luna Shen, for their invaluable support and kind help throughout the editing process.

Author Contributions: Conceptualization, W.-S.D., R.P.A., E.K., M.K. and J.C.; methodology, W.-S.D., R.P.A., E.K., M.K. and J.C.; software, W.-S.D.; validation, W.-S.D., R.P.A., E.K., M.K. and J.C.; formal analysis, W.-S.D., R.P.A., E.K., M.K. and J.C.; investigation, W.-S.D., R.P.A., E.K., M.K. and J.C.; writing—original draft preparation, W.-S.D.; writing—review and editing, W.-S.D., R.P.A., E.K., M.K. and J.C.; visualization, W.-S.D., R.P.A., E.K., M.K. and J.C.; supervision, W.-S.D., R.P.A., E.K., M.K. and J.C.; project administration, W.-S.D., R.P.A., E.K., M.K. and J.C. All authors have read and agreed to the published version of the manuscript.

Funding: Wei-Shih Du is partially supported by Grant No. NSTC 112-2115-M-017-002 of the National Science and Technology Council of the Republic of China. Marko Kostić is partially supported by grant 451-03-68/2020/14/200156 of Ministry of Science and Technological Development, Republic of Serbia. Jian Cao is partially supported by the Zhejiang Provincial Natural Science Foundation of China (Grant No. LY21A010019).

Institutional Review Board Statement: Not applicable.

Informed Consent Statement: Not applicable.

Data Availability Statement: Not applicable.

Acknowledgments: The authors wish to express their hearty thanks to the family of Professor Feng Qi for supplying his photograph and giving us permission to use it in this manuscript.

Conflicts of Interest: The authors declare no conflict of interest.

References

1. Liu, T.-P.; Wu, D.-C.; Lee, J.-H.; Chen, L.-C. Interview with Prof. Mourad Ismail. *Math Media* **2013**, *37*, 3–12. Available online: https://web.math.sinica.edu.tw/mathmedia/interview18_e.jsp?mID=37301 (accessed on 9 August 2023).
2. Bernstein, D.S. *Scalar, Vector, and Matrix Mathematics: Theory, Facts, and Formulas*, Revised and Expanded Edition; Princeton University Press: Princeton, NJ, USA, 2018. Available online: https://press.princeton.edu/books/hardcover/9780691151205/scalar-vector-and-matrix-mathematics (accessed on 9 August 2023).
3. Bernstein, D.S. *Matrix Mathematics: Theory, Facts, and Formulas*, 2nd ed.; Princeton University Press: Princeton, NJ, USA, 2009. [CrossRef]
4. Bullen, P.S. *Dictionary of Inequalities*, 2nd ed.; Monographs and Research Notes in Mathematics; CRC Press: Boca Raton, FL, USA, 2015. [CrossRef]
5. Bullen, P.S. *Handbook of Means and Their Inequalities*; Revised from the 1988 Original [P. S. Bullen, D. S. Mitrinović and P. M. Vasić, Means and Their Inequalities, Reidel, Dordrecht; MR0947142]; Mathematics and its Applications, 560; Kluwer Academic Publishers Group: Dordrecht, The Netherlands, 2003. [CrossRef]
6. Olver, F.W.J.; Lozier, D.W.; Boisvert, R.F.; Clark, C.W. (Eds.) *NIST Digital Library of Mathematical Functions*; U.S. Department of Commerce, National Institute of Standards and Technology: Washington, DC, USA; Cambridge University Press: Cambridge, UK, 2010. Available online: https://dlmf.nist.gov/ (accessed on 9 August 2023).
7. Olver, F.W.J.; Lozier, D.W.; Boisvert, R.F.; Clark, C.W. (Eds.) *NIST Handbook of Mathematical Functions*; U.S. Department of Commerce, National Institute of Standards and Technology: Washington, DC, USA; Cambridge University Press: Cambridge, UK, 2010. Available online: http://www.cambridge.org/catalogue/catalogue.asp?isbn=9780521192255 (accessed on 9 August 2023).
8. Schilling, R.L.; Song, R.; Vondraček, Z. *Bernstein Functions: Theory and Applications*, 2nd ed.; De Gruyter Studies in Mathematics, 37; Walter de Gruyter & Co.: Berlin, Germany, 2012. [CrossRef]
9. Schilling, R.L.; Song, R.; Vondraček, Z. *Bernstein Functions: Theory and Applications*; De Gruyter Studies in Mathematics, 37; De Gruyter: Berlin, Germany, 2010. [CrossRef]

Disclaimer/Publisher's Note: The statements, opinions and data contained in all publications are solely those of the individual author(s) and contributor(s) and not of MDPI and/or the editor(s). MDPI and/or the editor(s) disclaim responsibility for any injury to people or property resulting from any ideas, methods, instructions or products referred to in the content.

Editorial

A Brief Overview and Survey of the Scientific Work by Feng Qi

Ravi Prakash Agarwal [1,*], Erdal Karapinar [2,3,*], Marko Kostić [4], Jian Cao [5] and Wei-Shih Du [6]

1. Department of Mathematics, Texas A&M University-Kingsville, Kingsville, TX 78363-8202, USA
2. Department of Mathematics, Çankaya University, Etimesgut, Ankara 06790, Turkey
3. Department of Medical Research, China Medical University Hospital, China Medical University, Taichung 40402, Taiwan
4. Faculty of Technical Sciences, University of Novi Sad, 21125 Novi Sad, Serbia
5. School of Mathematics, Hangzhou Normal University, Hangzhou 311121, China
6. Department of Mathematics, National Kaohsiung Normal University, Kaohsiung 82444, Taiwan
* Correspondence: ravi.agarwal@tamuk.edu (R.P.A.); erdalkarapinar@yahoo.com (E.K.)

Abstract: In the paper, the authors present a brief overview and survey of the scientific work by Chinese mathematician Feng Qi and his coauthors.

Keywords: overview; survey; inequality; series expansion; partial Bell polynomial; convex function; special function; mathematical mean; Bernoulli number; matrix; completely monotonic degree; logarithmically completely monotonic function; gamma function; polygamma function; Bell number; Wallis ratio; additivity; complete elliptic integral; Pólya inequality; statistics

MSC: 00-02; 01-02; 05-02; 11-02; 12-02; 15-02; 26-02; 33-02; 40-02; 41-02; 44-02; 53-02

1. Introduction

Professor Feng Qi, whose ORCID profile is at https://orcid.org/0000-0001-6239-2968, received his PhD degree from the University of Science and Technology of China in 1999 and is currently a full Professor at Tiangong University and Henan Polytechnic University, China. On 17 May 2022, he moved to Dallas as an independent researcher in mathematics.

December 2017 in Dallas

Among other institutions and universities, he has visited Victoria University in Australia and the University of Hong Kong twice, the University of Copenhagen, Antalya IC Hotel for attending a conference, several universities in South Korea, Sun Yat-sen University, Kaohsiung Normal University, and so on. He is, or was, the editor-in-chief, an associate editor, or a member of the editorial board of over 40 reputable international journals. In 1993, Qi published his first academic paper in China. In 1996, Qi published his first academic paper abroad. To date, he has published over 670 papers in 220 journals, collections, or proceedings. Currently, his academic interests and research fields mainly include the theory of special functions, classical analysis, mathematical inequalities and applications, mathematical means and applications, analytic combinatorics, analytic number theory, the convex theory of functions, and so on.

Now, let us start out by briefly presenting an overview and survey of some research results obtained by Dr. Professor Feng Qi and his coauthors.

2. Concrete Contributions

2.1. Bell Numbers and Inequalities

From 2013 on, Dr. Qi began to consider some problems related to combinatorial number theory and applied the logarithmically complete monotonicity to combinatorial number theory.

December 2017 in Dallas

In the research article [1], Qi presented derivatives of the generating functions for the Bell numbers by induction and by the well-known Faà di Bruno formula. Using this approach, he recovered an explicit formula in terms of the Stirling numbers of the second kind, found the logarithmically absolute and complete monotonicity of the generating functions, and deduced some inequalities for the Bell numbers. The logarithmic convexity of the sequence of the Bell numbers is shown after that.

As is well known, the Bell number B_n is defined as the number of all equivalence relations on the set $\mathbb{N}_n = \{1, 2, \ldots, n\}$ for $n \in \mathbb{N}$. These numbers have been known already in medieval Japan, but they are named after Eric Temple Bell, who systematically analyzed them in the 1930s.

Let us recall that

$$B_1 = 1, \quad B_2 = 2, \quad B_3 = 5, \quad B_4 = 15, \quad B_5 = 52.$$

Since

$$e^{e^x} = e \sum_{k=0}^{\infty} B_k \frac{x^k}{k!} \quad \text{and} \quad e^{e^{-x}} = e \sum_{k=0}^{\infty} (-1)^k B_k \frac{x^k}{k!},$$

the functions $e^{e^{\pm x}}$ are called the generating functions for the Bell numbers B_k. The Bell numbers are also called exponential numbers.

It is known that, for every positive integer $n \in \mathbb{N}$, we have

$$\frac{d^n e^{e^x}}{d x^n} = e^{e^x} \sum_{k=1}^{n} S(n,k) e^{kx} \quad \text{and} \quad \frac{d^n e^{e^{-x}}}{d x^n} = (-1)^n e^{e^{-x}} \sum_{k=1}^{n} S(n,k) e^{-kx},$$

where $S(n,k)$ is the Stirling number of the second kind, which can be computed by

$$S(n,k) = \frac{1}{k!} \sum_{\ell=1}^{k} (-1)^{k-\ell} \binom{k}{\ell} \ell^n.$$

The Stirling numbers of the second kind satisfy the recurrence relation

$$S(n+1, k+1) = S(n,k) + (k+1)S(n, k+1), \quad 1 \le k \le n-1.$$

From the above, we have

$$B_n = \frac{1}{e} \lim_{x \to 0} \frac{d^n e^{e^x}}{d x^n}$$

and therefore
$$B_n = \sum_{k=1}^{n} S(n,k).$$
Several inequalities for the Bell numbers B_n have been proven, including the following ones:

1. Let $a = (a_1, a_2, \ldots, a_n)$ and $b = (b_1, b_2, \ldots, b_n)$ be two non-increasing tuples of non-negative integers such that $\sum_{i=1}^{k} a_i \geq \sum_{i=1}^{k} b_i$ for $1 \leq k \leq n-1$ and $\sum_{i=1}^{n} a_i = \sum_{i=1}^{n} b_i$. Then
$$B_{a_1} B_{a_2} \cdots B_{a_n} \geq B_{b_1} B_{b_2} \cdots B_{b_n}.$$

2. If $\ell \geq 0$ and $n \geq k \geq 0$, then we have
$$B_{n+\ell}^k B_\ell^{n-k} \geq B_{k+\ell}^n.$$

3. If $\ell \geq 0$, $n \geq k \geq m$, $2k \geq n$, and $2m \geq n$, then we have
$$B_{k+\ell} B_{n-k+\ell} \geq B_{m+\ell} B_{n-m+\ell}.$$

4. If $k \geq 0$ and $n \in \mathbb{N}$, then we have
$$\left(\prod_{\ell=0}^{n} B_{k+2\ell}\right)^{1/(n+1)} \geq \left(\prod_{\ell=0}^{n-1} B_{k+2\ell+1}\right)^{1/n}.$$

These results have been extended and generalized in [2–5] by Qi and his coauthors.

2.2. Partial Bell Polynomials

Partial Bell polynomials are also called the Bell polynomials of the second kind. They are usually denoted by $B_{n,k}(x_1, x_2, \ldots, x_{n-k+1})$. They are closely connected with the famous Faà di Bruno formula in combinatorics. In recent years, Qi and his coauthors creatively considered some special values of $B_{n,k}$ for special sequences $x_1, x_2, \ldots, x_{n-k+1}$ and successfully applied to some mathematical problems.

The survey article [6] is worth to be mentioned. We now just introduce the newest results obtained by Qi and his coauthors.

1. In the papers [7,8], the following conclusions were proved.
    (a) For $m \in \mathbb{N}$ and $|t| < 1$, the function $\left(\frac{\arcsin t}{t}\right)^m$, whose value at $t = 0$ is defined to be 1, has Maclaurin's series expansion
$$\left(\frac{\arcsin t}{t}\right)^m = 1 + \sum_{k=1}^{\infty} (-1)^k \frac{Q(m, 2k; 2)}{\binom{m+2k}{m}} \frac{(2t)^{2k}}{(2k)!}, \tag{1}$$
    where
$$Q(m, k; \alpha) = \sum_{\ell=0}^{k} \binom{m+\ell-1}{m-1} s(m+k-1, m+\ell-1) \left(\frac{m+k-\alpha}{2}\right)^\ell \tag{2}$$
    for $m, k \in \mathbb{N}$, the constant $\alpha \in \mathbb{R}$ such that $m + k \neq \alpha$, and the Stirling numbers of the first kind $s(m+k-1, m+\ell-1)$ are analytically generalized by
$$\frac{[\ln(1+x)]^k}{k!} = \sum_{n=k}^{\infty} s(n, k) \frac{x^n}{n!}, \quad |x| < 1.$$

(b) For $k, n \geq 0$ and $x_m \in \mathbb{C}$ with $m \in \mathbb{N}$, we have

$$B_{2n+1,k}\left(0, x_2, 0, x_4, \ldots, \frac{1+(-1)^k}{2} x_{2n-k+2}\right) = 0. \quad (3)$$

For $k, n \in \mathbb{N}$ such that $2n \geq k \in \mathbb{N}$, we have

$$B_{2n,k}\left(0, \frac{1}{3}, 0, \frac{9}{5}, 0, \frac{225}{7}, \ldots, \frac{1+(-1)^{k+1}}{2}\frac{[(2n-k)!!]^2}{2n-k+2}\right)$$

$$= (-1)^{n+k}\frac{(4n)!!}{(2n+k)!}\sum_{q=1}^{k}(-1)^q\binom{2n+k}{k-q}Q(q, 2n; 2), \quad (4)$$

where $Q(q, 2n; 2)$ is given by (2).

Maclaurin's series expansion (1) was recovered in (Section 6 [9]) and was generalized in (Section 4 [10]) as

$$\left(\frac{\arcsin t}{t}\right)^\alpha = 1 + \sum_{n=1}^{\infty}(-1)^n\left[\sum_{k=1}^{2n}\frac{(-\alpha)_k}{(2n+k)!}\sum_{q=1}^{k}(-1)^q\binom{2n+k}{k-q}Q(q, 2n; 2)\right](2t)^{2n} \quad (5)$$

for $\alpha \in \mathbb{R}$ and $|t| < 1$ by rediscovering a special case of (3) and the closed-form Formula (4), where $Q(q, 2n; 2)$ is given by (2) and the rising factorial of a complex number $\alpha \in \mathbb{C}$ is defined by

$$(\alpha)_m = \prod_{k=0}^{m-1}(\alpha+k) = \begin{cases}\alpha(\alpha+1)\cdots(\alpha+m-1), & m \in \mathbb{N}; \\ 1, & m = 0.\end{cases} \quad (6)$$

2. In [9], among other things, by establishing the Taylor series expansion

$$\left[\frac{(\arccos x)^2}{2(1-x)}\right]^k = 1 + (2k)!\sum_{n=1}^{\infty}\frac{Q(2k, 2n; 2)}{(2k+2n)!}[2(x-1)]^n \quad (7)$$

for $k \in \mathbb{N}$ and $|x| < 1$, Qi derived the specific value

$$B_{m,k}\left(-\frac{1}{12}, \frac{2}{45}, -\frac{3}{70}, \frac{32}{525}, -\frac{80}{693}, \ldots, \frac{(2m-2k+2)!!}{(2m-2k+4)!}Q(2, 2m-2k+2; 2)\right)$$

$$= (-1)^k[2(m-k)]!!\binom{m}{k}\sum_{j=1}^{k}(-1)^j(2j)!\binom{k}{j}\frac{Q(2j, 2m; 2)}{(2j+2m)!}$$

for $m \geq k \in \mathbb{N}$ and then generalized the series expansion (7) to

$$\left[\frac{(\arccos x)^2}{2(1-x)}\right]^\alpha = 1 + \sum_{n=1}^{\infty}\left[\sum_{j=1}^{n}\frac{(-\alpha)_j}{j!}\sum_{\ell=1}^{j}(-1)^\ell(2\ell)!\binom{j}{\ell}\frac{Q(2\ell, 2n; 2)}{(2\ell+2n)!}\right][2(x-1)]^n$$

for $\alpha \in \mathbb{R}$, where $Q(2j, 2m; 2)$ is defined by (2).

3. In [10], among other things, by establishing the specific values

$$B_{2r+k,k}(1, 0, 1, 0, 9, 0, 225, 0, \ldots, [(2r-3)!!]^2, 0, [(2r-1)!!]^2) = (-1)^r 2^{2r}Q(k, 2r; 2)$$

and

$$B_{2r+k-1,k}(1, 0, 1, 0, 9, 0, 225, 0, \ldots, [(2r-3)!!]^2, 0) = 0$$

for $r, k \in \mathbb{N}$, Qi concluded

$$\left(\frac{2\arccos t}{\pi}\right)^\alpha = 1 + \sum_{r=1}^{\infty}(-1)^r\left[\sum_{\ell=1}^{r}(-1)^\ell \frac{(-\alpha)_{2\ell-1}}{\pi^{2\ell-1}}Q(2\ell-1, 2r-2\ell; 2)\right]\frac{(2t)^{2r-1}}{(2r-1)!}$$
$$+ \frac{(-\alpha)_2}{\pi^2}\frac{(2t)^2}{2!} + \sum_{r=2}^{\infty}(-1)^r\left[\sum_{\ell=1}^{r}(-1)^\ell \frac{(-\alpha)_{2\ell}}{\pi^{2\ell}}Q(2\ell, 2r-2\ell; 2)\right]\frac{(2t)^{2r}}{(2r)!}$$

for $\alpha \in \mathbb{R}$ and $|t| < 1$, where $(\alpha)_r$ for $\alpha \in \mathbb{R}$ and $r \in \mathbb{N}$ is defined by (6) and $Q(k, 2r; 2)$ is given by (2).

4. In [11], among other things, by establishing a special case of (3) and the explicit formula

$$B_{2m,k}\left(0, -\frac{1}{3}, 0, \frac{1}{5}, \ldots, \frac{(-1)^m}{2m-k+2}\sin\frac{k\pi}{2}\right)$$
$$= (-1)^{m+k}\frac{2^{2m}}{k!}\sum_{j=1}^{k}(-1)^j\binom{k}{j}\frac{T(2m+j, j)}{\binom{2m+j}{j}}, \quad 2m \geq k \geq 1,$$

Qi showed that,

(a) when $\alpha \geq 0$, the series expansions

$$\operatorname{sinc}^\alpha z = 1 + \sum_{q=1}^{\infty}(-1)^q\left[\sum_{k=1}^{2q}\frac{(-\alpha)_k}{k!}\sum_{j=1}^{k}(-1)^j\binom{k}{j}\frac{T(2q+j, j)}{\binom{2q+j}{j}}\right]\frac{(2z)^{2q}}{(2q)!} \quad (8)$$

is convergent in $z \in \mathbb{C}$;

(b) when $\alpha < 0$, the series expansion (8) is convergent in $|z| < \pi$;

where

$$\operatorname{sinc} z = \begin{cases} \frac{\sin z}{z}, & z \neq 0 \\ 1, & z = 0 \end{cases}$$

is called the sinc function,

$$T(n, \ell) = \begin{cases} 1, & (n, \ell) = (0, 0) \\ 0, & n \in \mathbb{N}, \ell = 0 \\ \frac{1}{\ell!}\sum_{j=0}^{\ell}(-1)^j\binom{\ell}{j}\left(\frac{\ell}{2}-j\right)^n, & n, \ell \in \mathbb{N} \end{cases}$$

for $n \geq \ell \in \mathbb{N}_0 = \{0, 1, 2, \ldots\}$ is called the central factorial numbers of the second kind [12,13], and the rising factorial $(\alpha)_k$ is defined by (6).

On new results and applications of special values of partial Bell polynomials $B_{n,k}$ in recent years by Qi and his coauthors, please refer to [14–25] and closely related references therein.

2.3. Wallis Ratio

Starting from 1999, Qi began to be interested in special functions and applications. Through these work, he posed mathematical notions such as logarithmically completely monotonic function and completely monotonic degree.

The new approximation formula and the inequalities for the Wallis ratio

$$W_n = \frac{(2n-1)!!}{(2n)!!}, \quad n \in \mathbb{N}$$

have been examined in a joint research article [26] with C. Mortici. In (Theorems 4.1 and 4.2 [26]), the authors have proved the asymptotic formula

$$W_n \sim \sqrt{\frac{e}{n}}\left(1-\frac{1}{2n}\right)^n \frac{1}{\sqrt{n}} \exp\left(\frac{1}{24n^2}+\frac{1}{48n^3}+\frac{1}{160n^4}+\frac{1}{960n^5}+\cdots\right), \quad n\to\infty$$

and the inequality

$$W_n > \sqrt{\frac{e}{n}}\left(1-\frac{1}{2n}\right)^n \frac{1}{\sqrt{n}} \exp\left(\frac{1}{24n^2}+\frac{1}{48n^3}+\frac{1}{160n^4}+\frac{1}{960n^5}\right), \quad n\geq 1$$

respectively. In (Theorem 5.2 [26]), the double inequality

$$\sqrt{\frac{e}{\pi}}\left[1-\frac{1}{2(n+1/3)}\right]^{n+1/3}\frac{1}{\sqrt{n}} < W_n < \sqrt{\frac{e}{\pi}}\left[1-\frac{1}{2(n+1/3)}\right]^{n+1/3}\frac{e^{1/144n^3}}{\sqrt{n}}$$

has been proved for each integer $n \geq 1$.

In the branch of the Wallis ratio and inequalities, Qi and his coauthors published also the papers [27–33] and applied some results from [31] to the derivation of the series expansion (8).

2.4. Additivity of Polygamma Functions

The classical Euler gamma function $\Gamma(x)$ is defined for $x > 0$ by

$$\Gamma(x) = \int_0^\infty e^{-t} t^{x-1}\, dt.$$

The function $\psi(x) = \frac{\Gamma'(x)}{\Gamma(x)}$ is usually called the psi or digamma function, while the function $\psi^{(k)}(x)$ for $k \in \mathbb{N}$ is called the polygamma function.

August 2008 in Sydney

The properties of the gamma function, the digamma function, and the polygamma functions have been investigated in many research papers by now. In a joint work [34] with B.-N. Guo and Q.-M. Luo, F. Qi proved that for each positive integer $i \in \mathbb{N}$ the function $|\psi^{(i)}(e^x)|$ is subadditive on $(\ln\theta_i, \infty)$ and superadditive on $(-\infty, \ln\theta_i)$, where $\theta_i \in (0,1)$ is the unique root of the equation $2|\psi^{(i)}(\theta)| = |\psi^{(i)}(\theta^2)|$.

An earlier paper similar to [34] is [35] in which the convexity and concavity of the functions $\psi^{(k)}(e^x)$ and $\psi^{(k)}(x^c)$ for $x \in \mathbb{R}$ and $c \neq 0$ were considered by Qi and his two coauthors.

2.5. Bounds for Mathematical Means in Terms of Mathematical Means

In [36], a joint work with X.-T. Shi, F.-F. Liu, and Z.-H. Yang, Qi examined a double inequality for an integral mean in terms of the exponential and logarithmic means. Among many other results, it has been proved that, for every two distinct positive real numbers $a > 0$ and $b > 0$, we have

$$L(a,b) < \frac{2}{\pi} \int_0^{\pi/2} a^{\cos^2\theta} b^{\sin^2\theta} \, d\theta < I(a,b),$$

where

$$L(a,b) = \frac{b-a}{\ln b - \ln a} \quad \text{and} \quad I(a,b) = \frac{1}{e}\left(\frac{b^b}{a^a}\right)^{1/(b-a)}$$

are called [37] the logarithmic and exponential means, respectively.

The paper [36] is a starting point of [38,39] and many other papers such as [40–48] by other mathematicians.

In a joint research article [49] with W.-D. Jiang, F. Qi proved a double inequality for the combination of the Toader mean and the arithmetic mean in terms of the contraharmonic mean. Qi and his coauthors also published many other papers such as [50–56] in which some special means are bounded in terms of elementary and simple mathematical means.

2.6. Complete Elliptic Integrals

There is no need to say that the theory of complete elliptic integrals has attracted F. Qi and his coauthors, who provided many significant contributions in this field. Some new bounds for the complete elliptic integrals of the first and second kind and their generalizations were given in [57–62], for example.

2.7. Matrices

In [63], Qi and his two coauthors analytically discovered the inverse of the interesting matrix

$$A_n = (a_{i,j})_{n \times n} = \begin{pmatrix} \binom{1}{0} & 0 & 0 & 0 & \cdots & 0 & 0 & 0 & 0 \\ \binom{1}{1} & \binom{2}{0} & 0 & 0 & \cdots & 0 & 0 & 0 & 0 \\ 0 & \binom{2}{1} & \binom{3}{0} & 0 & \cdots & 0 & 0 & 0 & 0 \\ 0 & \binom{2}{2} & \binom{3}{1} & \binom{4}{0} & \cdots & 0 & 0 & 0 & 0 \\ 0 & 0 & \binom{3}{2} & \binom{4}{1} & \cdots & 0 & 0 & 0 & 0 \\ 0 & 0 & \binom{3}{3} & \binom{4}{2} & \cdots & 0 & 0 & 0 & 0 \\ 0 & 0 & 0 & \binom{4}{3} & \cdots & 0 & 0 & 0 & 0 \\ \vdots & \vdots & \vdots & \vdots & \ddots & \vdots & \vdots & \vdots & \vdots \\ 0 & 0 & 0 & 0 & \cdots & \binom{n-3}{0} & 0 & 0 & 0 \\ 0 & 0 & 0 & 0 & \cdots & \binom{n-3}{1} & \binom{n-2}{0} & 0 & 0 \\ 0 & 0 & 0 & 0 & \cdots & \binom{n-3}{2} & \binom{n-2}{1} & \binom{n-1}{0} & 0 \\ 0 & 0 & 0 & 0 & \cdots & \binom{n-3}{3} & \binom{n-2}{2} & \binom{n-1}{1} & \binom{n}{0} \end{pmatrix}_{n \times n} \quad (9)$$

for $n \in \mathbb{N}$, where

$$a_{i,j} = \begin{cases} 0, & i < j \\ \binom{j}{i-j}, & j \leq i \leq 2j \\ 0, & i > 2j \end{cases}$$

for $1 \leq i,j \leq n$. Basing on this result, they presented an inversion theorem which states that

$$\frac{S_n}{n!} = \sum_{k=1}^{n} (-1)^k \binom{k}{n-k} S_k \quad \text{if and only if} \quad nS_n = \sum_{k=1}^{n} \frac{(-1)^k}{(k-1)!} \binom{2n-k-1}{n-1} s_k,$$

where s_k and S_k are two sequences independent of n such that $n \geq k \geq 1$. Moreover, they deduced several identities, including

$$\sum_{\ell=0}^{\lfloor (j-1)/2 \rfloor} (-1)^\ell \binom{j-\ell-1}{\ell} C_{i-\ell-1} = \frac{j}{i}\binom{2i-j-1}{i-1}, \quad i \geq j \geq 1$$

and

$$\frac{\sum_{\ell=0}^{m-1}(-1)^\ell \binom{2m-\ell-1}{\ell}\frac{n+2\ell+1}{n-\ell+1}C_{n-\ell-1}}{\sum_{\ell=0}^{m-1}(-1)^\ell \binom{2m-\ell-2}{\ell}\frac{1}{2m-2\ell-1}C_{n-\ell-1}} = m(2m-1), \quad n \geq 2m \geq 2, \tag{10}$$

relating to the Catalan numbers $C_n = \frac{1}{n+1}\binom{2n}{n}$, where $\lfloor x \rfloor$ denotes the floor function whose value is the largest integer less than or equal to x.

We remark that the inverse of the matrix A_n defined in (9) was also combinatorially studied and connected in ([64] p. 8), while the identity in (10) was also combinatorially discussed and compared at the end on ([65] p. 3162). We emphasize that the approaches and methods used in [64,65] are quite different from those in [63]. This means that the approaches and methods used by Qi and his coauthors in [63] are novel and innovative.

October 2007 at Weinan Normal University, China

By the way, as for the Catalan numbers C_n, we recommend the new papers [66–69] by Qi and his coauthors. In these papers, the Catalan numbers C_n were generalized, some new properties of C_n were discovered by considering logarithmically complete monotonicity of their generating functions, integral representations of C_n were surveyed in [70] and applied in [63].

In [71], Hong and Qi clarified several new inequalities for generalized eigenvalues of perturbation problems on Hermitian matrices. If $A \in \mathbb{C}^{n \times n}$ is a Hermitian complex matrix of format $n \times n$, then A has the pure real spectrum. Let us denote its eigenvalues by $\lambda_1(A), \lambda_2(A), \ldots, \lambda_n(A)$ and assume that

$$\lambda_1(A) \geq \lambda_2(A) \geq \cdots \geq \lambda_n(A).$$

By $\|\cdot\|_2$ we denote the spectral norm of a matrix. If $E \in \mathbb{C}^{n \times n}$ is also a Hermitian complex matrix of format $n \times n$, then the famous Weyl theorem states that

$$\max_{1 \leq i \leq n} |\lambda_i(A) - \lambda_i(A+E)| \leq \|E\|_2.$$

Besides this result, we know that the following inequalities hold: If $A, B \in \mathbb{C}^{n \times n}$ are Hermitian complex matrices of format $n \times n$ and $i, j, k, \ell, m \in \mathbb{N}$ satisfy $j + k - 1 \leq i \leq \ell + m - n - 1$, then we have

$$\lambda_\ell(A) + \lambda_m(B) \leq \lambda_i(A+B) \leq \lambda_j(A) + \lambda_k(B).$$

In particular,
$$\lambda_i(A) + \lambda_n(B) \leq \lambda_i(A+B) \leq \lambda_j(A) + \lambda_1(B).$$

Accurately, Hong and Qi proved in [71] the following results:

1. Suppose that $A, B, H, E \in \mathbb{C}^{n \times n}$ are Hermitian complex matrices of format $n \times n$, that B is positive definite, that $\nu = \|E\|_2 / \lambda_n(B) < 1$, and that the positive integers $i, j, k, \ell, m \in \mathbb{N}$ satisfy $j + k - 1 \leq i \leq \ell + m - n - 1$.

    (a) If $\lambda_i(A + H) \geq 0$, then

    $$\frac{\lambda_\ell(AB^{-1}) + \lambda_m(HB^{-1})}{1 + \nu} \leq \lambda_i\big((A+H)(B+H)^{-1}\big) \leq \frac{\lambda_j(AB^{-1}) + \lambda_k(HB^{-1})}{1 - \nu}.$$

    (b) If $\lambda_i(A + H) \leq 0$, then

    $$\frac{\lambda_j(AB^{-1}) + \lambda_k(HB^{-1})}{1 - \nu} \leq \lambda_i\big((A+H)(B+H)^{-1}\big) \leq \frac{\lambda_\ell(AB^{-1}) + \lambda_m(HB^{-1})}{1 + \nu}.$$

2. Suppose that $A, B, H, E \in \mathbb{C}^{n \times n}$ are Hermitian complex matrices of format $n \times n$, that B is positive definite, and that $\nu = \|E\|_2 / \lambda_n(B) < 1$. Then we have

    $$\beta_i(A)\lambda_i(AB^{-1}) + \beta_n(H)\lambda_n(HB^{-1}) \leq \lambda_i\big((A+H)(B+H)^{-1}\big)$$
    $$\leq \alpha_i(A)\lambda_i(AB^{-1}) + \alpha_1(H)\lambda_1(HB^{-1}).$$

For more information on this topic, see also the joint papers [72,73] with Y. Hong, in which the authors considered determinantal inequalities of the Hua–Marcus–Zhang type for quaternion matrices and refined two determinantal inequalities for positive semidefinite matrices.

2.8. Bounds for Ratio of Bernoulli Numbers

One of the most influential scientific results of F. Qi was presented in [74], in which Qi considered a double inequality for the ratio of two non-zero neighboring Bernoulli numbers. This result has been quoted almost one hundred times in recent years.

It is well known that the Bernoulli numbers B_n can be generated by

$$\frac{z}{e^z - 1} = 1 - \frac{z}{2} + \sum_{k=1}^{\infty} B_{2k} \frac{z^{2k}}{(2k)!}, \quad |z| < 2\pi.$$

Since the function $\frac{x}{e^x - 1} - 1 + \frac{x}{2}$ is even on $\mathbb{R}$, all of the Bernoulli numbers B_{2n+1} for $n \in \mathbb{N}$ are equal to 0. Due to (Theorem 1.1 [74]), we have

$$\frac{2^{2k-1} - 1}{2^{2k+1} - 1} \frac{(2k+1)(2k+2)}{\pi^2} < \frac{|B_{2k+2}|}{|B_{2k}|} < \frac{2^{2k} - 1}{2^{2k+2} - 1} \frac{(2k+1)(2k+2)}{\pi^2}, \quad k \in \mathbb{N}. \quad (11)$$

This double inequality immediately implies

$$\lim_{k \to \infty} \frac{|B_{2k+2}|}{k^2 |B_{2k}|} = \frac{1}{\pi^2}.$$

In order to achieve his aims, Qi used the well-known identity

$$B_{2k} = 2 \frac{(-1)^{k+1}(2k)!}{(2\pi)^{2k}} \zeta(2k), \quad k \in \mathbb{N},$$

where $\zeta(\cdot)$ is the Riemann zeta function.

The double inequality (11) and related results in [75,76] have been extended, refined, generalized, improved, non-self-cited, and applied in over 50 preprints and papers such as [77–92] by many mathematicians, combinatorists, and physicists around the world.

2.9. Special Polynomials

The Boole polynomials $Bl_n(x;\alpha)$ are defined by

$$\frac{(1+t)^x}{1+(1+t)^\alpha} = \sum_{n=0}^{\infty} Bl_n(x;\alpha)\frac{t^n}{n!}.$$

The Peters polynomials (or higher-order Boole polynomials) $s_n(x;\alpha,\nu)$, defined by

$$\frac{(1+t)^x}{[1+(1+t)^\alpha]^\nu} = \sum_{n=0}^{\infty} s_n(x;\alpha,\nu)\frac{t^n}{n!},$$

clearly generalize the Boole polynomials. It is also known that the Peters polynomials can be further generalized. For example, the degenerate Peters polynomials $s_n(x;\alpha,\nu;\lambda)$, which are defined by

$$\frac{e^{x[(1+t)^\lambda 1]/\lambda}}{\left(1+e^{\alpha[(1+t)^\lambda 1]/\lambda}\right)^\nu} = \sum_{n=0}^{\infty} s_n(x;\alpha,\nu;\lambda)\frac{t^n}{n!},$$

generalize the Peters polynomials.

In a joint research article [93] with Y.-W. Li and M. C. Dağlı, F. Qi showed that

$$s_n(x;\alpha,\nu;\lambda) = (n-1)!\sum_{k=1}^{n}\left[\frac{(-1)^k}{\lambda^{k-1}k!}\sum_{\ell=1}^{k}(-1)^\ell \ell\binom{k}{\ell}\binom{\lambda\ell-1}{n-1}\right]$$

$$\times\left[\sum_{\ell=1}^{k}\frac{\langle-\nu\rangle_\ell}{2^{\nu+\ell}}\sum_{r+s=\ell}\sum_{i+j=k}\binom{k}{i}\left(-\frac{x}{\nu}\right)^i\left(\alpha-\frac{x}{\nu}\right)^j S(i,r)S(j,s)\right],$$

where the falling factorial $\langle z\rangle_n$ is defined for $z\in\mathbb{C}$ by

$$\langle z\rangle_n = \prod_{k=0}^{n-1}(z-k) = \begin{cases} z(z-1)\cdots(z-n+1), & n\geq 1; \\ 1, & n=0. \end{cases}$$

Setting $x=0$ in this formula, we obtain the special result stated in (Theorem 4.1 [93]).

In addition to the paper [93], Dr. Feng Qi and his coauthors conducted more work in the papers [94–114], for example, in this branch. Many of these papers are related to partial Bell polynomials $B_{n,k}$ mentioned above.

2.10. Complete Monotonicity Properties Related to Polygamma Functions

In [115], Qi employed the convolution theorem for the Laplace transform, Bernstein's theorem for completely monotonic functions, and some other analytic techniques to reveal some necessary and sufficient conditions for two functions defined by two derivatives of a function involving trigamma function to be completely monotonic or monotonic. See also a joint paper [116] with R. P. Agarwal, where the authors analyzed the complete monotonicity for several classes of functions related to ratios of gamma functions, and a joint paper [117] with D. Lim, where the authors investigated a ratio of finite many gamma functions and its monotonicity properties. We notice that the papers [115,117] are companions of the papers [118–126]. This series of articles originate from the paper [127] and its preprints.

2008 at Victoria University, Footscray, Melbourne, Australia

2.11. Convex Functions and Inequalities

From 2012 on, F. Qi collaborated with Professor Bo-Yan Xi and his academic group at Inner Mongolia University for Nationalities and paid much attention on generalizations of convex functions and on establishment of integral inequalities of the Hermite–Hadamard type.

The theory of convex functions is extremely significant in many areas of pure and applied sciences. The Jensen inequality and the Hermite–Hadamard type inequalities are still very attractive fields of research within the theory of convex functions. Concerning the scientific work of Professor Feng Qi in this area, we would like to mention the research articles [128–140] and references cited therein.

In this issue, we will briefly describe the results obtained in collaboration of Professor Feng Qi with Y. Wang and M.-M. Zheng in [133] only. Suppose that $\alpha \in (0,1]$ and $m \in (0,1]$. Let us recall that a function $f : [0,b] \to \mathbb{R}$, where $0 < b < \infty$, is said to be (α, m)-convex if and only if

$$f(tx + m(1-t)y) \leq t^\alpha f(x) + m(1-t^\alpha) f(y)$$

for $x, y \in [0, b]$ and $t \in [0, 1]$. If $\alpha = 1$, then an (α, m)-convex function $f : [0, b] \to \mathbb{R}$ is also said to be m-convex. Further on, a non-empty set $S \subseteq \mathbb{R}^n$ is said to be invex with respect to the map $v : S \times S \to \mathbb{R}^n$ if and only if $x + tv(x, y) \in S$ for all $t \in [0, 1]$ and $x, y \in S$. If this is the case, a function $f : S \to \mathbb{R}$ is said to be preinvex with respect to v if and only if

$$f(y + tv(x,y)) \leq tf(x) + (1-t)f(y), \quad x, y \in S, \quad t \in [0,1].$$

We know the following conclusions:

1. If $-\infty < c < a < b < d < \infty$, the function $f : [c, d] \to \mathbb{R}$ is differentiable, and the derivative $|f'|$ is convex on $[a, b]$, then we have

$$\left| \frac{f(a) + f(b)}{2} - \frac{1}{b-a} \int_a^b f(x) \, dx \right| \leq \frac{b-a}{8} (|f'(a)| + |f'(b)|).$$

2. For $0 \leq a < b < \infty$, if the function $f : [0, b] \to \mathbb{R}$ is m-convex for $m \in (0, 1]$ and the Lebesgue integrable, then we have

$$\left| \frac{1}{b-a} \int_a^b f(x) \, dx \right| \leq \min\left\{ \frac{f(a) + mf(b/m)}{2}, \frac{f(b) + mf(a/m)}{2} \right\}.$$

3. For $0 \leq a < b < \infty$ and $\alpha, m \in (0, 1]$, if the function $f : [0, b] \to \mathbb{R}$ is (α, m)-convex and differentiable and its first derivative is the Lebesgue integrable, then we have

$$\left| \frac{f(a)+f(b)}{2} - \frac{1}{b-a}\int_a^b f(x)\,dx \right| \le \frac{b-a}{2}\frac{1}{2^{1-1/q}}$$
$$\times \min\left\{ \left[v_1|f'(a)|^q + v_2 m|f'(b)|^q\right]^{1/q}, \left[v_1|f'(b)|^q + v_2 m|f'(a)|^q\right]^{1/q} \right\},$$

provided that the function $|f'|^q$ is (α, m)-convex for some real number $q \ge 1$, where

$$v_1 = \frac{\alpha + 1/2^\alpha}{(\alpha+1)(\alpha+2)} \quad \text{and} \quad v_2 = \frac{1}{(\alpha+1)(\alpha+2)}\left(\frac{\alpha^2+\alpha+2}{2} - \frac{1}{2^\alpha}\right).$$

August 2014 in China

In (Definition 7 [133]), the authors introduced the following notion: Suppose that a non-empty set $S \subseteq \mathbb{R}^n$ is invex with respect to v for $\alpha \in (0,1]$. We say that a function $f : S \to \mathbb{R}$ is α-preinvex with respect to v if and only if

$$f(y + tv(x,y)) \le t^\alpha f(x) + m(1-t^\alpha)f(y)$$

for $x, y \in S$ and $t \in [0,1]$. The main results are the Hermite–Hadamard type inequalities in (Theorems 5 to 9 [133]), where the authors mainly use the assumption that the function $|f'|^q$ is α-preinvex for some real number $\alpha \in (0,1]$ and $q \ge 1$. Until now, Qi and Xi's academic group have jointly published over 120 papers in reputable peer-review journals. Due to their better work in generalizing convex functions and in establishing the Hermite–Hadamard type inequalities, Qi and Xi's group acquired financial support from the National Natural Science Foundation of China with Grant No. 11361038 between 2014 and 2017.

2.12. Fractional Derivatives and Integrals

Let us note that Professor F. Qi analyzed, in three joint work [141–143] with W.-S. Du, A. Ghaffar, C.-J. Huang, S. M. Hussain, K. S. Nisar, and G. Rahman, the Čebyšev and Grüss type inequalities for conformable k-fractional integral operators, where the authors investigated the Hermite–Hadamard type inequalities for k-fractional conformable integrals.

Concerning the integral inequalities, it is also worth noting that F. Qi and his coauthors have generalized, in [144–147], the Young integral inequality using the Taylor theorems in terms of higher order derivatives and their norms; the authors have applied their results for the estimation of several concrete definite integrals.

2.13. Differential Geometry

From September 1982 to July 1986, F. Qi majored in mathematical education as a bachelor student at Department of Mathematics, Henan University, China. From September 1986 to June 1989, he majored in differential geometry as his master's research supervised by Professor Yi-Pei Chen at the Department of Mathematics, Xiamen University, China.

From March 1996 to January 1999, he majored in analysis and topology as his doctoral supervised by Professor Sen-Lin Xu at the Department of Mathematics, University of Science and Technology of China. In this period, he jointly published over 10 papers, including [148–152], in differential geometry.

2.14. Pólya Type Integral Inequalities

Starting from 1993, Qi's research was extended to mathematical inequalities and applications, including generalizations of the Pólya integral inequality [153]. As for the Pólya type integral inequalities, his first paper is [154], his last paper is [155]. On this topic, he also published the papers [156–163]. Then, he surveyed the Pólya type integral inequalities from the origin to date in [164]. Some of these results have been applied to refine the famous Young's integral inequality in the papers [145–147].

October 2015 in Huizhou, Guangdong, China

2.15. Properties of Special Mathematical Means

Starting from 1997, Qi's research was further extended to mathematical means and applications. He started out by publishing [165,166]. His newest and creative papers in this area are [38,167–178], for example. In these papers, he discovered logarithmic convexity and Schur convexity of the extended mean values (or say, Stolarsky's means), considered the logarithmically complete monotonicity of special mathematical means, established integral and Lévy–Khintchine representations of some special mathematical means and their reciprocals. Concretely speaking, for example, Qi and his coauthors obtained the following results:

1. Let $n \in \mathbb{N}$ be not less than 2 and $a = (a_1, a_2, \ldots, a_n)$ be a positive sequence, that is, $a_k > 0$ for $1 \leq k \leq n$. The arithmetic and geometric means $A_n(a)$ and $G_n(a)$ of the positive sequence a are defined, respectively, as

$$A_n(a) = \frac{1}{n} \sum_{k=1}^{n} a_k \quad \text{and} \quad G_n(a) = \left(\prod_{k=1}^{n} a_k \right)^{1/n}.$$

For $z \in \mathbb{C} \setminus (-\infty, -\min\{a_k, 1 \leq k \leq n\}]$ and $n \geq 2$, let $e = \overbrace{(1,1,\ldots,1)}^{n}$ and

$$G_n(a + ze) = \left[\prod_{k=1}^{n} (a_k + z) \right]^{1/n}.$$

In (Theorem 1.1 [176]), by virtue of the Cauchy integral formula in the theory of complex functions, the following integral representation was established.

Let σ be a permutation of the sequence $\{1,2,\ldots,n\}$ such that the sequence $\sigma(a) = (a_{\sigma(1)}, a_{\sigma(2)}, \ldots, a_{\sigma(n)})$ is a rearrangement of a in an ascending order $a_{\sigma(1)} \leq a_{\sigma(2)} \leq \cdots \leq a_{\sigma(n)}$. Then the principal branch of the geometric mean $G_n(a + ze)$ has the integral representation

$$G_n(a + ze) = A_n(a) + z - \frac{1}{\pi} \sum_{\ell=1}^{n-1} \sin \frac{\ell \pi}{n} \int_{a_{\sigma(\ell)}}^{a_{\sigma(\ell+1)}} \left| \prod_{k=1}^{n} (a_k - t) \right|^{1/n} \frac{dt}{t + z} \quad (12)$$

for $z \in \mathbb{C} \setminus (-\infty, -\min\{a_k, 1 \leq k \leq n\}]$.

Taking $z = 0$ in the integral representation (12) yields the fundamental inequality

$$G_n(a) = A_n(a) - \frac{1}{\pi} \sum_{\ell=1}^{n-1} \sin \frac{\ell \pi}{n} \int_{a_{\sigma(\ell)}}^{a_{\sigma(\ell+1)}} \left[\prod_{k=1}^{n} |a_k - t| \right]^{1/n} \frac{dt}{t} \leq A_n(a). \quad (13)$$

For $0 < a_1 \leq a_2 \leq a_3$, taking $n = 2, 3$ in (13) gives

$$\frac{a_1 + a_2}{2} - \sqrt{a_1 a_2} = \frac{1}{\pi} \int_{a_1}^{a_2} \sqrt{\left(1 - \frac{a_1}{t}\right)\left(\frac{a_2}{t} - 1\right)} \, dt \geq 0$$

and

$$\frac{a_1 + a_2 + a_3}{3} - \sqrt[3]{a_1 a_2 a_3} = \frac{\sqrt{3}}{2\pi} \int_{a_1}^{a_3} \sqrt[3]{\left|\left(1 - \frac{a_1}{t}\right)\left(1 - \frac{a_2}{t}\right)\left(1 - \frac{a_3}{t}\right)\right|} \, dt \geq 0.$$

These texts are excerpted from the site https://math.stackexchange.com/a/4256320/945479 on 10 July 2022.

2. The weighted version of the integral representation (12) can be found in the paper (Theorem 3.1 [175]). We recite the weighted version as follows.

For $n \geq 2$, $a = (a_1, a_2, \ldots, a_n)$, and $w = (w_1, w_2, \ldots, w_n)$ with $a_k, w_k > 0$ and $\sum_{k=1}^{n} w_k = 1$, the weighted arithmetic and geometric means $A_{w,n}(a)$ and $G_{w,n}(a)$ of a with the positive weight w are defined, respectively, as

$$A_{w,n}(a) = \sum_{k=1}^{n} w_k a_k \quad \text{and} \quad G_{w,n}(a) = \prod_{k=1}^{n} a_k^{w_k}.$$

Let us denote $\alpha = \min\{a_k, 1 \leq k \leq n\}$. For a complex variable $z \in \mathbb{C} \setminus (-\infty, -\alpha]$, we introduce the complex function

$$G_{w,n}(a + z) = \prod_{k=1}^{n} (a_k + z)^{w_k}.$$

With the aid of the Cauchy integral formula in the theory of complex functions, the following integral representation was established in (Theorem 3.1 [175]).

Let $0 < a_k \leq a_{k+1}$ for $1 \leq k \leq n-1$ and $z \in \mathbb{C} \setminus (-\infty, -a_1]$. Then the principal branch of the weighted geometric mean $G_{w,n}(a + z)$ with a positive weight $w = (w_1, w_2, \ldots, w_n)$ has the integral representation

$$G_{w,n}(a + z) - A_{w,n}(a)$$
$$= z - \frac{1}{\pi} \sum_{\ell=1}^{n-1} \sin \left[\left(\sum_{k=1}^{\ell} w_k \right) \pi \right] \int_{a_\ell}^{a_{\ell+1}} \prod_{k=1}^{n} |a_k - t|^{w_k} \frac{dt}{t + z}. \quad (14)$$

Letting $z = 0$ in the integral representation (14) gives the fundamental inequality

$$G_{w,n}(a) = A_{w,n}(a) - \frac{1}{\pi} \sum_{\ell=1}^{n-1} \sin\left[\left(\sum_{k=1}^{\ell} w_k\right)\pi\right] \int_{a_\ell}^{a_{\ell+1}} \prod_{k=1}^{n} |a_k - t|^{w_k} \frac{dt}{t} \quad (15)$$
$$\leq A_{w,n}(a).$$

Setting $n = 2$ in (15) leads to

$$a_1^{w_1} a_2^{w_2} = w_1 a_1 + w_2 a_2 - \frac{\sin(w_1 \pi)}{\pi} \int_{a_1}^{a_2} \left(1 - \frac{a_1}{t}\right)^{w_1} \left(\frac{a_2}{t} - 1\right)^{w_2} dt$$
$$\leq w_1 a_1 + w_2 a_2 \quad (16)$$

for $w_1, w_2 > 0$ such that $w_1 + w_2 = 1$. These texts are excerpted from the site https://math.stackexchange.com/a/4256320/945479 on 10 July 2022.

3. For $a_k < a_{k+1}$ and $w_k > 0$ with $\sum_{k=1}^{n} w_k = 1$ and $n \geq 2$, the principal branch of the reciprocal $H_{a,w,n}(z)$ of the weighted geometric mean $G_{w,n}(a+z)$ can be represented by

$$H_{a,w,n}(z) = \frac{1}{\prod_{k=1}^{n}(z+a_k)^{w_k}}$$
$$= \frac{1}{\pi} \sum_{\ell=1}^{n-1} \sin\left(\pi \sum_{k=1}^{\ell} w_k\right) \int_{a_\ell}^{a_{\ell+1}} \frac{1}{\prod_{k=1}^{n}|t-a_k|^{w_k}} \frac{dt}{t+z}, \quad (17)$$

where $z \in \mathbb{C} \setminus [-a_n, -a_1]$. Consequently, the reciprocal $H_{a,w,n}(t - a_1)$ of the weighted geometric mean $G_{w,n}(a + t - a_1)$ is a Stieltjes function and a logarithmically completely monotonic function. See (Theorem 2.1 [172]).

2.16. Invited Visits and Promotions

Due to his better work in mathematical inequalities and applications, F. Qi and his academic groups obtained support from the National Natural Science Foundation of China with Grant No. 10001016 between 2001 and 2003. Due to this, Qi obtained an invitation and support from Dr. Professor Sever S. Dragomir to visit Victoria University (Melbourne, Australia) for collaboration between November 2001 and January 2002. This is his first visit abroad. Supported by the China Scholarship Council, he visited Victoria University again to collaborate with Dr. Professor Pietro Cerone and Sever S. Dragomir between March 2008 and February 2009.

May 2017 in Jiaozuo, China

Due to inventing the notion of logarithmically completely monotonic functions and his better work in special functions, Qi obtained an invitation and support from Dr. Professor Christian Berg at Copenhagen University to attend the Workshop on Integral Transforms, Positivity and Applications between 1 and 3 September 2010.

Dr. Feng Qi was also invited and supported by Dr. Professor Ahmet Ocak Akdemir, Wing-Sum Cheung, Yeol Je Cho, Junesang Choi, Wei-Shih Du, Taekyun Kim, and Jen-Chih

Yao, to visit the University of Hong Kong twice in 2004, to visit Dongguk University at Gyeongju, Gyeongsang National University, Kwangwoon University, Kyungpook National University, and several other universities in South Korea from 2012 to 2015, to visit Antalya in Turkey in 2016, and to visit Sun Yat-sen University and Kaohsiung Normal University in Taiwan in 2018, for academic collaborations and international conferences, including taking part in the International Congress of Mathematicians 2014.

Due to his excellent works in university mathematics education, administration, and academic research, Qi was promptly and quicker promoted from a lecturer to an associate professor, to a full professor, and to a Specially-Appointed-Professor for Universities of Henan Province at Henan Polytechnic University in November 1995, October 1999, and November 2005.

2.17. Editorial and Refereeing Appointments

Currently, Dr. Qi is editors-in-chief, associate editor, editor, member of editorial board for over 25 internationally-reputed and peer-reviewed journals such as the Journal of Inequalities and Applications which is being indexed by the Science Citation Index-Expanded and Scopus.

The first academic journal specializing in mathematical inequalities, the Journal of Inequalities and Applications, was found by Dr. Professor Ravi Prakash Agarwal in 1997. This history was cultivated in Qi's survey article [164]. In addition, the following seven journals have also specialized in mathematical inequalities:

1. *Advances in Inequalities and Applications* (since 2012);
2. *Advances in Nonlinear Variational Inequalities* (since 1998);
3. *Journal of Inequalities and Special Functions* (since 2010);
4. *Journal of Inequalities in Pure and Applied Mathematics* (since 2000 to 2009);
5. *Journal of Mathematical Inequalities* (since 2007);
6. *Mathematical Inequalities and Applications* (since 1998);
7. *Turkish Journal of Inequalities* (since 2017).

It is also worth to mentioning the Monographs in Inequalities: Series in Inequalities at the site http://books.ele-math.com/ accessed on 10 July 2022.

Professor Qi was a recipient of the Top Peer Reviewer powered by Publons in the years 2016 and 2019. See Certificates in Figure 1.

Figure 1. Qi's Certificates for Top Peer Reviewer powered by Publons in 2016 and 2019.

3. Statistics of Qi's Contributions

Since 1993, Qi has published over 670 peer-reviewed articles, including over 42 papers published in Chinese, in over 220 journals, book chapters, collections, and conference proceedings in mathematics, see Table 1.

Table 1. The year distribution of Qi's papers formally published since 1993.

Year	Papers	Year	Papers	Year	Papers	Year	Papers
1993	9	1994	5	1995	5	1996	6
1997	7	1998	9	1999	14	2000	7
2001	7	2002	7	2003	37	2004	21
2005	23	2006	31	2007	21	2008	22
2009	14	2010	14	2011	7	2012	26
2013	38	2014	51	2015	52	2016	43
2017	35	2018	45	2019	39	2020	23
2021	26	2022	23	2023	3	2024	1

In Feng Qi's Google Scholar profile dated on 2 August 2022, his over 850 papers, preprints, and other works were indexed and they were totally cited 16858 times. See the screenshot in Figure 2.

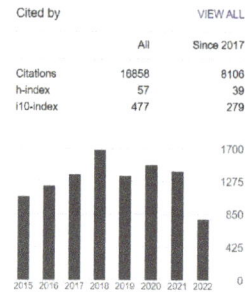

Figure 2. Statistics from Qi's Google Scholar profile dated on 2 August 2022.

In Feng Qi's Scopus profile dated on 2 August 2022, his 417 articles were indexed and they were cited 6590 times by 2007 documents. See the screenshot in Figure 3.

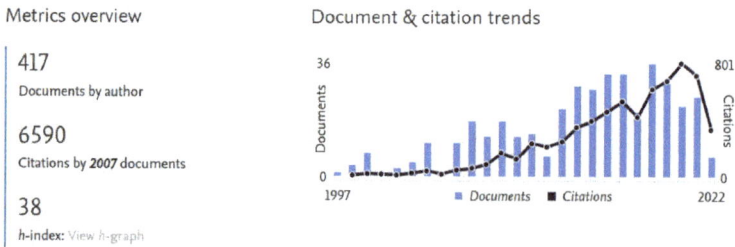

Figure 3. Statistics from Qi's Scopus profile dated on 2 August 2022.

In Qi's Publons profile dated on 2 August 2022, his 412 papers were indexed by the Web of Science Core Collection and they were cited 5915 times. See the screenshots in Figure 4.

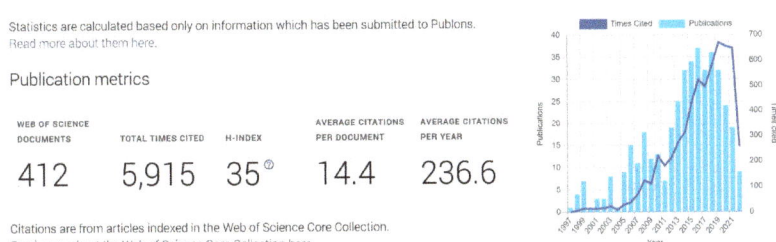

Figure 4. Statistics from Qi's Publons profile dated on 2 August 2022.

From 2014 to 2021, Qi consecutively ranked as the Most Cited Chinese Researchers in Mathematics. These rankings were carried out jointly by Elsevier and ShanghaiRanking Consultancy. See Figure 5.

Figure 5. Certificate of the 2021 Most Cited Chinese Researchers.

In the Stanford University's 2021 list of World's Top 2% Scientists, Qi ranked 61510/190064 in the Single Year Impact Data (2020) and ranked 96040/186178 in the Career-long Data (1960–2020). For more data, please click the link https://doi.org/10.17632/btchxktzyw.3 accessed on 10 July 2022.

In the 2022 edition of the World's Top Mathematics Scientists by Research.com dated on 2 August 2022, Qi ranked 330 worldwide and his 580 papers were indexed and were cited 11291 times. See Figure 6 or click the link https://research.com/u/feng-qi accessed on 8 July 2022.

H-Index & Metrics

Discipline name	H-index	Citations	Publications	World Ranking	National Ranking
Mathematics	57	11,291	580	330	12

Figure 6. Statistics from Qi's Research.com profile dated on 2 August 2022.

Since the year 1992, Qi took charge of and participated in two national research projects supported by the National Natural Science Foundation of China, several provincial scientific projects supported by Henan Province, and several university scientific projects supported by Henan Polytechnic University and Tianjin Polytechnic University. Totally he acquired about one and a half millions CNY of funding support.

Since 2002, his names "Feng Qi", "F. Qi", and "Qi" have appeared in titles of over 89 papers or preprints which were published or announced by hundreds of mathematicians in the globe. See, for example, the papers [40–48,88,179–185].

Currently, Qi's 49 papers or preprints were cited at the Wikipedia site https://en.wikipedia.org/wiki/Euler_numbers accessed on 10 July 2022 and in eight monographs or handbooks [37,186–192].

After the notion "logarithmically completely monotonic function" was explicitly defined in the preprints [193,194] and the papers [195,196], an important paper on logarithmically completely monotonic functions is [197], and the notion has been seemingly and gradually becoming a standard terminology in mathematical community. Currently, except over 60 preprints and papers by Qi and his coauthors, there have been over 40 papers and preprints whose titles contain the phrases "logarithmically completely monotonic function", "logarithmically complete monotonicity", and "logarithmically completely monotone" by other mathematicians. See, for example, the monographs [191,192] and the papers [198–201]. Qi pointed out several times that the terminology of the logarithmically completely monotonic function was first used without explicit definition in the paper [202].

By the Web of Science Core Collection, Feng Qi's papers have been cited at least in the following 50 research areas: mathematics, science technology other topics, computer science, plant sciences, mathematical computational biology, engineering, business economics, physics, mechanics, communication, telecommunications, biochemistry molecular biology, agriculture, operations research management science, food science technology, genetics heredity, life sciences biomedicine other topics, materials science, nutrition dietetics, anatomy morphology, chemistry, pharmacology pharmacy, biodiversity conservation, cell biology, environmental sciences ecology, instruments instrumentation, mathematical methods in social sciences, physiology, psychology, thermodynamics, transportation, acoustics, astronomy astrophysics, behavioral sciences, biophysics, biotechnology applied microbiology, cardiovascular system cardiology, developmental biology, energy fuels, government law, health care sciences services, infectious diseases, pathology, polymer science, psychiatry, public administration, public environmental occupational health, social issues, sociology, toxicology, and the like.

4. Conclusions

Recommended by Dr. Professor Ravi Prakash Agarwal, Dr. Professor Feng Qi is currently an editor of the *Journal of Inequalities and Applications*, the first academic journal specializing in mathematical inequalities in the world and in the history, founded by Dr. Professor Ravi Prakash Agarwal in 1997, as mentioned in Section 2.17. As one of the first two master students supervised by Dr. Professor Feng Qi between September 2004 and June 2007, Dr. Professor Jian Cao published the papers [27,35,66,203–218] jointly with Qi. As one of academic friends, Dr. Professor Wei-Shih Du published the papers [95,101,110,142] jointly with Qi. Currently Dr. Professor Feng Qi is an editor of the journal *Results in Nonlinear Analysis* founded by Dr. Professor Erdal Karapinar. As one of international colleagues, Dr. Professor Marko Kostić and his coauthors published the papers [77–79,82,84] in which Qi's results mentioned in Section 2.8 were cited and applied many times.

There have been more mathematical studies by Dr. Professor Feng Qi and his coauthors than those summarized in this paper. From the review articles [116,164,219–224], for example, we can also see more systematic contributions by F. Qi and his coauthors in mathematics. We think that we just summarized a small part of works and ideas created by Dr. Professor Feng Qi. This manuscript is the survey of the scientific work by Feng Qi and his coauthors, but not a total survey of all the topics Feng Qi and his coauthors have worked on. If this manuscript were an overall survey of or an almost complete overview of Qi's work, then it would be a book of more than 500 pages.

Author Contributions: Writing—original draft, R.P.A., J.C., W.-S.D., E.K., and M.K. All authors contributed equally to the manuscript and read and approved the final manuscript.

Funding: Marco Kostić is partially supported by Grant No. 451-03-68/2020/14/200156 of Ministry of Science and Technological Development, Republic of Serbia. Jian Cao is partially supported by Grant No. LY21A010019 of the Zhejiang Provincial Natural Science Foundation of China. Wei-Shih Du is partially supported by Grant No. MOST 111-2115-M-017-002 of the Ministry of Science and Technology of the Republic of China.

Institutional Review Board Statement: Not applicable.

Informed Consent Statement: Not applicable.

Data Availability Statement: The study did not report any data.

Acknowledgments: The authors thank anonymous referees for their careful corrections to and valuable comments on the original version of this paper.

Conflicts of Interest: The authors declare no conflicts of interest.

References

1. Qi, F. Some inequalities for the Bell numbers. *Proc. Indian Acad. Sci. Math. Sci.* **2017**, *127*, 551–564. [CrossRef]
2. Qi, F. Integral representations for multivariate logarithmic polynomials. *J. Comput. Appl. Math.* **2018**, *336*, 54–62. [CrossRef]
3. Qi, F. On multivariate logarithmic polynomials and their properties. *Indag. Math.* **2018**, *29*, 1179–1192. [CrossRef]
4. Qi, F. Some inequalities and an application of exponential polynomials. *Math. Inequal. Appl.* **2020**, *23*, 123–135. [CrossRef]
5. Qi, F.; Niu, D.-W.; Lim, D.; Guo, B.-N. Some properties and an application of multivariate exponential polynomials. *Math. Methods Appl. Sci.* **2020**, *43*, 2967–2983. [CrossRef]
6. Qi, F.; Niu, D.-W.; Lim, D.; Yao, Y.-H. Special values of the Bell polynomials of the second kind for some sequences and functions. *J. Math. Anal. Appl.* **2020**, *491*, 124382. [CrossRef]
7. Guo, B.-N.; Lim, D.; Qi, F. Maclaurin's series expansions for positive integer powers of inverse (hyperbolic) sine and tangent functions, closed-form formula of specific partial Bell polynomials, and series representation of generalized logsine function. *Appl. Anal. Discrete Math.* **2023**, *17*, in press. [CrossRef]
8. Guo, B.-N.; Lim, D.; Qi, F. Series expansions of powers of arcsine, closed forms for special values of Bell polynomials, and series representations of generalized logsine functions. *AIMS Math.* **2021**, *6*, 7494–7517. [CrossRef]
9. Qi, F. Taylor's series expansions for real powers of two functions containing squares of inverse cosine function, closed-form formula for specific partial Bell polynomials, and series representations for real powers of Pi. *Demonstr. Math.* **2022**, *55*, in press.
10. Qi, F. Explicit formulas for partial Bell polynomials, Maclaurin's series expansions of real powers of inverse (hyperbolic) cosine and sine, and series representations of powers of Pi. *Res. Sq.* **2021**. [CrossRef]
11. Qi, F.; Taylor, P. Several series expansions for real powers and several formulas for partial Bell polynomials of sinc and sinhc functions in terms of central factorial and Stirling numbers of second kind. *arXiv* **2022**, https://arxiv.org/abs/2204.05612v4.
12. Qi, F.; Guo, B.-N. Relations among Bell polynomials, central factorial numbers, and central Bell polynomials. *Math. Sci. Appl. E-Notes* **2019**, *7*, 191–194. [CrossRef]
13. Qi, F.; Wu, G.-S.; Guo, B.-N. An alternative proof of a closed formula for central factorial numbers of the second kind. *Turkish J. Anal. Number Theory* **2019**, *7*, 56–58. [CrossRef]
14. Guo, B.-N.; Qi, F. Viewing some ordinary differential equations from the angle of derivative polynomials. *Iran. J. Math. Sci. Inform.* **2021**, *16*, 77–95. [CrossRef]
15. Jin, S.; Guo, B.-N.; Qi, F. Partial Bell polynomials, falling and rising factorials, Stirling numbers, and combinatorial identities. *CMES Comput. Model. Eng. Sci.* **2022**, *132*, 781–799. [CrossRef]
16. Qi, F. Simplifying coefficients in a family of ordinary differential equations related to the generating function of the Laguerre polynomials. *Appl. Appl. Math.* **2018**, *13*, 750–755.
17. Qi, F.; Guo, B.-N. Explicit formulas for special values of the Bell polynomials of the second kind and for the Euler numbers and polynomials. *Mediterr. J. Math.* **2017**, *14*, 140. [CrossRef]
18. Qi, F.; Lim, D. Closed formulas for special Bell polynomials by Stirling numbers and associate Stirling numbers. *Publ. Inst. Math. (Beograd) (N.S.)* **2020**, *108*, 131–136. [CrossRef]
19. Qi, F.; Lim, D.; Guo, B.-N. Explicit formulas and identities for the Bell polynomials and a sequence of polynomials applied to differential equations. *Rev. R. Acad. Cienc. Exactas Fís. Nat. Ser. A Mat. RACSAM* **2019**, *113*, 1–9. [CrossRef]
20. Qi, F.; Lim, D.; Yao, Y.-H. Notes on two kinds of special values for the Bell polynomials of the second kind. *Miskolc Math. Notes* **2019**, *20*, 465–474. [CrossRef]
21. Qi, F.; Natalini, P.; Ricci, P.E. Recurrences of Stirling and Lah numbers via second kind Bell polynomials. *Discrete Math. Lett.* **2020**, *3*, 31–36.
22. Qi, F.; Niu, D.-W.; Lim, D.; Guo, B.-N. Closed formulas and identities for the Bell polynomials and falling factorials. *Contrib. Discrete Math.* **2020**, *15*, 163–174. [CrossRef]
23. Qi, F.; Shi, X.-T.; Liu, F.-F.; Kruchinin, D.V. Several formulas for special values of the Bell polynomials of the second kind and applications,. *J. Appl. Anal. Comput.* **2017**, *7*, 857–871. [CrossRef]
24. Qi, F.; Wan, A. A closed-form expression of a remarkable sequence of polynomials originating from a family of entire functions connecting the Bessel and Lambert functions. *São Paulo J. Math. Sci.* **2021**, *15*, in press. [CrossRef]
25. Qi, F.; Zheng, M.-M. Explicit expressions for a family of the Bell polynomials and applications. *Appl. Math. Comput.* **2015**, *258*, 597–607. [CrossRef]
26. Qi, F.; Mortici, C. Some best approximation formulas and inequalities for the Wallis ratio. *Appl. Math. Comput.* **2015**, *253*, 363–368. [CrossRef]
27. Cao, J.; Niu, D.-W.; Qi, F. A Wallis type inequality and a double inequality for probability integral. *Aust. J. Math. Anal. Appl.* **2007**, *4*, 3. Available online: http://ajmaa.org/cgi-bin/paper.pl?string=v4n1/V4I1P3.tex (accessed on 10 July 2022).
28. Chen, C.-P.; Qi, F. Best upper and lower bounds in Wallis' inequality. *J. Indones. Math. Soc. (MIHMI)* **2005**, *11*, 137–141.
29. Chen, C.-P.; Qi, F. Completely monotonic function associated with the gamma function and proof of Wallis' inequality. *Tamkang J. Math.* **2005**, *36*, 303–307. [CrossRef]

30. Chen, C.-P.; Qi, F. The best bounds in Wallis' inequality. *Proc. Am. Math. Soc.* **2005**, *133*, 397–401. [CrossRef]
31. Guo, B.-N.; Qi, F. On the Wallis formula. *Internat. J. Anal. Appl.* **2015**, *8*, 30–38.
32. Guo, S.; Xu, J.-G.; Qi, F. Some exact constants for the approximation of the quantity in the Wallis' formula. *J. Inequal. Appl.* **2013**, *2013*, 7. [CrossRef]
33. Qi, F. An improper integral, the beta function, the Wallis ratio, and the Catalan numbers. *Probl. Anal. Issues Anal.* **2018**, *7*, 104–115. [CrossRef]
34. Guo, B.-N.; Qi, F.; Luo, Q.-M. The additivity of polygamma functions. *Filomat* **2015**, *29*, 1063–1066. FIL1505063G. [CrossRef]
35. Cao, J.; Niu, D.-W.; Qi, F. Convexities of some functions involving the polygamma functions. *Appl. Math. E-Notes* **2008**, *8*, 53–57.
36. Qi, F.; Shi, X.-T.; Liu, F.-F.; Yang, Z.-H. A double inequality for an integral mean in terms of the exponential and logarithmic means. *Period. Math. Hungar.* **2017**, *75*, 180–189. [CrossRef]
37. Bullen, P.S. *Handbook of Means and Their Inequalities*; Mathematics and Its Application; Kluwer Academic Publishers Group: Dordrecht, The Netherlands, 2003; Volume 560. [CrossRef]
38. Qi, F.; Guo, B.-N. Lévy–Khintchine representation of Toader–Qi mean. *Math. Inequal. Appl.* **2018**, *21*, 421–431. [CrossRef]
39. Qi, F.; Yao, S.-W.; Guo, B.-N. Arithmetic means for a class of functions and the modified Bessel functions of the first kind. *Mathematics* **2019**, *7*, 60. [CrossRef]
40. Qian, W.-M.; Zhang, W.; Chu, Y.-M. Optimal bounds for Toader–Qi mean with applications. *J. Comput. Anal. Appl.* **2020**, *28*, 526–536.
41. Qian, W.-M.; Zhang, X.-H.; Chu, Y.-M. Sharp bounds for the Toader–Qi mean in terms of harmonic and geometric means. *J. Math. Inequal.* **2017**, *11*, 121–127. [CrossRef]
42. Xu, H.Z.; Qian, W.M. Some sharp bounds for Toader–Qi mean and other bivariate means. *J. Zhejiang Univ. Sci. Ed. (Zhejiang Daxue Xuebao, Lixue Ban)* **2017**, *44*, 526–530. (In Chinese) [CrossRef]
43. Yang, Z.-H.; Chu, Y.-M. A sharp lower bound for Toader–Qi mean with applications. *J. Funct. Spaces* **2016**, *2016*, 4165601. [CrossRef]
44. Yang, Z.-H.; Chu, Y.-M. On approximating the modified Bessel function of the first kind and Toader–Qi mean. *J. Inequal. Appl.* **2016**, *2016*, 21. [CrossRef]
45. Yang, Z.-H.; Chu, Y.-M.; Song, Y.-Q. Sharp bounds for Toader–Qi mean in terms of logarithmic and identric means. *Math. Inequal. Appl.* **2016**, *19*, 721–730. [CrossRef]
46. Yang, Z.-H.; Tian, J.-F. A new chain of inequalities involving the Toader–Qi, logarithmic and exponential means. *Appl. Anal. Discrete Math.* **2021**, *15*, 467–485. [CrossRef]
47. Yang, Z.-H.; Tian, J.-F.; Zhu, Y.-R. New sharp bounds for the modified Bessel function of the first kind and Toader–Qi mean. *Mathematics* **2020**, *8*, 901. [CrossRef]
48. Zhu, L. New bounds for the modified Bessel function of the first kind and Toader–Qi mean. *Mathematics* **2021**, *9*, 2867. [CrossRef]
49. Jiang, W.-D.; Qi, F. A double inequality for the combination of Toader mean and the arithmetic mean in terms of the contraharmonic mean. *Publ. Inst. Math. (Beograd) (N.S.)* **2016**, *99*, 237–242. [CrossRef]
50. Hua, Y.; Qi, F. A double inequality for bounding Toader mean by the centroidal mean. *Proc. Indian Acad. Sci. Math. Sci.* **2014**, *124*, 527–531. [CrossRef]
51. Hua, Y.; Qi, F. The best bounds for Toader mean in terms of the centroidal and arithmetic means. *Filomat* **2014**, *28*, 775–780. [CrossRef]
52. Jiang, W.-D.; Qi, F. Sharp bounds for the Neuman—Sándor mean in terms of the power and contraharmonic means. *Cogent Math.* **2015**, *2*, 7. [CrossRef]
53. Jiang, W.-D.; Qi, F. Sharp bounds for Neuman—Sándor's mean in terms of the root-mean-square. *Period. Math. Hungar.* **2014**, *69*, 134–138. [CrossRef]
54. Li, W.-H.; Miao, P.; Guo, B.-N. Bounds for the Neuman—Sándor mean in terms of the arithmetic and contra-harmonic means. *Axioms* **2022**, *11*, 236. [CrossRef]
55. Li, W.-H.; Shen, Q.-X.; Guo, B.-N. Several double inequalities for integer powers of the sinc and sinhc functions with applications to the Neuman–Sándor mean and the first Seiffert mean. *Axioms* **2022**, *11*, 304. [CrossRef]
56. Qi, F.; Li, W.-H. A unified proof of inequalities and some new inequalities involving Neuman-Sándor mean. *Miskolc Math. Notes* **2014**, *15*, 665–675. [CrossRef]
57. Guo, B.-N.; Qi, F. Some bounds for the complete elliptic integrals of the first and second kind. *Math. Inequal. Appl.* **2011**, *14*, 323–334. [CrossRef]
58. Qi, F.; Huang, Z. Inequalities of the complete elliptic integrals. *Tamkang J. Math.* **1998**, *29*, 165–169. [CrossRef]
59. Wang, F.; Guo, B.-N.; Qi, F. Monotonicity and inequalities related to complete elliptic integrals of the second kind. *AIMS Math.* **2020**, *5*, 2732–2742. [CrossRef]
60. Wang, F.; Qi, F. Monotonicity and sharp inequalities related to complete (p,q)-elliptic integrals of the first kind. *C. R. Math. Acad. Sci. Paris* **2020**, *358*, 961–970. [CrossRef]
61. Yin, L.; Lin, X.-L.; Qi, F. Monotonicity, convexity and inequalities related to complete (p,q,r)-elliptic integrals and generalized trigonometric functions. *Publ. Math. Debrecen* **2020**, *97*, 181–199. [CrossRef]
62. Yin, L.; Qi, F. Some inequalities for complete elliptic integrals. *Appl. Math. E-Notes* **2014**, *14*, 192–199.

63. Qi, F.; Zou, Q.; Guo, B.-N. The inverse of a triangular matrix and several identities of the Catalan numbers. *Appl. Anal. Discrete Math.* **2019**, *13*, 518–541. [CrossRef]
64. Beck, G.; Dilcher, K. A matrix related to Stern polynomials and the Prouhet–Thue–Morse sequence. *Integers* **2022**, *22*, 30.
65. Chu, W. Further identities on Catalan numbers. *Discrete Math.* **2018**, *341*, 3159–3164. [CrossRef]
66. Li, W.-H.; Cao, J.; Niu, D.-W.; Zhao, J.-L.; Qi, F. An analytic generalization of the Catalan numbers and its integral representation. *arXiv* **2005**. https://arxiv.org/abs/2005.13515v2.
67. Qi, F.; Cerone, P. Some properties of the Fuss–Catalan numbers. *Mathematics* **2018**, *6*, 277. [CrossRef]
68. Qi, F.; Shi, X.-T.; Cerone, P. A unified generalization of the Catalan, Fuss, and Fuss–Catalan numbers. *Math. Comput. Appl.* **2019**, *24*, 49. [CrossRef]
69. Qi, F.; Shi, X.-T.; Liu, F.-F. An integral representation, complete monotonicity, and inequalities of the Catalan numbers. *Filomat* **2018**, *32*, 575–587. [CrossRef]
70. Qi, F.; Guo, B.-N. Integral representations of the Catalan numbers and their applications. *Mathematics* **2017**, *5*, 40. [CrossRef]
71. Hong, Y.; Lim, D.; Qi, F. Some inequalities for generalized eigenvalues of perturbation problems on Hermitian matrices. *J. Inequal. Appl.* **2018**, *2018*, 6. [CrossRef]
72. Hong, Y.; Qi, F. Determinantal inequalities of Hua-Marcus-Zhang type for quaternion matrices. *Open Math.* **2021**, *19*, 562–568. [CrossRef]
73. Hong, Y.; Qi, F. Refinements of two determinantal inequalities for positive semidefinite matrices. *Math. Inequal. Appl.* **2022**, *25*, 673–678. [CrossRef]
74. Qi, F. A double inequality for the ratio of two non-zero neighbouring Bernoulli numbers. *J. Comput. Appl. Math.* **2019**, *351*, 1–5. [CrossRef]
75. Qi, F. Notes on a double inequality for ratios of any two neighbouring non-zero Bernoulli numbers. *Turkish J. Anal. Number Theory* **2018**, *6*, 129–131. [CrossRef]
76. Shuang, Y.; Guo, B.-N.; Qi, F. Logarithmic convexity and increasing property of the Bernoulli numbers and their ratios. *Rev. R. Acad. Cienc. Exactas Fís. Nat. Ser. A Mat. RACSAM* **2021**, *115*, 12. [CrossRef]
77. Bagul, Y.J.; Banjac, B.; Chesneau, C.; Kostić, M.; Malešević, B. New refinements of Cusa–Huygens inequality. *Results Math.* **2021**, *76*, 16. [CrossRef]
78. Bagul, Y.J.; Chesneau, C.; Kostić, M. The Cusa-Huygens inequality revisited. *Novi Sad J. Math.* **2020**, *50*, 149–159. [CrossRef]
79. Bagul, Y.J.; Kostić, M.; Chesneau, C.; Dhaigude, R.M. On the generalized Becker-Stark type inequalities. *Acta Univ. Sapientiae Math.* **2021**, *13*, 88–104. [CrossRef]
80. Bouali, M. Double inequalities for complete monotonicity degrees of remainders of asymptotic expansions of the gamma and digamma functions. *arXiv* **2022**, https://arxiv.org/abs/2202.01801v1.
81. Chen, X.-D.; Wang, H.; Yu, J.; Cheng, Z.; Zhu, P. New bounds of Sinc function by using a family of exponential functions. *Rev. R. Acad. Cienc. Exactas Fís. Nat. Ser. A Mat. RACSAM* **2022**, *116*, 17. [CrossRef]
82. Chouchi, B.; Fedorov, V.; Kostić, M. Monotonicity of certain classes of functions related with Cusa–Huygens inequality. *Chelyab. Fiz.-Mat. Zh. (Chelyabinsk Phys. Math. J.)* **2021**, *6*, 331–337.
83. Englert, C.; Giudice, G.F.; Greljo, A.; McCullough, M. The $\hat{H}$-parameter: An oblique Higgs view. *J. High Energy Phys.* **2019**, 28. [CrossRef]
84. Kostić, M.; Pilipović, S.; Velinov, D.; Fedorov, V.E. c-almost periodic type distributions. *Chelyab. Fiz.-Mat. Zh. (Chelyabinsk Phys. Math. J.)* **2021**, *6*, 190–207. [CrossRef]
85. Liu, J.-C. On two supercongruences for sums of Apéry-like numbers. *Rev. R. Acad. Cienc. Exactas Fís. Nat. Ser. A Mat. RACSAM* **2021**, *115*, 7. [CrossRef]
86. Tan, S.-Y.; Huang, T.-R.; Chu, Y.-M. Functional inequalities for Gaussian hypergeometric function and generalized elliptic integral of the first kind. *Math. Slovaca* **2021**, *71*, 667–682. [CrossRef]
87. Volkov, Y.S. Efficient computation of Favard constants and their connection to Euler polynomials and numbers. *Sib. Èlektron. Mat. Izv. (Sib. Electron. Math. Rep.)* **2020**, *17*, 1921–1942. [CrossRef]
88. Xu, A.-M.; Cen, Z.-D. Qi's conjectures on completely monotonic degrees of remainders of asymptotic formulas of di- and tri-gamma functions. *J. Inequal. Appl.* **2020**, 10. [CrossRef]
89. Yang, Z.-H. Approximations for certain hyperbolic functions by partial sums of their Taylor series and completely monotonic functions related to gamma function. *J. Math. Anal. Appl.* **2016**, *441*, 549–564. [CrossRef]
90. Yang, Z.-H.; Tian, J.-F. Sharp bounds for the ratio of two zeta functions. *J. Comput. Appl. Math.* **2020**, *364*, 112359. [CrossRef]
91. Zhao, T.-H.; Qian, W.-M.; Chu, Y.-M. Sharp power mean bounds for the tangent and hyperbolic sine means. *J. Math. Inequal.* **2021**, *15*, 1459–1472. [CrossRef]
92. Zhu, L. New bounds for arithmetic mean by the Seiffert-like means. *Mathematics* **2022**, *10*, 14. [CrossRef]
93. Li, Y.-W.; Dağlı, M.C.; Qi, F. Two explicit formulas for degenerate Peters numbers and polynomials. *Discrete Math. Lett.* **2022**, *8*, 1–5. [CrossRef]
94. Guo, B.-N.; Polatlı, E.; Qi, F. *Determinantal Formulas and Recurrent Relations for Bi-Periodic Fibonacci and Lucas Polynomials*; Chapter 18 in the Springer Proceedings of the International Conference on Advances in Mathematics and Computing (ICAMC-2020) organized by Veer Surendra Sai University of Technology, Odisha, India, during 7–8 February 2020; Paikray, S.K., Dutta, H., Mordeson, J.N., Eds.; New Trends in Applied Analysis and Computational Mathematics; Springer Book Series; Advances in Intelligent Systems and Computing; Springer: Singapore, 2021; Volume 1356. [CrossRef]

95. Kızılateş, C.; Du, W.-S.; Qi, F. Several determinantal expressions of generalized Tribonacci polynomials and sequences. *Tamkang J. Math.* **2022**, *53*, in press. [CrossRef]
96. Qi, F. Determinantal expressions and recurrence relations for Fubini and Eulerian polynomials. *J. Interdiscip. Math.* **2019**, *22*, 317–335. [CrossRef]
97. Qi, F.; Determinantal expressions and recursive relations of Delannoy polynomials and generalized Fibonacci polynomials. *J. Nonlinear Convex Anal.* **2021**, *22*, 1225–1239.
98. Qi, F. Simplifying coefficients in differential equations related to generating functions of reverse Bessel and partially degenerate Bell polynomials. *Bol. Soc. Paran. Mat.* **2021**, *39*, 73–82. [CrossRef]
99. Qi, F.; Čerňanová, V.; Semenov, Y.S. Some tridiagonal determinants related to central Delannoy numbers, the Chebyshev polynomials, and the Fibonacci polynomials. *Politehn. Univ. Bucharest Sci. Bull. Ser. A Appl. Math. Phys.* **2019**, *81*, 123–136.
100. Qi, F.; Chapman, R.J. Two closed forms for the Bernoulli polynomials. *J. Number Theory* **2016**, *159*, 89–100. [CrossRef]
101. Qi, F.; Dağlı, M.C.; Du, W.-S. Determinantal forms and recursive relations of the Delannoy two-functional sequence. *Adv. Theory Nonlinear Anal. Appl.* **2020**, *4*, 184–193. [CrossRef]
102. Qi, F.; Dağlı, M.C.; Lim, D. Several explicit formulas for (degenerate) Narumi and Cauchy polynomials and numbers. *Open Math.* **2021**, *19*, 833–849. [CrossRef]
103. Qi, F.; Guo, B.-N. A closed form for the Stirling polynomials in terms of the Stirling numbers. *Tbilisi Math. J.* **2017**, *10*, 153–158. [CrossRef]
104. Qi, F.; Guo, B.-N. A determinantal expression and a recurrence relation for the Euler polynomials. *Adv. Appl. Math. Sci.* **2017**, *16*, 297–309.
105. Qi, F.; Guo, B.-N. Explicit formulas and recurrence relations for higher order Eulerian polynomials. *Indag. Math.* **2017**, *28*, 884–891. [CrossRef]
106. Qi, F.; Guo, B.-N. Expressing the generalized Fibonacci polynomials in terms of a tridiagonal determinant. *Matematiche (Catania)* **2017**, *72*, 167–175. [CrossRef]
107. Qi, F.; Guo, B.-N. Some determinantal expressions and recurrence relations of the Bernoulli polynomials. *Mathematics* **2016**, *4*, 65. [CrossRef]
108. Qi, F.; Guo, B.-N. Some properties of the Hermite polynomials. *Georgian Math. J.* **2022**, *28*, 925–935. [CrossRef]
109. Qi, F.; Guo, B.-N. Two nice determinantal expressions and a recurrence relation for the Apostol–Bernoulli polynomials. *J. Indones. Math. Soc. (MIHMI)* **2017**, *23*, 81–87. [CrossRef]
110. Qi, F.; Kızılateş, C.; Du, W.-S. A closed formula for the Horadam polynomials in terms of a tridiagonal determinant. *Symmetry* **2019**, *11*, 8. [CrossRef]
111. Qi, F.; Lim, D.; Guo, B.-N. Some identities related to Eulerian polynomials and involving the Stirling numbers. *Appl. Anal. Discrete Math.* **2018**, *12*, 467–480. [CrossRef]
112. Wang, Y.; Dağlı, M.C.; Liu, X.-M.; Qi, F. Explicit, determinantal, and recurrent formulas of generalized Eulerian polynomials. *Axioms* **2021**, *10*, 37. [CrossRef]
113. Wu, L.; Chen, X.-Y.; Dağlı, M.C.; Qi, F. On degenerate array type polynomials. *CMES Comput. Model. Eng. Sci.* **2022**, *131*, 295–305. [CrossRef]
114. Zhao, J.-L.; Wang, J.-L.; Qi, F. Derivative polynomials of a function related to the Apostol–Euler and Frobenius–Euler numbers. *J. Nonlinear Sci. Appl.* **2017**, *10*, 1345–1349. [CrossRef]
115. Qi, F.; Necessary and sufficient conditions for complete monotonicity and monotonicity of two functions defined by two derivatives of a function involving trigamma function. *Appl. Anal. Discrete Math.* **2021**, *15*, 378–392. [CrossRef]
116. Qi, F.; Agarwal, R.P. On complete monotonicity for several classes of functions related to ratios of gamma functions. *J. Inequal. Appl.* **2019**, Paper No. 36, 42 pages. [CrossRef]
117. Qi, F.; Lim, D. Monotonicity properties for a ratio of finite many gamma functions. *Adv. Differ. Equ.* **2020**, 193. [CrossRef] [PubMed]
118. Qi, F. Alternative proofs for monotonicity of some functions related to sectional curvature of Fisher–Rao manifold of beta distributions. In *Applied Nonlinear Analysis and Soft Computing: Proceedings of ANASC 2020, Guwahati, India, 22–23 December 2020*; Advance in Intelligent Systems and Computing; Springer: Singapore, 2022; in press.
119. Qi, F. Decreasing properties of two ratios defined by three and four polygamma functions. *C. R. Math. Acad. Sci. Paris* **2022**, *360*, 89–101. [CrossRef]
120. Qi, F. Decreasing property and complete monotonicity of two functions constituted via three derivatives of a function involving trigamma function. *Math. Slovaca* **2022**, *72*, in press. [CrossRef]
121. Qi, F. Lower bound of sectional curvature of Fisher–Rao manifold of beta distributions and complete monotonicity of functions involving polygamma functions. *Results Math.* **2021**, *76*, 217. [CrossRef]
122. Qi, F. Necessary and sufficient conditions for a difference constituted by four derivatives of a function involving trigamma function to be completely monotonic. *Math. Inequal. Appl.* **2021**, *24*, 845–855. [CrossRef]
123. Qi, F. Necessary and sufficient conditions for a difference defined by four derivatives of a function containing trigamma function to be completely monotonic. *Appl. Comput. Math.* **2022**, *21*, 61–70. [CrossRef]
124. Qi, F. Necessary and sufficient conditions for a ratio involving trigamma and tetragamma functions to be monotonic. *Turkish J. Inequal.* **2021**, *5*, 50–59.

125. Qi, F. Some properties of several functions involving polygamma functions and originating from the sectional curvature of the beta manifold. *São Paulo J. Math. Sci.* **2020**, *14*, 614–630. [CrossRef]
126. Qi, F. Two monotonic functions defined by two derivatives of a function involving trigamma function. *TWMS J. Pure Appl. Math.* **2022**, *13*, 91–104.
127. Brigant, A.L.; Preston, S.C.; Puechmorel, S. Fisher–Rao geometry of Dirichlet distributions. *Differ. Geom. Appl.* **2021**, *74*, 16. [CrossRef]
128. Bai, Y.-M.; Qi, F. Some integral inequalities of the Hermite–Hadamard type for log-convex functions on co-ordinates. *J. Nonlinear Sci. Appl.* **2016**, *9*, 5900–5908. [CrossRef]
129. Bai, S.-P.; Wang, S.-H.; Qi, F. On HT-convexity and Hadamard-type inequalities. *J. Inequal. Appl.* **2020**, 1–12.[CrossRef]
130. Hua, J.; Xi, B.-Y.; Qi, F. Some new inequalities of Simpson type for strongly s-convex functions. *Afr. Mat.* **2015**, *26*, 741–752. [CrossRef]
131. Qi, F.; Zhang, T.-Y.; Xi, B.-Y. Hermite–Hadamard-type integral inequalities for functions whose first derivatives are convex. *Ukrainian Math. J.* **2015**, *67*, 625–640. [CrossRef]
132. Shuang, Y.; Qi, F. Integral inequalities of the Hermite–Hadamard type for (α, m)-GA-convex functions. *J. Nonlinear Sci. Appl.* **2017**, *10*, 1854–1860. [CrossRef]
133. Wang, Y.; Zheng, M.-M.; Qi, F. Integral inequalities of Hermite–Hadamard type for functions whose derivatives are (α, m)-preinvex. *J. Inequal. Appl.* **2014**, *2014*, 10. [CrossRef]
134. Wu, Y.; Qi, F. Discussions on two integral inequalities of Hermite–Hadamard type for convex functions. *J. Comput. Appl. Math.* **2022**, *406*, 6. [CrossRef]
135. Wu, Y.; Qi, F.; Pei, Z.-L.; Bai, S.-P. Hermite–Hadamard type integral inequalities via (s, m)-P-convexity on co-ordinates. *J. Nonlinear Sci. Appl.* **2016**, *9*, 876–884. [CrossRef]
136. Xi, B.-Y.; Bai, S.-P.; Qi, F. On integral inequalities of the Hermite–Hadamard type for co-ordinated (α, m_1)-(s, m_2)-convex functions. *J. Interdiscip. Math.* **2018**, *21*, 1505–1518. [CrossRef]
137. Xi, B.-Y.; Gao, D.-D.; Qi, F. Integral inequalities of Hermite–Hadamard type for (α, s)-convex and (α, s, m)-convex functions. *Ital. J. Pure Appl. Math.* **2020**, *44*, 499–510.
138. Xi, B.-Y.; Qi, F. Inequalities of Hermite–Hadamard type for extended s-convex functions and applications to means. *J. Nonlinear Convex Anal.* **2015**, *16*, 873–890.
139. Xi, B.-Y.; Qi, F. Properties and inequalities for the (h_1, h_2)- and (h_1, h_2, m)-GA-convex functions. *Cogent Math.* **2016**, *3*, 1176620. [CrossRef]
140. Xi, B.-Y.; Qi, F. Some inequalities of Hermite–Hadamard type for geometrically P-convex functions. *Adv. Stud. Contemp. Math. (Kyungshang)* **2016**, *26*, 211–220.
141. Huang, C.-J.; Rahman, G.; Nisar, K.S.; Ghaffar, A.; Qi, F. Some inequalities of the Hermite–Hadamard type for k-fractional conformable integrals. *Austral. J. Math. Anal. Appl.* **2019**, *16*, 7. Available online: http://ajmaa.org/cgi-bin/paper.pl?string=v16n1/V16I1P7.tex (accessed on 10 July 2022).
142. Qi, F.; Rahman, G.; Hussain, S.M.; Du, W.-S.; Nisar, K.S. Some inequalities of Čebyšev type for conformable k-fractional integral operators. *Symmetry* **2018**, *10*, 614. [CrossRef]
143. Rahman, G.; Nisar, K.S.; Ghaffar, A.; Qi, F. Some inequalities of the Grüss type for conformable k-fractional integral operators. *Rev. R. Acad. Cienc. Exactas Fís. Nat. Ser. A Mat. RACSAM* **2020**, *114*, 9. [CrossRef]
144. Hoorfar, A.; Qi, F. A new refinement of Young's inequality. *Math. Inequal. Appl.* **2008**, *11*, 689–692. [CrossRef]
145. Qi, F.; Li, W.-H.; Wu, G.-S.; Guo, B.-N. Refinements of Young's integral inequality via fundamental inequalities and mean value theorems for derivatives. In *Topics in Contemporary Mathematical Analysis and Applications*; Dutt, H., Ed.; CRC Press: Boca Raton, FL, USA, 2021; Chapter 8, pp. 193–227. [CrossRef]
146. Qi, F.; Wan, A. Geometric interpretations and reversed versions of Young's integral inequality. *Adv. Theory Nonlinear Anal. Appl.* **2021**, *5*, 1–6. [CrossRef]
147. Wang, J.-Q.; Guo, B.-N.; Qi, F. Generalizations and applications of Young's integral inequality by higher order derivatives. *J. Inequal. Appl.* **2019**, 18. [CrossRef]
148. Mei, J.-Q.; Xu, S.-L.; Qi, F. Curvature pinching for minimal submanifolds in unit spheres. *Math. Appl. (Wuhan)* **1999**, *12*, 5–10.
149. Qi, F.; Guo, B.-N. Lower bound of the first eigenvalue for the Laplace operator on compact Riemannian manifold. *Chinese Quart. J. Math.* **1993**, *8*, 40–49.
150. Qi, F.; Yu, L.-Q.; Luo, Q.-M. Estimates for the upper bounds of the first eigenvalue on submanifolds. *Chin. Quart. Math.* **1994**, *9*, 40–43.
151. Qi, F.; Zheng, M.-M. Absolute monotonicity of functions related to estimates of first eigenvalue of Laplace operator on Riemannian manifolds. *Int. J. Anal. Appl.* **2014**, *6*, 123–131.
152. Xu, S.-L.; Huang, Z.; Qi, F. A rigidity theorem for manifold with a nice submanifold. *Math. Appl. (Wuhan)* **1999**, *12*, 72–75.
153. Pólya, G. Ein mittelwertsatz für Funktionen mehrerer Veränderlichen. *Tôhoku Math. J.* **1921**, *19*, 1–3.
154. Qi, F. Inequalities for an integral. *Math. Gaz.* **1996**, *80*, 376–377. [CrossRef]
155. Sun, Y.; Yang, H.-T.; Qi, F. Some inequalities for multiple integrals on the n-dimensional ellipsoid, spherical shell, and ball. *Abstr. Appl. Anal.* **2013**, *2013*, 904721. [CrossRef]
156. Guo, B.-N.; Qi, F. *Estimates for An Integral in L^p Norm of the $(n+1)$-th Derivative of Its Integrand, Inequality Theory and Applications*; Cho, Y.J., Kim, J.K., Dragomir, S.S., Eds.; Nova Science Publishers: Hauppauge, NY, USA, 2003; Volume 3, pp. 127–131..

157. Guo, B.-N.; Qi, F. Proofs of an integral inequality. *Math. Informatics Q.* **1997**, *7*, 182–184.
158. Guo, B.-N.; Qi, F. Some estimates of an integral in terms of the L^p-norm of the $(n+1)$st derivative of its integrand. *Anal. Math.* **2003**, *29*, 1–6. http://dx.doi.org/10.1023/A:1022894413541. [CrossRef]
159. Qi, F. Further generalizations of inequalities for an integral. *Univ. Beograd. Publ. Elektrotehn. Fak. Ser. Mat.* **1997**, *8*, 79–83. Available online: https://www.jstor.org/stable/i40147167 (accessed on 10 July 2022).
160. Qi, F. Inequalities for a multiple integral. *Acta Math. Hungar.* **1999**, *84*, 19–26.:1006642601341. [CrossRef]
161. Qi, F. Inequalities for a weighted multiple integral. *J. Math. Anal. Appl.* **2001**, *253*, 381–388. [CrossRef]
162. Qi, F.; Cerone, P.; Dragomir, S.S. Some new Iyengar type inequalities. *Rocky Mountain J. Math.* **2005**, *35*, 997–1015. [CrossRef]
163. Qi, F.; Zhang, Y.-J. Inequalities for a weighted integral. *Adv. Stud. Contemp. Math. (Kyungshang)* **2002**, *4*, 93–101.
164. Qi, F. Pólya type integral inequalities: Origin, variants, proofs, refinements, generalizations, equivalences, and applications. *Math. Inequal. Appl.* **2015**, *18*, 1–38. [CrossRef]
165. Qi, F.; Luo, Q.-M. Refinements and extensions of an inequality. *Math. Inform. Q.* **1999**, *9*, 23–25.
166. Qi, F.; Xu, S.-L. Refinements and extensions of an inequality, II. *J. Math. Anal. Appl.* **1997**, *211*, 616–620. [CrossRef]
167. Guo, B.-N.; Qi, F. On the degree of the weighted geometric mean as a complete Bernstein function. *Afr. Mat.* **2015**, *26*, 1253–1262. [CrossRef]
168. Qi, F. Bounding the difference and ratio between the weighted arithmetic and geometric means. *Int. J. Anal. Appl.* **2017**, *13*, 132–135.
169. Qi, F.; Chen, S.-X. Complete monotonicity of the logarithmic mean. *Math. Inequal. Appl.* **2007**, *10*, 799–804. [CrossRef]
170. Qi, F.; Guo, B.-N. The reciprocal of the geometric mean of many positive numbers is a Stieltjes transform. *J. Comput. Appl. Math.* **2017**, *311*, 165–170. [CrossRef]
171. Qi, F.; Guo, B.-N. The reciprocal of the weighted geometric mean is a Stieltjes function. *Bol. Soc. Mat. Mex. (3)* **2018**, *24*, 181–202. [CrossRef]
172. Qi, F.; Guo, B.-N. The reciprocal of the weighted geometric mean of many positive numbers is a Stieltjes function. *Quaest. Math.* **2018**, *41*, 653–664. [CrossRef]
173. Qi, F.; Lim, D. Integral representations of bivariate complex geometric mean and their applications. *J. Comput. Appl. Math.* **2018**, *330*, 41–58. [CrossRef]
174. Qi, F.; Zhang, X.-J.; Li, W.-H. An elementary proof of the weighted geometric mean being a Bernstein function. *Politehn. Univ. Bucharest Sci. Bull. Ser. A Appl. Math. Phys.* **2015**, *77*, 35–38.
175. Qi, F.; Zhang, X.-J.; Li, W.-H. An integral representation for the weighted geometric mean and its applications. *Acta Math. Sin. (Engl. Ser.)* **2014**, *30*, 61–68. [CrossRef]
176. Qi, F.; Zhang, X.-J.; Li, W.-H. Lévy–Khintchine representation of the geometric mean of many positive numbers and applications. *Math. Inequal. Appl.* **2014**, *17*, 719–729. [CrossRef]
177. Qi, F.; Zhang, X.-J.; Li, W.-H. Lévy–Khintchine representations of the weighted geometric mean and the logarithmic mean. *Mediterr. J. Math.* **2014**, *11*, 315–327. [CrossRef]
178. Qi, F.; Zhang, X.-J.; Li, W.-H. The harmonic and geometric means are Bernstein functions. *Bol. Soc. Mat. Mex. (3)* **2017**, *23*, 713–736. [CrossRef]
179. Aljinović, A.A.; Pečarić, J. Note on an integral inequality similar to Qi's inequality. *Math. Maced.* **2009**, *7*, 1–7.
180. Chammam, W. Catalan–Qi numbers, series involving the Catalan–Qi numbers and a Hankel determinant evaluation. *J. Math.* **2020**, 8101725. [CrossRef]
181. Corcino, R.B.; Vega, M.A.R.P.; Dibagulun, A.M. A (p,q)-analogue of Qi-type formula for r-Dowling numbers. *J. Math. Computer Sci.* **2022**, *24*, 273–286. [CrossRef]
182. Mao, Z.-X.; Zhu, Y.-R.; Guo, B.-H.; Wang, F.-H.; Yang, Y.-H.; Zhao, H.-Q. Qi type diamond-alpha integral inequalities. *Mathematics* **2021**, *9*, 24. [CrossRef]
183. Nemes, G. A solution to an open problem on Mathieu series posed by Hoorfar and Qi. *Acta Math. Vietnam.* **2012**, *37*, 301–310.
184. Pečarić, J.; T Pejković, T. Note on Feng Qi's integral inequality. *J. Inequal. Pure Appl. Math.* **2004**, *5*, 51. Available online: http://www.emis.de/journals/JIPAM/article418.html (accessed on 10 July 2022).
185. Pogány, T.K. On an open problem of F. Qi. *J. Inequal. Pure Appl. Math.* **2002**, *3*, 54. Available online: http://www.emis.de/journals/JIPAM/article206.html (accessed on 10 July 2022).
186. Bernstein, D.S. *Scalar, Vector, and Matrix Mathematics: Theory, Facts, and Formulas-Revised and Expanded Edition*; Expanded, R.A., Ed.; Princeton University Press: Princeton, NJ, USA, 2018. Available online: https://press.princeton.edu/books/hardcover/9780691151205/scalar-vector-and-matrix-mathematics (accessed on 10 July 2022).
187. Bernstein, D.S. *Matrix Mathematics: Theory, Facts, and Formulas*, 2nd ed.; Princeton University Press: Princeton, NJ, USA, 2009. [CrossRef]
188. Bullen, P.S. *Dictionary of Inequalities*, 2nd ed.; Monographs and Research Notes in Mathematics; CRC Press: Boca Raton, FL, USA, 2015. [CrossRef]
189. Olver, F.W.J.; Lozier, D.W.; Boisvert, R.F.; Clark, C.W. (Eds.) *NIST Digital Library of Mathematical Functions*; U.S. Department of Commerce, National Institute of Standards and Technology: Washington, DC, USA; Cambridge University Press: Cambridge, UK, 2010–2020. Available online: https://dlmf.nist.gov/ (accessed on 10 July 2022).

190. Olver, F.W.J.; Lozier, D.W.; Boisvert, R.F.; Clark, C.W. (Eds.) *NIST Handbook of Mathematical Functions*; U.S. Department of Commerce, National Institute of Standards and Technology: Washington, DC, USA; Cambridge University Press, Cambridge, UK, 2010. Available online: http://www.cambridge.org/catalogue/catalogue.asp?isbn=9780521192255 (accessed on 10 July 2022).
191. Schilling, R.L.; Song, R.; Vondraček, Z. *Bernstein Functions. Theory and Applications*, de Gruyter Studies in Mathematics; Walter de Gruyter & Co.: Berlin, Germany, 2010; Volume 37.
192. Schilling, R.L.; Song, R.; Vondraček, Z. *Bernstein Functions: Theory and Applications*, 2nd ed.; De Gruyter Studies in Mathematics; Walter de Gruyter & Co.: Berlin, Germany, 2012; Volume 37. [CrossRef]
193. Qi, F.; Guo, B.-N. Complete monotonicities of functions involving the gamma and digamma functions. *RGMIA Res. Rep. Coll.* **2004**, *7*, 63–72. Available online: http://rgmia.org/v7n1.php (accessed on 10 July 2022).
194. Qi, F.; Guo, B.-N.; Chen, C.-P. Some completely monotonic functions involving the gamma and polygamma functions. *RGMIA Res. Rep. Coll.* **2004**, *7*, 31–36. Available online: http://rgmia.org/v7n1.php (accessed on 10 July 2022). [CrossRef]
195. Qi, F.; Chen, C.-P. A complete monotonicity property of the gamma function. *J. Math. Anal. Appl.* **2004**, *296*, 603–607. [CrossRef]
196. Qi, F.; Guo, B.-N.; Chen, C.-P. Some completely monotonic functions involving the gamma and polygamma functions. *J. Aust. Math. Soc.* **2006**, *80*, 81–88. [CrossRef]
197. Berg, C. Integral representation of some functions related to the gamma function. *Mediterr. J. Math.* **2004**, *1*, 433–439. [CrossRef]
198. Guo, S.; Srivastava, H.M.; Cheung, W.-S. Some properties of functions related to certain classes of completely monotonic functions and logarithmically completely monotonic functions. *Filomat* **2014**, *28*, 821–828. [CrossRef]
199. Li, A.-J.; Zhao, W.-Z.; Chen, C.-P. Logarithmically complete monotonicity properties for the ratio of gamma function. *Adv. Stud. Contemp. Math. (Kyungshang)* **2006**, *13*, 183–191.
200. Mehrez, K.; Das, S. Logarithmically completely monotonic functions related to the q-gamma function and its applications. *Anal. Math. Phys.* **2022**, *12*, 20. [CrossRef]
201. Tian, J.-F.; Yang, Z.-H. Logarithmically complete monotonicity of ratios of q-gamma functions. *J. Math. Anal. Appl.* **2022**, *508*, 13. [CrossRef]
202. Atanassov, R.D.; Tsoukrovski, U.V. Some properties of a class of logarithmically completely monotonic functions. *C. R. Acad. Bulgare Sci.* **1988**, *41*, 21–23.
203. Cao, J.; Niu, D.-W.; Qi, F. A refinement of Carleman's inequality. *Adv. Stud. Contemp. Math. (Kyungshang)* **2006**, *13*, 57–62.
204. Cao, J.; Niu, D.-W.; Qi, F. An extension and a refinement of van der Corput's inequality. *Internat. J. Math. Math. Sci.* **2006**, 70786. [CrossRef]
205. Huo, Z.-H.; Niu, D.-W.; Cao, J.; Qi, F. A generalization of Jordan's inequality and an application. *Hacet. J. Math. Stat.* **2011**, *40*, 53–61.
206. Jiang, W.-D.; Cao, J.; Qi, F. Sharp inequalities for bounding Seiffert mean in terms of the arithmetic, centroidal, and contra-harmonic means. *Math. Slovaca* **2016**, *66*, 1115–1118. [CrossRef]
207. Niu, D.-W.; Cao, J.; Qi, F. A class of logarithmically completely monotonic functions related to $(1 + 1/x)^x$ and an application. *Gen. Math.* **2006**, *14*, 97–112.
208. Niu, D.-W.; Cao, J.; Qi, F. A refinement of van der Corput's inequality. *J. Inequal. Pure Appl. Math.* **2006**, *7*, 127. Available online: http://www.emis.de/journals/JIPAM/article744.html (accessed on 10 July 2022).
209. Niu, D.-W.; Cao, J.; Qi, F. Generalizations of Jordan's inequality and concerned relations. *Politehn. Univ. Bucharest Sci. Bull. Ser. A Appl. Math. Phys.* **2010**, *72*, 85–98.
210. Niu, D.-W.; Huo, Z.-H.; Cao, J.; Qi, F. A general refinement of Jordan's inequality and a refinement of L. Yang's inequality. *Integral Transforms Spec. Funct.* **2008**, *19*, 157–164. [CrossRef]
211. Qi, F.; Cao, J.; Niu, D.-W. A generalization of van der Corput's inequality. *Appl. Math. Comput.* **2008**, *203*, 770–777. [CrossRef]
212. Qi, F.; Cao, J.; Niu, D.-W. More notes on a functional equation. *Internat. J. Math. Ed. Sci. Tech.* **2006**, *37*, 865–868. [CrossRef]
213. Qi, F.; Cao, J.; Niu, D.-W.; Ujević, N. An upper bound of a function with two independent variables. *Appl. Math. E-Notes* **2006**, *6*, 17.
214. Qi, F.; Jiang, W.-D.; Cao, J. Two double inequalities for the Seiffert mean in terms of the arithmetic, centroidal, and contra-harmonic means. *Adv. Stud. Contemp. Math. (Kyungshang)* **2015**, *25*, 547–552.
215. Qi, F.; Li, A.-J.; Zhao, W.-Z.; Niu, D.-W.; Cao, J. Extensions of several integral inequalities. *J. Inequal. Pure Appl. Math.* **2006**, *7*, 107. Available online: http://www.emis.de/journals/JIPAM/article706.html (accessed on 10 July 2022).
216. Qi, F.; Niu, D.-W.; Cao, J. An infimum and an upper bound of a function with two independent variables. *Octogon Math. Mag.* **2006**, *14*, 248–250.
217. Qi, F.; Niu, D.-W.; Cao, J. Logarithmically completely monotonic functions involving gamma and polygamma functions. *J. Math. Anal. Approx. Theory* **2006**, *1*, 66–74.
218. Qi, F.; Niu, D.-W.; Cao, J.; Chen, S.-X. Four logarithmically completely monotonic functions involving gamma function. *J. Korean Math. Soc.* **2008**, *45*, 559–573. [CrossRef]
219. Mahmoud, M.; Qi, F. Bounds for completely monotonic degrees of remainders in asymptotic expansions of the digamma function. *Math. Inequal. Appl.* **2022**, *25*, 291–306. [CrossRef]
220. Ouimet, F.; Qi, F. Logarithmically complete monotonicity of a matrix-parametrized analogue of the multinomial distribution. *Math. Inequal. Appl.* **2022**, *25*, 703–714. [CrossRef]
221. Qi, F. Bounds for the ratio of two gamma functions. *J. Inequal. Appl.* **2010**, *2010*, 493058. [CrossRef]

222. Qi, F. Bounds for the ratio of two gamma functions: from Gautschi's and Kershaw's inequalities to complete monotonicity. *Turkish J. Anal. Number Theory* **2014**, *2*, 152–164. [CrossRef]
223. Qi, F. Complete monotonicity for a new ratio of finitely many gamma functions. *Acta Math. Sci. Ser. B (Engl. Ed.)* **2022**, *42B*, 511–520. [CrossRef]
224. Qi, F.; Niu, D.-W.; Guo, B.-N. Refinements, generalizations, and applications of Jordan's inequality and related problems. *J. Inequal. Appl.* **2009**, *2009*, 271923. [CrossRef]

Article

Bounds for the Neuman–Sándor Mean in Terms of the Arithmetic and Contra-Harmonic Means

Wen-Hui Li [1], Peng Miao [1] and Bai-Ni Guo [2,*]

[1] Department of Basic Courses, Zhengzhou University of Science and Technology, Zhengzhou 450064, China; wen.hui.li102@gmail.com (W.-H.L.); miaopeng881026@163.com (P.M.)
[2] School of Mathematics and Informatics, Henan Polytechnic University, Jiaozuo 454010, China
* Correspondence: bai.ni.guo@gmail.com

Abstract: In this paper, the authors provide several sharp upper and lower bounds for the Neuman–Sándor mean in terms of the arithmetic and contra-harmonic means, and present some new sharp inequalities involving hyperbolic sine function and hyperbolic cosine function.

Keywords: Neuman–Sándor mean; arithmetic mean; contra-harmonic mean; bound; inequality; hyperbolic sine function; hyperbolic cosine function

MSC: Primary 26E60; Secondary 26D07; 33B10; 41A30

Citation: Li, W.-H.; Miao, P.; Guo, B.-N. Bounds for the Neuman–Sándor Mean in Terms of the Arithmetic and Contra-Harmonic Means. *Axioms* **2022**, *11*, 236. https://doi.org/10.3390/axioms11050236

Academic Editor: Wei-Shih Du

Received: 28 April 2022
Accepted: 16 May 2022
Published: 19 May 2022

Publisher's Note: MDPI stays neutral with regard to jurisdictional claims in published maps and institutional affiliations.

Copyright: © 2022 by the authors. Licensee MDPI, Basel, Switzerland. This article is an open access article distributed under the terms and conditions of the Creative Commons Attribution (CC BY) license (https://creativecommons.org/licenses/by/4.0/).

1. Introduction

In the literature, the quantities

$$A(s,t) = \frac{s+t}{2}, \quad G(s,t) = \sqrt{st}, \quad H(s,t) = \frac{2st}{s+t},$$

$$\overline{C}(s,t) = \frac{2(s^2+st+t^2)}{3(s+t)}, \quad C(s,t) = \frac{s^2+t^2}{s+t},$$

$$S(s,t) = \sqrt{\frac{s^2+t^2}{2}}, \quad M_p(s,t) = \begin{cases} \left(\dfrac{s^p+t^p}{2}\right)^{1/p}, & p \neq 0; \\ \sqrt{st}, & p = 0 \end{cases}$$

are called in [1–3], for example, the arithmetic mean, geometric mean, harmonic mean, centroidal mean, contra-harmonic mean, root-square mean, and the power mean of order p of two positive numbers s and t, respectively.

For $s,t > 0$ with $s \neq t$, the first Seiffert means $P(s,t)$, the second Seiffert means $T(s,t)$, and Neuman–Sándor mean $M(s,t)$ are, respectively, defined [4–6] by

$$P(s,t) = \frac{s-t}{4\arctan\left(\sqrt{\frac{s}{t}}\right) - \pi}, \quad T(s,t) = \frac{s-t}{2\arctan\frac{s-t}{s+t}}, \quad M(s,t) = \frac{s-t}{2\operatorname{arsinh}\frac{s-t}{s+t}},$$

where $\operatorname{arsinh} v = \ln(v + \sqrt{v^2+1})$ is the inverse hyperbolic sine function.
The first Seiffert mean $P(s,t)$ can be rewritten [6] (Equation (2.4)) as

$$P(s,t) = \frac{s-t}{2\arcsin\frac{s-t}{s+t}}.$$

A chain of inequalities

$$G(s,t) < L_{-1}(s,t) < P(s,t) < A(s,t) < M(s,t) < T(s,t) < Q(s,t)$$

were given in [6], where

$$L_p(s,t) = \begin{cases} \left[\dfrac{t^{p+1} - s^{p+1}}{(p+1)(t-s)}\right]^{1/p}, & p \neq -1, 0; \\ \dfrac{1}{e}\left(\dfrac{t^t}{s^s}\right)^{1/(t-s)}, & p = 0; \\ \dfrac{t-s}{\ln t - \ln s}, & p = -1 \end{cases}$$

is the p-th generalized logarithmic mean of s and t with $s \neq t$.

In [6,7], three double inequalities

$$A(s,t) < M(s,t) < T(s,t), \quad P(s,t) < M(s,t) < T^2(s,t),$$

and

$$A(s,t)T(s,t) < M^2(s,t) < \dfrac{A^2(s,t) + T^2(s,t)}{2}$$

were established for $s, t > 0$ with $s \neq t$.

For $0 < s, t < \tfrac{1}{2}$ with $s \neq t$, the inequalities

$$\dfrac{G(s,t)}{G(1-s, 1-t)} < \dfrac{L_{-1}(s,t)}{L_{-1}(1-s, 1-t)} < \dfrac{P(s,t)}{P(1-s, 1-t)}$$

$$< \dfrac{A(s,t)}{A(1-s, 1-t)} < \dfrac{M(s,t)}{M(1-s, 1-t)} < \dfrac{T(s,t)}{T(1-s, 1-t)}$$

of Ky Fan type were presented in [6] (Proposition 2.2).

In [8], Li and their two coauthors showed that the double inequality

$$L_{p_0}(s,t) < M(s,t) < L_2(s,t)$$

holds for all $s, t > 0$ with $s \neq t$ and for $p_0 = 1.843\ldots$, where p_0 is the unique solution of the equation $(p+1)^{1/p} = 2\ln(1 + \sqrt{2})$.

In [9], Neuman proved that the double inequalities

$$\alpha Q(s,t) + (1-\alpha)A(s,t) < M(s,t) < \beta Q(s,t) + (1-\beta)A(s,t)$$

and

$$\lambda C(s,t) + (1-\lambda)A(s,t) < M(s,t) < \mu C(s,t) + (1-\mu)A(s,t)$$

hold for all $s, t > 0$ with $s \neq t$ if and only if

$$\alpha \leq \dfrac{1 - \ln(1 + \sqrt{2})}{(\sqrt{2} - 1)\ln(1 + \sqrt{2})} = 0.3249\ldots, \quad \beta \geq \dfrac{1}{3}$$

and

$$\lambda \leq \dfrac{1 - \ln(1 + \sqrt{2})}{\ln(1 + \sqrt{2})} = 0.1345\ldots, \quad \mu \geq \dfrac{1}{6}.$$

In [10], (Theorems 1.1 to 1.3), it was found that the double inequalities

$$\alpha_1 H(s,t) + (1-\alpha_1)Q(s,t) < M(s,t) < \beta_1 H(s,t) + (1-\beta_1)Q(s,t),$$

$$\alpha_2 G(s,t) + (1-\alpha_2)Q(s,t) < M(s,t) < \beta_2 G(s,t) + (1-\beta_2)Q(s,t),$$

and

$$\alpha_3 H(s,t) + (1-\alpha_3)C(s,t) < M(s,t) < \beta_3 H(s,t) + (1-\beta_3)C(s,t)$$

hold for all $s, t > 0$ with $s \neq t$ if and only if

$$\alpha_1 \geq \frac{2}{9} = 0.2222\ldots, \quad \beta_1 \leq 1 - \frac{1}{\sqrt{2}\ln(1+\sqrt{2})} = 0.1977\ldots,$$

$$\alpha_2 \geq \frac{1}{3} = 0.3333\ldots, \quad \beta_2 \leq 1 - \frac{1}{\sqrt{2}\ln(1+\sqrt{2})} = 0.1977\ldots,$$

and

$$\alpha_3 \geq 1 - \frac{1}{2\ln(1+\sqrt{2})} = 0.4327\ldots, \quad \beta_3 \leq \frac{5}{12} = 0.4166\ldots$$

In 2017, Chen and their two coauthors [11] established bounds for Neuman–Sándor mean $M(s,t)$ in terms of the convex combination of the logarithmic mean and the second Seiffert mean $T(s,t)$. In 2022, Wang and Yin [12] obtained bounds for the reciprocals of the Neuman–Sándor mean $M(s,t)$.

In [13], it was showed that the double inequality

$$\frac{\alpha}{A(s,t)} + \frac{1-\alpha}{C(s,t)} < \frac{1}{TD(s,t)} < \frac{\beta}{A(s,t)} + \frac{1-\beta}{C(s,t)} \tag{1}$$

holds for all $s, t > 0$ with $s \neq t$ if and only if $\alpha \leq \pi - 3$ and $\beta \geq \frac{1}{4}$, where $TD(s,t)$ is the Toader mean introduced in [14] by

$$TD(s,t) = \frac{2}{\pi} \int_0^{\pi/2} \sqrt{s^2 \cos^2 \phi + t^2 \sin^2 \phi} \, d\phi.$$

In this paper, motivated by the double inequality (1), we will aim to find out the largest values α_1, α_2, and α_3 and the smallest values β_1, β_2, and β_3 such that the double inequalities

$$\frac{\alpha_1}{C(s,t)} + \frac{1-\alpha_1}{A(s,t)} < \frac{1}{M(s,t)} < \frac{\beta_1}{C(s,t)} + \frac{1-\beta_1}{A(s,t)}, \tag{2}$$

$$\frac{\alpha_2}{C^2(s,t)} + \frac{1-\alpha_2}{A^2(s,t)} < \frac{1}{M^2(s,t)} < \frac{\beta_2}{C^2(s,t)} + \frac{1-\beta_2}{A^2(s,t)}, \tag{3}$$

and

$$\alpha_3 C^2(s,t) + (1-\alpha_3)A^2(s,t) < M^2(s,t) < \beta_3 C^2(s,t) + (1-\beta_3)A^2(s,t) \tag{4}$$

hold for all positive real numbers s and t with $s \neq t$.

2. Lemmas

To attain our main purposes, we need the following lemmas.

Lemma 1 ([15] (Theorem 1.25)). *For $-\infty < s < t < \infty$, let $f, g : [s,t] \to \mathbb{R}$ be continuous on $[s,t]$, differentiable on (s,t), and $g'(v) \neq 0$ on (s,t). If $\frac{f'(v)}{g'(v)}$ is (strictly) increasing (or strictly) decreasing, respectively) on (s,t), so are the functions*

$$\frac{f(v)-f(s)}{g(v)-g(s)} \quad \text{and} \quad \frac{f(v)-f(t)}{g(v)-g(t)}.$$

Lemma 2 ([16] (Lemma 1.1)). *Suppose that the power series $f(v) = \sum_{\ell=0}^{\infty} u_\ell v^\ell$ and $g(v) = \sum_{\ell=0}^{\infty} w_\ell v^\ell$ have the convergent radius $r > 0$ and $w_\ell > 0$ for all $\ell \in \mathbb{N} = \{0,1,2,\ldots\}$. Let $h(v) = \frac{f(v)}{g(v)}$. Then the following statements are true.*

1. *If the sequence $\{\frac{u_\ell}{w_\ell}\}_{\ell=0}^{\infty}$ is (strictly) increasing (or decreasing, respectively), then $h(v)$ is also (strictly) increasing (or decreasing, respectively) on $(0,r)$.*
2. *If the sequence $\{\frac{u_\ell}{w_\ell}\}_{\ell=0}^{\infty}$ is (strictly) increasing (or decreasing resepctively) for $0 < \ell \leq \ell_0$ and (strictly) decreasing (or increasing resepctively) for $\ell > \ell_0$, then there exists $x_0 \in (0,r)$*

such that $h(v)$ is (strictly) increasing (decreasing) on $(0, x_0)$ and (strictly) decreasing (or increasing resepctively) on (x_0, r).

Lemma 3. Let
$$h_1(v) = \frac{2v \sinh v + \cosh v - 1}{3 \sinh^2 v}.$$
Then $h_1(v)$ is strictly decreasing on $(0, \infty)$ with $\lim_{v \to 0^+} h_1(v) = \frac{5}{6}$ and $\lim_{v \to \infty} h_1(v) = 0$.

Proof. Let
$$f_1(v) = 2v \sinh v + \cosh v - 1 \quad \text{and} \quad f_2(v) = 3 \sinh^2 v = \frac{3}{2}[\cosh(2v) - 1].$$

Using the power series
$$\sinh v = \sum_{\ell=0}^{\infty} \frac{v^{2\ell+1}}{(2\ell+1)!} \quad \text{and} \quad \cosh v = \sum_{\ell=0}^{\infty} \frac{v^{2\ell}}{(2\ell)!}, \tag{5}$$

we can express the functions $f_1(v)$ and $f_2(v)$ as
$$f_1(v) = \sum_{\ell=0}^{\infty} \frac{2(2\ell+2)! + (2\ell+1)!}{(2\ell+1)!(2\ell+2)!} v^{2\ell+2} \quad \text{and} \quad f_2(v) = \frac{3}{2} \sum_{\ell=0}^{\infty} \frac{2^{2\ell+2} v^{2\ell+2}}{(2\ell+2)!}.$$

Hence, we have
$$h_1(v) = \frac{\sum_{\ell=0}^{\infty} u_\ell v^{2\ell+2}}{\sum_{\ell=0}^{\infty} w_\ell v^{2\ell+2}}, \tag{6}$$

where $u_\ell = \frac{2(2\ell+2)! + (2\ell+1)!}{(2\ell+1)!(2\ell+2)!}$ and $w_\ell = \frac{3 \times 2^{2\ell+1}}{(2\ell+2)!}$.
Let $c_\ell = \frac{u_\ell}{w_\ell}$. Then
$$c_\ell = \frac{2(2\ell+2)! + (2\ell+1)!}{3(2\ell+1)! 2^{2\ell+1}} \quad \text{and} \quad c_{\ell+1} - c_\ell = -\frac{4(3\ell+4)(2\ell+2)! + 3(2\ell+3)!}{3(2\ell+3)! 2^{2\ell+3}} < 0.$$

As a result, by Lemma 2, it follows that the function $h_1(v)$ is strictly decreasing on $(0, \infty)$. From (6), it is easy to see that $\lim_{v \to 0^+} h_1(v) = \frac{u_0}{w_0} = \frac{5}{6}$.
Using the L'Hospital rule leads to $\lim_{v \to \infty} h_1(v) = 0$ immediately. The proof of Lemma 3 is complete. □

Lemma 4. Let
$$h_2(v) = \frac{(\sinh^2 v - v^2) \cosh^4 v}{(\cosh^2 v + 1) \sinh^4 v}.$$

Then $h_2(v)$ is strictly increasing on $v \in (0, \infty)$ and has the limit $\lim_{v \to 0^+} h_2(v) = \frac{1}{6}$ and $\lim_{v \to \infty} h_2(v) = 1$.

Proof. Let
$$f_3(v) = (\sinh^2 v - v^2) \cosh^4 v \quad \text{and} \quad f_4(v) = (\cosh^2 v + 1) \sinh^4 v.$$

Since
$$f_3'(v) = 2(\sinh v + 3 \sinh^3 v - v \cosh v - 2v^2 \sinh v) \cosh^3 v$$

and
$$f_4'(v) = 2(3 \cosh^2 v + 1) \sinh^3 v \cosh v,$$

we obtain

$$\frac{f_3'(v)}{f_4'(v)} = \frac{(\sinh v + 3\sinh^3 v - v\cosh v - 2v^2 \sinh v)\cosh^2 v}{(3\cosh^2 v + 1)\sinh^3 v}$$

$$= \frac{\cosh^2 v}{3\cosh^2 v + 1} \cdot \frac{\sinh v + 3\sinh^3 v - v\cosh v - 2v^2 \sinh v}{\sinh^3 v}$$

$$= \frac{1}{3 + \frac{1}{\cosh^2 v}} \left(3 + \frac{\sinh v - v\cosh v - 2v^2 \sinh v}{\sinh^3 v}\right)$$

$$= \frac{1}{3 + \frac{1}{\cosh^2 v}} [3 + g(v)],$$

where

$$g(v) = \frac{\sinh v - v\cosh v - 2v^2 \sinh v}{\sinh^3 v}.$$

By using the identity that $\sinh(3v) = 3\sinh v + 4\sinh^3 v$, we arrive at

$$g(v) = 4 \frac{\sinh v - v\cosh v - 2v^2 \sinh v}{\sinh(3v) - 3\sinh v} \triangleq 4\frac{g_1(v)}{g_2(v)},$$

where $g_1(v) = \sinh v - v\cosh v - 2v^2 \sinh v$ and $g_2(v) = \sinh(3v) - 3\sinh v$.
Straightforward computation gives

$$g_1'(v) = -(5v\sinh v + 2v^2 \cosh v), \qquad g_2'(v) = 3[\cosh(3v) - \cosh v],$$
$$g_1''(v) = -(5\sinh v + 9v\cosh v + 2v^2 \sinh v), \qquad g_2''(v) = 3[3\sinh(3v) - \sinh v],$$

and

$$g_1(0^+) = g_2(0^+) = g_1'(0^+) = g_2'(0^+) = g_1''(0^+) = g_2''(0^+) = 0.$$

Consequently, we obtain

$$\frac{g_1''(v)}{g_2''(v)} = -\frac{5\sinh v + 9v\cosh v + 2v^2 \sinh v}{3[3\sinh(3v) - \sinh v]} \triangleq -\frac{1}{3}\frac{g_3(v)}{g_4(v)}.$$

Using the power series of $\sinh v$ and $\cosh v$, we deduce

$$g_3(v) = 5\sum_{\ell=0}^{\infty} \frac{v^{2\ell+1}}{(2\ell+1)!} + 9\sum_{\ell=0}^{\infty} \frac{v^{2\ell+1}}{(2\ell)!} + 2\sum_{\ell=0}^{\infty} \frac{v^{2\ell+3}}{(2\ell+1)!}$$

$$= 14v + \sum_{\ell=1}^{\infty} \left[\frac{5}{(2\ell+1)!} + \frac{9}{(2\ell)!} + \frac{2}{(2\ell-1)!}\right] v^{2\ell+1}$$

$$= 14v + \sum_{\ell=1}^{\infty} \left[\frac{(4\ell+7)(2\ell)! + 9(2\ell+1)!}{(2\ell)!(2\ell+1)!}\right] v^{2\ell+1}$$

and

$$g_4(v) = 3\sum_{\ell=0}^{\infty} \frac{(3v)^{2\ell+1}}{(2\ell+1)!} - \sum_{\ell=0}^{\infty} \frac{v^{2\ell+1}}{(2\ell+1)!} = \sum_{\ell=0}^{\infty} \left[\frac{3^{2\ell+2}-1}{(2\ell+1)!}\right] v^{2\ell+1}.$$

Therefore, we find

$$\frac{g_3(v)}{g_4(v)} = \frac{\sum_{\ell=0}^{\infty} u_\ell v^{2\ell+1}}{\sum_{\ell=0}^{\infty} w_\ell v^{2\ell+1}},$$

where

$$u_\ell = \begin{cases} 14, & \ell = 0; \\ \dfrac{(4\ell+7)(2\ell)! + 9(2\ell+1)!}{(2\ell)!(2\ell+1)!}, & \ell \geq 1 \end{cases} \quad \text{and} \quad w_\ell = \begin{cases} 8 > 0, & \ell = 0; \\ \dfrac{3^{2\ell+2}-1}{(2\ell+1)!}, & \ell \geq 1. \end{cases}$$

Let $c_\ell = \dfrac{u_\ell}{w_\ell}$. Then

$$c_\ell = \begin{cases} \dfrac{7}{4}, & \ell = 0; \\ \dfrac{(4\ell+7)(2\ell)! + 9(2\ell+1)!}{(3^{2\ell+2}-1)(2\ell)!}, & \ell \geq 1. \end{cases}$$

When $\ell = 0$, we have $c_1 - c_0 = -\dfrac{51}{40} < 0$. When $\ell \geq 1$, it follows that

$$c_{\ell+1} - c_\ell = \dfrac{(4\ell+11)(2\ell+2)! + 9(2\ell+3)!}{(3^{2\ell+4}-1)(2\ell+2)!} - \dfrac{(4\ell+7)(2\ell)! + 9(2\ell+1)!}{(3^{2\ell+2}-1)(2\ell)!}$$

$$= \dfrac{1}{(3^{2\ell+2}-1)(3^{2\ell+4}-1)(2\ell+2)!}\{[(4\ell+11)(2\ell+2)!$$
$$+ 9(2\ell+3)!](3^{2\ell+2}-1) - [(4\ell+7)(2\ell)! + 9(2\ell+1)!](2\ell+2)(3^{2\ell+4}-1)\}$$

$$= \dfrac{1}{(3^{2\ell+2}-1)(3^{2\ell+4}-1)(2\ell+2)!}\{[(4\ell+11)(2\ell+2)!$$
$$+ 9(2\ell+3)!]3^{2\ell+2} - [(4\ell+7)(2\ell)! + 9(2\ell+1)!](2\ell+2)3^{2\ell+4}$$
$$+ (2\ell+2)[(4\ell+7)(2\ell)! + 9(2\ell+1)!] - [(4\ell+11)(2\ell+2)! + 9(2\ell+3)!]\}$$

$$= -\dfrac{1}{(3^{2\ell+2}-1)(3^{2\ell+4}-1)(2\ell+2)!}\{[(8\ell+13)(2\ell+2)!$$
$$+ 9(16\ell+15)(2\ell+1)!]3^{2\ell+2} + 9(2\ell+1)! + 4(2\ell+2)!\}$$
$$< 0.$$

By Lemma 2, it follows that the function $\dfrac{g_3(v)}{g_4(v)}$ is strictly decreasing on $(0, \infty)$, so the function $\dfrac{g_1''(v)}{g_2''(v)}$ is strictly increasing on $(0, \infty)$. Applying Lemma 1, it follows that the function $g(v)$ is strictly increasing on $(0, \infty)$. By the L'Hospital rule, we have

$$\lim_{v \to 0^+} g(v) = -\dfrac{7}{3} \quad \text{and} \quad \lim_{v \to \infty} g(v) = 0.$$

It is common knowledge that the function $\cosh v$ is strictly increasing on $(0, \infty)$. Hence, the function $\dfrac{1}{3+\frac{1}{\cosh^2 v}}$ is strictly increasing on $(0, \infty)$. Therefore, the function $h_2(v)$ is strictly increasing on $(0, \infty)$ with the limits

$$\lim_{v \to 0} h_2(v) = \dfrac{1}{6} \quad \text{and} \quad \lim_{v \to \infty} h_2(v) = 1.$$

The proof of Lemma 3 is complete. □

Lemma 5. *Let*

$$h_3(v) = \dfrac{2v \cosh^2 v}{\sinh v}.$$

Then $h_3(v)$ is strictly increasing on $(0, \infty)$ and has the limit $\lim_{v \to 0^+} h_3(v) = 2$.

Proof. Let $k_1(v) = 2v \cosh^2 v = v \cosh(2v) + v$ and $k_2(v) = \sinh v$. By Equation (5), we have

$$k_1(v) = 2v + \sum_{\ell=1}^{\infty} \frac{2^{2\ell}}{(2\ell)!} v^{2\ell+1} \quad \text{and} \quad k_2(v) = \sum_{\ell=0}^{\infty} \frac{v^{2\ell+1}}{(2\ell+1)!}.$$

Hence,

$$h_3(v) = \frac{2v + \sum_{\ell=1}^{\infty} u_\ell v^{2\ell+1}}{\sum_{\ell=0}^{\infty} w_\ell v^{2\ell+1}}, \qquad (7)$$

where

$$u_\ell = \begin{cases} 2, & \ell = 0; \\ \dfrac{2^{2\ell}}{(2\ell)!}, & \ell \geq 1 \end{cases} \quad \text{and} \quad w_\ell = \frac{1}{(2\ell+1)!}.$$

Let $c_\ell = \frac{u_\ell}{w_\ell}$. Then

$$c_\ell = \begin{cases} 2, & \ell = 0; \\ \dfrac{(2\ell+1)! 2^{2\ell}}{(2\ell)!}, & \ell \geq 1 \end{cases} \quad \text{and} \quad c_{\ell+1} - c_\ell = \begin{cases} 10, & \ell = 0; \\ \dfrac{(3\ell+5)(2\ell+1)! 2^{2\ell+1}}{(2\ell+2)!} > 0, & \ell \geq 1. \end{cases}$$

Thus, by Lemma 2, it follows that the function $h_3(v)$ is strictly increasing on $(0, \infty)$. From (7), it is easy to see that $\lim_{v \to 0^+} h_3(v) = \frac{u_0}{w_0} = 2$. The proof of Lemma 5 is complete. □

3. Bounds for Neuman–Sándor Mean

Now we are in a position to state and prove our main results.

Theorem 1. *For $s, t > 0$ with $s \neq t$, the double inequality (2) holds if and only if*

$$\alpha_1 \geq 2[1 - \ln(1 + \sqrt{2})] = 0.237253\ldots \quad \text{and} \quad \beta_1 \leq \frac{1}{6}.$$

Proof. Without loss of generality, we assume that $s > t > 0$. Let $q = \frac{s-t}{s+t}$. Then $q \in (0, 1)$ and

$$\frac{\frac{1}{M(s,t)} - \frac{1}{A(s,t)}}{\frac{1}{C(s,t)} - \frac{1}{A(s,t)}} = \frac{\frac{\operatorname{arsinh} q}{q} - 1}{\frac{1}{1+q^2} - 1}.$$

Let $q = \sinh \phi$. Then $\phi \in (0, \ln(1 + \sqrt{2}))$ and

$$\frac{\frac{1}{M(s,t)} - \frac{1}{A(s,t)}}{\frac{1}{C(s,t)} - \frac{1}{A(s,t)}} = \frac{\frac{\phi}{\sinh \phi} - 1}{\frac{1}{\cosh^2 \phi} - 1} = \frac{(\sinh \phi - \phi) \cosh^2 \phi}{\sinh^3 \phi} \triangleq F(\phi) = \frac{k_1(\phi)}{k_2(\phi)}.$$

Let

$$k_1(\phi) = (\sinh \phi - \phi) \cosh^2 \phi \quad \text{and} \quad k_2(\phi) = \sinh^3 \phi.$$

Then elaborated computations lead to $k_1(0^+) = k_2(0^+) = 0$ and

$$\frac{k_1'(\phi)}{k_2'(\phi)} = \frac{2(\sinh \phi - \phi) \sinh \phi + (\cosh \phi - 1) \cosh \phi}{3 \sinh^2 \phi} = 1 - \frac{2\phi \sinh \phi + \cosh \phi - 1}{3 \sinh^2 \phi}.$$

Combining this with Lemmas 1 and 3 reveals that the function $F(\phi)$ is strictly increasing on $(0, \ln(1 + \sqrt{2}))$. Moreover, it is easy to compute the limits

$$\lim_{\phi \to 0^+} F(\phi) = \frac{1}{6} \quad \text{and} \quad \lim_{\phi \to \ln(1+\sqrt{2})^-} F(\phi) = 2 - 2\ln(1 + \sqrt{2}).$$

The proof of Theorem 1 is thus complete. □

Corollary 1. *For all $\phi \in (0, \ln(1+\sqrt{2}))$, the double inequality*

$$1 - \beta_1\left(1 - \frac{1}{\cosh^2\phi}\right) < \frac{\phi}{\sinh\phi} < 1 - \alpha_1\left(1 - \frac{1}{\cosh^2\phi}\right) \quad (8)$$

holds if and only if

$$\alpha_1 \leq \frac{1}{6} \quad \text{and} \quad \beta_1 \geq 2[1 - \ln(1+\sqrt{2})] = 0.237253\ldots.$$

Theorem 2. *For $s, t > 0$ with $s \neq t$, the double inequality (3) holds if and only if*

$$\alpha_2 \geq \frac{4}{3}[1 - \ln^2(1+\sqrt{2})] = 0.297574\ldots \quad \text{and} \quad \beta_2 \leq \frac{1}{6}.$$

Proof. Without loss of generality, we assume that $s > t > 0$. Let $q = \frac{s-t}{s+t}$. Then $q \in (0,1)$ and

$$\frac{\frac{1}{M^2(s,t)} - \frac{1}{A^2(s,t)}}{\frac{1}{C^2(s,t)} - \frac{1}{A^2(s,t)}} = \frac{\frac{\operatorname{arsinh}^2 q}{q^2} - 1}{\frac{1}{(1+q^2)^2} - 1}.$$

Let $q = \sinh\phi$. Then $\phi \in (0, \ln(1+\sqrt{2}))$ and

$$\frac{\frac{1}{M^2(s,t)} - \frac{1}{A^2(s,t)}}{\frac{1}{C^2(s,t)} - \frac{1}{A^2(s,t)}} = \frac{\frac{\phi^2}{\sinh^2\phi} - 1}{\frac{1}{\cosh^4\phi} - 1} = \frac{(\sinh^2\phi - \phi^2)\cosh^4\phi}{(\cosh^2\phi + 1)\sinh^4\phi} \triangleq H(\phi).$$

By Lemma 4, it is easy to show that $H(\phi)$ is strictly increasing on $(0, \ln(1+\sqrt{2}))$. Moreover, the limits

$$\lim_{\phi \to 0^+} H(\phi) = \frac{1}{6} \quad \text{and} \quad \lim_{\phi \to \ln(1+\sqrt{2})^-} H(\phi) = \frac{4}{3}[1 - \ln^2(1+\sqrt{2})]$$

can be computed readily. The double inequality (3) is thus proved. □

Corollary 2. *For all $\phi \in (0, \ln(1+\sqrt{2}))$, the double inequality*

$$1 - \beta_2\left(1 - \frac{1}{\cosh^4\phi}\right) < \left(\frac{\phi}{\sinh\phi}\right)^2 < 1 - \alpha_2\left(1 - \frac{1}{\cosh^4\phi}\right) \quad (9)$$

holds if and only if

$$\alpha_2 \leq \frac{1}{6} \quad \text{and} \quad \beta_2 \geq \frac{4}{3}[1 - \ln^2(1+\sqrt{2})] = 0.297574\ldots.$$

Theorem 3. *For $s, t > 0$ with $s \neq t$, the double inequality (4) holds if and only if*

$$\alpha_3 \leq \frac{1 - \ln^2(1+\sqrt{2})}{3\ln^2(1+\sqrt{2})} = 0.095767\ldots \quad \text{and} \quad \beta_3 \geq \frac{1}{6}.$$

Proof. Without loss of generality, we assume that $s > t > 0$. Let $q = \frac{s-t}{s+t}$. Then $q \in (0,1)$ and

$$\frac{M^2(s,t) - A^2(s,t)}{C^2(s,t) - A^2(s,t)} = \frac{\frac{q^2}{\operatorname{arsinh}^2 q} - 1}{(1+q^2)^2 - 1}.$$

Let $q = \sinh\phi$. Then $\phi \in (0, \ln(1+\sqrt{2}))$ and

$$\frac{M^2(s,t) - A^2(s,t)}{C^2(s,t) - A^2(s,t)} = \frac{\frac{\sinh^2\phi}{\phi^2} - 1}{\cosh^4\phi - 1} \triangleq G(\phi) = \frac{k_1(\phi)}{k_2(\phi)},$$

where

$$k_1(\phi) = \frac{\sinh^2\phi}{\phi^2} - 1 \quad \text{and} \quad k_2(\phi) = \cosh^4\phi - 1.$$

Then $k_1(0^+) = k_2(0^+) = 0$ and

$$\frac{k_1'(\phi)}{k_2'(\phi)} = \frac{\phi\cosh\phi - \sinh\phi}{2\phi^3 \cosh^3\phi}.$$

Denote

$$k_3(\phi) = \phi\cosh\phi - \sinh\phi \quad \text{and} \quad k_4(\phi) = 2\phi^3 \cosh^3\phi,$$

it is easy to obtain $k_3(0^+) = k_4(0^+) = 0$ and

$$\frac{k_4'(\phi)}{k_3'(\phi)} = \frac{6\phi\cosh^2\phi}{\sinh\phi} + 6\phi^2 \cosh^2\phi. \tag{10}$$

Since the function $v^2 \cosh^2 v$ is strictly increasing on $(0, \infty)$, by Lemma 5, we see that the ratio in (10) is strictly increasing and $\frac{k_3'(\phi)}{k_4'(\phi)}$ is strictly decreasing on $(0, \ln(1+\sqrt{2}))$. Consequently, from Lemma 1, it follows that $G(\phi)$ is strictly decreasing on $(0, \ln(1+\sqrt{2}))$. The limits

$$\lim_{\phi \to 0^+} G(\phi) = \frac{1}{6} \quad \text{and} \quad \lim_{\phi \to \ln(1+\sqrt{2})^-} G(\phi) = \frac{1 - \ln^2(1+\sqrt{2})}{3\ln^2(1+\sqrt{2})}$$

can be computed easily. The proof of Theorem 3 is thus complete. □

Corollary 3. *For all $\phi \in (0, \ln(1+\sqrt{2}))$, the double inequality*

$$1 + \alpha_3(\cosh^4\phi - 1) < \left(\frac{\sinh\phi}{\phi}\right)^2 < 1 + \beta_3(\cosh^4\phi - 1) \tag{11}$$

holds if and only if

$$\alpha_3 \leq \frac{1 - \ln^2(1+\sqrt{2})}{3\ln^2(1+\sqrt{2})} = 0.095767\ldots \quad \text{and} \quad \beta_3 \geq \frac{1}{6}.$$

4. A Double Inequality

From Lemma 5, we can deduce

$$\frac{\sinh v}{v} < \cosh^2 v \quad \text{and} \quad \frac{\sinh v}{v} > \frac{\tanh^2 x}{v^2} \tag{12}$$

for $v \in (0, \infty)$. The inequality

$$\left(\frac{\sinh v}{v}\right)^3 > \cosh v \tag{13}$$

for $v \in (0, \infty)$ can be found and has been applied in [17] (p. 65), [18] (p. 300), [19] (pp. 279, 3.6.9), and [20] (p. 260). In [21], (Lemma 3), Zhu recovered the fact stated in [19] (pp. 279, 3.6.9) that the exponent 3 in the inequality (13) is the least possible, that is, the inequality

$$\left(\frac{\sinh v}{v}\right)^p > \cosh v \qquad (14)$$

for $x > 0$ holds if and only if $p \leq 3$.

Inspired by (12) and (14), we find out the following double inequality.

Theorem 4. *The inequality*

$$\cosh^\alpha v < \frac{\sinh v}{v} < \cosh^\beta v \qquad (15)$$

for $v \neq 0$ holds if and only if $\alpha \leq \frac{1}{3}$ and $\beta \geq 1$.

Proof. Let

$$h(v) = \frac{\ln \sinh v - \ln v}{\ln \cosh v} \triangleq \frac{f_1(v)}{f_2(v)}.$$

Direct calculation yields

$$\frac{f_1'(v)}{f_2'(v)} = \frac{v \cosh^2 v - \sinh v \cosh v}{v \sinh^2 v} = \frac{v \cosh(2v) + v - \sinh(2v)}{v \cosh(2v) - v} \triangleq \frac{f_3(v)}{f_4(v)}.$$

Using the power series of $\sinh v$ and $\cosh v$, we obtain

$$f_3(v) = v + v \sum_{\ell=0}^{\infty} \frac{(2v)^{2\ell}}{(2\ell)!} - \sum_{\ell=0}^{\infty} \frac{(2v)^{2\ell+1}}{(2\ell+1)!} = \sum_{\ell=1}^{\infty} \left[\frac{2^{2\ell}}{(2\ell)!} - \frac{2^{2\ell+1}}{(2\ell+1)!}\right] v^{2\ell+1}$$

$$= \sum_{\ell=0}^{\infty} \frac{(2\ell+1) 2^{2\ell+2}}{(2\ell+3)!} v^{2\ell+3} \triangleq \sum_{\ell=0}^{\infty} u_\ell v^{2\ell+3}$$

and

$$f_4(v) = v \sum_{\ell=0}^{\infty} \frac{(2v)^{2\ell}}{(2\ell)!} - v = \sum_{\ell=1}^{\infty} \frac{2^{2\ell}}{(2\ell)!} v^{2\ell+1} = \sum_{\ell=0}^{\infty} \frac{2^{2\ell+2}}{(2\ell+2)!} v^{2\ell+3} \triangleq \sum_{\ell=0}^{\infty} w_\ell v^{2\ell+3},$$

where

$$u_\ell = \frac{(2\ell+1) 2^{2\ell+2}}{(2\ell+3)!} \quad \text{and} \quad w_\ell = \frac{2^{2\ell+2}}{(2\ell+2)!}.$$

When setting $c_\ell = \frac{u_\ell}{w_\ell}$, we obtain

$$c_\ell = \frac{2\ell+1}{2\ell+3} = 1 - \frac{2}{2\ell+3}$$

is increasing on $\ell \in \mathbb{N}$. Therefore, by Lemma 2, the ratio $\frac{f_3(v)}{f_4(v)}$ is increasing on $(0, \infty)$. Using Lemma 1, we obtain that

$$h(v) = \frac{f_1(v)}{f_2(v)} = \frac{f_1(v) - f_1(0^+)}{f_2(v) - f_2(0^+)}$$

is increasing on $(0, \infty)$.

Moreover, the limits $\lim_{v \to 0^+} h_1 = \frac{1}{3}$ and $\lim_{v \to \infty} h_1 = 1$ are obvious. The proof of Lemma 4 is thus complete. □

5. A Remark

For $v, r \in \mathbb{R}$, we have

$$\left(\frac{\sinh v}{v}\right)^r = 1 + \sum_{m=1}^{\infty}\left[\sum_{k=1}^{2m} \frac{(-r)_k}{k!} \sum_{j=1}^{k}(-1)^j \binom{k}{j}\frac{T(2m+j,j)}{\binom{2m+j}{j}}\right]\frac{(2v)^{2m}}{(2m)!}, \qquad (16)$$

where the rising factorial $(r)_k$ is defined by

$$(r)_k = \prod_{\ell=0}^{k-1}(r+\ell) = \begin{cases} r(r+1)\cdots(r+k-1), & k \geq 1 \\ 1, & k = 0 \end{cases}$$

and $T(2m+j,j)$ is called central factorial numbers of the second kind and can be computed by

$$T(n,\ell) = \frac{1}{\ell!}\sum_{j=0}^{\ell}(-1)^j\binom{\ell}{j}\left(\frac{\ell}{2}-j\right)^n.$$

for $n \geq \ell \geq 0$.

The series expansion (16) was recently derived in [22] (Corollary 4.1).
Can one find bounds of the function $\left(\frac{\sinh v}{v}\right)^r$ for $v, r \in \mathbb{R}\setminus\{0\}$?

6. Conclusions

In this paper, we found out the largest values $\alpha_1, \alpha_2, \alpha_3$ and the smallest values $\beta_1, \beta_2, \beta_3$ such that the double inequalities (2), (3), and (4) hold for all positive real number $s, t > 0$ with $s \neq t$. Moreover, we presented some new sharp inequalities (8), (9), (11), and (15) involving the hyperbolic sine function $\sinh\phi$ and the hyperbolic cosine function $\cosh\phi$.

Author Contributions: Writing—original draft, W.-H.L., P.M. and B.-N.G. All authors have read and agreed to the published version of the manuscript.

Funding: This research received no external funding.

Institutional Review Board Statement: Not applicable.

Informed Consent Statement: Not applicable.

Data Availability Statement: Data sharing is not applicable to this article as no new data were created or analyzed in this study.

Acknowledgments: The authors thank anonymous referees for their careful corrections to and valuable comments on the original version of this paper.

Conflicts of Interest: The authors declare no conflict of interest.

References

1. Jiang, W.-D.; Qi, F. Sharp bounds for Neuman–Sándor's mean in terms of the root-mean-square. *Period. Math. Hung.* **2014**, *69*, 134–138. [CrossRef]
2. Jiang, W.-D.; Qi, F. Sharp bounds in terms of the power of the contra-harmonic mean for Neuman–Sándor mean. *Cogent Math.* **2015**, *2*, 995951. [CrossRef]
3. Qi, F.; Li, W.-H. A unified proof of inequalities and some new inequalities involving Neuman–Sándor mean. *Miskolc Math. Notes* **2014**, *15*, 665–675. [CrossRef]
4. Seiffert, H.-J. Problem 887. *Nieuw Arch. Wiskd.* **1993**, *11*, 176.
5. Seiffert, H.-J. Aufgabe β 16. *Wurzel* **1995**, *29*, 221–222.
6. Neuman, E.; Sándor, J. On the Schwab–Borchardt mean. *Math. Pannon.* **2003**, *14*, 253–266.
7. Neuman, E.; Sándor, J. On the Schwab–Borchardt mean II. *Math. Pannon.* **2006**, *17*, 49–59.
8. Li, Y.-M.; Long, B.-Y.; Chu, Y.-M. Sharp bounds for the Neuman–Sándor mean in terms of generalized logarithmic mean. *J. Math. Inequal.* **2012**, *6*, 567–577. [CrossRef]
9. Neuman, E. A note on a certain bivariate mean. *J. Math. Inequal.* **2012**, *6*, 637–643. [CrossRef]
10. Zhao, T.-H.; Chu, Y.-M.; Liu, B.-Y. Optimal bounds for Neuman–Sándor mean in terms of the convex combinations of harmonic, geometric, quadratic, and contraharmonic means. *Abstr. Appl. Anal.* **2012**, *2012*, 302635. [CrossRef]

11. Chen, J.-J.; Lei, J.-J.; Long, B.-Y. Optimal bounds for Neuman–Sándor mean in terms of the convex combination of the logarithmic and the second Seiffert means. *J. Inequal. Appl.* **2017**, *2017*, 251. [CrossRef] [PubMed]
12. Wang, X.-L.; Yin, L. Sharp bounds for the reciprocals of the Neuman–Sándor mean. *J. Interdiscip. Math.* **2022**.
13. Hua, Y.; Qi, F. The best bounds for Toader mean in terms of the centroidal and arithmetic means. *Filomat* **2014**, *28*, 775–59780. [CrossRef]
14. Toader, G. Some mean values related to the arithmetic-geometric mean. *J. Math. Anal. Appl.* **1998**, *218*, 358–368. [CrossRef]
15. Anderson, G.D.; Vamanamurthy, M.K.; Vuorinen, M. *Conformal Invariants, Inequalities, and Quasiconformal Maps*; John Wiley & Sons: New York, NY, USA, 1997,
16. Simić, S.; Vuorinen, M. Landen inequalities for zero-balanced hypergeometric functions. *Abstr. Appl. Anal.* **2012**, *2012*, 932061. [CrossRef]
17. Guo, B.-N.; Qi, F. The function $(b^x - a^x)/x$: Logarithmic convexity and applications to extended mean values. *Filomat* **2011**, *25*, 63–73. [CrossRef]
18. Kuang, J.C. *Applied Inequalities*, 3rd ed.; Shangdong Science and Technology Press: Jinan, China, 2004; pp. 300–301.
19. Mitrinović, D.S. *Analytic Inequalities*; Springer: Berlin/Heidelberg, Germany, 1970.
20. Qi, F. On bounds for norms of sine and cosine along a circle on the complex plane. *Kragujevac J. Math.* **2024**, *48*, 255–266. [CrossRef]
21. Zhu, L. On Wilker-type inequalities. *Math. Inequal. Appl.* **2007**, *10*, 727–731. [CrossRef]
22. Qi, F.; Taylor, P. Several series expansions for real powers and several formulas for partial Bell polynomials of sinc and sinhc functions in terms of central factorial and Stirling numbers of second kind. *arXiv* **2022**, arxiv:2204.05612v4.

Article

New Inequalities and Generalizations for Symmetric Means Induced by Majorization Theory

Huan-Nan Shi [1] and Wei-Shih Du [2,*]

[1] Department of Electronic Information, Teacher's College, Beijing Union University, Beijing 100011, China; sfthuannan@buu.edu.cn
[2] Department of Mathematics, National Kaohsiung Normal University, Kaohsiung 82444, Taiwan
* Correspondence: wsdu@mail.nknu.edu.tw

Abstract: In this paper, the authors study new inequalities and generalizations for symmetric means and give new proofs for some known results by applying majorization theory.

Keywords: majorization; inequality; log-concave sequence; symmetric function; symmetric mean

MSC: Primary 05E05; Secondary 26A09; 26A51; 26D15

1. Introduction and Preliminaries

Convex analysis has wide applications to many areas of mathematics and science. In the past nearly 80 years, convex analysis has reached a high level of maturity, and an increasing number of connections have been identified between mathematics, physics, economics and finance, automatic control systems, estimation and signal processing, communications and networks and so forth. Several authors have studied a large number of new concepts of generalized convexity and concavity; see, for example, [1–7] and the references therein. Majorization theory has contributed greatly to many branches of pure and applied mathematics, especially in the field of inequalities; for more details, one can refer to [4–6,8–13] and the references therein.

Definition 1 (see [5] (p. 4)). *A finite sequence $\{x_k\}_{k=1}^n$ or an infinite sequence $\{x_k\}_{k=1}^\infty$ of nonnegative real numbers is said to be*

(i) *logarithmically convex (abbreviated as log-convex) if*

$$x_k^2 \leq x_{k-1} x_{k+1}$$

for all $k = 2, \ldots, n-1$ or for all $k \geq 2$; and

(ii) *logarithmically concave (abbreviated as log-concave) if*

$$x_k^2 \geq x_{k-1} x_{k+1}$$

for all $k = 2, \ldots, n-1$ or for all $k \geq 2$.

The following characterizations of logarithmic convexity are crucial to our proofs.

Lemma 1 (see [5] (p. 4)). *Let*

$$\mathbb{N}_0^n = \underbrace{\{0, 1, 2, \ldots\} \times \{0, 1, 2, \ldots\} \times \cdots \times \{0, 1, 2, \ldots\}}_{n}.$$

The necessary and sufficient condition for a non-negative sequence $\{a_k\}$ to be log-convex is that, for any $p = (p_1, p_2, \ldots, p_n)$, $q = (q_1, q_2, \ldots, q_n) \in \mathbb{N}_0^n$ with $p \prec q$, we have

$$\prod_{i=1}^n a_{p_i} \leq \prod_{i=1}^n a_{q_i}.$$

Corollary 1. *Let $\{a_k\}$ be a positive sequence. If $\{a_k\}$ is log-concave, then, for any $p = (p_1, p_2, \ldots, p_n)$, $q = (q_1, q_2, \ldots, q_n) \in \mathbb{N}_0^n$ with $p \prec q$, we have*

$$\prod_{i=1}^n a_{p_i} \geq \prod_{i=1}^n a_{q_i}.$$

Proof. Since $\{a_k\}$ is a positive log-concave sequence, $\{\frac{1}{a_k}\}$ is a positive log-convex sequence. According to Lemma 1, we have $\prod_{i=1}^n \frac{1}{a_{q_i}} \leq \prod_{i=1}^n \frac{1}{a_{p_i}}$, this is $\prod_{i=1}^n a_{p_i} \geq \prod_{i=1}^n a_{q_i}$, so that and Corollary 1 holds. □

Definition 2 (see [10,12]). *Let $x = (x_1, x_2, \ldots, x_n)$ and $y = (y_1, y_2, \ldots, y_n) \in \mathbb{R}^n$. A vector x is said to be majorized by y, denoted by $x \prec y$, if*

$$\sum_{i=1}^k x_{[i]} \leq \sum_{i=1}^k y_{[i]} \quad \text{for } 1 \leq k \leq n-1,$$

and

$$\sum_{i=1}^n x_i = \sum_{i=1}^n y_i,$$

where $x_{[1]} \geq \cdots \geq x_{[n]}$ and $y_{[1]} \geq \cdots \geq y_{[n]}$ are rearrangements of x and y in a descending order.

We now recall the concepts of symmetric function and symmetric mean as follows.

Definition 3 (see, e.g., [9,11]). *Let $x = (x_1, x_2, \ldots, x_n) \in \mathbb{R}^n$.*
(i) *The kth symmetric function $s_k(x)$ for $1 \leq k \leq n$ is defined by*

$$s_k(x) = s_k(x_1, x_2, \ldots, x_n) = \sum_{1 \leq i_1 < i_2 < \cdots < i_k \leq n} \prod_{j=1}^k x_{i_j}.$$

In particular, $s_n(x) = \prod_{i=1}^n x_i$ and $s_1(x) = \sum_{i=1}^n x_i$. We assume that $s_0(x) = 1$ and $s_k(x) = 0$ for $k < 0$ or $k > n$.
(ii) *The kth symmetric mean is defined by*

$$B_k(x) = \frac{s_k(x)}{\binom{n}{k}} \quad \text{for } k = 0, 1, \ldots, n.$$

The following lemma is important and will be used for proving our main results.

Lemma 2 (see [9] (p. 458) or [11] (p. 95)). *Let $x = (x_1, x_2, \ldots, x_n) \in \mathbb{R}^n$ with $x_i \geq 0$ for $i = 1, 2, \ldots, n$. Then,*

$$B_{k+1}(x) B_{k-1}(x) \leq B_k^2(x)$$

for all $1 \leq k \leq n$. Equivalently speaking, the sequence $\{B_k(x)\}$ is log-concave.

Remark 1. (i) *In particular, for $n \geq 2$ and $x_i > 0$ with $i = 1, 2, \ldots, n$, we have*

$$B_1(x) = \frac{s_1(x)}{\binom{n}{1}} = A_n(x) = \frac{x_1 + x_2 + \cdots + x_n}{n},$$

$$\sqrt[n]{B_n(x)} = \sqrt[n]{\frac{s_n(x)}{\binom{n}{n}}} = G_n(x) = \sqrt[n]{x_1 x_2 \cdots x_n}$$

and

$$\frac{B_n(x)}{B_{n-1}(x)} = H_n(x) = \frac{n}{\frac{1}{x_1} + \frac{1}{x_2} + \cdots + \frac{1}{x_n}},$$

where $A_n(x)$, $G_n(x)$ and $H_n(x)$ denote the arithmetic mean, geometric mean and harmonic mean of the n positive numbers $x_i > 0$ for $i = 1, 2, \ldots, n$, respectively. See the famous monograph [8].

(ii) Let $x_i > 0$ for $i = 1, 2, \ldots, n$. When $n \geq 2$, the double inequality between the arithmetic, geometric and harmonic means reads that

$$A_n(x) \geq G_n(x) \geq H_n(x). \tag{1}$$

The double inequality (1) is fundamental and important in all areas of mathematical sciences. There have been over one hundred proofs for the double inequality (1). See the related texts and references in the paper [2], for example.

In the history of the research process of inequality theory, many important generalization studies have come from simple inequalities that have wide applications. In 1995, by virtue of the Lagrange multiplier method, Zhu [13] proved the following interesting inequality

$$n^{n-2}(x_1 x_2 \cdots x_{n-1} + x_2 x_3 \cdots x_n + \cdots + x_n x_1 \cdots x_{n-2}) \leq (x_1 + x_2 + \cdots + x_n)^{n-1},$$

which is equivalent to

$$B_{n-1}(x) \leq B_1^{n-1}(x), \tag{2}$$

where $x = (x_1, x_2, \ldots, x_n) \in \mathbb{R}^n$ with $x_i \geq 0$ for $i = 1, 2, \ldots, n$ with $n \geq 3$. In 2022, Hu [14] established the following inequality by mathematical induction:

$$(s_{n-1}(x))^{n-1} \geq n^{n-2}(s_n(x))^{n-2} s_1(x), \tag{3}$$

where $x = (x_1, x_2, \ldots, x_n) \in \mathbb{R}^n$ with $x_i > 0$ for $i = 1, 2, \ldots, n$. It is easy to see that inequality (3) is equivalent to

$$B_{n-1}^{n-1}(x) \geq B_n^{n-2}(x) B_1(x).$$

Motivated by the works mentioned above, in this paper, we study and investigate new inequalities and generalizations for symmetric means by applying majorization theory. We also give new proofs for some known results proven by difficult typical elementary or analytical methods. Our new proofs given in this paper are novel and concise.

2. Main Results

In this section, we establish the following new inequalities for symmetric means.

Theorem 1. Let $x = (x_1, x_2, \ldots, x_n) \in \mathbb{R}^n$ with $x_i > 0$ for $i = 1, 2, \ldots, n$. Then, the following hold:

(i) $B_{n-k}^{n-k}(x) \geq B_n^{n-2k}(x) B_k^k(x)$ for all $2 \leq 2k \leq n$;

(ii) $B_{n-k}^{n-k+1}(x) \geq B_{n-k+1}^{n-k}(x)$ for all $1 \leq k \leq n$;

(iii) $B_{n-k}^{n-k}(x) B_n^{2k}(x) \geq B_k^k(x) B_n^n(x)$ for all $2 \leq 2k \leq n$;

(iv) $B_{k_1}^{1/k_1}(x) \geq B_{k_2}^{1/k_2}(x)$ for all $1 \leq k_1 < k_2 \leq n$.

Proof. (i) Let $2 \leq 2k \leq n$. It is easy to verify that

$$\Big(\underbrace{n-k, n-k, \ldots, n-k}_{n-k}\Big) \prec \Big(\underbrace{n, n, \ldots, n}_{n-2k}, \underbrace{k, k, \ldots, k}_{k}\Big).$$

According to Lemma 2, the sequence $\{B_k(x)\}$ is log-concave, and by Corollary 1, it follows that
$$B_{n-k}^{n-k}(x) \geq B_n^{n-2k}(x)B_k^k(x).$$

(ii) Let $1 \leq k \leq n$. Since
$$(\underbrace{n-k,\ldots,n-k}_{n-k+1},\underbrace{0,\ldots,0}_{k-1}) \prec (\underbrace{n-k+1,\ldots,n-k+1}_{n-k},\underbrace{0,\ldots,0}_{k}),$$
by the logarithmic concavity of the sequence $\{B_k(x)\}$, from Corollary 1, we have
$$B_{n-k}^{n-k+1}(x) = B_{n-k}^{n-k+1}(x)B_0^{k-1}(x) \geq B_{n-k+1}^{n-k}(x)B_0^k(x) = B_{n-k+1}^{n-k}(x).$$

(iii) Let $2 \leq 2k \leq n$. Since
$$(\underbrace{n-k,\ldots,n-k}_{n-k},\underbrace{n,\ldots,n}_{2k}) \prec (\underbrace{k,\ldots,k}_{k},\underbrace{n,\ldots,n}_{n}),$$
by the logarithmic concavity of the sequence $\{B_k(x)\}$, we obtain
$$B_{n-k}^{n-k}(x)B_n^{2k}(x) \geq B_k^k(x)B_n^n(x).$$

(iv) Let $1 \leq k_1 < k_2 \leq n$. Since
$$(\underbrace{k_1,\ldots,k_1}_{k_2},\underbrace{0,\ldots,0}_{k_1-k_2}) \prec (\underbrace{k_2,\ldots,k_2}_{k_1}),$$
from the logarithmic concavity of the sequence $\{B_k(x)\}$, we obtain
$$B_{k_1}^{k_2}(x)B_0^{k_1-k_2}(x) = \left[\frac{s_{k_1}(x)}{\binom{n}{k_1}}\right]^{k_2}\left[\frac{s_0(x)}{\binom{n}{0}}\right]^{k_1-k_2} \geq B_{k_2}^{k_1}(x) = \left[\frac{s_{k_2}(x)}{\binom{n}{k_2}}\right]^{k_1},$$
which implies
$$B_{k_1}^{1/k_1}(x) \geq B_{k_2}^{1/k_2}(x).$$

The proof is completed. □

Remark 2. *When $k_1 = k$ and $k_2 = k+1$ in (iv) of Theorem 1, the inequality*
$$B_{k_1}^{1/k_1}(x) \geq B_{k_2}^{1/k_2}(x)$$
becomes the famous Maclaurin's inequality
$$\left[\frac{s_k(x)}{\binom{n}{k}}\right]^{1/k} \leq \left[\frac{s_{k-1}(x)}{\binom{n}{k-1}}\right]^{1/(k-1)}.$$

In terms of the symmetric means $B_1(x)$, $B_{n-1}(x)$ and $B_n(x)$, the double inequality (1) can be reformulated as follows.

Theorem 2. *Let $n \geq 2$ and $x = (x_1, x_2, \ldots, x_n) \in \mathbb{R}^n$ with $x_i > 0$ for $i = 1, 2, \ldots, n$. Then,*
$$B_1^n(x) \geq B_n(x) \qquad (4)$$
and
$$B_{n-1}^n(x) \geq B_n^{n-1}(x). \qquad (5)$$

Proof. According to Lemma 2, the sequence $\{B_k(x)\}$ is log-concave. Since the majorization relation

$$(\underbrace{1,1,1,\ldots,1}_{n}) \prec (n,\underbrace{0,0,\ldots,0}_{n-1})$$

is valid, by Corollary 1, we acquire

$$B_1^n(x) \geq B_n(x) B_0^{n-1}(x) = B_n(x).$$

Next, we varify $B_{n-1}^n(x) \geq B_n^{n-1}(x)$. It is not difficult to see that

$$(\underbrace{n-1, n-1, \ldots, n-1}_{n}) \prec (\underbrace{n, n, \ldots, n}_{n-1}, 0).$$

From the logarithmic concavity of the sequence $\{B_k(x)\}$, we have

$$B_{n-1}^n(x) \geq B_n^{n-1}(x) B_0(x) = B_n^{n-1}(x).$$

The proof is completed. □

The following result is a generalization of inequality (2).

Theorem 3. *Let $x = (x_1, x_2, \ldots, x_n) \in \mathbb{R}^n$ with $x_i > 0$ for $i = 1, 2, \ldots, n$. Then, for $n \geq 2k \geq 2$,*

$$B_k^{n-k}(x) \geq B_{n-k}^k(x). \tag{6}$$

Proof. According to Lemma 2, the sequence $\{B_k(x)\}$ is log-concave. Note that, for $n \geq 2k$, this is, for $k \leq n - k$,

$$(\underbrace{k, k, \ldots, k}_{n-k}) \prec (\underbrace{n-k, n-k, \ldots, n-k}_{k}, \underbrace{0, 0, \ldots, 0}_{n-2k}).$$

By Corollary 1, we obtain

$$B_k^{n-k}(x) = \left[\frac{S_k(x)}{\binom{n}{k}}\right]^{n-k} \geq B_{n-k}^k(x) B_0^{n-2k}(x) = \left[\frac{S_{n-k}(x)}{\binom{n}{n-k}}\right]^k \left[\frac{S_0(x)}{\binom{n}{0}}\right]^{n-2k}.$$

The inequality (6) is thus proved. □

Theorem 4. *Let $x = (x_1, x_2, \ldots, x_n) \in \mathbb{R}^n$ with $x_i > 0$ for $i = 1, 2, \ldots, n$. Then, we have*

$$\sqrt[n]{\prod_{k=1}^{n} B_{2k}(x)} \geq \sqrt[n+1]{\prod_{k=1}^{n} B_{2k-1}(x)}. \tag{7}$$

Proof. The majorization relation

$$(\underbrace{2,\ldots,2}_{n+1}, \underbrace{4,\ldots,4}_{n+1}, \ldots, \underbrace{2n,\ldots,2n}_{n+1}) \prec (\underbrace{1,\ldots,1}_{n}, \underbrace{3,\ldots,3}_{n}, \ldots, \underbrace{2n+1,\ldots,2n+1}_{n})$$

is shown in [4] (p. 40). By the logarithmic concavity of the sequence $\{B_k(x)\}$, we obtain

$$\prod_{k=1}^{n} B_{2k}^{n+1}(x) \geq \prod_{k=0}^{n} B_{2k+1}^n(x),$$

which deduces (11). □

The arithmetic mean $A_n(x)$, geometric mean $G_n(x)$ and harmonic mean $H_n(x)$ also satisfy Sierpinski's inequality [9] (p. 62) below. In this paper, we give a new proof for Sierpinski's inequality via majorization.

Theorem 5 (Sierpinski's inequality [9] (p. 62)). *Let $x = (x_1, x_2, \ldots, x_n) \in \mathbb{R}^n$ with $x_i > 0$ for $i = 1, 2, \ldots, n$ with $n \geq 2$. Then,*

$$A_n(x) H_n^{n-1}(x) \leq G_n^n(x) \leq A_n^{n-1}(x) H_n(x). \tag{8}$$

Proof. In terms of symmetric means $B_1(x)$, $B_{n-1}(x)$ and $B_n(x)$, the left and right inequalities in the double inequality (8) can be reformulated as

$$B_1(x) B_n^{n-1}(x) \leq B_n(x) B_{n-1}^{n-1}(x)$$

and

$$B_n(x) B_{n-1}(x) \leq B_1^{n-1}(x) B_n(x).$$

By the logarithmic concavity of the sequence $\{B_k(x)\}$, the above two inequalities can be obtained from two majorization relations

$$(n, \underbrace{n-1, n-1, \ldots, n-1}_{n-1}, 0) \prec (n, \underbrace{n, n, \ldots, n}_{n-1}, 1)$$

and

$$(n, \underbrace{1, 1, \ldots, 1}_{n-1}) \prec (n, n-1, \underbrace{0, 0, \ldots, 0}_{n-2}),$$

respectively. This proves the inequality (8). □

Theorem 6 ([9] (p. 260)). *Let $x = (x_1, x_2, \ldots, x_n) \in \mathbb{R}^n$ with $x_i > 0$ for $i = 1, 2, \ldots, n$. Then,*

$$s_n(x) \leq \frac{s_1(x) s_{n-1}(x)}{n^2} \leq \frac{s_1^n(x)}{n^2}. \tag{9}$$

Proof. It is clear that $(n-1, 1) \prec (n, 0)$ and

$$(\underbrace{1, 1, 1, \ldots, 1}_{n}) \prec (n-1, 1, \underbrace{0, \ldots, 0}_{n-2}).$$

From the logarithmic concavity of the sequence $\{B_k(x)\}$, it follows that

$$B_{n-1}(x) B_1(x) = \frac{s_{n-1}(x)}{\binom{n}{n-1}} \frac{s_1(x)}{\binom{n}{1}} \geq B_n(x) B_0(x) = \frac{s_n(x)}{\binom{n}{n}} \frac{s_0(x)}{\binom{n}{0}}$$

and

$$B_1^n(x) = \left[\frac{s_1(x)}{\binom{n}{1}}\right]^n \geq B_{n-1}(x) B_1(x) B_0^{n-2}(x) = \frac{s_{n-1}(x)}{\binom{n}{n-1}} \frac{s_1(x)}{\binom{n}{1}} \left[\frac{s_0(x)}{\binom{n}{0}}\right]^{n-2}.$$

This proves the double inequality (9). □

Theorem 7. *Let $x = (x_1, x_2, \ldots, x_n) \in \mathbb{R}^n$ with $x_i > 0$ for $i = 1, 2, \ldots, n$. Then,*

$$s_k(x) s_{n-k}(x) \geq \binom{n}{k}^2 s_n(x) \tag{10}$$

and

$$(s_k(x))^n \geq \binom{n}{k}^n (s_n(x))^k \tag{11}$$

for $k = 1, 2, \ldots, n-1$.

Proof. It is clear that $(n-k, k) \prec (n, 0)$. From the logarithmic concavity of the sequence $\{B_k(x)\}$, we find

$$\frac{s_k(x)}{\binom{n}{k}} \frac{s_{n-k}(x)}{\binom{n}{n-k}} = B_k(x) B_{n-k}(x) \geq B_n(x) B_0(x) = \frac{s_n(x)}{\binom{n}{n}} \frac{s_0(x)}{\binom{n}{0}},$$

which show inequality (10). From the majorization relation

$$\Big(\underbrace{k, k, \ldots, k, 0}_{n}\Big) \prec \Big(\underbrace{n, n, \ldots, n}_{k}, \underbrace{0, 0, \ldots, 0}_{n-k}\Big),$$

it follows that inequality (11) holds. □

3. Conclusions

As a discrete form of logarithmic convex (concave) functions, logarithmic convex (concave) sequences play an important role in mathematical analysis and inequality theory. Lemma 1 and Corollary 1 are important conclusion about logarithmic convex (concave) sequences in majorization theory. In this paper, in view of the logarithmic concavity of symmetric mean sequences, we use Corollary 1 and various majorization relations to establish new inequalities and generalizations for symmetric means and give concise, novel and unique proofs for some known results.

Author Contributions: Writing original draft, H.-N.S. and W.-S.D. All authors have read and agreed to the published version of the manuscript.

Funding: The second author is partially supported by Grant No. MOST 110-2115-M-017-001 of the Ministry of Science and Technology of the Republic of China.

Institutional Review Board Statement: Not applicable.

Informed Consent Statement: Not applicable.

Data Availability Statement: Not applicable.

Acknowledgments: The authors wish to express their hearty thanks to Feng Qi for their valuable suggestions and comments.

Conflicts of Interest: The authors declare no conflict of interest.

References

1. Komlósi, S. Generalized Convexity and Generalized Derivatives. In *Handbook of Generalized Convexity and Generalized Monotonicity*; Hadjisavvas, N., Komlosi, S., Schaible, S., Eds.; Kluwer Academic Publishers: Alphen aan den Rijn, The Netherlands, 2005; pp. 421–464.
2. Qi, F.; Guo, B.-N. The reciprocal of the geometric mean of many positive numbers is a Stieltjes transform. *J. Comput. Appl. Math.* **2017**, *311*, 165–170. [CrossRef]
3. Rockafellar, R.T. *Convex Analysis*; Princeton University Press: Princeton, NJ, USA, 1970.
4. Shi, H.-N. *Schur-Convex Functions and Inequalities: Volume 1: Concepts, Properties, and Applications in Symmetric Function Inequalities*; Harbin Institute of Technology Press Ltd.: Harbin, China; Walter de Gruyter GmbH: Berlin/Boston, Germany, 2019.
5. Shi, H.-N. *Schur-Convex Functions and Inequalities: Volume 2: Applications in Inequalities*; Harbin Institute of Technology Press Ltd.: Harbin, China; Walter de Gruyter GmbH: Berlin/Boston, Germany, 2019.
6. Shi, H.-N.; Du, W.-S. Schur-power convexity of a completely symmetric function dual. *Symmetry* **2019**, *11*, 897. [CrossRef]
7. Zălinescu, C. *Convex Analysis in General Vector Spaces*; World Scientific: Singapore, 2002.
8. Bullen, P.S. *Handbook of Means and Their Inequalities*; Revised from the 1988 original [P. S. Bullen, D. S. Mitrinović and P. M. Vasić, Means and Their Inequalities, Reidel, Dordrecht; MR0947142]. Mathematics and its Applications, 560; Kluwer Academic Publishers Group: Dordrecht, The Netherlands, 2003.
9. Kuang, J.-C. *Applied Inequalities (Chang Yong Bu Deng Shi)*, 5th ed.; Shandong Press of Science and Technology: Jinan, China, 2021. (In Chinese)

10. Marshall, A.W.; Olkin, I.; Arnold, B.C. *Inequalities: Theory of Majorization and Its Applications*, 2nd ed.; Springer: New York, NY, USA; Dordrecht, The Netherlands; Heidelberg, Germany; London, UK, 2011.
11. Mitrinović, D.S. *Analytic Inequalities*; In cooperation with P. M. Vasić, Die Grundlehren der mathematischen Wissenschaften, Band 165; Springer: New York, NY, USA; Berlin, Germany, 1970.
12. Wang, B.-Y. *Foundations of Majorization Inequalities*; Beijing Normal University Press: Beijing, China, 1990. (In Chinese)
13. Zhu, M. Proposition and proof of a class of inequalities. *J. Huaibei Coal Normal Univ.* **1995**, *16*, 86–87. (In Chinese)
14. Hu, F. A generalization of a five-element inequality. *Middle Sch. Math. Res.* **2022**, *3*, 34. (In Chinese)

Article
Context-Free Grammars for Several Triangular Arrays

Roberta Rui Zhou [1,*], Jean Yeh [2,*] and Fuquan Ren [3]

[1] School of Mathematics and Statistics, Northeastern University at Qinhuangdao, Qinhuangdao 066004, China
[2] Department of Mathematics, National Kaohsiung Normal University, Kaohsiung 000800, Taiwan
[3] School of Science, Yanshan University, Qinhuangdao 066004, China; renfu_quan@ysu.edu.cn
* Correspondence: zhourui@neuq.edu.cn (R.R.Z.); chunchenyeh@nknu.edu.tw (J.Y.)

Abstract: In this paper, we present a unified grammatical interpretation of the numbers that satisfy a kind of four-term recurrence relation, including the Bell triangle, the coefficients of modified Hermite polynomials, and the Bessel polynomials. Additionally, as an application, a criterion for real zeros of row-generating polynomials is also presented.

Keywords: recurrence relations; grammars; real zeros; Bell triangular array

MSC: 05A05; 05A15

1. Introduction

Let A denote an alphabet, the letters of which are considered as independent commutative indeterminates. Then, the context-free grammar G over A is defined as a set of replacement rules that substitute the letters in A with formal functions on A. The formal derivative D is a linear operator, which is defined relative to a context-free grammar G (see [1]). For example, for $A = \{u,v\}$ and $G = \{u \to uv, v \to v\}$, then $D(u) = uv, D^2(u) = u(v+v^2), D^n(u) = u\sum_{k=1}^{n} S(n,k)v^k$, where $S(n,k)$ is the Stirling number of the second kind, i.e., the number of ways to partition $[n]$ into k blocks.

In [2], Hao, Wang, and Yang presented a grammatical interpretation of the numbers $T(n,k)$ that satisfy the following three-term recurrence relation:

$$T(n,k) = (a_1 n + a_2 k + a_3)T(n-1,k) + (b_1 n + b_2 k + b_3)T(n-1,k-1).$$

Very recently, there is a large literature devoted to the numbers $t(n,k)$ that satisfy the following four-term recurrence relation (see [3–7]):

$$t_{n,k} = (a_1 n + a_2 k + a_3)t_{n-1,k} + (b_1 n + b_2 k + b_3)t_{n-1,k-1} + (c_1 n + c_2 k + c_3)t_{n-1,k-2}, \quad (1)$$

with $t_{0,0} = 1$ and $t_{n,k} = 0$, unless $0 \leq k \leq n$. For example, Ma [8] showed that if $G = \{x \to xy, y \to yz, z \to y^2\}$, then $D^n(x^2) = x^2 \sum_{k=0}^{n} R(n+1,k)y^k z^{n-k}$, where $R(n,k)$ is the number of permutations in S_n with k alternating runs, and it satisfies the recurrence relation

$$R(n,k) = kR(n-1,k) + 2R(n-1,k-1) + (n-k)R(n-1,k-2)$$

with the initial conditions $R(1,0) = 1$ and $R(1,k) = 0$ for $k \geq 1$.
Let

$$a(n,k) = \sum_{i=0}^{n} S(n,i)\binom{i}{k}$$

for $0 \leq k \leq n$. Clearly, $a(n,k)$ is the number of set partitions of $\{1,2,\ldots,n\}$ in which exactly k of the blocks have been distinguished. The numbers $a(n,k)$ satisfy the recurrence relation

$$a(n+1,k) = a(n,k-1) + (k+1)a(n,k) + (k+1)a(n,k+1), \quad (2)$$

with $a(0,0) = 1$, $a(0,k) = 0$ for $k \neq 0$ (see [9,10]). The triangular array $\{a(n,k)\}_{n,k}$ is known as the classical Bell triangle and is given as follows:

$$\begin{pmatrix} 1 & & & & & \\ 1 & 1 & & & & \\ 2 & 3 & 1 & & & \\ 5 & 10 & 6 & 1 & & \\ 15 & 37 & 31 & 10 & 1 & \\ \vdots & & & & & \ddots \end{pmatrix}.$$

It appears that $a(n,0) = \sum_{i=0}^{n} S(n,i) = B_n$, which implies that the first column of the triangle array is made up of the Bell numbers B_n. A natural question is whether there exists a grammatical interpretation of the numbers $a(n,k)$.

This paper is motivated by exploring the grammatical interpretation of the triangular array $\{B(n,k)\}_{0 \leq k \leq n}$ that satisfies the following four-term recurrence relation

$$B(n+1,k) = (a_1 n + a_2 k + a_3) B(n, k-1) + (b_1 n + b_2 k + b_3) B(n,k) \\ + (k+1) c B(n, k+1), \tag{3}$$

where a_i, b_i, and c are integers for $1 \leq i \leq 3$ with $B(0,0) = 1$ and $B(0,k) = 0$ if $k \neq 0$. In Section 2, we present grammatical interpretations of the triangular array $\{B(n,k)\}$. In Section 3, we present grammatical interpretations of several combinatorial sequences, including the Bell triangle, the modified Hermite polynomials, the Bessel polynomials, and so on. In Section 4, we show the result of the real-rootedness of row-generating functions for $\{B(n,k)\}$, and apply the proposed criteria to the Bell triangular array as an example.

2. Grammatical Interpretations of the Triangular Array $B(n,k)$

We now present the first main result of this paper.

Theorem 1. *Suppose that a_i, b_i, and c are integers for $1 \leq i \leq 3$. Let*

$$G = \{I \to (a_2 + a_3)IX + b_3 IY; X \to (a_1 + a_2)X^2 + (b_1 + b_2)XY + cY^2; Y \to a_1 XY + b_1 Y^2\}.$$

Then, we have

$$D^n(I) = I \sum_{k \geq 0} B(n,k) X^k Y^{n-k}, \tag{4}$$

where the coefficients $B(n,k)$ satisfy the recurrence relation (3).

Proof. Note that $D(I) = (a_2 + a_3)IX + b_3 IY$. Suppose that (4) holds for n. Then, by induction, we obtain

$$D^{n+1}(I) = D\{D^n(I)\} = \sum_{k \geq 0} B(n,k) D(I) X^k Y^{n-k} \\ + \sum_{k \geq 0} B(n,k) ID(X^k) Y^{n-k} + \sum_{k \geq 0} B(n,k) IX^k D(Y^{n-k}).$$

Applying the rules of G, we can derive

$$\sum_{k \geq 0} B(n,k) I(a_2 + a_3) X^{k+1} Y^{n-k} + \sum_{k \geq 0} B(n,k) I b_3 X^k Y^{n+1-k} \\ + \sum_{k \geq 0} B(n,k) k I X^{k-1} Y^{n-k} \{(a_1 + a_2) X^2 + (b_1 + b_2) XY + cY^2\} \\ + \sum_{k \geq 0} B(n,k)(n-k) IX^k Y^{n-k} \{a_1 X + b_1 Y\}.$$

Collate and merge similar items

$$\sum_{k\geq 0} B(n,k)(a_2 + a_3 + k(a_1 + a_2) + (n-k)a_1)IX^{k+1}Y^{n-k}$$
$$+ \sum_{k\geq 0} B(n,k)((n-k)b_1 + k(b_1 + b_2) + b_3)IX^kY^{n+1-k}$$
$$+ \sum_{k\geq 0} B(n,k)kcIX^{k-1}Y^{n-k+2}.$$

Extracting the coefficient of IX^kY^{n+1-k}, we obtain (3). This completes the proof. □

Along the same lines of the proof of Theorem 1, one can easily derive the following result.

Proposition 1. *Let*

$$G = \{I \to (a_2+a_3)IX+b_3IY;\ X \to (a_1+a_2)X^2+(b_1+b_2)XY+cY^2;\ Y \to dX^2+a_1XY+b_1Y^2\}.$$

Then, we have

$$D^n(I) = I \sum_{k\geq 0} M(n,k)X^kY^{n-k},$$

where $M(n,k)$ satisfy the following five-term recursive relation:

$$\begin{aligned}M(n+1,k) &= (n-k+2)dM(n,k-2) + (a_1n + a_2k + a_3)M(n,k-1) \\ &\quad +(b_1n + b_2k + b_3)M(n,k) + (k+1)cM(n,k+1).\end{aligned} \quad (5)$$

where a_i, b_i, c, and d are integers for $1 \leq i \leq 3$.

When $d = 0$, the recurrence relation (5) is degenerated into (3).

3. Applications
3.1. The Bell Triangle

The Bell triangle was proposed by Aigner [9] to provide a characterization of the sequence of Bell numbers by means of the determinants of Hankel matrices. As a special case of Theorem 1, we now present a grammatical interpretations of the Bell triangle.

Proposition 2. *Let $G = \{I \to IX + IY; X \to XY + Y^2; Y \to 0\}$. Then, we have*

$$D^n(I) = I \sum_{k\geq 0} a(n,k)X^kY^{n-k} = IY^n a_n\left(\frac{X}{Y}\right).$$

Note $D^n(X) = XY^n + Y^{n+1}$, $D^n(Y) = 0$. From Leibniz's formula, we obtain the following corollary:

Corollary 1. *For $n \geq 0$, we have*

$$a_{n+1}(x) = \sum_{i=0}^{n} \binom{n}{k} a_k(x)(x+1)$$

Let $D^n(IX) = I\sum_{k=0}^{n+1} b(n+1,k)X^kY^{n+1-k}$. It is routine to verify that

$$b(n+2,k) = b(n+1,k-1) + (k+1)b(n+1,k) + (k+1)b(n+1,k+1),$$

with $b(1,1) = 1$ and $b(1,k) = 0$ when $k \neq 1$. Since $D^{n+1}(I) = D^n(IX) + D^n(IY)$, it follows that $a(n+1,k) = b(n+1,k) + a(n,k)$.

Note that $D^n(X) = Y^n(X+Y)$. Then,

$$b(n+1,k) = \sum_{i=0}^{n+1-k}\binom{n}{i+k-1}a(i+k-1,k-1) + \sum_{i=0}^{n-k}\binom{n}{i+k}a(i+k,k).$$

3.2. On the Coefficients of Modified Hermite Polynomials

The modified Hermite polynomials have the following form:

$$h(0,x) = 1$$
$$h(1,x) = x$$
$$h(2,x) = x^2 + 1$$
$$h(3,x) = x^3 + 3x$$
$$h(4,x) = x^4 + 6x^2 + 3$$
$$h(5,x) = x^5 + 10x^3 + 15x$$
$$h(6,x) = x^6 + 15x^4 + 45x^2 + 15$$

If $n - k \geq 0$ is even, let

$$T(n,k) = \frac{n!}{2^{\frac{n-k}{2}}(\frac{n-k}{2})!k!}.$$

Otherwise, set $T(n,k) = 0$. It should be noted that the numbers $T(n,k)$ are the coefficients of the modified Hermite polynomials (see A099174 [11]) and

$$T(n+1,k) = T(n,k-1) + (k+1)T(n,k+1).$$

Using Theorem 1, we obtain the following proposition.

Proposition 3. *Let $G = \{I \to IX; X \to Y^2; Y \to 0\}$. Then, we have*

$$D^n(I) = I \sum_{k \geq 0} T(n,k) X^k Y^{n-k} = IY^n h(n, \frac{X}{Y}).$$

Note that $D^n(X) = 0$ $(n \geq 2)$. From Leibniz's formula, we obtain the following corollaries:

Corollary 2. *For $n \geq 0$, we have*

$$h(n+1,x) = xh(n,x) + nh(n-1,x)$$

Corollary 3. *For $n \geq k \geq 1$, we have*

$$T(n+1,k) = T(n,k-1) + nT(n-1,k)$$

3.3. The Bessel Polynomials

As a well-known orthogonal sequence of polynomials, the Bessel polynomials $y_n(x)$ were introduced by Krall and Frink in [12], which can be defined as the polynomial solutions of the second-order differential equation

$$x^2 \frac{d^2 y_n(x)}{dx^2} + 2(x+1)\frac{dy_n(x)}{dx} = n(n+1)y_n(x)$$

After that, the Bessel polynomials have been extensively studied and applied (see [13–15]). Moreover, the polynomials $y_n(x)$ can be generated by using the Rodrigues formula (see [11] [A001498]):

$$y_n(x) = \frac{1}{2^n} e^{2/x} \frac{d^n}{dx^n}(x^{2n} e^{-2/x})$$

Explicitly, we can obtain

$$y_n(x) = \sum_{k=0}^{n} \frac{(n+k)!}{(n-k)!k!} \left(\frac{x}{2}\right)^k$$

Let

$$H(n,k) = \frac{(n+k)!}{2^k(n-k)!k!}$$

Then,

$$y_n(x) = \sum_{k=0}^{n} H(n,k) x^k$$

It is easy to verify that

$$H(n+1,k) = H(n,k) + (n+k)H(n,k-1)$$

The polynomials $y_n(x)$ satisfy the recurrence relation

$$y_{n+1}(x) = (2n+1)xy_n(x) + y_{n-1}(x), \quad \text{for } n \geqslant 0$$

with initial conditions $y_{-1}(x) = y_0(x) = 1$. The first three Bessel Polynomials are expressed as

$$y_1(x) = 1 + x,$$
$$y_2(x) = 1 + 3x + 3x^2,$$
$$y_3(x) = 1 + 6x + 15x^2 + 15x^3.$$

We present here a grammatical characterization of the Bessel polynomials $y_n(x)$.

Proposition 4. *Let $G = \{I \to IX + IY; X \to 2X^2; Y \to XY\}$. Then, we have*

$$D^n(I) = I \sum_{k \geq 0} H(n,k) X^k Y^{n-k} = IY^n y_n(X/Y).$$

Note that $D^n(X) = n!2^n X^{n+1}$ and $D^n(Y) = (2n-1)!!X^n Y$. From Leibniz's formula, we obtain the following corollary:

Corollary 4. *For $n \geq 0$, we have*

$$y_{n+1}(x) = \sum_{k=0}^{n} \binom{n}{k}(2n-2k-1)!! y_k(x) x^{n-k} + \sum_{k=0}^{n} \frac{n!2^{n-k}}{k!} y_k(x) x^{n-k+1}.$$

3.4. The Exponential Riordan Array $[\exp(x/(1-x)), x/(1-x)]$

Definition 1 (see [16]). *The exponential Riordan group G is a set of infinite lower-triangular integer matrices, and each matrix in G is defined by a pair of generating function $g(x) = g_0 + g_1 x + g_2 x^2 + \cdots$ and $f(x) = f_1 x + f_2 x^2 + \cdots$, with $g_0 \neq 0$ and $f_1 \neq 0$. The associated matrix is the matrix whose i-th column has exponential generating function $g(x)f(x)^i/i!$ (columns marked from 0). The matrix corresponding to the pair f, g is defined by $[g, f]$.*

Let $R(n,k)$ be the (n,k)-th element in the matrix $[\exp(x/(1-x)), x/(1-x)]$. The associated Riordan array is given as follows:

$$\begin{pmatrix} 1 & & & & & \\ 1 & 1 & & & & \\ 3 & 4 & 1 & & & \\ 13 & 21 & 9 & 1 & & \\ 73 & 136 & 78 & 16 & 1 & \\ \vdots & & & & & \ddots \end{pmatrix} \quad (6)$$

From A059110 [11], we see that

$$R(n,k) = \sum_{i=0}^{n} L'(n,i) \binom{i}{k}$$

for $0 \leq k \leq n$, where $L'(n,i) = \frac{n!}{i!}\binom{n-1}{i-1}$ are unsigned Lah numbers. It is routine to verify that

$$R(n+1,k) = R(n,k-1) + (n+k+1)R(n,k) + (k+1)R(n,k+1).$$

Hence, by Theorem 1, we obtain the following Proposition.

Proposition 5. *Let*

$$G = \{I \to IX + IY; X \to 2XY + Y^2; Y \to Y^2\}$$

Then, we have

$$D^n(I) = I \sum_{k \geq 0} R(n,k) X^k Y^{n-k} := IY^n r_n\left(\frac{X}{Y}\right).$$

Note $D^n(X) = (n+1)!xY^n + nn!Y^{n+1}$, $D^n(Y) = n!Y^{n+1}$. From Leibniz's formula, we obtain the following corollary:

Corollary 5. *For $n \geq 0$, we have*

$$r_{n+1}(x) = \sum_{k=1}^{n} \binom{n}{k}(n-k+1)!r_k(x)(x+1)$$

In Table 1, we list some combinatorial sequences that satisfy (3). More examples can be found in similar tables in [17–19]. By using Theorem 1, we give the grammatical interpretation of the corresponding sequences, so that we can obtain more convolution formulas.

4. Real Rootedness

In this section, as an application, we will pay attention to the property of real roots of the row-generating functions in the array $\{B(n,k)\}_{0 \leq k \leq n}$ in (3). For the sake of proving our results, some known results should be introduced beforehand.

Let $\{P_n(x)\}$ denote a Sturm sequence, which is a sequence of standard polynomials meeting the condition of $\deg P_n = n$ and $P_{n-1}(r)P_{n+1}(r) < 0$ whenever $P_n(r) = 0$ and $n \geq 1$. Let RZ represent the set of polynomials with only real roots. $\{P_n(x)\}$ is known as a generalized Sturm sequence (GSS) if $P_n \in RZ$ and zeros of $P_n(x)$ are separated by those of $P_{n-1}(x)$ for $n \geq 1$. As a special case of Corollary 2.4 in Liu and Wang [20] (also see Zhu, Yeh, and Lu [7]), the following result provides a unified method to many polynomials with only real zeros.

Table 1. Some combinatorial sequences satisfying formula (3).

$(a_1, a_2, a_3, b_1, b_2, b_3, c)$	Description	Entry
$(1,-1,1,0,1,1,0)$	Eulerian numbers	A173018
$(2,-1,1,0,1,1,0)$	Second-order Eulerian numbers	A008517
$(0,1,0,0,1,0,0)$	$\mathrm{Surj}(n,k)$	A019538
$(1,1,0,0,1,0,0)$	Ward numbers	A134991
$(0,0,1,0,1,0,0)$	Stirling subset numbers	A008277
$(0,0,-1,-1,-1,0,0)$	Lah numbers $L_{n,k}$	A008297
$(0,0,1,1,1,0,0)$	Unsigned Lah numbers $L(n,k)$	A105278
$(-2,1,-2,0,0,1,0)$	Coefficients of Laguerre polynomials in reverse order	A021010
$(0,0,1,0,0,1,0)$	Binomial coefficients	A007318
$(0,0,1,1,0,0,0)$	Stirling cycle numbers	A132393
$(0,0,1,-1,0,0,0)$	Stirling numbers of the 1st kind $s(n,k)$	A008275
$(0,0,1,0,1,2,1)$	Production of the triangle of Stirling numbers of the 2nd kind with the Pascal's triangle read by rows	A137597
$(0,0,1,0,1,0,1)$	Set partitions without singletons	A217537
$(0,0,1,0,2,1,2)$	Exponential Riordan Array $[\exp(\sinh(x)*\exp(x)), \sinh(x)*\exp(x)]$	A154602
$(0,1,0,0,2,1,1)$	$n!\binom{n}{k}$	A196347
$(0,1,0,0,2,2,1)$	Row-generating function is $n! \sum_{k=0}^{n} \frac{(1+x)^{n-k}}{k!}$	A073474
$(1,1,0,2,2,2,1)$	The number of (n,k) labeled rooted Greg trees $(n \geq 1, 0 \leq k \leq n-1)$	A048160
$(2,-1,2,0,0,0,1)$	The number of fixed-point-free involutions of $1,2,\ldots,2n$ having k cycles with entries of opposite parities $(0 \leq k \leq n)$	A161119

Lemma 1. *Let $\{P_n(x)\}$ be a sequence of polynomials with nonnegative coefficients and $0 \leq \deg P_n - \deg P_{n-1} \leq 1$. Suppose that*

$$P_n(x) = (a_n x + b_n) P_{n-1}(x) + x(c_n x + d_n) P'_{n-1}(x)$$

where $a_n, b_n \in \mathbb{R}$, and $c_n \leq 0, d_n \geq 0$. Then, $\{P_n(x)\}_{n \geq 0}$ is a generalized Sturm sequence.

For nonnegative array $B(n,k)$, which satisfies the recurrence relation (3), it is sufficient to assume that, for $n \geq 1$,

$$\begin{cases} a_1 n + a_2 k + a_3 - a_1 \geq 0 & \text{for } 1 \leq k \leq n, \\ b_1 n + b_2 k + b_3 - b_1 \geq 0 & \text{for } 0 \leq k \leq n-1, \\ c(k+1) \geq 0 & \text{for } 0 \leq k \leq n-2, \end{cases}$$

which is equivalent to

$$\begin{cases} a_1 \geq 0, a_1 + a_2 \geq 0, a_2 + a_3 \geq 0, \\ b_1 \geq 0, b_1 + b_2 \geq 0, b_3 \geq 0, \\ c \geq 0. \end{cases}$$

Define $B_n(x) = \sum_{k \geq 0}^{n} B(n,k) x^k$ $(n \geq 0)$ as the row-generating functions of $B(n,k)$. Thus, $B_0(x) = 1$ and

$$B_1(x) = b_3 + (a_2 + a_3)x.$$

Moreover, it turns out that $B_n(x)$ follows from the recurrence relation (3) as

$$B_n(x) = [b_1 n + b_3 - b_1 + (a_1 n + a_2 + a_3 - a_1)x]B_{n-1}(x) + (c + b_2 x + a_2 x^2)B'_{n-1}(x),$$

which implies that

$$\deg(B_n(x)) - \deg(B_{n-1}(x)) \leq 1$$

for each n.

Theorem 2. *Let $\{B(n,k)\}_{n,k\geq 0}$ be the array defined in (3). Assume that $b_2 = a_2 + c$. Then, we have the following results:*

(i) *There exist polynomials $A_n(x)$ for $n \geq 0$ such that*

$$B_n(x) = a^n (1+x)^n A_n\left(\frac{d}{1+x}\right),$$

where $A_n(x)$ satisfies the recurrence relation

$$\begin{aligned}A_n(x) &= \frac{1}{a}\{(a_1+a_2)n + a_3 - a_1 + \frac{(b_1+c-a_1-a_2)n-c+b_3-b_1-a_3+a_1}{d} x\} A_{n-1}(x) \\ &+ \frac{x}{a}\{\frac{(a_2-c)x}{d} - a_2\} A'_{n-1}(x)\end{aligned} \quad (7)$$

with $A_0(x) = 1$, $a > 0$ and $d > 0$.

(ii) *Assume $b_1 \geq a_1$ and $b_3 \geq a_2 + a_3$. If $a_2 \leq 0$, then $\{B_n(x)\}_{n\geq 0}$ is a generalized Sturm sequence.*

Proof. (i) Because $b_2 = a_2 + c$, it is obvious that

$$B_n(x) = [b_1 n + b_3 - b_1 + (a_1 n + a_2 + a_3 - a_1)x]B_{n-1}(x) + (c + a_2 x)(1+x)B'_{n-1}(x),$$

It can be proven that (i) holds by induction on n as follows.
As $n = 1$, we can obtain

$$A_1(x) = \frac{1}{a}\{a_2 + a_3 + \frac{b_3 - a_2 - a_3}{d} x\}$$
$$B_1(x) = b_3 + (a_2 + a_3)x.$$

Thus, we have

$$B_1(x) = a(1+x)A_1\left(\frac{d}{1+x}\right).$$

By the induction hypothesis, it now turns out that

$$\begin{aligned}B'_{n-1}(x) &= a^{n-1}(n-1)(x+1)^{n-2} A_{n-1}\left(\frac{d}{1+x}\right) - a^{n-1}(x+1)^{n-1} A'_{n-1}\left(\frac{d}{1+x}\right)\frac{d}{(1+x)^2} \\ &= \frac{(n-1)B_{n-1}(x)}{1+x} - da^{n-1}(x+1)^{n-3} A'_{n-1}\left(\frac{d}{1+x}\right).\end{aligned}$$

It follows from that recurrence relation (7) that, for $n \geq 2$,

$$\begin{aligned}&a^n(1+x)^n A_n\left(\frac{d}{1+x}\right) \\ &= \{((a_1+a_2)n + a_3 - a_1)(1+x) + (b_1 + c - a_1 - a_2)n - c + b_3 - b_1 - a_3 + a_1\}B_{n-1}(x) \\ &\quad - (c+a_2 x)(n-1)B_{n-1}(x) + (c+a_2 x)(1+x)B'_{n-1}(x) = B_n(x)\end{aligned}$$

Thus, for $n \geq 1$, we can prove that

$$B_n(x) = a^n(1+x)^n A_n\left(\frac{d}{1+x}\right).$$

(ii) Evidently, in light of (i), $B_n(x)$ forms a generalized Sturm sequence if and only if (iff) $A_n(x)$ forms a generalized Sturm sequence. The nonnegativity of the coefficients for $A_n(x)$ needs to be considered firstly. Let $A_n(x) = \sum_{k=0}^{n} A(n,k)x^k$ for $n \geq 0$. Then, according to the recurrence relation (7), we obtain

$$A(n,k) = \frac{(a_1+a_2)n - a_2 k + a_3 - a_1}{a} A(n-1,k)$$
$$+ \frac{(b_1+c-a_1-a_2)n - (c-a_2)k + b_3 - b_1 + a_1 - a_2 - a_3}{ad} A(n-1,k-1)$$

for $n \geq 1$. Following from the nonnegativity of $\{B(n,k)\}_{n,k\geq 0}$, it holds

$$a_1 + a_2 \geq 0, a_1 \geq 0, a_2 + a_3 \geq 0$$

Furthermore, by the hypothesis condition, we obtain

$$\begin{cases} b_1 + c - a_1 - a_2 \geq c - a_2 \geq 0, \\ (b_1 + c - a_1 - a_2) - (c - a_2) = b_1 - a_1 \geq 0, \\ (b_1 + c - a_1 - a_2) - (c - a_2) + b_3 - b_1 + a_1 - a_2 - a_3 \geq 0. \end{cases}$$

Thus, $\{B(n,k)\}_{n,k\geq 0}$ is a nonnegative array. According to the recurrence relation (7) and Lemma 1, we can conclude that the polynomials $A_n(x)$ form a generalized Sturm sequence if $a_2 \leq 0$. For the same reason, the polynomials $B_n(x)$ form a generalized Sturm sequence. □

For example, the row-generating function of the Bell triangle $a(n,k)$ in Section 3 is $a_n(x) = \sum_{k=0}^{n} a(n,k)x^k$. Then, the polynomials satisfy

$$a_n(x) = (1+x)a_{n-1}(x) + (1+x)a'_{n-1}(x),$$

with $a_0(x) = 1$. Using Theorem 2 (i), there exists an array $A(n,k)$ such that

$$a_n(x) = \sum_{k=0}^{n} a(n,k)x^k = (1+x)^n A_n\left(\frac{1}{1+x}\right)$$

where $A_n(x)$ for $n \geq 1$ satisfies the recurrence relation

$$A_n(x) = [(n-1)x + 1]A_{n-1}(x) - x^2 A'_{n-1}(x)$$

where $A_0(x) = 1$ and $A_1(x) = 1$. Obviously, $A(n,k) = S(n, n-k)$ for $n \geq 1$. Applying Theorem 2 (ii), it can be proven that $\{a_n(x)\}$ for $n \geq 0$ is a generalized Sturm sequence.

Author Contributions: Methodology, R.R.Z. and J.Y.; validation, F.R.; writing, R.R.Z. All authors have read and agreed to the published version of the manuscript.

Funding: The first author was supported by the National Natural Science Foundation of China (NSFC No. 11501090) and the Natural Science Foundation of Hebei Province (A2019501024). The second author was supported by MOST 110-2115-M-017-002-MY2; The third author's research was partially supported by the National Natural Science Foundation of China (NSFC No. 61807029).

Institutional Review Board Statement: Not applicable.

Informed Consent Statement: Not applicable.

Data Availability Statement: Not applicable.

Conflicts of Interest: The authors declare no conflict of interest.

References

1. Chen, W.Y.C. Context-free grammars, differential operators and formal power series. *Theor. Comput. Sci.* **1993**, *117*, 113–129. [CrossRef]
2. Hao, R.X.J.; Wang, L.X.W.; Yang, H.R.L. Context-free Grammars for Triangular Arrays. *Acta Math. Sin. Engl. Ser.* **2015**, *31*, 445–455. [CrossRef]
3. Bóna, M.; Ehrenborg, R. A combinatorial proof of the log-concavity of the numbers of permutations with k runs. *J. Combin. Theory Ser. A* **2000**, *90*, 293–303. [CrossRef]
4. Ma, S.-M.; Wang, Y. q-Eulerian polynomials and polynomials with only real zeros. *Electron. J. Combin.* **2008**, *15*, 17. [CrossRef]
5. Ma, S.-M. An explicit formula for the number of permutations with a given number of alternating runs. *J. Combin. Theory Ser. A* **2012**, *119*, 1660–1664. [CrossRef]
6. Stanley, R.P. Longest alternating subsequences of permutations. *Mich. Math. J.* **2008**, *57*, 675–687. [CrossRef]
7. Zhu, B.-X.; Yeh, Y.-N.; Lu, Q. Context-free grammars, generating functions and combinatorial arrays. *Eur. J. Comb.* **2019**, *78*, 236–255. [CrossRef]
8. Ma, S.-M. Enumeration of permutations by number of alternating runs. *Discret. Math.* **2013**, *313*, 1816–1822. [CrossRef]
9. Aigner, M. A characterization of the Bell numbers. *Discret. Math.* **1999**, *205*, 207–210. [CrossRef]
10. Chen, X.; Liang, H.; Wang, Y. Total positivity of recursive matrices. *Linear Algebra Its Appl.* **2015**, *471*, 383–393. [CrossRef]
11. Sloane, N.J.A. The On-Line Encyclopedia of Integer Sequences. Available online: http://oeis.org (accessed on 30 January 2022).
12. Krall, H.L.; Frink, O. A new class of orthogonal polynomials. *Trans. Amer. Math. Soc.* **1945**, *65*, 100–115. [CrossRef]
13. Goldman, J.; Haglund, J. Generalized rook polynomials. *J. Combin. Theory Ser. A* **2000**, *91*, 509–530. [CrossRef]
14. Han, H.; Seo, S. Combinatorial proofs of inverse relations and log-concavity for Bessel numbers. *Eur. J. Combin.* **2008**, *29*, 1544–1554. [CrossRef]
15. Ma, S.-M. Some combinatorial arrays generated by context-free grammars. *Eur. J. Comb.* **2013**, *34*, 1081–1091. [CrossRef]
16. Barry, P. Exponential Riordan Arrays and Permutation Enumeration. *J. Integer Seq.* **2010**, *13*, Article 10.9.1.
17. Barbero, J.F. Salas, G.J. Bivariate generating functions for a class of linear recurrences: General structure. *J. Comb. Theory Ser. A* **2014**, *125*, 146–165. [CrossRef]
18. Théorêt, P. Hyperbinomiales: Doubles Suites Satisfaisant à Des équations aux Différences Partielles de Dimension et D'ordre deux de la Forme $H(n,k) = p(n,k)H(n-1,k) + q(n,k)H(n-1,k-1)$. Ph.D. Thesis, Université du Québec à Montréal, Montreal, QC, Canada, May 1994.
19. Théorêt, P. Fonctions génératrices pour une classe déquations aux différences partielles. *Ann. Sci. Math. Québec* **1995**, *19*, 91–105.
20. Liu, L.L.; Wang, Y. A unified approach to polynomial sequences with only real zeros. *Adv. Appl. Math.* **2007**, *38*, 542–560. [CrossRef]

Article

Several Double Inequalities for Integer Powers of the Sinc and Sinhc Functions with Applications to the Neuman–Sándor Mean and the First Seiffert Mean

Wen-Hui Li [1], Qi-Xia Shen [1] and Bai-Ni Guo [2,3,*]

[1] Department of Basic Courses, Zhengzhou University of Science and Technology, Zhengzhou 450064, China; wen.hui.li@foxmail.com (W.-H.L.); shenqixia2004@163.com (Q.-X.S.)
[2] School of Mathematics and Informatics, Henan Polytechnic University, Jiaozuo 454010, China
[3] Independent Researcher, Dallas, TX 75252-8024, USA
* Correspondence: bai.ni.guo@gmail.com

Abstract: In the paper, the authors establish a general inequality for the hyperbolic functions, extend the newly-established inequality to trigonometric functions, obtain some new inequalities involving the inverse sine and inverse hyperbolic sine functions, and apply these inequalities to the Neuman–Sándor mean and the first Seiffert mean.

Keywords: Neuman–Sándor mean; Seiffert mean; inequality; sinc function; sinhc function; inverse hyperbolic function; trigonometric function; necessary and sufficient condition

MSC: 26D07; 26E60; 41A30

1. Introduction

For $s, t > 0$ with $s \neq t$, the Neuman–Sándor mean $M(s,t)$, the first Seiffert mean $P(s,t)$, and the second Seiffert mean $T(s,t)$ are, respectively, defined in [1–3] by

$$M(s,t) = \frac{s-t}{2\operatorname{arcsinh}\frac{s-t}{s+t}}, \quad P(s,t) = \frac{s-t}{4\arctan\sqrt{\frac{s}{t}} - \pi}, \quad T(s,t) = \frac{s-t}{2\arctan\frac{s-t}{s+t}},$$

where $\operatorname{arcsinh} x = \ln(x + \sqrt{x^2+1})$ denotes the inverse hyperbolic sine function. The first Seiffert mean $P(s,t)$ can be rewritten ([1], Equation (2.4)) as

$$P(s,t) = \frac{s-t}{2\arcsin\frac{s-t}{s+t}}.$$

Recently, these bivariate mean values have been the subject of intensive research. In particular, many remarkable inequalities and properties for the means $M(s,t)$, $P(s,t)$, and $T(s,t)$ can be found in the literature [4–20].

Let $A(s,t) = \frac{s+t}{2}$, $H(s,t) = \frac{2st}{s+t}$, and $C(s,t) = \frac{s^2+t^2}{s+t}$ be the arithmetic, harmonic, and contra-harmonic mean of two positive numbers s and t. The inequalities

$$H(s,t) < P(s,t) < A(s,t) < T(s,t) < C(s,t) \tag{1}$$

hold for all $s, t > 0$ with $s \neq t$.
In [1,21], it was established that

$$P(s,t) < M(s,t) < T^2(s,t), \quad A(s,t) < M(s,t) < T(s,t), \tag{2}$$

$$A(s,t) T(s,t) < M^2(s,t) < \frac{A^2(s,t) + T^2(s,t)}{2}$$

for $s, t > 0$ with $s \neq t$.

For $z \in \mathbb{C}$, the functions

$$\operatorname{sinc} z = \begin{cases} \dfrac{\sin z}{z}, & z \neq 0 \\ 1, & z = 0 \end{cases} \quad \text{and} \quad \operatorname{sinhc} z = \begin{cases} \dfrac{\sinh z}{z}, & z \neq 0 \\ 1, & z = 0 \end{cases}$$

are called the sinc function and hyperbolic sinc function, respectively. The function $\operatorname{sinc} z$ is also called the sine cardinal or sampling function, and the function $\operatorname{sinhc} z$ is also called the hyperbolic sine cardinal; see [22]. The sinc function $\operatorname{sinc} z$ arises frequently in signal processing, the theory of Fourier transforms, and other areas in mathematics, physics, and engineering. It is easy to see that these two functions $\operatorname{sinc} z$ and $\operatorname{sinhc} z$ are analytic on $\mathbb{C}$, that is, they are entire functions.

In [23], the authors obtained double inequalities of the Neuman–Sándor meansin terms of the arithmetic and contra-harmonic means, and they deduced that the inequalities

$$1 - \beta_1\left(1 - \dfrac{1}{\cosh^2 \theta}\right) < \dfrac{1}{\operatorname{sinhc} \theta} < 1 - \alpha_1\left(1 - \dfrac{1}{\cosh^2 \theta}\right),$$
$$1 - \beta_2\left(1 - \dfrac{1}{\cosh^4 \theta}\right) < \dfrac{1}{\operatorname{sinhc}^2 \theta} < 1 - \alpha_2\left(1 - \dfrac{1}{\cosh^4 \theta}\right), \quad (3)$$
$$1 + \alpha_3(\cosh^4 \theta - 1) < \operatorname{sinhc}^2 \theta < 1 + \beta_3(\cosh^4 \theta - 1)$$

hold for $\theta \in (0, \ln(1 + \sqrt{2}))$ if and only if

$$\alpha_1 \leq \dfrac{1}{6} \quad \text{and} \quad \beta_1 \geq 2[1 - \ln(1 + \sqrt{2})] = 0.237253\ldots,$$

$$\alpha_2 \leq \dfrac{1}{6} \quad \text{and} \quad \beta_2 \geq \dfrac{4}{3}[1 - \ln^2(1 + \sqrt{2})] = 0.297574\ldots,$$

$$\alpha_3 \leq \dfrac{1 - \ln^2(1 + \sqrt{2})}{3 \ln^2(1 + \sqrt{2})} = 0.095767\ldots \quad \text{and} \quad \beta_3 \geq \dfrac{1}{6}$$

respectively.

In this paper, motivated by those double inequalities in (3), we will obtain necessary and sufficient conditions on α and β such that double inequalities

$$1 - \alpha + \alpha \cosh^{2r} x < \operatorname{sinhc}^r x < 1 - \beta + \beta \cosh^{2r} x \quad (4)$$

and

$$1 - \alpha + \alpha \cos^{2r} x < \operatorname{sinc}^r x < 1 - \beta + \beta \cos^{2r} x \quad (5)$$

are valid on $(-\infty, \infty)$ for some ranges of $r \in \mathbb{R}$. Hereafter, substituting the double inequalities (4) and (5) into the Neuman–Sándor mean $M(s,t)$ and the first Seiffert means $P(s,t)$, we will derive generalizations of some inequalities for the Neuman–Sándor mean $M(s,t)$ and the first Seiffert means $P(s,t)$.

2. Lemmas

To achieve our main purposes, we need the following lemmas.

Lemma 1 ([24], Theorem 1.25). *For $-\infty < s < t < \infty$, let f, g be continuous on $[s,t]$, differentiable on (s,t), and $g'(x) \neq 0$ on (s,t). If the ratio $\dfrac{f'(x)}{g'(x)}$ is increasing on (s,t), so are the functions $\dfrac{f(x)-f(s)}{g(x)-g(s)}$ and $\dfrac{f(x)-f(t)}{g(x)-g(t)}$.*

Lemma 2 ([25], Lemma 1.1). *Suppose that the power series $f(x) = \sum_{n=0}^{\infty} a_n x^n$ and $g(x) = \sum_{n=0}^{\infty} b_n x^n$ have the radius $r > 0$ of convergence and $b_n > 0$ for all $n \in \mathbb{N}_0 = \{0, 1, 2, \dots\}$. Let $h(x) = \frac{f(x)}{g(x)}$. Then the following statements are true.*

1. *If the sequence $\{\frac{a_n}{b_n}\}_{n=0}^{\infty}$ is increasing, so is the function $h(x)$ on $(0, r)$.*
2. *If the sequence $\{\frac{a_n}{b_n}\}$ is increasing for $0 < n \le n_0$ and decreasing for $n > n_0$, then there exists $x_0 \in (0, r)$ such that $h(x)$ is increasing on $(0, x_0)$ and decreasing on (x_0, r).*

The classical Bernoulli numbers B_n for $n \ge 0$ are generated in ([26], p. 3) by

$$\frac{z}{e^z - 1} = \sum_{n=0}^{\infty} B_n \frac{z^n}{n!} = 1 - \frac{z}{2} + \sum_{n=1}^{\infty} B_{2n} \frac{z^{2n}}{(2n)!}, \quad |z| < 2\pi.$$

In the recent papers [27–29], some novel results for the even-indexed Bernoulli numbers B_{2n} were discovered.

Lemma 3 ([30]). *Let B_{2n} be the even-indexed Bernoulli numbers. Then*

$$\frac{x}{\sin x} = 1 + \sum_{n=1}^{\infty} \frac{2^{2n} - 2}{(2n)!} |B_{2n}| x^{2n}, \quad 0 < |x| < \pi. \tag{6}$$

Lemma 4 ([30–32]). *Let B_{2n} be the even-indexed Bernoulli numbers. Then*

$$\cot x = \frac{1}{x} - \sum_{n=1}^{\infty} \frac{2^{2n}}{(2n)!} |B_{2n}| x^{2n-1}$$

and

$$\frac{1}{\sin^2 x} = \csc^2 x = \frac{1}{x^2} + \sum_{n=1}^{\infty} \frac{2^{2n}(2n-1)}{(2n)!} |B_{2n}| x^{2n-2} \tag{7}$$

for $0 < |x| < \pi$.

Lemma 5. *The function*

$$h_1(x) = \frac{2 \sinh^2 x \cosh x - x \sinh x - x^2 \cosh^3 x}{(x - \sinh x \cosh x - x \sinh^2 x)(x \cosh x - \sinh x)}$$

is increasing on $(0, \infty)$ and has the limits

$$\lim_{x \to 0^+} h_1(x) = \frac{17}{25} \quad \text{and} \quad \lim_{x \to \infty} h_1(x) = 1. \tag{8}$$

Proof. Let

$$A(x) = 2 \sinh^2 x \cosh x - x \sinh x - x^2 \cosh^3 x$$

and

$$B(x) = (x - \sinh x \cosh x - x \sinh^2 x)(x \cosh x - \sinh x).$$

Straightforward computation gives

$$A(x) = 2 \cosh^3 x - 2 \cosh x - x \sinh x - x^2 \cosh^3 x$$

$$= \frac{\cosh 3x}{2} - \frac{\cosh x}{2} - \frac{x^2 \cosh 3x}{4} - \frac{3x^2 \cosh x}{4} - x \sinh x$$

$$= \frac{1}{2} \sum_{n=0}^{\infty} \frac{(3x)^{2n}}{(2n)!} - \frac{1}{2} \sum_{n=0}^{\infty} \frac{x^{2n}}{(2n)!} - \frac{x^2}{4} \sum_{n=0}^{\infty} \frac{(3x)^{2n}}{(2n)!} - \frac{3x^2}{4} \sum_{n=0}^{\infty} \frac{x^{2n}}{(2n)!} - x \sum_{n=0}^{\infty} \frac{x^{2n+1}}{(2n+1)!}$$

$$= \frac{1}{2}\sum_{n=0}^{\infty}\frac{(3x)^{2n+2}}{(2n+2)!} - \frac{1}{2}\sum_{n=0}^{\infty}\frac{x^{2n+2}}{(2n+2)!} - \frac{1}{4}\sum_{n=0}^{\infty}\frac{3^{2n}x^{2n+2}}{(2n)!}$$
$$- \frac{3}{4}\sum_{n=0}^{\infty}\frac{x^{2n+2}}{(2n)!} - \sum_{n=0}^{\infty}\frac{x^{2n+2}}{(2n+1)!}$$
$$= \frac{1}{2}\sum_{n=2}^{\infty}\frac{3^{2n}(-2n^2-3n+8)-6n^2-13n-8}{(2n+2)!}x^{2n+2}$$

and

$$B(x) = x^2\cosh x - 2x\sinh x - x^2\sinh^2 x\cosh x + \sinh^2 x\cosh x$$
$$= x^2\cosh x - 2x\sinh x - \frac{x^2\cosh 3x}{4} + \frac{x^2\cosh x}{4} + \frac{\cosh 3x}{4} - \frac{\cosh x}{4}$$
$$= \frac{5}{4}\sum_{n=0}^{\infty}\frac{x^{2n+2}}{(2n)!} - 2\sum_{n=0}^{\infty}\frac{x^{2n+2}}{(2n+1)!} - \frac{1}{4}\sum_{n=0}^{\infty}\frac{3^{2n}x^{2n+2}}{(2n)!} + \frac{1}{4}\sum_{n=0}^{\infty}\frac{(3x)^{2n}}{(2n)!} - \frac{1}{4}\sum_{n=0}^{\infty}\frac{x^{2n}}{(2n)!}$$
$$= \frac{1}{4}\sum_{n=2}^{\infty}\frac{3^{2n}(-4n^2-6n+7)+20n^2+14n-7}{(2n+2)!}x^{2n+2}.$$

Let

$$a_n = \frac{3^{2n}(-2n^2-3n+8)-6n^2-13n-8}{2(2n+2)!}$$

and

$$b_n = \frac{3^{2n}(-4n^2-6n+7)+20n^2+14n-7}{4(2n+2)!}.$$

Simple computation leads to

$$a_n = \frac{3^{2n}(-2n^2-3n+8)-6n^2-13n-8}{2(2n+2)!} \leq \frac{3^4(-2n^2-3n+8)-6n^2-13n-8}{2(2n+2)!}$$
$$= \frac{-168n^2-256n+640}{2(2n+2)!} \leq -\frac{272}{(2n+2)!} < 0$$

for all $n \in \mathbb{N}$ and $n \geq 2$, whereas, for all $n \in \mathbb{N}$ and $n \geq 2$,

$$b_n = \frac{3^{2n}(-4n^2-6n+7)+20n^2+14n-7}{4(2n+2)!} \leq \frac{3^4(-4n^2-6n+7)+20n^2+14n-7}{4(2n+2)!} \qquad (9)$$
$$= \frac{-304n^2-472n+560}{4(2n+2)!} \leq -\frac{400}{(2n+2)!} < 0.$$

Consequently, we obtain

$$c_n = \frac{-a_n}{-b_n} = 2 \times \frac{3^{2n}(2n^2+3n-8)+6n^2+13n+8}{3^{2n}(4n^2+6n-7)-20n^2-14n+7}$$
$$= \frac{9^n(4n^2+6n-16)+12n^2+26n+16}{9^n(4n^2+6n-7)-20n^2-14n+7} \qquad (10)$$
$$= 1 + \frac{-9^{n+1}+32n^2+40n+9}{9^n(4n^2+6n-7)-20n^2-14n+7}$$
$$\triangleq 1 + k(n)$$

for $n \in \mathbb{N}$ and $n \geq 2$. Let

$$k(x) = \frac{-9^{x+1}+32x^2+40x+9}{9^x(4x^2+6x-7)-20x^2-14x+7}$$

for $x \in [2, \infty)$. Then
$$k'(x) = \frac{\ell(x)}{[9^x(4x^2+6x-7)-20x^2-14x+7]^2},$$
where
$$\begin{aligned}
\ell(x) &= \left(-9^{x+1}\ln 9 + 64x + 40\right)\left[9^x(4x^2+6x-7)-20x^2-14x+7\right] \\
&\quad - \left(-9^{x+1}+32x^2+40x+9\right)\left[9^x(4x^2+6x-7)\ln 9 + 9^x(8x+6)-40x-14\right] \\
&= 9^{2x+1}(8x+6) + 9^x\left[9(20x^2+14x-7)-(4x^2+6x-7)(32x^2+40x+9)\right]\ln 9 \\
&\quad + 9^x\left[(64x+40)(4x^2+6x-7)-9(40x+14)-(8x+6)(32x^2+40x+9)\right] \\
&\quad - (64x+40)(20x^2+14x-7) + (40x+14)(32x^2+40x+9) \\
&= 9^{2x+1}(8x+6) + 9^x(352x+128x^2-352x^3-128x^4)\ln 9 \\
&\quad + 9^x \times 4(-115-220x+8x^2) + 406 + 808x + 352x^2 \\
&= 2 \times 9^x\left[9^{x+1}(3+4x) + (176x+64x^2-176x^3-64x^4)\ln 9 - 230 - 440x + 16x^2\right] \\
&\quad + 406 + 808x + 352x^2.
\end{aligned}$$

Let
$$m(x) = 9^{x+1}(3+4x) + (176x+64x^2-176x^3-64x^4)\ln 9 - 230 - 440x + 16x^2.$$

Then
$$m'(x) = 9^{x+1}\ln 9(3+4x) + 4 \times 9^{x+1} + (176+128x-528x^2-256x^3)\ln 9 - 440 + 32x,$$
$$m'(2) = 4219\ln 9 + 2412$$
$$> 0,$$
$$m''(x) = \ln^2 9 \times 9^{x+1}(3+4x) + 8\ln 9 \times 9^{x+1} + (128-1056x-768x^2)\ln 9 + 32,$$
$$m''(2) = 8019\ln^2 9 + 776\ln 9 + 32$$
$$> 0,$$
$$m^{(3)}(x) = \ln^3 9 \times 9^{x+1}(3+4x) + 12\ln^2 9 \times 9^{x+1} + (-1056-1536x)\ln 9,$$
$$m^{(3)}(2) = 8019\ln^3 9 + 8748\ln^2 9 - 2112\ln 9$$
$$> 0,$$
$$m^{(4)}(x) = \ln^4 9 \times 9^{x+1}(3+4x) + 16\ln^3 9 \times 9^{x+1} - 1536\ln 9$$
$$> \ln^4 9 \times 9^{x+1}(3+4x) + 11664\ln^3 9 - 1536\ln 9$$
$$> 0$$

on $[2, \infty)$. Therefore, the function $m(x)$ is increasing on $[2, \infty)$ and
$$m(2) = 6973 - 1824\ln 9 > 1501 > 0.$$

Hence, it follows that $\ell(x) > 0$ and the function $k(x)$ is increasing on $[2, \infty)$.
According to (10), we can observe that c_n is increasing for $n \in \mathbb{N}$ and $n \geq 2$. Thus, based on Lemma 2, the function $h_1(x) = \frac{A(x)}{B(x)}$ is increasing on $(0, \infty)$.
The limits in (8) are straightforward. The proof of Lemma 5 is complete. □

3. Necessary and Sufficient Conditions

Now we are in a position to state and prove our main results.

Theorem 1. *Let* $x, r \in \mathbb{R}$.

1. When $r \geq \frac{8}{25}$, the double inequality (4) holds if and only if $\alpha \leq 0$ and $\beta \geq \frac{1}{6}$.
2. When $r < 0$, the right-hand side of the inequality (4) holds if and only if $\beta \leq \frac{1}{6}$.

Proof. Let
$$F(x) = \frac{\operatorname{sinhc}^r x - 1}{\cosh^{2r} x - 1} \triangleq \frac{f_1(x)}{f_2(x)},$$
where $f_1(x) = \operatorname{sinhc}^r x - 1$ and $f_2(x) = \cosh^{2r} x - 1$. Then
$$\frac{f_1'(x)}{f_2'(x)} = \frac{\sinh^{r-2} x (x \cosh x - \sinh x)}{2 x^{r+1} \cosh^{2r-1} x}$$

and
$$\left[\frac{f_1'(x)}{f_2'(x)}\right]' = \frac{r-1}{2} \left(\frac{\sinh x}{x \cosh^2 x}\right)^{r-2} \frac{x - \sinh x \cosh x - x \sinh^2 x}{x^2 \cosh^3 x} \cdot \frac{x \cosh x - \sinh x}{x^2 \sinh x \cosh x}$$
$$+ \frac{1}{2} \left(\frac{\sinh x}{x \cosh^2 x}\right)^{r-1} \frac{2 \sinh^2 x \cosh x - x^2 \cosh^3 x - x \sinh x}{x^3 \sinh^2 x \cosh^2 x}$$
$$= \frac{1}{2} \left(\frac{\sinh x}{x \cosh^2 x}\right)^{r-2} \frac{1}{x^4 \sinh x \cosh^4 x} \left[(r-1)(x - \sinh x \cosh x - x \sinh^2 x)\right.$$
$$\times (x \cosh x - \sinh x) + \left(2 \sinh^2 x \cosh x - x \sinh x - x^2 \cosh^3 x\right)\bigg]$$
$$= \frac{1}{2} \left(\frac{\sinh x}{x \cosh^2 x}\right)^{r-2} \frac{(x - \sinh x \cosh x - x \sinh^2 x)(x \cosh x - \sinh x)}{x^4 \sinh x \cosh^4 x}$$
$$\times \left[r - 1 + \frac{2 \sinh^2 x \cosh x - x \sinh x - x^2 \cosh^3 x}{(x - \sinh x \cosh x - x \sinh^2 x)(x \cosh x - \sinh x)}\right]$$
$$= \frac{1}{2} \left(\frac{\sinh x}{x \cosh^2 x}\right)^{r-2} \frac{B(x)}{x^4 \sinh x \cosh^4 x} [r - 1 + h_1(x)].$$

Based on the result (9) in the proof of Lemma 5, we can observe that the function $B(x) < 0$.

When $r \geq \frac{8}{25}$ and $x \in (0, \infty)$, we have $r - 1 + h_1(x) > 0$, and then $\frac{f_1'(x)}{f_2'(x)}$ is decreasing on $(0, \infty)$. Accordingly, by Lemma 1, the function $F(x) = \frac{f_1(x)}{f_2(x)} = \frac{f_1(x) - f_1(0^+)}{f_2(x) - f_2(0^+)}$ is decreasing on $(0, \infty)$.

When $r < 0$ and $x \in (0, \infty)$, we have $r - 1 + h_1(x) < 0$, and then $\frac{f_1'(x)}{f_2'(x)}$ is increasing on $(0, \infty)$. Accordingly, based on Lemma 1, the function $F(x) = \frac{f_1(x)}{f_2(x)} = \frac{f_1(x) - f_1(0^+)}{f_2(x) - f_2(0^+)}$ is increasing on $(0, \infty)$.

It is straightforward that $\lim_{x \to 0^+} F(x) = \frac{1}{6}$. The proof of Theorem 1 is thus complete. □

Corollary 1. *Let $r > 0$ and $x \in \mathbb{R}$. Then the inequality*
$$\frac{1}{\operatorname{sinhc}^r x} < 1 - \alpha + \alpha \left(\frac{1}{\cosh x}\right)^{2r}$$
holds if and only if $\alpha \leq \frac{1}{6}$.

Corollary 2. *Let $x \in \mathbb{R}$. Then*
$$\frac{1}{\cosh^2 x} < \frac{1}{\operatorname{sinhc} x} < \frac{5}{6} + \frac{1}{6 \cosh^2 x} < 1 < \operatorname{sinhc} x < \frac{5}{6} + \frac{\cosh^2 x}{6} < \cosh^2 x.$$

Corollary 3. Let $t \neq 0$. Then

$$\frac{1}{1+t^2} < \frac{\operatorname{arcsinh} t}{t} < \frac{5}{6} + \frac{1}{6(1+t^2)} < 1 < \frac{t}{\operatorname{arcsinh} t} < \frac{5}{6} + \frac{1+t^2}{6} < 1+t^2.$$

Theorem 2. Let $r \in \mathbb{R}$. For $x \in \left(0, \frac{\pi}{2}\right)$,

1. when $r \geq \frac{1}{2}$, the double inequality (5) holds if and only if $\alpha \geq 1 - \left(\frac{2}{\pi}\right)^r$ and $\beta \leq \frac{1}{6}$;
2. when $0 < r \leq \frac{8}{25}$, the double inequality (5) holds if and only if $\alpha \geq \frac{1}{6}$ and $\beta \leq 1 - \left(\frac{2}{\pi}\right)^r$;
3. when $r < 0$, then the right-hand side inequality in (5) holds if and only if $\beta \geq \frac{1}{6}$.

Proof. Let

$$G(x) = \frac{\operatorname{sinc}^r x - 1}{\cos^{2r} x - 1} \triangleq \frac{g_1(x)}{g_2(x)},$$

where $g_1(x) = \operatorname{sinc}^r x - 1$ and $g_2(x) = \cos^{2r} x - 1$. Then

$$\frac{g_1'(x)}{g_2'(x)} = -\frac{1}{2}\left(\frac{\sin x}{x \cos^2 x}\right)^{r-1} \frac{x \cos x - \sin x}{x^2 \sin x \cos x}$$

and

$$\left[\frac{g_1'(x)}{g_2'(x)}\right]' = \frac{r-1}{2}\left(\frac{\sin x}{x \cos^2 x}\right)^{r-2} \frac{x - \sin x \cos x + x \sin^2 x}{x^2 \cos^3 x} \cdot \frac{\sin x - x \cos x}{x^2 \sin x \cos x}$$

$$+ \frac{1}{2}\left(\frac{\sin x}{x \cos^2 x}\right)^{r-1} \frac{x^2 \cos^3 x + x \sin x - 2 \sin^2 x \cos x}{x^3 \sin^2 x \cos^2 x}$$

$$= \frac{1}{2}\left(\frac{\sin x}{x \cos^2 x}\right)^{r-2} \frac{1}{x^4 \sin x \cos^4 x}[(r-1)(x - \sin x \cos x + x \sin^2 x)$$

$$\times (\sin x - x \cos x) + (x^2 \cos^3 x + x \sin x - 2 \sin^2 x \cos x)]$$

$$= \frac{1}{2}\left(\frac{\sin x}{x \cos^2 x}\right)^{r-2} \frac{2x \sin x - \sin^2 x \cos x - x^2 \cos x - x^2 \sin^2 x \cos x}{x^4 \sin x \cos^4 x}$$

$$\times \left(r + \frac{2x^2 \cos x - x \sin x - \sin^2 x \cos x}{2x \sin x - \sin^2 x \cos x - x^2 \cos x - x^2 \sin^2 x \cos x}\right)$$

$$= \frac{1}{2}\left(\frac{\sin x}{x \cos^2 x}\right)^{r-2} \frac{2x \sin x - \sin^2 x \cos x - x^2 \cos x - x^2 \sin^2 x \cos x}{x^4 \sin x \cos^4 x}[r + u(x)],$$

where

$$u(x) = \frac{2x^2 \cos x - x \sin x - \sin^2 x \cos x}{2x \sin x - \sin^2 x \cos x - x^2 \cos x - x^2 \sin^2 x \cos x}$$

$$= \frac{\frac{2x^2}{\sin^2 x} - \frac{2x}{\sin 2x} - 1}{\frac{4x}{\sin 2x} - 1 - \frac{x^2}{\sin^2 x} - x^2} \triangleq \frac{D(x)}{E(x)}$$

with

$$D(x) = \frac{2x^2}{\sin^2 x} - \frac{2x}{\sin 2x} - 1 \quad \text{and} \quad E(x) = \frac{4x}{\sin 2x} - 1 - \frac{x^2}{\sin^2 x} - x^2.$$

By virtue of (6) and (7), we have

$$D(x) = 2x^2\left[\frac{1}{x^2} + \sum_{n=1}^{\infty} \frac{2^{2n}(2n-1)}{(2n)!}|B_{2n}|x^{2n-2}\right] - \left[1 + \sum_{n=1}^{\infty} \frac{2^{2n}-2}{(2n)!}|B_{2n}|(2x)^{2n}\right] - 1$$

$$= \sum_{n=1}^{\infty} \frac{2^{2n+1}(2n-1)}{(2n)!}|B_{2n}|x^{2n} - \sum_{n=1}^{\infty} \frac{2^{2n}-2}{(2n)!}|B_{2n}|(2x)^{2n}$$

$$= \sum_{n=2}^{\infty} \frac{2^{2n}(4n-2^{2n})}{(2n)!}|B_{2n}|x^{2n} \triangleq \sum_{n=2}^{\infty} d_n x^{2n}$$

and

$$E(x) = 2\left[1 + \sum_{n=1}^{\infty} \frac{2^{2n}-2}{(2n)!}|B_{2n}|(2x)^{2n}\right] - x^2\left[\frac{1}{x^2} + \sum_{n=1}^{\infty} \frac{2^{2n}(2n-1)}{(2n)!}|B_{2n}|x^{2n-2}\right] - x^2 - 1$$

$$= \sum_{n=1}^{\infty} \frac{(2^{2n+1}-2n-3)2^{2n}}{(2n)!}|B_{2n}|x^{2n} - x^2$$

$$= \sum_{n=2}^{\infty} \frac{(2^{2n+1}-2n-3)2^{2n}}{(2n)!}|B_{2n}|x^{2n} \triangleq \sum_{n=2}^{\infty} e_n x^{2n},$$

where

$$d_n = \frac{2^{2n}(4n-2^{2n})}{(2n)!}|B_{2n}| \quad \text{and} \quad e_n = \frac{(2^{2n+1}-2n-3)2^{2n}}{(2n)!}|B_{2n}| > 0.$$

Since the sequence $c_n = \frac{d_n}{e_n} = \frac{4n-2^{2n}}{2^{2n+1}-2n-3}$ for $n = 2, 3, \ldots$ is decreasing, according to Lemma 2, the function $u(x) = \frac{D(x)}{E(x)}$ is decreasing from $(0, \frac{\pi}{2})$ onto $(-\frac{1}{2}, -\frac{8}{25})$. When $r \geq \frac{1}{2}$, the function $\frac{g_1'(x)}{g_2'(x)}$ is increasing on $(0, \frac{\pi}{2})$, and based on Lemma 1, the function $G(x) = \frac{g_1(x)}{g_2(x)} = \frac{g_1(x) - g_1(0^+)}{g_2(x) - g_2(0^+)}$ is increasing on $(0, \frac{\pi}{2})$. When $r \leq \frac{8}{25}$, the function $\frac{g_1'(x)}{g_2'(x)}$ is decreasing on $(0, \frac{\pi}{2})$, and according to Lemma 1, the function $G(x) = \frac{g_1(x)}{g_2(x)} = \frac{g_1(x) - g_1(0^+)}{g_2(x) - g_2(0^+)}$ is decreasing on $(0, \frac{\pi}{2})$.

It is straightforward that $\lim_{x \to 0^+} G(x) = \frac{1}{6}$. The proof of Theorem 2 is thus complete. □

Corollary 4. *Let $r > 0$ and $|x| < \pi/2$. Then the inequality*

$$\frac{1}{\operatorname{sinc}^r x} < 1 - \alpha + \alpha \left(\frac{1}{\cos x}\right)^{2r}$$

holds if and only if $\alpha \geq \frac{1}{6}$.

Corollary 5. *Let $|x| \leq \frac{\pi}{2}$. Then*

$$\cos^2 x < \cos x < \operatorname{sinc} x < \frac{5}{6} + \frac{\cos^2 x}{6} < 1 < \frac{1}{\operatorname{sinc} x} < \frac{5}{6} + \frac{1}{6\cos^2 x} < \frac{1}{\cos^2 x}.$$

Corollary 6. *Let $t \in (0,1)$. Then*

$$1 - t^2 < \frac{t}{\arcsin t} < \frac{5}{6} + \frac{1-t^2}{6} < 1 < \frac{\arcsin t}{t} < \frac{5}{6} + \frac{1}{6(1-t^2)} < \frac{1}{1-t^2}.$$

4. Applications of Necessary and Sufficient Conditions

In this section, using Theorems 1 and 2, we can obtain the following inequalities.

Theorem 3. *Let $s, t > 0$ with $s \neq t$. When $r \geq \frac{8}{25}$, the double inequality*

$$\alpha C^r(s,t) + (1-\alpha)A^r(s,t) < M^r(s,t) < \beta C^r(s,t) + (1-\beta)A^r(s,t) \tag{11}$$

holds if and only if $\alpha \leq \frac{1}{2^r-1}\frac{1-\ln^r(1+\sqrt{2})}{\ln^r(1+\sqrt{2})}$ and $\beta \geq \frac{1}{6}$; when $r < 0$, the inequality (11) holds if and only if $\alpha \geq \frac{1}{2^r-1}\frac{1-\ln^r(1+\sqrt{2})}{\ln^r(1+\sqrt{2})}$ and $\beta \leq \frac{1}{6}$.

Proof. Without loss of generality, we assume that $s > t > 0$. Let $u = \frac{s-t}{s+t}$. Then $u \in (0,1)$ and

$$\frac{M^r(s,t) - A^r(s,t)}{C^r(s,t) - A^r(s,t)} = \frac{\frac{u^r}{\operatorname{arcsinh}^r u} - 1}{(1+u^2)^r - 1}.$$

Let $t = \sinh \theta$. Then $\theta \in (0, \ln(1+\sqrt{2}))$ and

$$\frac{M^r(s,t) - A^r(s,t)}{C^r(s,t) - A^r(s,t)} = \frac{\frac{\sinh^r \theta}{\theta^r} - 1}{\cosh^{2r} \theta - 1} \triangleq F(\theta).$$

Using Theorem 1, we can observe that, when $r \geq \frac{8}{25}$, the function $F(\theta)$ is decreasing on the interval $(0, \ln(1+\sqrt{2}))$, whereas $F(\theta)$ is increasing on $(0, \ln(1+\sqrt{2}))$ for $r < 0$. According to L'Hospital's rule, we have

$$\lim_{\theta \to 0^+} F(\theta) = \frac{1}{6} \quad \text{and} \quad \lim_{\theta \to \ln(1+\sqrt{2})^-} F(\theta) = \frac{1}{2^r - 1} \frac{1 - \ln^r(1+\sqrt{2})}{\ln^r(1+\sqrt{2})}.$$

The proof of Theorem 3 is thus complete. □

Theorem 4. *Let $s, t > 0$ with $s \neq t$. Then the double inequality*

$$\alpha H^r(s,t) + (1-\alpha)A^r(s,t) < P^r(s,t) < \beta H^r(s,t) + (1-\beta)A^r(s,t)$$

holds if and only if

$$\begin{cases} \text{for } r \geq \frac{1}{2}, & \alpha \geq 1 - \left(\frac{2}{\pi}\right)^r \text{ and } \beta \leq \frac{1}{6}; \\ \text{for } 0 < r \leq \frac{8}{25}, & \alpha \geq \frac{1}{6} \text{ and } \beta \leq 1 - \left(\frac{2}{\pi}\right)^r; \\ \text{for } r < 0, & \alpha \leq 0 \text{ and } \beta \geq \frac{1}{6}. \end{cases}$$

Proof. Without the loss of generality, we assume that $s > t > 0$. Let $v = \frac{s-t}{s+t}$. Then $v \in (0,1)$ and

$$\frac{P^r(s,t) - A^r(s,t)}{H^r(s,t) - A^r(s,t)} = \frac{\frac{v^r}{\operatorname{arcsin}^r v} - 1}{(1-v^2)^r - 1}.$$

Let $v = \sin \theta$. Then $\theta \in (0, \frac{\pi}{2})$ and

$$\frac{P^r(s,t) - A^r(s,t)}{H^r(s,t) - A^r(s,t)} = \frac{\frac{\sin^r \theta}{\theta^r} - 1}{\cos^{2r} \theta - 1} \triangleq G(\theta).$$

By virtue of Theorem 2, we can observe that, when $r \in (-\infty, 0) \cup (0, \frac{8}{25}]$, the function $G(\theta)$ is decreasing on $(0, \frac{\pi}{2})$, whereas $G(\theta)$ is increasing on $(0, \frac{\pi}{2})$ for $r \geq \frac{1}{2}$. Using L'Hospital's rule, we obtain the limits $\lim_{\theta \to 0^+} G(\theta) = \frac{1}{6}$ and

$$\lim_{\theta \to (\pi/2)^-} G(\theta) = \begin{cases} 1 - \left(\frac{2}{\pi}\right)^r, & r > 0; \\ 0, & r < 0. \end{cases}$$

The proof of Theorem 4 is thus complete. □

Corollary 7. *For all $s, t > 0$ with $s \neq t$,*

1. The double inequality

$$\frac{\alpha_1}{H(s,t)} + \frac{1-\alpha_1}{A(s,t)} < \frac{1}{P(s,t)} < \frac{\beta_1}{H(s,t)} + \frac{1-\beta_1}{A(s,t)}$$

holds if and only if

$$\alpha_1 \leq 2[1-\ln(1+\sqrt{2})] = 0.237253\ldots \quad \text{and} \quad \beta_1 \geq \frac{1}{6};$$

2. The double inequality

$$\frac{\alpha_2}{H^2(s,t)} + \frac{1-\alpha_2}{A^2(s,t)} < \frac{1}{P^2(s,t)} < \frac{\beta_2}{H^2(s,t)} + \frac{1-\beta_2}{A^2(s,t)}$$

holds if and only if $\alpha_2 \leq 0$ and $\beta_2 \geq \frac{1}{6}$;

3. The double inequality

$$\alpha_3 H(s,t) + (1-\alpha_3)A(s,t) < P(s,t) < \beta_3 H(s,t) + (1-\beta_3)A(s,t)$$

holds if and only if

$$\alpha_3 \geq 1 - \frac{2}{\pi} = 0.36338\ldots, \quad \text{and} \quad \beta_3 \leq \frac{1}{6};$$

4. The double inequality

$$\alpha_4 H^2(s,t) + (1-\alpha_4)A^2(s,t) < P^2(s,t) < \beta_4 H^2(s,t) + (1-\beta_4)A^2(s,t)$$

holds if and only if

$$\alpha_4 \geq 1 - \left(\frac{2}{\pi}\right)^2 = 0.594715\ldots \quad \text{and} \quad \beta_4 \leq \frac{1}{6}.$$

Corollary 8. *For all* $s,t > 0$ *with* $s \neq t$, *then*

$$H(s,t) < \left(1-\frac{2}{\pi}\right)H(s,t) + \frac{2}{\pi}A(s,t) < P(s,t) < \frac{1}{6}H(s,t) + \frac{5}{6}A(s,t)$$

$$< A(s,t) < \frac{1-\ln(1+\sqrt{2})}{\ln(1+\sqrt{2})}C(s,t) + \frac{2\ln(1+\sqrt{2})-1}{\ln(1+\sqrt{2})}A(s,t) \qquad (12)$$

$$< M(s,t) < \frac{1}{6}C(s,t) + \frac{5}{6}A(s,t) < C(s,t).$$

5. Remarks

Remark 1. *When taking* $r = -2, -1, 1, 2$ *in Theorem 1, we can obtain the results reported in [13,23].*

Remark 2. *The inequality chain (12) improves the left-hand sides of inequalities (1) and (2).*

Remark 3. *From* $\sinh(z\mathrm{i}) = \mathrm{i}\sin z$, *it follows that* $\mathrm{sinhc}(z\mathrm{i}) = \mathrm{sinc}\, z$. *This relation is possibly available to simplify proofs of the main results in this paper.*

Remark 4. *In [33–36], series expansions of the functions*

$$\left(\frac{\arcsin t}{t}\right)^r, \quad \left(\frac{\mathrm{arcsinh}\, t}{t}\right)^r, \quad \left[\frac{(\arccos x)^2}{2(1-x)}\right]^r,$$

$$\left[\frac{(\operatorname{arccosh} x)^2}{2(1-x)}\right]^r, \quad (\arccos t)^r, \quad (\operatorname{arccosh} t)^r$$

for $r \in \mathbb{R}$ were established. These series expansions are possibly available to prove the main results presented in this paper.

6. Conclusions

In this paper, we have established some inequalities for the trigonometric functions and hyperbolic functions. These results can trigger further investigations on inequalities involving trigonometric and hyperbolic functions. The techniques used in this paper are suitable for proving and establishing many other inequalities involving the Neuman–Sándor mean, the Seiffert mean, the Toader mean, and so on.

Author Contributions: Writing—original draft, W.-H.L., Q.-X.S. and B.-N.G. All authors contributed equally to the manuscript. All authors have read and agreed to the published version of the manuscript.

Funding: This research received no external funding.

Institutional Review Board Statement: Not applicable.

Informed Consent Statement: Not applicable.

Data Availability Statement: Not applicable.

Acknowledgments: The authors thank anonymous referees for their careful corrections to and valuable comments on the original version of this paper.

Conflicts of Interest: The authors declare no conflict of interest.

References

1. Neuman, E.; Sándor, J. On the Schwab-Borchardt mean. *Math. Pannon.* **2003**, *14*, 253–266.
2. Seiffert, H.-J. Aufgabe β 16. *Wurzel* **1995**, *29*, 221–222.
3. Seiffert, H.-J. Problem 887. *Nieuw Arch. Wiskd.* **1993**, *11*, 176.
4. Chu, Y.-M.; Long, B.-L. Bounds of the Neuman–Sándor mean using power and identric means. *Abstr. Appl. Anal.* **2013**, *2013*, 6. [CrossRef]
5. Chu, Y.-M.; Long, B.-L.; Gong, W.-M.; Song, Y.-Q. Sharp bounds for Seiffert and Neuman–Sándor means in terms of generalized logarithmic means. *J. Inequal. Appl.* **2013**, *2013*, 13. [CrossRef]
6. Chu, Y.-M.; Wang, M.-K.; Gong, W.-M. Two sharp double inequalities for Seiffert mean. *J. Inequal. Appl.* **2011**, *2011*, 7. [CrossRef]
7. Chu, Y.-M.; Zong, C.; Wang, G.-D. Optimal convex combination bounds of Seiffert and geometric means for the arithmetic mean. *J. Math. Inequal.* **2011**, *5*, 429–434. [CrossRef]
8. Jiang, W.-D. Some sharp inequalities involving reciprocals of the Seiffert and other means. *J. Math. Inequal.* **2012**, *6*, 593–599. [CrossRef]
9. Jiang, W.-D.; Qi, F. Sharp bounds for Neuman-Sándor's mean in terms of the root-mean-square. *Period. Math. Hungar.* **2014**, *69*, 134–138. [CrossRef]
10. Jiang, W.-D.; Qi, F. Sharp bounds for the Neuman-Sándor mean in terms of the power and contraharmonic means. *Cogent Math.* **2015**, *2*, 7. [CrossRef]
11. Li, Y.-M.; Long, B.-Y.; Chu, Y.-M. Sharp bounds for the Neuman-Sándor mean in terms of generalized logarithmic mean. *J. Math. Inequal.* **2012**, *6*, 567–577. [CrossRef]
12. Liu, H.; Meng, X.-J. The optimal convex combination bounds for Seiffert's mean. *J. Inequal. Appl.* **2011**, *2011*, 9. [CrossRef]
13. Neuman, E. A note on a certain bivariate mean. *J. Math. Inequal.* **2012**, *6*, 637–643. [CrossRef]
14. Neuman, E. Inequalities for the Schwab-Borchardt mean and their applications. *J. Math. Inequal.* **2011**, *5*, 601–609. [CrossRef]
15. Qi, F.; Li, W.-H. A unified proof of inequalities and some new inequalities involving Neuman–Sándor mean. *Miskolc Math. Notes* **2014**, *15*, 665–675. [CrossRef]
16. Sun, H.; Shen, X.-H.; Zhao, T.-H.; Chu, Y.-M. Optimal bounds for the Neuman-Sándor means in terms of geometric and contraharmonic means. *Appl. Math. Sci. (Ruse)* **2013**, *7*, 4363–4373. [CrossRef]
17. Sun, H.; Zhao, T.-H.; Chu, Y.-M.; Liu, B.-Y. A note on the Neuman-Sándor mean. *J. Math. Inequal.* **2014**, *8*, 287–297. [CrossRef]
18. Wang, M.-K.; Chu, Y.-M.; Liu, B.-Y. Sharp inequalities for the Neuman-Sándor mean in terms of arithmetic and contra-harmonic means. *Rev. Anal. Numér. Théor. Approx.* **2013**, *42*, 115–120.
19. Zhao, T.-H.; Chu, Y.-M. A sharp double inequality involving identric, Neuman-Sándor, and quadratic means. *Sci. Sin. Math.* **2013**, *43*, 551–562. (In Chinese) [CrossRef]

20. Zhao, T.-H.; Chu, Y.-M.; Liu, B.-Y. Optimal bounds for Neuman-Sándor mean in terms of the convex cobinations of harmonic, geometric, quadratic, and contra-harmonic means. *Abstr. Appl. Anal.* **2012**, *2012*, 9. [CrossRef]
21. Neuman, E.; Sándor, J. On the Schwab-Borchardt mean II. *Math. Pannon.* **2006**, *17*, 49–59.
22. Sánchez-Reyes, J. The hyperbolic sine cardinal and the catenary. *Coll. Math. J.* **2012**, *43*, 285–290. [CrossRef]
23. Li, W.-H.; Miao, P.; Guo, B.-N. Bounds for the Neuman–Sándor mean in terms of the arithmetic and contra-harmonic means. *Axioms* **2022**, *11*, 236. [CrossRef]
24. Anderson, G.D.; Vamanamurthy, M.K.; Vuorinen, M. *Conformal Invariants, Inequalities, and Quasiconformal Maps*; John Wiley & Sons: New York, NY, USA, 1997.
25. Simić, S.; Vuorinen, M. Landen inequalities for zero-balanced hypergeometric function. *Abstr. Appl. Anal.* **2012**, *2012*, 11. [CrossRef]
26. Temme, N.M. *Special Functions: An Introduction to Classical Functions of Mathematical Physics*; A Wiley-Interscience Publication; John Wiley & Sons, Inc.: New York, NY, USA, 1996. [CrossRef]
27. Qi, F. A double inequality for the ratio of two non-zero neighbouring Bernoulli numbers. *J. Comput. Appl. Math.* **2019**, *351*, 1–5. [CrossRef]
28. Qi, F. On signs of certain Toeplitz–Hessenberg determinants whose elements involve Bernoulli numbers. *Contrib. Discrete Math.* **2022**, *17*, 2. Available online: https://www.researchgate.net/publication/356579520 (accessed on 22 June 2022).
29. Shuang, Y.; Guo, B.-N.; Qi, F. Logarithmic convexity and increasing property of the Bernoulli numbers and their ratios. *Rev. R. Acad. Cienc. Exactas Fís. Nat. Ser. A Mat.* **2021**, *115*, 12. [CrossRef]
30. Qi, F.; Taylor, P. Several series expansions for real powers and several formulas for partial Bell polynomials of sinc and sinhc functions in terms of central factorial and Stirling numbers of second kind. *arXiv* **2022**, arXiv:2204.05612.
31. Abramowitz, M.; Stegun, I.A. (Eds.) *Handbook of Mathematical Functions with Formulas, Graphs, and Mathematical Tables*; National Bureau of Standards, Applied Mathematics Series 55, 10th Printing; Dover Publications: New York, NY, USA; Washington, DC, USA, 1972.
32. Jeffrey, A. *Handbook of Mathematical Formulas and Integrals*, 3rd ed.; Elsevier Academic Press: San Diego, CA, USA, 2004.
33. Guo, B.-N.; Lim, D.; Qi, F. Maclaurin's series expansions for positive integer powers of inverse (hyperbolic) sine and tangent functions, closed-form formula of specific partial Bell polynomials, and series representation of generalized logsine function. *Appl. Anal. Discrete Math.* **2022**, *16*, 2. [CrossRef]
34. Guo, B.-N.; Lim, D.; Qi, F. Series expansions of powers of arcsine, closed forms for special values of Bell polynomials, and series representations of generalized logsine functions. *AIMS Math.* **2021**, *6*, 7494–7517. [CrossRef]
35. Qi, F. *Explicit Formulas for Partial Bell Polynomials, Maclaurin's Series Expansions of Real Powers of Inverse (Hyperbolic) Cosine and Sine, and Series Representations of Powers of Pi*; Research Square: Durham, NC, USA, 2021. [CrossRef]
36. Qi, F. Taylor's series expansions for real powers of functions containing squares of inverse (hyperbolic) cosine functions, explicit formulas for special partial Bell polynomials, and series representations for powers of circular constant. *arXiv* **2021**, arXiv:2110.02749.

Article

Hermite–Hadamard's Integral Inequalities of (α, s)-GA- and (α, s, m)-GA-Convex Functions

Jing-Yu Wang [1], Hong-Ping Yin [1], Wen-Long Sun [2] and Bai-Ni Guo [3,4,*]

1. College of Mathematics and Physics, Inner Mongolia Minzu University, Tongliao 028043, China
2. Department of Mathematics, School of Science, Shenyang University of Technology, Shenyang 110870, China
3. School of Mathematics and Informatics, Henan Polytechnic University, Jiaozuo 454003, China
4. Independent Researcher, Dallas, TX 75252-8024, USA
* Correspondence: bai.ni.guo@gmail.com

Abstract: In this paper, the authors propose the notions of (α, s)-geometric-arithmetically convex functions and (α, s, m)-geometric-arithmetically convex functions, while they establish some new integral inequalities of the Hermite–Hadamard type for (α, s)-geometric-arithmetically convex functions and for (α, s, m)-geometric-arithmetically convex functions.

Keywords: Hermite–Hadamard type integral inequality; (α, s)-geometric-arithmetically convex function; (α, s, m)-geometric-arithmetically convex function

MSC: Primary 26A51; Secondary 26D15; 41A55

1. Introduction

In this paper, we denote a nonempty and open interval with $I \subseteq \mathbb{R}$.

We first review some definitions of various convex functions and list some Hermite–Hadamard-type integral inequalities.

It is general knowledge that a function $f : I \subseteq \mathbb{R} \to \mathbb{R}$ is said to be convex if
$$f(tx + (1-t)y) \leq tf(x) + (1-t)f(y)$$
for all $x, y \in I$ and $t \in [0,1]$. One can find a lot of classical conclusions for convex functions in monographs [1,2].

In [3], Xi and his co-authors defined (α, s)-convex functions and (α, s, m)-convex functions and established some Hermite–Hadamard-type integral inequalities.

Definition 1 ([3]). *For some $s \in [-1,1]$ and $\alpha \in (0,1]$, a function $f : I \subseteq \mathbb{R} \to \mathbb{R}$ is said to be (α, s)-convex if*
$$f(tx + (1-t)y) \leq t^{\alpha s} f(x) + (1 - t^\alpha)^s f(y)$$
holds for all $x, y \in I$ and $t \in (0,1)$.

Definition 2 ([3]). *For some $s \in [-1,1]$ and $(\alpha, m) \in (0,1] \times (0,1]$, a function $f : [0,b] \to \mathbb{R}$ is said to be (α, s, m)-convex if*
$$f(tx + m(1-t)y) \leq t^{\alpha s} f(x) + m(1 - t^\alpha)^s f(y)$$
holds for all $x, y \in [0,b]$ and $t \in (0,1)$.

Definition 3 ([4,5]). *The function $f : I \subseteq \mathbb{R}_+ = (0, \infty) \to \mathbb{R}$ is said to be geometric-arithmetically convex, that is, GA-convex, on I if*
$$f(x^t y^{1-t}) \leq tf(x) + (1-t)f(y)$$

holds for all $x, y \in I$ and $t \in [0, 1]$.

In [6], Shuang and her co-authors, including the second author of this paper, introduced the notion of the geometric-arithmetically s-convex function and established some inequalities of the Hermite–Hadamard type for geometric-arithmetically s-convex functions.

Definition 4 ([6])**.** *Let $f : I \subseteq \mathbb{R}_+ \to \mathbb{R}_0 = [0, \infty)$ and $s \in (0, 1]$. A function $f(x)$ is said to be geometric-arithmetically s-convex on I if*

$$f(x^t y^{1-t}) \leq t^s f(x) + (1-t)^s f(y)$$

holds for all $x, y \in I$ and $t \in (0, 1]$.

Remark 1. *When $s = 1$, a geometric-arithmetically s-convex function becomes the GA-convex function defined in [4,5].*

Remark 2. *The integral estimates and applications of geometric-arithmetically convex functions have received renewed attention in recent years. A remarkable variety of refinements and generalizations have been found in, for example, [3–6]. In this paper, we will generalize the results of the above-mentioned literature and study the application problems.*

Let $f : I \subseteq \mathbb{R} \to \mathbb{R}$ be a convex function on I. Then, the Hermite–Hadamard integral inequality reads that

$$f\left(\frac{x+y}{2}\right) \leq \frac{1}{y-x} \int_x^y f(x) \, dx \leq \frac{f(x) + f(y)}{2}, \quad x, y \in I.$$

One can find a lot of classical conclusions for the Hermite–Hadamard integral inequality in the monograph [7].

Hermite–Hadamard-type integral inequalities are a very active research topic [8]. We now recall some known results below.

Theorem 1 ([9], Theorem 2.2)**.** *Let $f : I^\circ \subseteq \mathbb{R} \to \mathbb{R}$ be a differentiable mapping on I°, and let the points $a, b \in I^\circ$ with $a < b$. If $|f'|$ is convex on $[a, b]$, then*

$$\left| \frac{f(a) + f(b)}{2} - \frac{1}{b-a} \int_a^b f(x) \, dx \right| \leq \frac{(b-a)(|f'(a)| + |f'(b)|)}{8}.$$

Theorem 2 ([10], Theorems 1 and 2)**.** *Let $f : I \subseteq \mathbb{R} \to \mathbb{R}$ be differentiable on I°, and let $a, b \in I$ with $a < b$. If $|f'|^q$ is convex on $[a, b]$ for $q \geq 1$, then*

$$\left| \frac{f(a) + f(b)}{2} - \frac{1}{b-a} \int_a^b f(x) \, dx \right| \leq \frac{b-a}{4} \left(\frac{|f'(a)|^q + |f'(b)|^q}{2} \right)^{1/q}$$

and

$$\left| f\left(\frac{a+b}{2}\right) - \frac{1}{b-a} \int_a^b f(x) \, dx \right| \leq \frac{b-a}{4} \left(\frac{|f'(a)|^q + |f'(b)|^q}{2} \right)^{1/q}.$$

Theorem 3 ([11])**.** *Let $f : \mathbb{R}_0 \to \mathbb{R}$ be m-convex and $m \in (0, 1]$. If $f \in L_1([a, b])$ for $0 \leq a < b < \infty$, then*

$$\frac{1}{b-a} \int_a^b f(x) \, dx \leq \min \left\{ \frac{f(a) + mf(b/m)}{2}, \frac{mf(a/m) + f(b)}{2} \right\}.$$

Theorem 4 ([12]). *Let $f : I \subseteq \mathbb{R}_0 \to \mathbb{R}$ be differentiable on I°, the numbers $a, b \in I$ with $a < b$, and $f' \in L_1([a,b])$. If $|f'|^q$ is s-convex on $[a,b]$ for some fixed $s \in (0,1]$ and $q \geq 1$, then*

$$\left| \frac{f(a)+f(b)}{2} - \frac{1}{b-a} \int_a^b f(x)\,dx \right|$$
$$\leq \frac{b-a}{2} \left(\frac{1}{2}\right)^{1-1/q} \left[\frac{2+1/2^s}{(s+1)(s+2)} \right]^{1/q} [|f'(a)|^q + |f'(b)|^q]^{1/q}.$$

Theorem 5 ([13]). *Let $f : I \subseteq \mathbb{R}_0 \to \mathbb{R}$ be differentiable on I°, let $a, b \in I$ with $a < b$, and let $f' \in L_1([a,b])$. If $|f'|^q$ is s-convex on $[a,b]$ for some fixed $s \in (0,1]$ and $q > 1$, then*

$$\left| f\left(\frac{a+b}{2}\right) - \frac{1}{b-a}\int_a^b f(x)\,dx \right| \leq \frac{b-a}{4} \left[\frac{1}{(s+1)(s+2)}\right]^{1/q} \left(\frac{1}{2}\right)^{1/p} \Bigg\{ \left[|f'(a)|^q \right.$$
$$\left. + (s+1)\left|f'\left(\frac{a+b}{2}\right)\right|^q \right]^{1/q} + \left[|f'(b)|^q + (s+1)\left|f'\left(\frac{a+b}{2}\right)\right|^q \right]^{1/q} \Bigg\},$$

where $\frac{1}{p} + \frac{1}{q} = 1$.

Theorem 6 ([14]). *Let $f : I \subseteq \mathbb{R}_0 \to \mathbb{R}$ be differentiable on I°, let $a, b \in I$ with $a < b$, and let $f' \in L_1([a,b])$. If $|f'|$ is s-convex on $[a,b]$ for some $s \in (0,1]$, then*

$$\left| \frac{1}{6}\left[f(a) + 4f\left(\frac{a+b}{2}\right) + f(b)\right] - \frac{1}{b-a}\int_a^b f(x)\,dx \right|$$
$$\leq \frac{(s-4)6^{s+1} + 2 \times 5^{s+2} - 2 \times 3^{s+2} + 2}{6^{s+2}(s+1)(s+2)} (b-a)(|f'(a)| + |f'(b)|).$$

Motivated by the studies above, we will introduce the notions of "(α, s)-geometric-arithmetically convex functions" and "(α, s, m)-geometric-arithmetically convex functions", and we will establish some new inequalities of the Hermite–Hadamard type for (α, s)-geometric-arithmetically convex functions and for (α, s, m)-geometric-arithmetically convex functions.

2. Definitions

We now introduce the notions of "(α, s)-geometric-arithmetically convex functions" and "(α, s, m)-geometric-arithmetically convex functions".

Definition 5. *For some $s \in [-1,1]$ and $\alpha \in (0,1]$, a function $f : I \subseteq \mathbb{R}_+ \to \mathbb{R}$ is said to be (α, s)-geometric-arithmetically convex, or simply speaking, (α, s)-GA-convex if*

$$f(x^t y^{1-t}) \leq t^{\alpha s} f(x) + (1-t^\alpha)^s f(y)$$

holds for all $x, y \in I$ and $t \in (0,1)$.

Remark 3. *By Definition 5, we can see that,*
1. *If $\alpha = 1$, then $f(x)$ is an s-GA-convex function on I, see [6];*
2. *If $\alpha = s = 1$, then $f(x)$ is a GA-convex function on I, see [4,5].*

Definition 6. *For some $s \in [-1,1]$ and $(\alpha, m) \in (0,1] \times (0,1]$, a function $f : (0,b] \subseteq \mathbb{R}_+ \to \mathbb{R}$ is said to be (α, s, m)-geometric-arithmetically convex, or simply speaking, (α, s, m)-GA-convex if*

$$f(x^t y^{m(1-t)}) \leq t^{\alpha s} f(x) + m(1-t^\alpha)^s f(y)$$

holds for all $x, y \in (0,b]$ and $t \in (0,1)$.

Remark 4. By Definition 6, we can see that:
1. If $s = 1$, then $f(x)$ is an (α, m)-GA-convex function on $(0, b]$;
2. If $\alpha = 1$, then $f(x)$ is an (s, m)-GA-convex function on $(0, b]$;
3. If $m = 1$, then $f(x)$ is an (α, s)-GA-convex function on $(0, b]$.

It is obvious that:
1. When $r \in (0, 1)$, the function $f(x) = x^r$ is strictly concave with respect to $x \in (0, 1]$;
2. When $r \in (-\infty, 0] \cup [1, \infty)$, the function $f(x) = x^r$ is convex with respect to $x \in (0, 1]$.

Proposition 1. Let $\alpha \in (0, 1]$ and $s \in [-1, 0)$. Then, the function $f(x) = x^r$ for $r \in (0, 1)$ is (α, s)-geometric-arithmetically convex with respect to $x \in \mathbb{R}_+$.

Proof. We only need to verify the inequality

$$(x^r)^t (y^r)^{1-t} = f(x^t y^{1-t}) \leq t^{\alpha s} f(x) + (1-t^\alpha)^s f(y) = t^{\alpha s} x^r + (1-t^\alpha)^s y^r$$

for all $x, y \in \mathbb{R}$ and $t \in (0, 1)$.
For all $x, y \in \mathbb{R}$ and $t \in (0, 1)$:
1. When $x^r \leq y^r$, let $u = \frac{x^r}{y^r}$, then $0 \leq u \leq 1$ and $(1-t^\alpha)^s > 1$; thus,

$$u^t \leq 1 < (1-t^\alpha)^s < t^{\alpha s} u + (1-t^\alpha)^s,$$

that is,

$$f(x^t y^{1-t}) \leq t^{\alpha s} f(x) + (1-t^\alpha)^s f(y);$$

2. When $x^r \geq y^r$, we have

$$f(x^t y^{1-t}) = (x^r)^t (y^r)^{1-t} \leq x^r < t^{\alpha s} f(x) < t^{\alpha s} f(x) + (1-t^\alpha)^s f(y).$$

The proof of Proposition 1 is complete. □

3. Lemmas

The following lemmas are necessary for us.

Lemma 1 ([15]). Let $f : I \subseteq \mathbb{R} \to \mathbb{R}$ be differentiable on I° and let $a, b \in I$ with $a < b$. If $f' \in L_1([a, b])$, then for $x \in [a, b]$, we have

$$\frac{(b-x)f(b) + (x-a)f(a)}{b-a} - \frac{1}{b-a} \int_a^b f(u) \, du$$

$$= \frac{(x-a)^2}{b-a} \int_0^1 (t-1) f'(tx + (1-t)a) \, dt + \frac{(b-x)^2}{b-a} \int_0^1 (1-t) f'(tx + (1-t)b) \, dt.$$

Lemma 2. Let $\alpha \in (0, 1)$. Then,

$$R_{-1}(\alpha) \triangleq \int_0^1 \frac{1-t}{t^\alpha} \, dt = \frac{1}{(1-\alpha)(2-\alpha)}$$

and

$$T_{-1}(\alpha) \triangleq \int_0^1 \frac{1-t}{1-t^\alpha} \, dt = \frac{1}{\alpha} \left[\psi\left(\frac{2}{\alpha}\right) - \psi\left(\frac{1}{\alpha}\right) \right],$$

where $\psi(z) = \frac{d \ln \Gamma(z)}{dz}$, and

$$\Gamma(z) = \int_0^1 t^{z-1} e^{-t} \, dt, \quad \Re(z) > 0$$

denotes the classical Euler gamma function.

Proof. By letting $u = t^\alpha$ for $t \in (0,1)$ and using the formulas

$$\psi(z) + \gamma = \int_0^1 \frac{1 - t^{z-1}}{1 - t} \, dt$$

and

$$\gamma = \int_0^\infty \left(\frac{1}{1+t} - e^{-t} \right) \frac{dt}{t}$$

in [16] (p. 259, 6.3.22), it is easy to show that

$$\int_0^1 \frac{1-t}{1-t^\alpha} \, dt = \frac{1}{\alpha} \int_0^1 \frac{u^{1/\alpha - 1} - u^{2/\alpha - 1}}{1 - u} \, du = \frac{1}{\alpha} \left[\psi\left(\frac{2}{\alpha}\right) - \psi\left(\frac{1}{\alpha}\right) \right].$$

The proof of Lemma 2 is complete. □

4. Hermite–Hadamard-Type Integral Inequalities

In this section, we turn our attention to the establishment of integral inequalities of the Hermite–Hadamard type for (α, s)-GA-convex and (α, s, m)-GA-convex functions.

Theorem 7. *For some $s \in [-1, 1]$ and $\alpha \in (0, 1]$, let $f : I \subseteq \mathbb{R}_+ \to \mathbb{R}$ be a differentiable function on I°, let $a, b \in I^\circ$ with $a < b$ and $x \in [a, b]$, and let $f' \in L_1([a, b])$ and $|f'|$ be decreasing on $[a, b]$. If $|f'|^q$ is (α, s)-GA-convex on $[a, b]$ for $q \geq 1$, then the following conclusions are valid:*

1. *When $s \in (-1, 1]$ and $\alpha \in (0, 1]$, we have*

$$\left| \frac{(b - x)f(b) + (x - a)f(a)}{b - a} - \frac{1}{b - a} \int_a^b f(u) \, du \right|$$

$$\leq \left(\frac{1}{2}\right)^{1 - 1/q} \left\{ \frac{(x - a)^2}{b - a} \left[R(\alpha, s)|f'(x)|^q + T(\alpha, s)|f'(a)|^q \right]^{1/q} \right.$$

$$\left. + \frac{(b - x)^2}{b - a} \left[R(\alpha, s)|f'(x)|^q + T(\alpha, s)|f'(b)|^q \right]^{1/q} \right\}, \quad (1)$$

where $R(\alpha, s)$ and $T(\alpha, s)$ are defined by

$$R(\alpha, s) \triangleq \frac{1}{(\alpha s + 1)(\alpha s + 2)}$$

and

$$T(\alpha, s) \triangleq \frac{1}{\alpha} \left[B\left(s + 1, \frac{1}{\alpha}\right) - B\left(s + 1, \frac{2}{\alpha}\right) \right]$$

for $s \in (-1, 1]$;

2. *When $s = -1$ and $\alpha \in (0, 1)$, we have*

$$\left| \frac{(b - x)f(b) + (x - a)f(a)}{b - a} - \frac{1}{b - a} \int_a^b f(u) \, du \right|$$

$$\leq \left(\frac{1}{2}\right)^{1 - 1/q} \left\{ \frac{(x - a)^2}{b - a} \left[R_{-1}(\alpha)|f'(x)|^q + T_{-1}(\alpha)|f'(a)|^q \right]^{1/q} \right.$$

$$\left. + \frac{(b - x)^2}{b - a} \left[R_{-1}(\alpha)|f'(x)|^q + T_{-1}(\alpha)|f'(b)|^q \right]^{1/q} \right\},$$

where $R_{-1}(\alpha)$, $T_{-1}(\alpha)$ are defined in Lemma 2 and

$$B(x,y) = \int_0^1 t^{x-1}(1-t)^{y-1}\,dt, \quad \Re(x), \Re(y) > 0 \qquad (2)$$

denotes the classical beta function.

Proof. For $s \in (-1, 1]$ and $\alpha \in (0, 1]$, since $|f'|$ is decreasing on $[a, b]$, by Lemma 1 and the Hölder integral inequality, we have

$$\left| \frac{(b-x)f(b) + (x-a)f(a)}{b-a} - \frac{1}{b-a}\int_a^b f(u)\,du \right|$$
$$\leq \frac{(x-a)^2}{b-a} \int_0^1 (1-t)|f'(tx + (1-t)a)|\,dt$$
$$+ \frac{(b-x)^2}{b-a} \int_0^1 (1-t)|f'(tx + (1-t)b)|\,dt$$
$$\leq \frac{(x-a)^2}{b-a} \int_0^1 (1-t)|f'(x^t a^{1-t})|\,dt + \frac{(b-x)^2}{b-a} \int_0^1 (1-t)|f'(x^t b^{1-t})|\,dt \qquad (3)$$
$$\leq \frac{(x-a)^2}{b-a} \left[\int_0^1 (1-t)\,dt\right]^{1-1/q} \left[\int_0^1 (1-t)|f'(x^t a^{1-t})|^q\,dt\right]^{1/q}$$
$$+ \frac{(b-x)^2}{b-a} \left[\int_0^1 (1-t)\,dt\right]^{1-1/q} \left[\int_0^1 (1-t)|f'(x^t b^{1-t})|^q\,dt\right]^{1/q}.$$

Making use of the (α, s)-GA-convexity of $|f'|^q$, we have

$$\int_0^1 (1-t)|f'(x^t a^{1-t})|^q\,dt \leq \int_0^1 (1-t)\left[t^{\alpha s}|f'(x)|^q + (1-t^\alpha)^s|f'(a)|^q\right]dt$$
$$= R(\alpha, s)|f'(x)|^q + T(\alpha, s)|f'(a)|^q$$

and

$$\int_0^1 (1-t)|f'(x^t b^{1-t})|^q\,dt \leq \int_0^1 (1-t)\left[t^{\alpha s}|f'(x)|^q + (1-t^\alpha)^s|f'(b)|^q\right]dt \qquad (4)$$
$$= R(\alpha, s)|f'(x)|^q + T(\alpha, s)|f'(b)|^q.$$

By using the above inequalities between (3) and (4) and then simplifying them, we obtain the required inequality (1).

When $s = -1$ and $\alpha \in (0, 1)$, by the inequalities between (3) and (4) and by Lemma 2, we have

$$\left| \frac{(b-x)f(b) + (x-a)f(a)}{b-a} - \frac{1}{b-a}\int_a^b f(u)\,du \right|$$

$$\leq \frac{(x-a)^2}{b-a}\left(\frac{1}{2}\right)^{1-1/q}\left[\int_0^1 (1-t)|f'(x^t a^{1-t})|^q\,dt\right]^{1/q}$$

$$+ \frac{(b-x)^2}{b-a}\left(\frac{1}{2}\right)^{1-1/q}\left[\int_0^1 (1-t)|f'(x^t b^{1-t})|^q\,dt\right]^{1/q}$$

$$\leq \frac{(x-a)^2}{b-a}\left(\frac{1}{2}\right)^{1-1/q}\left[\int_0^1 (1-t)\left[t^{-\alpha}|f'(x)|^q + (1-t^\alpha)^{-1}|f'(a)|^q\right]dt\right]^{1/q}$$

$$+ \frac{(b-x)^2}{b-a}\left(\frac{1}{2}\right)^{1-1/q}\left[\int_0^1 (1-t)\left[t^{-\alpha}|f'(x)|^q + (1-t^\alpha)^{-1}|f'(b)|^q\right]dt\right]^{1/q}$$

$$= \left(\frac{1}{2}\right)^{1-1/q}\left\{\frac{(x-a)^2}{b-a}\left[R_{-1}(\alpha)|f'(x)|^q + T_{-1}(\alpha)|f'(a)|^q\right]^{1/q}\right.$$

$$\left. + \frac{(b-x)^2}{b-a}\left[R_{-1}(\alpha)|f'(x)|^q + T_{-1}(\alpha)|f'(b)|^q\right]^{1/q}\right\}.$$

The proof of Theorem 7 is complete. □

In Theorem 7, when taking $\alpha = 1$ and $s \in (0,1]$, we derive the same result as in [6].

Corollary 1. *Under the conditions of Theorem 7, with $\alpha = 1$ and $s \in (-1,1]$, we have*

$$\left| \frac{(b-x)f(b) + (x-a)f(a)}{b-a} - \frac{1}{b-a}\int_a^b f(u)\,du \right|$$

$$\leq \frac{(x-a)^2}{b-a}\left(\frac{1}{2}\right)^{1-1/q}\left[\frac{|f'(x)|^q + (s+1)|f'(a)|^q}{(s+1)(s+2)}\right]^{1/q}$$

$$+ \frac{(b-x)^2}{b-a}\left(\frac{1}{2}\right)^{1-1/q}\left[\frac{|f'(x)|^q + (s+1)|f'(b)|^q}{(s+1)(s+2)}\right]^{1/q}.$$

In Theorem 7, when setting $\alpha = s = 1$, we deduce the following integral inequalities of the Hermite–Hadamard type for the GA-convex function.

Corollary 2. *Under the conditions of Theorem 7, with $\alpha = s = 1$, we have*

$$\left| \frac{(b-x)f(b) + (x-a)f(a)}{b-a} - \frac{1}{b-a}\int_a^b f(u)\,du \right|$$

$$\leq \left(\frac{1}{2}\right)^{1-1/q}\left\{\frac{(x-a)^2}{b-a}\left[\frac{|f'(x)|^q + 2|f'(a)|^q}{6}\right]^{1/q}\right.$$

$$\left. + \frac{(b-x)^2}{b-a}\left[\frac{|f'(x)|^q + 2|f'(b)|^q}{6}\right]^{1/q}\right\}.$$

Corollary 3. *Under the conditions of Theorem 7, with $q = 1$ and $s \in (-1,1]$, we obtain*

$$\left| \frac{(b-x)f(b) + (x-a)f(a)}{b-a} - \frac{1}{b-a}\int_a^b f(u)\,du \right|$$

$$\leq \frac{(x-a)^2}{b-a}\left[R(\alpha,s)|f'(x)| + T(\alpha,s)|f'(a)|\right]$$

$$+ \frac{(b-x)^2}{b-a}\left[R(\alpha,s)|f'(x)| + T(\alpha,s)|f'(b)|\right].$$

By making use of the same method as that in the proof of Theorem 7, we obtain the following integral inequalities for (α, s, m)-GA-convex functions.

Theorem 8. *For some fixed $(\alpha, m) \in (0,1] \times (0,1]$ and $s \in (-1,1]$, let $a, b \in \mathbb{R}_+$ with $b > a$ and $x \in [a,b]$, let $f : (0, \max\{b, b^{1/m}\}] \to \mathbb{R}$ be a differentiable function, let $f' \in L_1([a, \max\{b, b^{1/m}\}])$, and let $|f'|$ be decreasing on $[a,b]$. If $|f'|^q$ is (α, s, m)-GA-convex on $(0, \max\{b, b^{1/m}\}]$ for $q \geq 1$, then:*

1. *When $s \in (-1, 1]$ and $\alpha \in (0,1]$, we have*

$$\left| \frac{(b-x)f(b) + (x-a)f(a)}{b-a} - \frac{1}{b-a} \int_a^b f(u) \, du \right|$$
$$\leq \left(\frac{1}{2}\right)^{1-1/q} \left\{ \frac{(x-a)^2}{b-a} \left[R(\alpha, s)|f'(x)|^q + mT(\alpha, s)|f'(a^{1/m})|^q \right]^{1/q} \right.$$
$$\left. + \frac{(b-x)^2}{b-a} \left[R(\alpha, s)|f'(x)|^q + mT(\alpha, s)|f'(b^{1/m})|^q \right]^{1/q} \right\}; \quad (5)$$

2. *When $s = -1$ and $\alpha \in (0,1)$, we have*

$$\left| \frac{(b-x)f(b) + (x-a)f(a)}{b-a} - \frac{1}{b-a} \int_a^b f(u) \, du \right|$$
$$\leq \left(\frac{1}{2}\right)^{1-1/q} \left\{ \frac{(x-a)^2}{b-a} \left[R_{-1}(\alpha)|f'(x)|^q + mT_{-1}(\alpha)|f'(a^{1/m})|^q \right]^{1/q} \right.$$
$$\left. + \frac{(b-x)^2}{b-a} \left[R_{-1}(\alpha)|f'(x)|^q + mT_{-1}(\alpha)|f'(b^{1/m})|^q \right]^{1/q} \right\}, \quad (6)$$

where $R(\alpha, s)$, $T(\alpha, s)$, $R_{-1}(\alpha)$, and $T_{-1}(\alpha)$ are defined respectively in Theorem 7 and Lemma 2.

Proof. Using (3), we have

$$\left| \frac{(b-x)f(b) + (x-a)f(a)}{b-a} - \frac{1}{b-a} \int_a^b f(u) \, du \right|$$
$$\leq \frac{(x-a)^2}{b-a} \left[\int_0^1 (1-t) \, dt \right]^{1-1/q} \left[\int_0^1 (1-t)|f'(x^t a^{1-t})|^q \, dt \right]^{1/q}$$
$$+ \frac{(b-x)^2}{b-a} \left[\int_0^1 (1-t) \, dt \right]^{1-1/q} \left[\int_0^1 (1-t)|f'(x^t b^{1-t})|^q \, dt \right]^{1/q}. \quad (7)$$

Making use of the (α, s, m)-GA-convexity of $|f'|^q$ on $(0, \max\{b, b^{1/m}\}]$ once again yields

$$\int_0^1 (1-t)|f'(x^t a^{1-t})|^q \, dt = \int_0^1 (1-t)|f'(x^t a^{m(1-t)/m})|^q \, dt$$
$$\leq \int_0^1 \left[(1-t)t^{\alpha s}|f'(x)|^q + m(1-t)(1-t^\alpha)^s|f'(a^{1/m})|^q \right] dt$$
$$= R(\alpha, s)|f'(x)|^q + mT(\alpha, s)|f'(a^{1/m})|^q$$

and

$$\int_0^1 (1-t)|f'(x^t b^{1-t})|^q \, dt \leq R(\alpha, s)|f'(x)|^q + mT(\alpha, s)|f'(b^{1/m})|^q.$$

We then substitute the two inequalities above into (7) and simplify the result in the required inequality (5).

Similarly, we can prove inequality (6). The proof of Theorem 8 is complete. □

Corollary 4. In Theorem 8, if $q = 1$ and $s \in (-1, 1]$, then

$$\left| \frac{(b-x)f(b) + (x-a)f(a)}{b-a} - \frac{1}{b-a} \int_a^b f(u)\,du \right|$$
$$\leq \frac{(x-a)^2}{b-a} \left[R(\alpha, s)|f'(x)| + mT(\alpha, s)|f'(a^{1/m})| \right]$$
$$+ \frac{(b-x)^2}{b-a} \left[R(\alpha, s)|f'(x)| + mT(\alpha, s)|f'(b^{1/m})| \right].$$

Theorem 9. For some fixed $(\alpha, m) \in (0, 1] \times (0, 1]$ and $s \in (-1, 1]$, let $a, b \in \mathbb{R}_+$ with $b > a$ and $x \in [a, b]$, let $f : (0, \max\{b, b^{1/m}\}] \to \mathbb{R}$ be a differentiable function, and let $f' \in L_1([a, \max\{b, b^{1/m}\}])$ and $|f'|$ be decreasing on $[a, b]$. If $|f'|^q$ is (α, s, m)-GA-convex on $(0, \max\{b, b^{1/m}\}]$ for $q > 1$, then

$$\left| \frac{(b-x)f(b) + (x-a)f(a)}{b-a} - \frac{1}{b-a} \int_a^b f(u)\,du \right|$$
$$\leq \left(\frac{q-1}{2q-1} \right)^{1-1/q} \left\{ \frac{(x-a)^2}{b-a} \left[\frac{\alpha|f'(x)|^q + m(\alpha s + 1)B(\frac{1}{\alpha}, s+1)|f'(a^{1/m})|^q}{\alpha(\alpha s + 1)} \right]^{1/q} \right.$$
$$\left. + \frac{(b-x)^2}{b-a} \left[\frac{\alpha|f'(x)|^q + m(\alpha s + 1)B(\frac{1}{\alpha}, s+1)|f'(b^{1/m})|^q}{\alpha(\alpha s + 1)} \right]^{1/q} \right\}, \quad (8)$$

where $B(x, y)$ is defined by (2) in Theorem 7.

Proof. Since $|f'|$ is decreasing on $[a, b]$, by Lemma 1 and the Hölder integral inequality, we obtain

$$\left| \frac{(b-x)f(b) + (x-a)f(a)}{b-a} - \frac{1}{b-a} \int_a^b f(u)\,du \right|$$
$$\leq \frac{(x-a)^2}{b-a} \left[\int_0^1 (1-t)^{q/(q-1)}\,dt \right]^{1-1/q} \left[\int_0^1 |f'(x^t a^{1-t})|^q\,dt \right]^{1/q}$$
$$+ \frac{(b-x)^2}{b-a} \left[\int_0^1 (1-t)^{q/(q-1)}\,dt \right]^{1-1/q} \left[\int_0^1 |f'(x^t b^{1-t})|^q\,dt \right]^{1/q}, \quad (9)$$

where

$$\int_0^1 (1-t)^{q/(q-1)}\,dt = \frac{q-1}{2q-1},$$
$$\int_0^1 |f'(x^t a^{1-t})|^q\,dt \leq \int_0^1 \left[t^{\alpha s}|f'(x)|^q + m(1-t^\alpha)^s|f'(a^{1/m})|^q \right] dt$$
$$= \frac{\alpha|f'(x)|^q + m(\alpha s + 1)B(\frac{1}{\alpha}, s+1)|f'(a^{1/m})|^q}{\alpha(\alpha s + 1)},$$

and

$$\int_0^1 |f'(x^t b^{1-t})|^q\,dt \leq \frac{\alpha|f'(x)|^q + m(\alpha s + 1)B(\frac{1}{\alpha}, s+1)|f'(b^{1/m})|^q}{\alpha(\alpha s + 1)}.$$

Note that in the above arguments, we used the fact that the function $|f'|^q$ is (α, s, m)-GA-convex on $(0, \max\{b, b^{1/m}\}]$. Applying the above equality and inequalities into (9) and then simplifying them lead to the required inequality (8). The proof of Theorem 9 is complete. □

Using the same method as that in the proof of Theorem 9, we obtain the following inequalities of (α, s)-GA-convex functions.

Theorem 10. *For some* $s \in (-1, 1]$ *and* $\alpha \in (0, 1]$, *let* $f : I \subseteq \mathbb{R}_+ \to \mathbb{R}$ *be a differentiable function on* I°, *let* $a, b \in I^\circ$ *with* $a < b$ *and* $x \in [a, b]$, *and let* $f' \in L_1([a, b])$ *and* $|f'|$ *be decreasing on* $[a, b]$. *If* $|f'|^q$ *is* (α, s)-*GA-convex on* $[a, b]$ *for* $q > 1$, *then*

$$\left| \frac{(b-x)f(b) + (x-a)f(a)}{b-a} - \frac{1}{b-a} \int_a^b f(u) \, du \right|$$

$$\leq \left(\frac{q-1}{2q-1} \right)^{1-1/q} \left\{ \frac{(x-a)^2}{b-a} \left[\frac{\alpha |f'(x)|^q + (\alpha s + 1) B(\frac{1}{\alpha}, s+1) |f'(a)|^q}{\alpha(\alpha s + 1)} \right]^{1/q} \right.$$

$$\left. + \frac{(b-x)^2}{b-a} \left[\frac{\alpha |f'(x)|^q + (\alpha s + 1) B(\frac{1}{\alpha}, s+1) |f'(b)|^q}{\alpha(\alpha s + 1)} \right]^{1/q} \right\},$$

where $B(x, y)$ *is defined by* (2) *in Theorem 7.*

In Theorem 10, when $\alpha = 1$, the Hermite–Hadamard-type integral inequality is the same as the result in [6].

Corollary 5 ([6])**.** *Under the conditions of Theorem 10, if we take* $\alpha = 1$, *then*

$$\left| \frac{(b-x)f(b) + (x-a)f(a)}{b-a} - \frac{1}{b-a} \int_a^b f(u) \, du \right| \leq \left(\frac{q-1}{2q-1} \right)^{1-1/q}$$

$$\times \left[\frac{(x-a)^2}{b-a} \left(\frac{|f'(x)|^q + |f'(a)|^q}{s+1} \right)^{1/q} + \frac{(b-x)^2}{b-a} \left(\frac{|f'(x)|^q + |f'(b)|^q}{s+1} \right)^{1/q} \right].$$

5. Applications to Special Means

For two positive numbers $a, b \in \mathbb{R}_+$ with $b > a$, define

$$A(a, b) = \frac{a+b}{2}, \quad H(a, b) = \frac{2ab}{a+b}, \quad L(a, b) = \frac{b-a}{\ln b - \ln a}$$

and

$$L_r(a, b) = \begin{cases} \left[\dfrac{b^{r+1} - a^{r+1}}{(r+1)(b-a)} \right]^{1/r}, & r \neq 0, -1; \\ L(a, b), & r = -1; \\ \dfrac{1}{e} \left(\dfrac{b^b}{a^a} \right)^{1/(b-a)}, & r = 0. \end{cases}$$

These means are respectively called the arithmetic, harmonic, logarithmic, and generalized logarithmic means of $a, b \in \mathbb{R}_+$.

Theorem 11. *Let* $a, b \in \mathbb{R}_+$ *with* $a < b$, *let* $0 \neq r \leq 1$, *and let* $q \geq 1$.
1. *If* $r \neq -1$, *we have*

$$|A(a^r, b^r) - L_r^r(a, b)|$$

$$\leq \frac{(b-a)|r|}{2} \left(\frac{1}{2} \right)^{2(1-1/q)} \left[\left(\frac{2A^{(r-1)q}(a, b) + a^{(r-1)q}}{3} \right)^{1/q} \right.$$

$$\left. + \left(\frac{2A^{(r-1)q}(a, b) + b^{(r-1)q}}{3} \right)^{1/q} \right].$$

2. If $r = -1$, we have

$$\left| \frac{1}{H(a,b)} - \frac{1}{L(a,b)} \right| \leq \frac{b-a}{2} \left(\frac{1}{2} \right)^{-2/q} \left[\left(\frac{2A^{-2q}(a,b) + a^{-2q}}{3} \right)^{1/q} + \left(\frac{2A^{-2q}(a,b) + b^{-2q}}{3} \right)^{1/q} \right].$$

Proof. In Corollary 1, let $x = \frac{a+b}{2}$ and $s = -\frac{1}{2}$. If $r \leq 1$ and $q \geq 1$, the $|f'(x)| = |r|x^{r-1}$ is decreasing on $[a,b]$. By Proposition 1, we can derive the inequalities in Theorem 11. □

Corollary 6. *Under the conditions of Theorem 11, with $q = 1$:*

1. If $r \neq -1$, we have

$$|A(a^r, b^r) - L_r^r(a,b)| \leq (b-a)|r| \left[\frac{a^{r-1} + 4[A(a,b)]^{r-1} + b^{r-1}}{6} \right];$$

2. If $r = -1$, we have

$$\left| \frac{1}{H(a,b)} - \frac{1}{L(a,b)} \right| \leq (b-a)|r| \left[\frac{a^{-2} + 4[A(a,b)]^{-2} + b^{-2}}{6} \right].$$

6. Conclusions

Integral inequalities are important for the prediction of upper and lower bounds in various aspects of applied sciences such as in Probability Theory, Functional Inequalities, and Information Theory.

In this paper, after recalling some convexities and the Hermite–Hadamard-type integral inequalities, we introduced the notions of (α, s)-geometric-arithmetically convex functions and (α, s, m)-geometric-arithmetically convex functions, established several integral inequalities of the Hermite–Hadamard type for (α, s)-GA-convex and (α, s, m)-GA-convex functions, and applied several results in the construction of several inequalities of special means.

Author Contributions: Writing—original draft, J.-Y.W., H.-P.Y., W.-L.S. and B.-N.G. All authors contributed equally to the writing of the manuscript and read and approved the final version of the manuscript.

Funding: This work was partially supported by the Research Program of Science and Technology at Universities of Inner Mongolia Autonomous Region (Grant No. NJZY20119), China.

Data Availability Statement: The study did not report any data.

Acknowledgments: The authors thank the anonymous referees for their careful corrections and valuable comments on the original version of this paper.

Conflicts of Interest: The authors declare no conflict of interest.

References

1. Niculescu, C.P.; Persson, L.-E. *Convex Functions and Their Applications: A Contemporary Approach*, 2nd ed.; CMS Books in Mathematics/Ouvrages de Mathématiques de la SMC; Springer: Cham, Swizerlands, 2018. [CrossRef]
2. Pečarić, J.; Proschan, F.; Tong, Y.L. *Convex Functions, Partial Orderings, and Statistical Applications*; Mathematics in Science and Engineering; Academic Press, Inc.: Boston, MA, USA, 1992; Volume 187.
3. Xi, B.-Y.; Gao, D.-D.; Qi, F. Integral inequalities of Hermite–Hadamard type for (α, s)-convex and (α, s, m)-convex functions. *Ital. J. Pure Appl. Math.* **2020**, *44*, 499–510.
4. Niculescu, C.P. Convexity according to the geometric mean. *Math. Inequal. Appl.* **2020**, *3*, 155–167. [CrossRef]

5. Niculescu, C.P. Convexity according to means. *Math. Inequal. Appl.* **2003**, *6*, 571–579. [CrossRef]
6. Shuang, Y.; Yin, H.-P.; Qi, F. Hermite–Hadamard type integral inequalities for geometric-arithmetically s-convex functions. *Analysis (Munich)* **2013**, *33*, 197–208. [CrossRef]
7. Dragomir, S.S.; Pearce, C.E.M. *Selected Topics on Hermite-Hadamard Type Inequalities and Applications*; RGMIA Monographs, Victoria University: Footscray, Australia, 2000. Available online: http://rgmia.org/monographs/hermite_hadamard.html (accessed on 27 September 2022).
8. Wu, Y.; Qi, F. Discussions on two integral inequalities of Hermite–Hadamard type for convex functions. *J. Comput. Appl. Math.* **2022**, *406*, 114049. [CrossRef]
9. Dragomir, S.S.; Agarwal, R.P. Two inequalities for differentiable mappings and applications to special means of real numbers and to trapezoidal formula. *Appl. Math. Lett.* **1998**, *11*, 91–95. [CrossRef]
10. Pearce, C.E.M.; Pećarixcx, J. Inequalities for differentiable mappings with application to special means and quadrature formulae. *Appl. Math. Lett.* **2000**, *13*, 51–55. [CrossRef]
11. Dragomir, S.S.; Toader, G. Some inequalities for m-convex functions. *Studia Univ. Babeş-Bolyai Math.* **1993**, *38*, 21–28.
12. Kirmaci, U.S.; Bakula, M.K.; Özdemir, M.E.; Pećarixcx, J. Hadamard-type inequalities for s-convex functions. *Appl. Math. Comput.* **2007**, *193*, 26–35. [CrossRef]
13. Hussain, S.; Bhatti, M.I.; Iqbal, M. Hadamard-type inequalities for s-convex functions, I. *Punjab Univ. J. Math.* **2009**, *41*, 51–60.
14. Sarikaya, M.Z.; Set, E.; Özdemir, M.E. On new inequalities of Simpson's type for s-convex functions. *Comput. Math. Appl.* **2010**, *60*, 2191–2199. [CrossRef]
15. Avci, M.; Kavurmaci, H.; Özdemir, M.E. New inequalities of Hermite–Hadamard type via s-convex functions in the second sense with applications. *Appl. Math. Comput.* **2011**, *217*, 5171–5176. [CrossRef]
16. Abramowitz, M.; Stegun, I.A. (Eds.) *Handbook of Mathematical Functions with Formulas, Graphs, and Mathematical Tables*; National Bureau of Standards, Applied Mathematics Series, Reprint of the 1972 edition; Dover Publications, Inc.: New York, NY, USA, 1992; Volume 55.

Article

Schur-Convexity of the Mean of Convex Functions for Two Variables

Huan-Nan Shi [1], Dong-Sheng Wang [2] and Chun-Ru Fu [3,*]

1 Department of Electronic Information, Teacher's College, Beijing Union University, Beijing 100011, China
2 Basic Courses Department, Beijing Polytechnic, Beijing 100176, China
3 Applied College of Science and Technology, Beijing Union University, Beijing 102200, China
* Correspondence: fuchunru2008@163.com

Abstract: The results of Schur convexity established by Elezovic and Pecaric for the average of convex functions are generalized relative to the case of the means for two-variable convex functions. As an application, some binary mean inequalities are given.

Keywords: inequality; Schur-convex function; Hadamard's inequality; convex functions of two variables; mean

MSC: 26A51; 26D15; B25

1. Introduction

Let $\mathbb{R}$ be a set of real numbers, g be a convex function defined on the interval $I \subseteq \mathbb{R} \to \mathbb{R}$ and $c, d \in I, c < d$. Then

$$g\left(\frac{d+c}{2}\right) \leq \frac{1}{d-c} \int_c^d g(t)\, dt \leq \frac{g(d)+g(c)}{2}. \tag{1}$$

This is the famous Hadamard's inequality for convex functions.

In 2000, utilizing Hadamard's inequality, Elezovic and Pecaric [1] researched Schur-convexity on the lower and upper limit of the integral for the mean of the convex functions and obtained the following important and profound theorem.

Theorem 1 ([1]). *Let I be an interval with nonempty interior on $\mathbb{R}$ and g be a continuous function on I. Then,*

$$\Phi(c,d) = \begin{cases} \frac{1}{d-c} \int_c^d g(s)\, ds, & c, d \in I,\ d \neq c \\ g(c), & d = c \end{cases}$$

is Schur convex (Schur concave, resp.) on $I \times I$ iff g is convex (concave, resp.) on I.

In recent years, this result attracted the attention of many scholars (see references [2–12] and Chapter II of the monograph [13] and its references).

In this paper, the result of theorem 1 is generalized to the case of bivariate convex functions, and some bivariate mean inequalities are established.

Theorem 2. *Let I be an interval with non-empty interior on $\mathbb{R}$ and $g(s,t)$ be a continuous function on $I \times I$. If g is convex (or concave resp.) on $I \times I$, then*

$$G(u,v) = \begin{cases} \frac{1}{(v-u)^2} \int_u^v \int_u^v g(s,t)\, ds\, dt, & (u,v) \in I \times I,\ u \neq v \\ g(u,u), & (u,v) \in I \times I,\ u = v \end{cases} \tag{2}$$

is Schur convex (or Schur concave, resp.) on $I \times I$.

2. Definitions and Lemmas

To prove Theorem 2, we provide the following lemmas and definitions.

Definition 1. *Let (x_1, x_2) and $(y_1, y_2) \in \mathbb{R} \times \mathbb{R}$.*
(1) *A set $\Omega \subset \mathbb{R} \times \mathbb{R}$ is said to be convex if $(x_1, x_2), (y_1, y_2) \in \Omega$ and $0 \leq \beta \leq 1$ implies*

$$(\beta x_1 + (1-\beta)y_1, \beta x_2 + (1-\beta)y_2) \in \Omega.$$

(2) *Let $\Omega \subset \mathbb{R} \times \mathbb{R}$ be convex set. A function $\psi: \Omega \to \mathbb{R}$ is said to be a convex function on Ω if, for all $\beta \in [0,1]$ and all $(x_1, x_2), (y_1, y_2) \in \Omega$, inequality*

$$\psi(\beta x_1 + (1-\beta)y_1, \beta x_2 + (1-\beta)y_2) \leq \beta \psi(x_1, x_2) + (1-\beta)\psi(y_1, y_2) \quad (3)$$

holds. If, for all $\beta \in [0,1]$ and all $(x_1, x_2), (y_1, y_2) \in \Omega$, the strict inequality in (3) holds, then ψ is said to be strictly convex. ψ is called concave (or strictly concave, resp.) iff $-\psi$ is convex (or strictly convex, resp.)

Definition 2 ([14,15]). *Let $\Omega \subseteq \mathbb{R} \times \mathbb{R}$, (x_1, x_2) and $(y_1, y_2) \in \Omega$, and let $\varphi: \Omega \to \mathbb{R}$:*
(1) *(x_1, x_2) is said to be majorized by (y_1, y_2) (in symbols $(x_1, x_2) \prec (y_1, y_2)$) if $\max\{x_1, x_2\} \leq \max\{y_1, y_2\}$ and $x_1 + x_2 = y_1 + y_2$.*
(2) *ψ is said to be a Schur-convex function on Ω if $(x_1, x_2) \prec (y_1, y_2)$ on Ω implies $\psi(x_1, x_2) \prec \psi(y_1, y_2)$, and ψ is said to be a Schur-concave function on Ω iff $-\psi$ is a Schur-convex function.*

Lemma 1 ([14] (p. 5)). *Let $(x_1, x_2) \in \mathbb{R} \times \mathbb{R}$. Then*

$$\left(\frac{x_1+x_2}{2}, \frac{x_1+x_2}{2}\right) \prec (x_1, x_2).$$

Lemma 2 ([14] (p. 5)). *Let $\Omega \subseteq \mathbb{R} \times \mathbb{R}$ be symmetric set with a nonempty interior $\Omega°$. $\psi: \Omega \to \mathbb{R}$ is continuous on Ω and differentiable in $\Omega°$. Then, function ψ is Schur convex (or Schur concave, resp.) iff ψ is symmetric on Ω and*

$$(x_1 - x_2)\left(\frac{\partial \psi}{\partial x_1} - \frac{\partial \psi}{\partial x_2}\right) \geq 0 (or \leq 0, resp.)$$

holds for any $(x_1, x_2) \in \Omega°$.

Lemma 3 ([16]). *Let $\varphi(x, w)$ and $\frac{\partial \varphi(x,w)}{\partial w}$ be continuous on*

$$D = \{(x, w) : a \leq x \leq b, c \leq w \leq d\}; let$$

$a(w), b(w)$ and their derivatives be continuous on $[c, d]$; $v \in [c, d]$ implies $a(w), b(w) \in [a, b]$. Then,

$$\frac{d}{dw}\int_{a(w)}^{b(w)} \varphi(x,w)\,dx = \int_{a(w)}^{b(w)} \frac{\partial \varphi(x,w)}{\partial w}\,dx + \varphi(b(w), u)b'(w) - \varphi(a(w), w)a'(w). \quad (4)$$

Lemma 4. *Let $g(s,t)$ be continuous on rectangle $[a, p; a, q]$, $G(c,d) = \int_c^d \int_c^d g(s,t)\,ds\,dt$. If $c = c(b)$ and $d = d(b)$ are differentiable with b, $a \leq c(b) \leq p$ and $a \leq d(b) \leq q$, then*

$$\frac{\partial G}{\partial b} = \int_c^d g(s,d)d'(b)\,ds - \int_c^d g(s,c)c'(b)\,ds$$
$$+ d'(b)\int_c^d g(d,t)\,dt - c'(b)\int_c^d g(c,t)\,dt. \quad (5)$$

Proof. Let $\varphi(s,b) = \int_c^d g(s,t)\,dt$. Then,

$$\frac{\partial \varphi(s,b)}{\partial b} = g(s,d)d'(b) - g(s,c)c'(b).$$

By Lemma 3, we have

$$\begin{aligned}\frac{\partial G}{\partial b} &= \frac{d}{db}\int_c^d \varphi(s,b)\,ds \\ &= \int_c^d \frac{\partial \varphi(s,b)}{\partial b}\,ds + \varphi(d,b)d'(b) - \varphi(c,b)c'(b) \\ &= \int_c^d g(s,d)d'(b)\,ds - \int_c^d g(s,c)c'(b)\,ds \\ &\quad + d'(b)\int_c^d g(d,s)\,ds - c'(b)\int_c^d g(c,s)\,ds.\end{aligned}$$

□

Remark 1. *In passing, it is pointed out that (9) in Lemma 5 of reference [2] is incorrect and should be replaced by (4) of this paper.*

Lemma 5. *Let I be an interval with nonempty interior on $\mathbb{R}$ and $g(s,t)$ be a continuous function on $I \times I$. For $(u,v) \in I \times I, u \neq v$, let $G(u,v) = \int_u^v \int_u^v g(s,t)\,ds\,dt$. Then,*

$$\frac{\partial G}{\partial v} = \int_u^v g(s,v)\,ds + \int_u^v g(v,t)\,dt, \tag{6}$$

$$\frac{\partial G}{\partial u} = -\left(\int_u^v g(s,u)\,ds + \int_u^v g(u,t)\,dt\right). \tag{7}$$

Proof. By taking $c(b) = a$ and $d(b) = b$, we have $c'(b) = 0$ and $d'(b) = 1$. By (5) in Lemma 4, we obtain (6).

Notice that $G(u,v) = \int_v^u \int_v^u g(s,t)\,ds\,dt$; from (5), we have

$$\frac{\partial G}{\partial u} = \int_v^u g(s,u)\,ds + \int_v^u g(u,t)\,dt = -\left(\int_u^v g(s,u)\,ds + \int_u^v g(u,t)\,dt\right).$$

□

Lemma 6 ([14] (p. 38, Proposition 4.3) and [15] (p. 644, B.3.d)). *Let $\Omega \subset \mathbb{R} \times \mathbb{R}$ be an open convex set and let $\psi(x,y) : \Omega \to \mathbb{R}$ be twice differentiable. Then, ψ is convex on Ω iff the Hessian matrix*

$$H(x,y) = \begin{pmatrix} \frac{\partial^2 \psi}{\partial x \partial x} & \frac{\partial^2 \psi}{\partial x \partial y} \\ \frac{\partial^2 \psi}{\partial y \partial x} & \frac{\partial^2 \psi}{\partial y \partial y} \end{pmatrix}$$

is non-negative definite on Ω. If $H(x)$ is positive definite on Ω, then ψ is strictly convex on Ω.

3. Proofs of Main Results

Proof of Theorem 2. Let $g(s,t)$ be convex on $I \times I$. $G(u,v)$ is evidently symmetric. By Lemma 5, we have

$$\frac{\partial G(u,v)}{\partial v} = \frac{-2}{(v-u)^3}\int_u^v \int_u^v g(s,t)\,ds\,dt + \frac{1}{(v-u)^2}\left(\int_u^v g(s,v)\,ds + \int_u^v g(v,t)\,dt\right).$$

$$\frac{\partial G(u,v)}{\partial u} = \frac{2}{(v-u)^3}\int_u^v \int_u^v g(s,t)\,ds\,dt - \frac{1}{(v-u)^2}\left(\int_u^v g(s,u)\,ds + \int_u^v g(u,t)\,dt\right).$$

$$\Delta := (v-u)\left(\frac{\partial G(u,v)}{\partial v} - \frac{\partial G(u,v)}{\partial u}\right) = -\frac{4}{(v-u)^2}\int_u^v\int_u^v g(s,t)\,ds\,dt$$
$$+ \frac{1}{v-u}\int_u^v (g(s,v)+g(s,u))\,ds + \frac{1}{v-u}\int_u^v (g(u,t)+g(v,t))\,dt$$

By Hadamards inequality, we have

$$\frac{2}{(v-u)^2}\int_u^v\int_u^v g(s,t)\,ds\,dt = \frac{2}{v-u}\int_u^v \left(\frac{1}{v-u}\int_u^v g(s,t)\,ds\right)dt$$
$$\leq \frac{2}{v-ua}\int_u^v \frac{g(u,t)+g(v,t)}{2}\,dt = \frac{1}{v-u}\int_u^v a(g(u,t)+g(v,t))\,dt$$

and

$$\frac{2}{(v-u)^2}\int_u^v\int_u^v g(s,t)\,ds\,dt = \frac{2}{v-u}\int_u^v\left(\frac{1}{v-u}\int_u^v g(s,t)\,dt\right)ds$$
$$\leq \frac{2}{v-u}\int_u^v \frac{g(s,u)+g(s,v)}{2}\,ds = \frac{1}{v-u}\int_u^v (g(s,u)+g(s,v))\,ds.$$

Moreover, we have

$$\frac{4}{(v-u)^2}\int_u^v\int_u^v g(s,t)\,ds\,dt$$
$$\leq \frac{1}{v-u}\int_u^v (g(s,v)+g(s,u))\,ds + \frac{1}{v-u}\int_u^v (g(u,t)+g(v,t))\,dt.$$

Therefore, $\Delta \geq 0$, so $G(u,v)$ is Schur-convex on $I \times I$.
When $g(s,t)$ is a concave function on $I \times I$, it can be proved with similar methods. □

4. Application on Binary Mean

Theorem 3. *Let $c > 0$ and $d > 0$. If $c \neq d$, $0 < s < 1$, then*

$$A(d,c) \geq S_{s+1}^s(d,c)S_s^{s-1}(d,c) \geq \frac{(c+d)^{2s-1}}{s(s+1)}, \tag{8}$$

where $A(d,c) = \frac{c+d}{2}$ and $S_s(d,c) = \left(\frac{d^s-c^s}{s(d-c)}\right)^{\frac{1}{s-1}}$ are the arithmetic mean and the s-order Stolarsky mean of positive numbers c and d, respectively.

Proof. Let $x > 0, y > 0$ and $0 < s < 1$. From Theorem 4 in the reference [17], we know that $g(x,y) = x^s y^{1-s}$ is concave on $(0,+\infty) \times (0,+\infty)$. For $c \neq d$, by Theorem 2, from $\left(\frac{d+c}{2}, \frac{d+c}{2}\right) \prec (c,d) \prec (d+c,0)$, it follows that

$$G(d+c,0) = \frac{1}{(d+c-0)^2}\int_c^d\int_0^{d+c} x^s y^{1-s}\,dx\,dy$$
$$= \frac{1}{(d+c)^2}\int_0^{d+c} x^s\,dx \int_0^{d+c} y^{1-s}\,dy$$
$$= \frac{1}{(d+c)^2}\frac{(c+d)^{s+1}}{s+1}\frac{(c+d)^s}{s} = \frac{(c+d)^{2s-1}}{s(s+1)}$$
$$\leq G(c,d) = \frac{1}{(d-c)^2}\int_c^d\int_c^d x^s y^{1-s}\,dx\,dy$$
$$= \frac{1}{(d-c)^2}\int_c^d x^s\,dx \int_c^d y^{1-s}\,dy$$
$$= \frac{1}{(d-c)^2}\frac{d^{s+1}-c^{s+1}}{s+1}\frac{d^s-c^s}{s}$$
$$\leq G\left(\frac{d+c}{2},\frac{d+c}{2}\right) = \frac{d+c}{2},$$

That is, we obtain the following.

$$\frac{(c+d)^{2s-1}}{s(s+1)} \leq S_{s+1}^s(d,c)S_s^{s-1}(d,c) = \frac{d^{s+1}-c^{s+1}}{(s+1)(d-c)} \cdot \frac{d^s-c^s}{s(d-c)} \leq \frac{d+c}{2} = A(d,c).$$

□

Theorem 4. *Let $c > 0, d > 0$. Then,*

$$\log\left(\frac{A(d,c)}{B(d,c)}\right)^2 \geq \left(\frac{c-d}{d+c}\right)^2, \qquad (9)$$

where $B(d,c) = \sqrt{dc}$ is the geometric mean of of positive numbers c and d.

Proof. From reference [17], we know that the function $g(x,y) = \frac{1}{(x+y)^2}$ is convex on $(0,+\infty) \times (0,+\infty)$. For $c > 0, d > 0$ and $d \neq c$, by Theorem 2, from $(\frac{d+c}{2}, \frac{d+c}{2}) \prec (d,c)$, it follows that

$$G(c,d) = \frac{1}{(d-c)^2} \int_c^d \int_c^d \frac{1}{(x+y)^2} dx\,dy$$

$$= \frac{1}{(d-c)^2} \int_c^d \left(\frac{1}{c+y} - \frac{1}{d+y}\right) dy$$

$$= \frac{1}{(d-c)^2}[(\log(d+c) - \log(2c)) - (\log(2d) - \log(d+c))]$$

$$\geq G\left(\frac{d+c}{2}, \frac{d+c}{2}\right) = \frac{1}{(d+c)^2},$$

That is, we obtain the following.

$$\log\left(\frac{A(d,c)}{B(d,c)}\right)^2 = \log\frac{(d+c)^2}{4dc} \geq \left(\frac{c-d}{d+c}\right)^2.$$

□

Theorem 5. *Let $c > 0, d > 0$. Then,*

$$H_e(c^2, d^2) \geq A^2(c,d), \qquad (10)$$

where $H_e(c,d) = \frac{c+\sqrt{cd}+d}{3}$ is the Heronian mean of positive numbers c and d.

Proof. From reference [18], we know that the function of two variables

$$\psi(x,y) = \frac{x^2}{2r^2} + \frac{y^2}{2s^2}$$

is a convex function on $(0,+\infty) \times (0,+\infty)$, where $s > 0$ and $r > 0$. For $d > 0, c > 0$, and $c \neq d$, by Theorem 2, from $(\frac{d+c}{2}, \frac{d+c}{2}) \prec (d,c)$, it follows that

$$G(c,d) = \frac{1}{(d-c)^2} \int_c^d \int_c^d \left(\frac{x^2}{2r^2} + \frac{y^2}{2s^2}\right) dx\,dy$$

$$= \frac{1}{(d-c)^2} \int_c^d \left(\frac{d^3 - c^3}{6r^2} + \frac{y^2(d-c)}{2s^2}\right) dy$$

$$= \frac{1}{(d-c)^2} \left(\frac{(d^3-c^3)(d-c)}{6r^2} + \frac{(d^3-c^3)(d-c)}{6s^2}\right)$$

$$= \frac{1}{(d-c)^2} \cdot \frac{(d^3-c^3)(d-c)}{6} \left(\frac{1}{r^2} + \frac{1}{s^2}\right)$$

$$\geq G\left(\frac{d+c}{2}, \frac{d+c}{2}\right) = \frac{(c+d)^2}{8} \left(\frac{1}{r^2} + \frac{1}{s^2}\right),$$

namely

$$H_e(c^2, d^2) = \frac{c^2 + cd + d^2}{3} = \frac{(d^3-c^3)}{3(d-c)} \geq \frac{(d+c)^2}{4} = A^2(d,c).$$

□

Theorem 6. *Let $c > 0, d > 0$. We have*

$$H_e(c^2, d^2) \geq L(d,c) A(d,c), \tag{11}$$

where $L(d,c) = \frac{d-c}{\log d - \log c}$ is the logarithmic mean of positive numbers c and d.

Proof. Let $g(x,y) = y^2 x^{-1}, x > 0, y > 0$. Then,

$$g_{xx} = 2x^{-3} y^2, \quad g_{xy} = -2x^{-2} y = g_{yx}, g_{yy} = 2x^{-1}.$$

The Hesse matrix of $g(x,y)$ is

$$H = \begin{pmatrix} 2x^{-3} y^2 & -2x^{-2} y \\ -2x^{-2} y & 2x^{-1} \end{pmatrix}.$$

$$\det(H - \lambda I) = \det \begin{pmatrix} 2x^{-3} y^2 - \lambda & -2x^{-2} y \\ -2x^{-2} y & 2x^{-1} - \lambda \end{pmatrix} = 0$$

$$\Rightarrow \lambda(\lambda - 2x^{-3} y^2 - 2x^{-1}) = 0 \Rightarrow \lambda_1 = 0, \lambda_2 = 2x^{-3} y^2 + 2x^{-1} > 0.$$

Therefore, matrix H is positive semidefinite, so it is known that $g(x,y)$ is a convex function on $(0, +\infty) \times (0, +\infty)$. For $d > 0, c > 0$ and $d \neq c$, by Theorem 2, from $\left(\frac{d+c}{2}, \frac{d+c}{2}\right) \prec (d,c)$, it follows that

$$G(c,d) = \frac{1}{(d-c)^2} \int_c^d \int_c^d y^2 x^{-1} dx\,dy$$

$$= \frac{\log d - \log c}{d-c} \cdot \frac{d^2 + cd + c^2}{3} \geq \frac{\left(\frac{d+c}{2}\right)^2}{\frac{c+c}{2}} = \frac{d+c}{2},$$

which is

$$H_e(c^2, d^2) \geq L(d,c) A(d,c).$$

□

Theorem 7. Let $d > 0, c > 0, d \neq c$. Then

$$\tilde{E}(d,c) \leq A(d,c)e^{(d+c)}\left(\frac{d-c}{e^d - e^c}\right)^2 \leq A(d,c), \tag{12}$$

where

$$\tilde{E}(d,c) = \begin{cases} \frac{ce^d - de^c}{e^d - e^c} + 1, & d, c \in I, \ d \neq c \\ c, & c = d \end{cases}$$

is exponent type mean of positive numbers c and d (see [13] (p. 134)).

Proof. Let $g(x,y) = xe^{-(x+y)}, y > 0, x > 0$. From reference [19], we know that function $g(x,y)$ is convex on $\mathbb{R} \times \mathbb{R}$. For $d > 0, c > 0$, and $d \neq c$ by Theorem 2 from $(\frac{d+c}{2}, \frac{d+c}{2}) \prec (d,c)$, it follows that

$$G(c,d) = \frac{1}{(c-d)^2} \int_c^d \int_c^d xe^{-x-y} \, dx \, dy$$

$$= \frac{1}{(c-d)^2} \int_c^d xe^{-x} \, dx \int_c^d e^{-y} \, dy$$

$$= \frac{1}{(c-d)^2} \left(\frac{c+1}{e^c} - \frac{d+1}{e^d}\right) \cdot \left(\frac{1}{e^c} - \frac{1}{e^d}\right)$$

$$= \frac{1}{(d-c)^2} \frac{(ce^d - de^c) + (e^d - e^c)}{e^{(c+d)}} \cdot \frac{e^d - e^c}{e^{(c+d)}}$$

$$\leq G\left(\frac{d+c}{2}, \frac{d+c}{2}\right) = \frac{c+d}{2} \frac{1}{e^{(d+c)}},$$

which is

$$\frac{ce^d - de^c}{e^d - e^c} + 1 \leq \frac{d+c}{2} e^{(d+c)} \left(\frac{d-c}{e^d - e^c}\right)^2.$$

For the rest, we only need to prove that

$$e^{(c+d)}\left(\frac{d-c}{e^d - e^c}\right)^2 \leq 1. \tag{13}$$

We write $e^d = u$ and $e^c = v$; then, the above inequality is equivalent to the well-known log-geometric mean inequality.

$$L(v,u) = \frac{v-u}{\log v - \log u} \geq \sqrt{vu} = B(v,u).$$

□

Author Contributions: Conceptualization, H.-N.S., D.-S.W. and C.-R.F.; Methodology, H.-N.S.; Validation, C.-R.F.; Formal analysis, H.-N.S. and D.-S.W.; Investigation, D.-S.W.; Resources, C.-R.F.; Writing—original draft, D.-S.W.; Funding acquisition, C.-R.F. All authors have read and agreed to the published version of the manuscript.

Funding: This research received no external funding.

Institutional Review Board Statement: Not applicable.

Informed Consent Statement: Not applicable.

Data Availability Statement: Not applicable.

Acknowledgments: The authors sincerely thanks Chen Dirong and Chen Jihang for their valuable opinions and suggestions.

Conflicts of Interest: The authors declare no conflict of interest.

References

1. Elezovic, N.; Pečarić, J. A note on schur-convex fuctions. *Rocky Mt. J. Math.* **2000**, *30*, 853–856. [CrossRef]
2. Shi, H.N. Schur-convex functions relate to Hadamard-type inequalities. *J. Math. Inequal.* **2007**, *1*, 127–136. [CrossRef]
3. Čuljak, V.; Franjić, I.; Ghulam, R.; Pečarić, J. Schur-convexity of averages of convex functions. *J. Inequal. Appl.* **2011**, *2011*, 581918. [CrossRef]
4. Long, B.-Y.; Jiang, Y.-P.; Chu, Y.-M. Schur convexity properties of the weighted arithmetic integral mean and Chebyshev functional. *Rev. Anal. Numr. Thor. Approx.* **2013**, *42*, 72–81.
5. Sun, J.; Sun, Z.-L.; Xi, B.-Y.; Qi, F. Schur-geometric and Schur harmonic convexity of an integral mean for convex functions. *Turk. J. Anal. Number Theory* **2015**, *3*, 87–89. [CrossRef]
6. Zhang, X.-M.; Chu, Y.-M. Convexity of the integral arithmetic mean of a convex function. *Rocky Mt. J. Math.* **2010**, *40*, 1061–1068. [CrossRef]
7. Chu, Y.-M.; Wang, G.-D.; Zhang, X.-H. Schur convexity and Hadmards inequality. *Math. Inequal. Appl.* **2010**, *13*, 725–731.
8. Sun, Y.-J.; Wang, D.; Shi, H.-N. Two Schur-convex functions related to the generalized integral quasiarithmetic means. *Adv. Inequal. Appl.* **2017**, *2017*, 7.
9. Nozar, S.; Ali, B. Schur-convexity of integral arithmetic means of co-ordinated convex functions in R^3. *Math. Anal. Convex Optim.* **2020**, *1*, 15–24. [CrossRef]
10. Sever, D.S. Inequalities for double integrals of Schur convex functions on symmetric and convex domains. *Mat. Vesnik* **2021**, *73*, 63–74.
11. Kovač, S. Schur-geometric and Schur-harmonic convexity of weighted integral mean. *Trans. Razmadze Math. Inst.* **2021**, *175*, 225–233.
12. Dragomir, S.S. Operator Schur convexity and some integral inequalities. *Linear Multilinear Algebra* **2019**, *69*, 2733–2748. [CrossRef]
13. Shi, H.-N. *Schur-Convex Functions and Inequalities: Volume 2: Applications in Inequalities*; Harbin Institute of Technology Press Ltd.: Harbin, China, 2019.
14. Wang, B.Y. *Foundations of Majorization Inequalities*; Beijing Normal University Press: Beijing, China, 1990. (In Chinese)
15. Marshall, A.W.; Olkin, I. *Inequalities: Theory of Majorization and Its Application*; Academies Press: New York, NY, USA, 1979.
16. Ye, Q.; Shen, Y. *Handbook of Practical Mathematics*, 2nd ed.; Science Press: Beijing, China, 2019; pp. 246–247.
17. Shi, H.-N.; Wang, P.; Zhang, J.; Du, W.-S. Notes on judgment criteria of convex functions of several variables. *Results Nonlinear Anal.* **2021**, *4*, 235–243. [CrossRef]
18. Shi, H.-N. *Schur-Convex Functions and Inequalities: Volume 1: Concepts, Properties, and Applications in Symmetric Function Inequalities*; Harbin Institute of Technology Press Ltd.: Harbin, China, 2019.
19. You, X. The properties and applications of convex function of many variables. *J. Beijing Inst. Petrochem. Technol.* **2008**, *16*, 61–64. (In Chinese)

Article

Inequalities and Reverse Inequalities for the Joint A-Numerical Radius of Operators

Najla Altwaijry [1,*,†], Silvestru Sever Dragomir [2,†] and Kais Feki [3,4,†]

1. Department of Mathematics, College of Science, King Saud University, P.O. Box 2455, Riyadh 11451, Saudi Arabia
2. College of Engineering and Science, Victoria University, Melbourne, VIC 8000, Australia
3. Faculty of Economic Sciences and Management of Mahdia, University of Monastir, Mahdia 5111, Tunisia
4. Laboratory Physics-Mathematics and Applications (LR/13/ES-22), Faculty of Sciences of Sfax, University of Sfax, Sfax 3018, Tunisia
* Correspondence: najla@ksu.edu.sa
† These authors contributed equally to this work.

Abstract: In this paper, we aim to establish several estimates concerning the generalized Euclidean operator radius of d-tuples of A-bounded linear operators acting on a complex Hilbert space $\mathcal{H}$, which leads to the special case of the well-known A-numerical radius for $d = 1$. Here, A is a positive operator on $\mathcal{H}$. Some inequalities related to the Euclidean operator A-seminorm of d-tuples of A-bounded operators are proved. In addition, under appropriate conditions, several reverse bounds for the A-numerical radius in single and multivariable settings are also stated.

Keywords: positive operator; joint A-numerical radius; Euclidean operator A-seminorm; joint operator A-seminorm

MSC: 47B65; 47A12; 47A13; 47A30

1. Introduction

The theory of inequalities remains a very attractive area of research in the last few decades. In particular, the investigation of numerical radius inequalities in Hilbert and semi-Hilbert spaces has occupied an important and central role in the theory of operator inequalities. For further details, interested readers are referred to the very recent book by Bhunia et al. [1].

Throughout the present article, $\mathcal{H}$ stands for a non-trivial complex Hilbert space with inner product $\langle \cdot, \cdot \rangle$ and the corresponding norm $\|\cdot\|$. By $\mathbb{B}(\mathcal{H})$, we denote the C^*-algebra of all bounded linear operators acting on $\mathcal{H}$. The identity operator on $\mathcal{H}$ will be simply written as I. Let $T \in \mathbb{B}(\mathcal{H})$. The range and the adjoint of T will be denoted by $\mathcal{R}(T)$ and T^*, respectively. An operator $T \in \mathbb{B}(\mathcal{H})$ is called positive and we write $T \geq 0$ if $\langle Tx, x \rangle \geq 0$ for all $x \in \mathcal{H}$. If $T \geq 0$, then $T^{1/2}$ denotes the square root of T.

If $\mathcal{S}$ is a subspace of $\mathcal{H}$, then we mean by $\overline{\mathcal{S}}$ the closure of $\mathcal{S}$ in the norm topology of $\mathcal{H}$. Let $\mathcal{C}$ be a closed subspace of $\mathcal{H}$. We denote by $P_\mathcal{C}$ the orthogonal projection onto $\mathcal{C}$.

For the rest of this work, by an operator, we mean a bounded linear operator acting on $\mathcal{H}$. We also assume that $A \in \mathbb{B}(\mathcal{H})$ is a non-zero, positive operator. Such an A defines the following semi-inner product on $\mathcal{H}$:

$$\langle x, y \rangle_A = \langle Ax, y \rangle = \langle A^{1/2}x, A^{1/2}y \rangle,$$

for all $x, y \in \mathcal{H}$. The seminorm on $\mathcal{H}$ induced by $\langle \cdot, \cdot \rangle_A$ is stated as: $\|x\|_A = \|A^{1/2}x\|$ for every $x \in \mathcal{H}$. Hence, we see that the above seminorm is a norm on $\mathcal{H}$ if and only if A is a one-to-one operator. Furthermore, one can prove that the semi-Hilbert space $(\mathcal{H}, \|\cdot\|_A)$ is a complete space if and only if $\overline{\mathcal{R}(A)} = \mathcal{R}(A)$. The A-unit sphere of $\mathcal{H}$ is defined as

$$\mathbb{S}_A^1 = \{y \in \mathcal{H}\,;\, \|y\|_A = 1\}.$$

We refer the reader to the following list of recent works on the theory of semi-Hilbert spaces [1–6].

Let $T \in \mathbb{B}(\mathcal{H})$. We recall from [7] that an operator $R \in \mathbb{B}(\mathcal{H})$ is called an A-adjoint of T if the equality

$$\langle Ty, z \rangle_A = \langle y, Rz \rangle_A$$

holds for all $y, z \in \mathcal{H}$, that is, $AR = T^*A$. In general, the existence and the uniqueness of an A-adjoint of an arbitrary bounded operator T are not guaranteed. By using a famous theorem due to Douglas [8], we see that the sets of all operators that admit A-adjoint and $A^{1/2}$-adjoint operators are, respectively, given by

$$\mathbb{B}_A(\mathcal{H}) = \{S \in \mathbb{B}(\mathcal{H})\,;\, \mathcal{R}(S^*A) \subset \mathcal{R}(A)\},$$

and

$$\mathbb{B}_{A^{1/2}}(\mathcal{H}) = \{S \in \mathbb{B}(\mathcal{H})\,;\, \exists \zeta > 0 \text{ such that } \|Sx\|_A \leq \zeta \|x\|_A,\, \forall x \in \mathcal{H}\}.$$

When an operator S belongs to $\mathbb{B}_{A^{1/2}}(\mathcal{H})$, we say that S is A-bounded. It is not difficult to check that $\mathbb{B}_A(\mathcal{H})$ and $\mathbb{B}_{A^{1/2}}(\mathcal{H})$ represent two subalgebras of $\mathbb{B}(\mathcal{H})$. Moreover, the following inclusions

$$\mathbb{B}_A(\mathcal{H}) \subseteq \mathbb{B}_{A^{1/2}}(\mathcal{H}) \subseteq \mathbb{B}(\mathcal{H})$$

hold and are, in general, proper. For more details, we refer to [7,9–11] and the references therein. We recall now that an operator $S \in \mathbb{B}(\mathcal{H})$ is called A-self-adjoint if AS is self-adjoint. Clearly the fact that S is A-self-adjoint implies that $S \in \mathbb{B}_A(\mathcal{H})$. Furthermore, we say that an operator S is called A-positive (and we write $S \geq_A 0$) if $AS \geq 0$. Obviously, A-positive operators are A-self-adjoint. For $S \in \mathbb{B}_{A^{1/2}}(\mathcal{H})$, the operator A-seminorm and the A-numerical radius of S are given, respectively, by

$$\|S\|_A = \sup_{x \in \mathbb{S}_A^1} \|Sx\|_A \quad \text{and} \quad \omega_A(S) = \sup_{x \in \mathbb{S}_A^1} |\langle Sx, x \rangle_A|. \qquad (1)$$

The quantities in (1) are also intensively studied when $A = I$, and the reader is referred to [12–22] as a recent list of references treating the numerical radius and operator norm of operators on complex Hilbert spaces.

If $S \in \mathbb{B}_A(\mathcal{H})$, then by the Douglas theorem [8], there exists a unique solution, denoted by $S^{\dagger_A}$, of the problem: $AX = S^*A$ and $\mathcal{R}(X) \subseteq \overline{\mathcal{R}(A)}$. We emphasize here that if $S \in \mathbb{B}_A(\mathcal{H})$, then $S^{\dagger_A} \in \mathbb{B}_A(\mathcal{H})$ and $(S^{\dagger_A})^{\dagger_A} = P_{\overline{\mathcal{R}(A)}} S P_{\overline{\mathcal{R}(A)}}$.

Now, let $\mathcal{T} = (T_1, \ldots, T_d) \in \mathbb{B}_{A^{1/2}}(\mathcal{H})^d$ be a d-tuple of operators. According to [23], the following two quantities

$$\omega_A(\mathcal{T}) := \sup_{y \in \mathbb{S}_A^1} \sqrt{\sum_{k=1}^{d} |\langle T_k y, y \rangle_A|^2},$$

and

$$\|\mathcal{T}\|_A := \sup_{y \in \mathbb{S}_A^1} \sqrt{\sum_{k=1}^{d} \|T_k y\|_A^2}$$

generalize the notions in (1) and define two equivalent norms on $\mathbb{B}_{A^{1/2}}(\mathcal{H})^d$. Namely, we have

$$\frac{1}{2\sqrt{d}}\|\mathcal{T}\|_A \leq \omega_A(\mathcal{T}) \leq \|\mathcal{T}\|_A, \qquad (2)$$

for every operator tuple $\mathcal{T} = (T_1,\ldots,T_d) \in \mathbb{B}_{A^{1/2}}(\mathcal{H})^d$. Note that $\omega_A(\mathcal{T})$ and $\|\mathcal{T}\|_A$ are called the joint A-numerical radius and joint operator A-seminorm of $\mathcal{T}$, respectively. The above two quantities have been investigated by several authors when $A = I$ (see for instance [24–27]). Another joint A-seminorm of A-bounded operators has been recently introduced [28]. Namely, the Euclidean A-seminorm of an operator tuple $\mathcal{T} = (T_1,\ldots,T_d) \in \mathbb{B}_{A^{1/2}}(\mathcal{H})^d$ is given by

$$\|\mathcal{T}\|_{e,A} = \sup_{(\nu_1,\ldots,\nu_d)\in\overline{\mathcal{B}}_d} \|\nu_1 T_1 + \ldots + \nu_d T_d\|_A, \qquad (3)$$

where $\overline{\mathcal{B}}_d$ denotes the closed unit ball of $\mathbb{C}^d$, i.e.,

$$\overline{\mathcal{B}}_d := \left\{ \nu = (\nu_1,\ldots,\nu_d) \in \mathbb{C}^d ;\; \|\nu\|_2^2 := \sum_{k=1}^d |\nu_k|^2 \leq 1 \right\},$$

where $\mathbb{C}$ denotes the set of all complex numbers. It is important to note that the following inequalities,

$$\frac{1}{\sqrt{d}}\|\mathcal{T}\|_A \leq \|\mathcal{T}\|_{e,A} \leq \|\mathcal{T}\|_A,$$

hold for any d-tuple of operators $\mathcal{T} = (T_1,\ldots,T_d) \in \mathbb{B}_{A^{1/2}}(\mathcal{H})^d$ (see [28]).

Our aim in the present article is to establish several estimates involving the quantities $\omega_A(\mathcal{T})$, $\|\mathcal{T}\|_A$ and $\|\mathcal{T}\|_{e,A}$, where $\mathcal{T} = (T_1,\ldots,T_d)$ is a d-tuple of A-bounded operators. Some inequalities connecting the A-numerical radius and operator A-seminorm for A-bounded operators are established. One main target of this work is to derive, under appropriate conditions, several reverse bounds for $\omega_A(\mathcal{T})$ in both single and multivariable settings. In particular, for $T \in \mathbb{B}_{A^{1/2}}(\mathcal{H})$, $\nu \in \mathbb{C}$ and $r > 0$, we will demonstrate under appropriate conditions on T, ν and r that

$$\|T\|_A^2 \leq \omega_A^2(T) + \frac{2r^2}{|\nu| + \sqrt{|\nu|^2 - r^2}} \omega_A(T).$$

2. Results

This section is devoted to present our contributions. By $\Re z$, we will denote the real part of any complex number $z \in \mathbb{C}$. In the next theorem, we state our first result.

Theorem 1. Let $T \in \mathbb{B}_{A^{1/2}}(\mathcal{H})$ and $\rho, \sigma \in \mathbb{C}$ with $\rho \neq \sigma$. If

$$\Re\langle \rho x - Tx, Tx - \sigma x\rangle_A \geq 0 \quad \text{for any} \quad x \in \mathbb{S}_A^1 \qquad (4)$$

or, equivalently

$$\left\|Tx - \frac{\rho+\sigma}{2}x\right\|_A \leq \frac{1}{2}|\rho - \sigma| \text{ for any } x \in \mathbb{S}_A^1, \qquad (5)$$

then

$$\|T\|_A^2 \leq \omega_A^2(T) + \frac{1}{4}|\rho - \sigma|^2. \qquad (6)$$

Proof. Notice first that the following assertions,

(i) $\Re\langle u - y, y - z\rangle_A \geq 0$,
(ii) $\left\|y - \frac{z+u}{2}\right\|_A \leq \frac{1}{2}\|u - z\|_A$,

are equivalent for every $y, z, u \in \mathscr{H}$. Indeed, one can see that

$$\frac{1}{4}\|u-z\|_A^2 - \left\|y - \frac{z+u}{2}\right\|_A^2 = \frac{1}{4}\|u-y+y-z\|_A^2 - \frac{1}{4}\|y-z+y-u\|_A^2$$

$$= \frac{1}{4}\left(\|u-y\|_A^2 + 2\Re\langle u-y, y-z\rangle_A + \|y-z\|_A^2\right)$$

$$- \frac{1}{4}\left(\|y-z\|_A^2 + 2\Re\langle y-z, y-u\rangle_A + \|u-y\|_A^2\right)$$

$$= \frac{1}{2}\left(\Re\langle u-y, y-z\rangle_A - \Re\langle y-z, y-u\rangle_A\right)$$

$$= \frac{1}{2}\left(\Re\langle u-y, y-z\rangle_A - \overline{\Re\langle y-u, y-z\rangle_A}\right)$$

$$= \Re\langle u-y, y-z\rangle_A.$$

Hence, the equivalence is proved.

By taking $u = \rho x$, $z = \sigma x$ and $y = Tx$ in the statements (i) and (ii), we deduce that (4) and (5) are equivalent.

Now, for $x \in \mathbb{S}_A^1$, we define

$$I_1 := \Re\left[\left(\rho - \langle Tx, x\rangle_A\right)\left(\overline{\langle Tx, x\rangle_A} - \overline{\sigma}\right)\right]$$

and

$$I_2 := \Re\langle \rho x - Tx, Tx - \sigma x\rangle_A.$$

Then,

$$I_1 = \Re\left[\rho\overline{\langle Tx, x\rangle_A} + \overline{\sigma}\langle Tx, x\rangle_A\right] - \left|\langle Tx, x\rangle_A\right|^2 - \Re(\rho\overline{\sigma})$$

and

$$I_2 = \Re\left[\rho\overline{\langle Tx, x\rangle_A} + \overline{\sigma}\langle Tx, x\rangle_A\right] - \|Tx\|_A^2 - \Re(\rho\overline{\sigma}).$$

This gives

$$I_1 - I_2 = \|Tx\|_A^2 - \left|\langle Tx, x\rangle_A\right|^2,$$

for any $x \in \mathbb{S}_A^1$ and $\sigma, \rho \in \mathbb{C}$. This is an interesting identity itself as well.
If (4) holds, then $I_2 \geq 0$ and thus

$$\|Tx\|_A^2 - \left|\langle Tx, x\rangle_A\right|^2 \leq \Re\left[\left(\rho - \langle Tx, x\rangle_A\right)\left(\overline{\langle Tx, x\rangle_A} - \overline{\sigma}\right)\right]. \quad (7)$$

Furthermore, it can be checked that for every $u, v \in \mathbb{C}$, we have

$$\Re(u\overline{v}) \leq \frac{1}{4}|u+v|^2.$$

By letting

$$u := \rho - \langle Tx, x\rangle_A, \quad v := \langle Tx, x\rangle_A - \sigma$$

in the above elementary inequality, we obtain

$$\Re\left[\left(\rho - \langle Tx, x\rangle_A\right)\left(\overline{\langle Tx, x\rangle_A} - \overline{\sigma}\right)\right] \leq \frac{1}{4}|\rho - \sigma|^2. \quad (8)$$

Making use of the inequalities (7) and (8), we deduce that

$$\|Tx\|_A^2 \leq \left|\langle Tx, x\rangle_A\right|^2 + \frac{1}{4}|\rho - \sigma|^2 \quad (9)$$

and by taking the supremum over all $x \in \mathbb{S}_A^1$ in (9), we obtain the required result (6). □

Remark 1. Let $S \in \mathbb{B}(\mathscr{H})$. We say that S is an A-accretive operator, if

$$\Re\langle Sx, x\rangle_A \geq 0, \quad \text{for all } x \in \mathscr{H}.$$

Now, let $T \in \mathbb{B}_A(\mathscr{H})$. If $\theta \geq \mu > 0$ are such that either $(T^{\dagger_A} - \mu I)(\theta I - T)$ is A-accretive or $(T^{\dagger_A} - \mu I)(\theta I - T) \geq_A 0$, then by (6), we obtain

$$\|T\|_A^2 \leq \omega_A^2(T) + \frac{1}{4}(\theta - \mu)^2,$$

which gives

$$\|T\|_A \leq \sqrt{\omega_A^2(T) + \frac{1}{4}(\theta - \mu)^2}.$$

As an application of Theorem 1, we state the following result.

Corollary 1. Let $\mathcal{T} = (T_1, \ldots, T_d) \in \mathbb{B}_{A^{1/2}}(\mathscr{H})^d$ and $\rho, \sigma \in \mathbb{C}$ be such that $\rho \neq \sigma$ and

$$\left\| T_i x - \frac{\rho + \sigma}{2} x \right\|_A \leq \frac{1}{2}|\rho - \sigma|,$$

for any $x \in \mathbb{S}_A^1$ and every $i \in \{1, \ldots, d\}$. Then,

$$\|\mathcal{T}\|_{e,A}^2 \leq d \left(\max_{k \in \{1,\ldots,d\}} \omega_A^2(T_k) + \frac{1}{4}|\rho - \sigma|^2 \right). \tag{10}$$

Proof. Let $(\nu_1, \ldots, \nu_d) \in \overline{\mathcal{B}}_d$. From Theorem 1, we have

$$\|T_i\|_A^2 \leq \omega_A^2(T_i) + \frac{1}{4}|\rho - \sigma|^2$$

for $i \in \{1, \ldots, d\}$. This gives,

$$\sum_{i=1}^d |\nu_i|^2 \|T_i\|_A^2 \leq \sum_{i=1}^d |\nu_i|^2 \omega_A^2(T_i) + \frac{1}{4}|\rho - \sigma|^2 \sum_{i=1}^d |\nu_i|^2. \tag{11}$$

By using the triangle and Cauchy–Schwarz inequalities, we have

$$\frac{1}{d} \left\| \sum_{i=1}^d \nu_i T_i \right\|_A^2 \leq \frac{1}{d} \left(\sum_{i=1}^d \|\nu_i T_i\|_A \right)^2 \leq \sum_{i=1}^d |\nu_i|^2 \|T_i\|_A^2. \tag{12}$$

Moreover, since

$$\sum_{i=1}^d |\nu_i|^2 \omega_A^2(T_i) \leq \max_{k \in \{1,\ldots,d\}} \omega_A^2(T_k) \sum_{i=1}^d |\nu_i|^2,$$

then, by applying (11) and (12), we obtain

$$\frac{1}{d} \left\| \sum_{i=1}^d \nu_i T_i \right\|_A^2 \leq \max_{k \in \{1,\ldots,d\}} \omega_A^2(T_k) \sum_{i=1}^d |\nu_i|^2 + \frac{1}{4}|\rho - \sigma|^2 \sum_{i=1}^d |\nu_i|^2$$

for all $(\nu_1, \ldots, \nu_d) \in \overline{\mathcal{B}}_d$.

By taking the supremum over all $(\nu_1, \ldots, \nu_d) \in \overline{\mathcal{B}}_d$ in the last inequality and then using the identity in (3), we reach (10) as desired. □

An important application of the inequality (9) can be stated as follows.

Corollary 2. Let $\mathcal{T} = (T_1, \ldots, T_d) \in \mathbb{B}_{A^{1/2}}(\mathcal{H})^d$ and $\rho_i, \sigma_i \in \mathbb{C}$ with $\rho_i \neq \sigma_i$ for $i \in \{1, \ldots, d\}$. Assume that for every $x \in \mathbb{S}_A^1$, we have

$$\left\| T_i x - \frac{\rho_i + \sigma_i}{2} x \right\|_A \leq \frac{1}{2} |\rho_i - \sigma_i|, \quad \forall i \in \{1, \ldots, d\}. \tag{13}$$

Then,

$$\|\mathcal{T}\|_A \leq \sqrt{\omega_A^2(\mathcal{T}) + \frac{1}{4} \sum_{i=1}^d |\rho_i - \sigma_i|^2}. \tag{14}$$

Proof. Let $x \in \mathbb{S}_A^1$. By applying (9), we obtain

$$\|T x_i\|_A^2 \leq \left| \langle T_i x, x \rangle_A \right|^2 + \frac{1}{4} |\rho_i - \sigma_i|^2$$

for $i \in \{1, \ldots, d\}$.

By summing over $i = 1, \ldots, d$, we obtain

$$\sum_{i=1}^d \|T x_i\|_A^2 \leq \sum_{i=1}^d \left| \langle T_i x, x \rangle_A \right|^2 + \frac{1}{4} \sum_{i=1}^d |\rho_i - \sigma_i|^2$$

Finally, by taking the supremum over $x \in \mathbb{S}_A^1$, we obtain

$$\|\mathcal{T}\|_A^2 \leq \omega_A^2(\mathcal{T}) + \frac{1}{4} \sum_{i=1}^d |\rho_i - \sigma_i|^2.$$

This establishes (14). □

The following lemma is needed for the sequel.

Lemma 1 ([29] p. 9). Let $\sigma, \rho \in \mathbb{C}$ and $\zeta_j \in \mathbb{C}$ be such that

$$\left| \zeta_j - \frac{\sigma + \rho}{2} \right| \leq \frac{1}{2} |\rho - \sigma|$$

for all $j \in \{1, \ldots, d\}$. Then,

$$d \sum_{j=1}^d |\zeta_j|^2 - \left| \sum_{j=1}^d \zeta_j \right|^2 \leq \frac{1}{4} d^2 |\rho - \sigma|^2. \tag{15}$$

We can now prove the next proposition.

Proposition 1. Let $\mathcal{T} = (T_1, \ldots, T_d) \in \mathbb{B}_{A^{1/2}}(\mathcal{H})^d$ and $\rho, \sigma \in \mathbb{C}$ with $\rho \neq \sigma$. Assume that

$$\omega_A\left(T_j - \frac{\sigma + \rho}{2} I\right) \leq \frac{1}{2} |\rho - \sigma| \text{ for any } j \in \{1, \ldots, d\}. \tag{16}$$

Then,

$$\omega_A^2(\mathcal{T}) \leq \frac{1}{d} \omega_A^2 \left(\sum_{j=1}^d T_j \right) + \frac{1}{4} d |\rho - \sigma|^2. \tag{17}$$

Proof. Assume that (16) is valid. Let $x \in \mathbb{S}_A^1$ and take $\zeta_j = \langle T_j x, x \rangle_A$ for all $j \in \{1, \ldots, d\}$. Then, we see that

$$\left| \zeta_j - \frac{\sigma + \rho}{2} \right| = \left| \langle T_j x, x \rangle_A - \frac{\sigma + \rho}{2} \langle x, x \rangle_A \right|$$

$$= \left| \left\langle \left(T_j - \frac{\sigma + \rho}{2} I \right) x, x \right\rangle_A \right|$$

$$\leq \sup_{x \in \mathbb{S}_A^1} \left| \left\langle \left(T_j - \frac{\sigma + \rho}{2} I \right) x, x \right\rangle_A \right|$$

$$= \omega_A \left(T_j - \frac{\sigma + \rho}{2} \right) \leq \frac{1}{2} |\rho - \sigma|,$$

for any $j \in \{1, \ldots, d\}$.

By using (15), we obtain

$$\sum_{j=1}^d \left| \langle T_j x, x \rangle_A \right|^2 \leq \frac{1}{d} \left| \left\langle \sum_{j=1}^d T_j x, x \right\rangle_A \right|^2 + \frac{1}{4} d |\rho - \sigma|^2.$$

So, by taking the supremum over all $x \in \mathbb{S}_A^1$, we obtain (17) as desired. □

We now have the following result.

Theorem 2. *Let $T \in \mathbb{B}_{A^{1/2}}(\mathcal{H})$. If $v \in \mathbb{C} \setminus \{0\}$ and $r > 0$ are such that*

$$\|T - vI\|_A \leq r. \tag{18}$$

Then,

$$\|T\|_A \leq \omega_A(T) + \frac{1}{2} \cdot \frac{r^2}{|v|}.$$

Proof. Let $x \in \mathbb{S}_A^1$. It follows from (18) that

$$\|Tx - vx\|_A \leq \|T - vI\|_A \leq r.$$

This implies that

$$\|Tx\|_A^2 + |v|^2 \leq 2 \Re e \left[\overline{v} \langle Tx, x \rangle_A \right] + r^2 \leq 2|v| \left| \langle Tx, x \rangle_A \right| + r^2.$$

Taking the supremum over $x \in \mathbb{S}_A^1$ in the last inequality, we obtain

$$\|T\|_A^2 + |v|^2 \leq 2 \omega_A(T) |v| + r^2. \tag{19}$$

Moreover, it is clear that

$$2 \|T\|_A |v| \leq \|T\|_A^2 + |v|^2, \tag{20}$$

thus, by applying (19) and (20), we infer that

$$2 \|T\|_A |v| \leq 2 \omega_A(T) |v| + r^2.$$

So, we immediately obtain the desired result. □

The following corollary is now in order.

Corollary 3. Let $T \in \mathbb{B}_{A^{1/2}}(\mathscr{H})$ and $\alpha, \beta \in \mathbb{C}$ with $\alpha \notin \{-\beta, \beta\}$. Assume that

$$\Re\langle \alpha x - Tx, Tx - \beta x\rangle_A \geq 0 \quad \forall x \in \mathbb{S}_A^1. \tag{21}$$

Then,

$$\|T\|_A \leq \omega_A(T) + \frac{1}{4}\frac{|\alpha - \beta|^2}{|\alpha + \beta|}. \tag{22}$$

Proof. According to the proof of Theorem 1, we observe that (21) is equivalent to

$$\left\|Tx - \frac{\alpha+\beta}{2}x\right\|_A \leq \frac{1}{2}|\alpha - \beta| \text{ for any } x \in \mathbb{S}_A^1, \tag{23}$$

which is, in turn, equivalent to the following operator norm inequality:

$$\left\|T - \frac{\alpha+\beta}{2}I\right\|_A \leq \frac{1}{2}|\alpha - \beta|.$$

Now, applying Theorem 2 for $\nu = \frac{\alpha+\beta}{2}$ and $r = \frac{1}{2}|\alpha - \beta|$, we deduce the desired result. □

Another sufficient condition under which the inequality (22) hold is presented in terms of A-positive operators and reads as follows.

Corollary 4. Let $\alpha, \beta \in \mathbb{C}$ with $\alpha \notin \{-\beta, \beta\}$ and $T \in \mathbb{B}_A(\mathscr{H})$. If

$$\left(T^{\dagger_A} - \bar{\beta}I\right)(\alpha I - T) \geq_A 0,$$

then

$$\|T\|_A \leq \omega_A(T) + \frac{1}{4}\frac{|\alpha - \beta|^2}{|\alpha + \beta|}.$$

Corollary 5. Suppose that T, ν and r are as in Theorem 2. If, in addition,

$$\left||\nu| - \omega_A(T)\right| \geq \rho, \tag{24}$$

for some $\rho > 0$, then

$$(0 \leq)\|T\|_A^2 - \omega_A^2(T) \leq r^2 - \rho^2.$$

Proof. From the inequality (19), we see that

$$\|T\|_A^2 - \omega_A^2(T) \leq r^2 - \omega_A^2(T) + 2\omega_A(T)|\nu| - |\nu|^2$$
$$= r^2 - (|\nu| - \omega_A(T))^2.$$

Hence, an application of (24) leads to the desired inequality. □

Remark 2. If, in particular, $\|T - \nu I\|_A \leq r$ with $|\nu| = \omega_A(T), \nu \in \mathbb{C}$, then

$$(0 \leq)\|T\|_A^2 - \omega_A^2(T) \leq r^2.$$

Our next result reads as follows.

Theorem 3. Let $\mathcal{T} = (T_1, \ldots, T_d) \in \mathbb{B}_{A^{1/2}}(\mathscr{H})^d$ and $\alpha_i, \beta_i \in \mathbb{C}$ with $\alpha_i \notin \{-\beta_i, \beta_i\}$ for $i \in \{1, \ldots, d\}$. If

$$\left\|T_i - \frac{\alpha_i + \beta_i}{2}I\right\|_A \leq \frac{1}{2}|\alpha_i - \beta_i|, \tag{25}$$

for $i \in \{1, \ldots, d\}$, then

$$\|\mathcal{T}\|_{e,A} \leq \left(\sum_{i=1}^{d} \omega_A^2(T_i)\right)^{\frac{1}{2}} + \frac{1}{4}\left(\sum_{i=1}^{d} \frac{|\alpha_i - \beta_i|^4}{|\alpha_i + \beta_i|^2}\right)^{\frac{1}{2}} \quad (26)$$

and

$$\|\mathcal{T}\|_A \leq \omega_A(\mathcal{T}) + \frac{1}{4} \frac{\sum_{i=1}^{d} |\alpha_i - \beta_i|^2}{\left(\sum_{i=1}^{d} |\alpha_i + \beta_i|^2\right)^{\frac{1}{2}}}. \quad (27)$$

Proof. Using Corollary 3, we have

$$\|T_i\|_A \leq \omega_A(T_i) + \frac{1}{4} \frac{|\alpha_i - \beta_i|^2}{|\alpha_i + \beta_i|}$$

for $i \in \{1, \ldots, d\}$.

Let $(\nu_1, \ldots, \nu_d) \in \overline{\mathcal{B}}_d$, multiply by $|\nu_i|$ and sum to obtain

$$\sum_{i=1}^{d} \|\nu_i T_i\|_A \leq \sum_{i=1}^{d} |\nu_i| \omega_A(T_i) + \frac{1}{4} \sum_{i=1}^{d} |\nu_i| \frac{|\alpha_i - \beta_i|^2}{|\alpha_i + \beta_i|}. \quad (28)$$

By the triangle inequality, we have

$$\left\|\sum_{i=1}^{d} \nu_i T_i\right\|_A \leq \sum_{i=1}^{d} \|\nu_i T_i\|_A,$$

while by the Cauchy–Schwarz inequality, we obtain

$$\sum_{i=1}^{d} |\nu_i| \omega_A(T_i) \leq \left(\sum_{i=1}^{d} |\nu_i|^2\right)^{\frac{1}{2}} \left(\sum_{i=1}^{d} \omega_A^2(T_i)\right)^{\frac{1}{2}} \leq \left(\sum_{i=1}^{d} \omega_A^2(T_i)\right)^{\frac{1}{2}}$$

and

$$\sum_{i=1}^{d} |\nu_i| \frac{|\alpha_i - \beta_i|^2}{|\alpha_i + \beta_i|} \leq \left(\sum_{i=1}^{d} |\nu_i|^2\right)^{\frac{1}{2}} \left(\sum_{i=1}^{d} \frac{|\alpha_i - \beta_i|^4}{|\alpha_i + \beta_i|^2}\right)^{\frac{1}{2}}$$

$$\leq \left(\sum_{i=1}^{d} \frac{|\alpha_i - \beta_i|^4}{|\alpha_i + \beta_i|^2}\right)^{\frac{1}{2}}.$$

From (28), we then obtain

$$\left\|\sum_{i=1}^{d} \nu_i T_i\right\|_A \leq \left(\sum_{i=1}^{d} \omega_A^2(T_i)\right)^{\frac{1}{2}} + \frac{1}{4}\left(\sum_{i=1}^{d} \frac{|\alpha_i - \beta_i|^4}{|\alpha_i + \beta_i|^2}\right)^{\frac{1}{2}}$$

for all $(\nu_1, \ldots, \nu_d) \in \overline{\mathcal{B}}_d$.

By taking the supremum over $(\nu_1, \ldots, \nu_d) \in \overline{\mathcal{B}}_d$ and using the representation (3), we obtain (26).

The inequality (25) is equivalent for $x \in \mathbb{S}_A^1$ to

$$\|T_i x\|_A^2 - 2\Re\mathfrak{e}\left[\frac{\overline{\alpha_i + \beta_i}}{2} \langle T_i x, x \rangle_A\right] + \frac{1}{4}|\alpha_i + \beta_i|^2 \leq \frac{1}{4}|\alpha_i - \beta_i|^2$$

for $i \in \{1,\ldots,d\}$. Therefore,

$$\|T_i x\|_A^2 + \frac{1}{4}|\alpha_i + \beta_i|^2 \leq \frac{1}{4}|\alpha_i - \beta_i|^2 + 2\Re e\left[\frac{\overline{\alpha_i + \beta_i}}{2}\langle T_i x, x\rangle_A\right] \quad (29)$$

$$\leq \frac{1}{4}|\alpha_i - \beta_i|^2 + |\alpha_i + \beta_i|\left|\langle T_i x, x\rangle_A\right|$$

for $i \in \{1,\ldots,d\}$.

If we sum and apply the Cauchy–Schwarz inequality, we then obtain

$$\sum_{i=1}^{d}\|T_i x\|_A^2 + \frac{1}{4}\sum_{i=1}^{d}|\alpha_i + \beta_i|^2$$

$$\leq \frac{1}{4}\sum_{i=1}^{d}|\alpha_i - \beta_i|^2 + \sum_{i=1}^{d}|\alpha_i + \beta_i|\left|\langle T_i x, x\rangle_A\right|$$

$$\leq \frac{1}{4}\sum_{i=1}^{d}|\alpha_i - \beta_i|^2 + \left(\sum_{i=1}^{d}|\alpha_i + \beta_i|^2\right)^{\frac{1}{2}}\left(\sum_{i=1}^{d}\left|\langle T_i x, x\rangle_A\right|^2\right)^{\frac{1}{2}}.$$

On the other hand, an application of the arithmetic-geometric mean inequality shows that

$$\left(\sum_{i=1}^{d}\|T_i x\|_A^2\right)^{\frac{1}{2}}\left(\sum_{i=1}^{d}|\alpha_i + \beta_i|^2\right)^{\frac{1}{2}} \leq \sum_{i=1}^{d}\|T_i x\|_A^2 + \frac{1}{4}\sum_{i=1}^{d}|\alpha_i + \beta_i|^2.$$

Therefore, we deduce that

$$\left(\sum_{i=1}^{d}\|T_i x\|_A^2\right)^{\frac{1}{2}}\left(\sum_{i=1}^{d}|\alpha_i + \beta_i|^2\right)^{\frac{1}{2}}$$

$$\leq \frac{1}{4}\sum_{i=1}^{d}|\alpha_i - \beta_i|^2 + \left(\sum_{i=1}^{d}|\alpha_i + \beta_i|^2\right)^{\frac{1}{2}}\left(\sum_{i=1}^{d}\left|\langle T_i x, x\rangle_A\right|^2\right)^{\frac{1}{2}}.$$

If we take the supremum over all $x \in \mathbb{S}_A^1$, we obtain

$$\|\mathcal{T}\|_A\left(\sum_{i=1}^{d}|\alpha_i + \beta_i|^2\right)^{\frac{1}{2}} \leq \frac{1}{4}\sum_{i=1}^{d}|\alpha_i - \beta_i|^2 + \left(\sum_{i=1}^{d}|\alpha_i + \beta_i|^2\right)^{\frac{1}{2}}\omega_A(\mathcal{T}),$$

which gives (27). Hence, the proof is complete. □

An immediate application of Theorem 3 is derived in the next corollary.

Corollary 6. *Let* $\mathcal{T} = (T_1,\ldots,T_d) \in \mathbb{B}_{A^{1/2}}(\mathscr{H})^d$ *and* $\sigma, \rho \in \mathbb{C}$ *with* $\rho \neq \pm\sigma$. *Assume that*

$$\left\|T_j - \frac{\sigma + \rho}{2}I\right\|_A \leq \frac{1}{2}|\rho - \sigma| \quad (30)$$

for $i \in \{1,\ldots,d\}$. *Then,*

$$\|\mathcal{T}\|_{e,A} \leq \left(\sum_{i=1}^{d}\omega_A^2(T_i)\right)^{\frac{1}{2}} + \frac{1}{4}\sqrt{d}\frac{|\rho - \sigma|^2}{|\sigma + \rho|}$$

and

$$\|\mathcal{T}\|_A \leq \omega_A(\mathcal{T}) + \frac{1}{4}\sqrt{d}\frac{|\rho - \sigma|^2}{|\sigma + \rho|}.$$

Now, we state in the next lemma a reverse of the Cauchy–Schwarz inequality (see for instance ([29] p. 32) for a more general result).

Lemma 2. *Under the same assumptions of Lemma 1, we have*

$$\left(\sum_{j=1}^{d}|\zeta_j|^2\right)^{\frac{1}{2}} \leq \frac{1}{\sqrt{d}}\left(\left|\sum_{j=1}^{d}\zeta_j\right| + \frac{1}{4}d\frac{|\rho-\sigma|^2}{|\rho+\sigma|}\right). \tag{31}$$

We state our next result as follows.

Theorem 4. *Let $\mathcal{T} = (T_1,\ldots,T_d) \in \mathbb{B}_{A^{1/2}}(\mathcal{H})^d$ and $\sigma,\rho \in \mathbb{C}$ with $\rho \neq \pm\sigma$. Assume that*

$$\omega_A\left(T_j - \frac{\sigma+\rho}{2}I\right) \leq \frac{1}{2}|\rho-\sigma| \text{ for any } j \in \{1,\ldots,d\}. \tag{32}$$

Then,

$$\omega_A(\mathcal{T}) \leq \frac{1}{\sqrt{d}}\omega_A\left(\sum_{j=1}^{d}T_j\right) + \frac{1}{4}\sqrt{d}\frac{|\rho-\sigma|^2}{|\rho+\sigma|}.$$

Proof. Let $x \in \mathbb{S}_A^1$ and $\mathcal{T} = (T_1,\ldots,T_d) \in \mathbb{B}_{A^{1/2}}(\mathcal{H})^d$ with the property (32). By letting $\zeta_j = \langle T_j x, x\rangle_A$ and then proceeding as in the proof of Proposition 1, we see that

$$\left|\zeta_j - \frac{\sigma+\rho}{2}\right| \leq \omega_A\left(T_j - \frac{\sigma+\rho}{2}\right) \leq \frac{1}{2}|\rho-\sigma|,$$

for any $j \in \{1,\ldots,d\}$. So, by employing (31), we obtain

$$\left(\sum_{j=1}^{d}|\langle T_j x,x\rangle_A|^2\right)^{\frac{1}{2}} \leq \frac{1}{\sqrt{d}}\left(\left|\sum_{j=1}^{d}\langle T_j x,x\rangle_A\right| + \frac{1}{4}d\frac{|\rho-\sigma|^2}{|\rho+\sigma|}\right)$$

$$= \frac{1}{\sqrt{d}}\left(\left|\left\langle \sum_{j=1}^{d}T_j x,x\right\rangle_A\right| + \frac{1}{4}d\frac{|\rho-\sigma|^2}{|\rho+\sigma|}\right)$$

for every $x \in \mathbb{S}_A^1$. By taking the supremum over all $x \in \mathbb{S}_A^1$ in the last inequality, we reach the desired result. □

Remark 3. *Since $\omega_A(\mathcal{T}) \leq \|\mathcal{T}\|_A$, then (30) implies (32).*

Now, we aim to establish several reverse inequalities for the A-numerical radius of operators acting on semi-Hilbert spaces in both single and multivariable settings under some boundedness conditions for the operators. Our first new result in this context may be stated as follows.

Theorem 5. *Let $T \in \mathbb{B}_{A^{1/2}}(\mathcal{H})$ be such that $AT \neq 0$. If $\nu \in \mathbb{C}\setminus\{0\}$ and $r > 0$ are such that $|\nu| > r$ and*

$$\|T - \nu I\|_A \leq r,$$

then

$$\sqrt{1 - \frac{r^2}{|\nu|^2}} \leq \frac{\omega_A(T)}{\|T\|_A} \quad (\leq 1). \tag{33}$$

Proof. By (19), we have

$$\|T\|_A^2 + |\nu|^2 - r^2 \leq 2|\nu|\omega_A(T).$$

Dividing by $\sqrt{|v|^2 - r^2} > 0$, we obtain

$$\frac{\|T\|_A^2}{\sqrt{|v|^2 - r^2}} + \sqrt{|v|^2 - r^2} \leq \frac{2|v|\omega_A(T)}{\sqrt{|v|^2 - r^2}}. \tag{34}$$

Further, it is easy to verify that

$$2\|T\|_A \leq \frac{\|T\|_A^2}{\sqrt{|v|^2 - r^2}} + \sqrt{|v|^2 - r^2}.$$

So, by using (34), we deduce

$$\|T\|_A \leq \frac{\omega_A(T)|v|}{\sqrt{|v|^2 - r^2}},$$

which is immediately equivalent to (33). □

Remark 4. (1) Squaring the inequality (33), we obtain the following inequality:

$$(0 \leq) \|T\|_A^2 - \omega_A^2(T) \leq \frac{r^2}{|v|^2} \|T\|_A^2.$$

(2) For every operator $T \in \mathbb{B}_{A^{1/2}}(\mathscr{H})$, we have the relation $\omega_A(T) \geq \frac{1}{2}\|T\|_A$ (see [23]). Inequality (33) would produce an improvement of the above classic fact only in the case when

$$\frac{1}{2} \leq \left(1 - \frac{r^2}{|v|^2}\right)^{\frac{1}{2}},$$

which is, in turn, equivalent to $\frac{r}{|v|} \leq \frac{\sqrt{3}}{2}$.

The next corollary holds.

Corollary 7. Let $\alpha, \beta \in \mathbb{C}$ with $\mathfrak{Re}(\alpha\bar{\beta}) > 0$. Additionally, let $T \in \mathbb{B}_{A^{1/2}}(\mathscr{H})$ be such that $AT \neq 0$. Assume that either (21) or (23) holds. Then, we have

$$\frac{2\sqrt{\mathfrak{Re}(\alpha\bar{\beta})}}{|\alpha + \beta|} \leq \frac{\omega_A(T)}{\|T\|_A} (\leq 1) \tag{35}$$

and

$$(0 \leq) \|T\|_A^2 - \omega_A^2(T) \leq \left|\frac{\alpha - \beta}{\alpha + \beta}\right|^2 \|T\|_A^2.$$

Proof. If we consider $v = \frac{\alpha + \beta}{2}$ and $r = \frac{1}{2}|\alpha - \beta|$, then

$$|v|^2 - r^2 = \left|\frac{\alpha + \beta}{2}\right|^2 - \left|\frac{\alpha - \beta}{2}\right|^2 = \mathfrak{Re}(\alpha\bar{\beta}) > 0.$$

Now, by applying Theorem 5, we deduce the desired result. □

Remark 5. If $|\alpha - \beta| \leq \frac{\sqrt{3}}{2}|\alpha + \beta|$ and $\mathfrak{Re}(\alpha\bar{\beta}) > 0$, then (35) is a refinement of the inequality $\omega_A(T) \geq \frac{1}{2}\|T\|_A$.

Corollary 8. Let $\alpha, \beta \in \mathbb{C}$ with $\Re(\alpha\bar{\beta}) > 0$. Additionally, let $\mathcal{T} = (T_1, \ldots, T_d) \in \mathbb{B}_{A^{1/2}}(\mathcal{H})^d$ be such that the condition

$$\left\|T_j - \frac{\alpha + \beta}{2} I\right\|_A \leq \frac{1}{2}|\alpha - \beta| \tag{36}$$

is true for $i \in \{1, \ldots, d\}$. Then,

$$\|\mathcal{T}\|_{e,A} \leq \frac{|\alpha + \beta|}{2\sqrt{\Re(\alpha\bar{\beta})}} \left(\sum_{i=1}^{d} \omega_A^2(T_i)\right)^{\frac{1}{2}}. \tag{37}$$

Proof. Notice, first, that since (36) holds, then we infer that

$$\left\|T_i x - \frac{\alpha + \beta}{2} x\right\|_A \leq \frac{1}{2}|\alpha - \beta|,$$

for any $x \in \mathbb{S}_A^1$ and all $i \in \{1, \ldots, d\}$. Therefore, it follows from (35) that

$$\|T_i\|_A \leq \frac{|\alpha + \beta|}{2\sqrt{\Re(\alpha\bar{\beta})}} \omega_A(T_i)$$

for $i \in \{1, \ldots, d\}$.

Let $(v_1, \ldots, v_d) \in \overline{\mathbb{B}}_d$, multiply by $|v_i|$ and sum to obtain

$$\sum_{i=1}^{d} \|v_i T_i\|_A \leq \frac{|\alpha + \beta|}{2\sqrt{\Re(\alpha\bar{\beta})}} \sum_{i=1}^{d} |v_i| \omega_A(T_i).$$

Therefore, we see that

$$\left\|\sum_{i=1}^{d} v_i T_i\right\|_A \leq \sum_{i=1}^{d} \|v_i T_i\|_A$$

$$\leq \frac{|\alpha + \beta|}{2\sqrt{\Re(\alpha\bar{\beta})}} \sum_{i=1}^{d} |v_i| \omega_A(T_i).$$

$$\leq \frac{|\alpha + \beta|}{2\sqrt{\Re(\alpha\bar{\beta})}} \left(\sum_{i=1}^{d} |v_i|^2\right)^{\frac{1}{2}} \left(\sum_{i=1}^{d} \omega_A^2(T_i)\right)^{\frac{1}{2}}.$$

By taking the supremum over $(v_1, \ldots, v_d) \in \overline{\mathbb{B}}_d$ and using the representation (3), we obtain (37). □

In the next result, we prove under appropriate conditions a new relation connecting the joint A-seminorms $\|\cdot\|_A$ and $\omega_A(\cdot)$.

Proposition 2. Let $\alpha_i, \beta_i \in \mathbb{C}$ with $\Re(\alpha_i\bar{\beta}_i) > 0$ for all $i \in \{1, \ldots, d\}$. Additionally, let $\mathcal{T} = (T_1, \ldots, T_d) \in \mathbb{B}_{A^{1/2}}(\mathcal{H})^d$ be such that (25) is valid for $i \in \{1, \ldots, d\}$. Then,

$$\|\mathcal{T}\|_A \leq \frac{1}{2} \frac{\left(\sum_{i=1}^{d}|\alpha_i + \beta_i|^2\right)^{\frac{1}{2}}}{\left(\sum_{i=1}^{d}\Re(\alpha_i\bar{\beta}_i)\right)^{\frac{1}{2}}} \omega_A(\mathcal{T}). \tag{38}$$

Proof. From (29), we obtain

$$\|T_ix\|_A^2 + \frac{1}{4}|\alpha_i + \beta_i|^2 - \frac{1}{4}|\alpha_i - \beta_i|^2 \leq |\alpha_i + \beta_i|\left|\langle T_ix, x\rangle_A\right|$$

for $i \in \{1,\ldots,d\}$. This is equivalent to

$$\|T_ix\|_A^2 + \Re e(\alpha_i\bar{\beta}_i) \leq |\alpha_i + \beta_i|\left|\langle T_ix, x\rangle_A\right|$$

for $i \in \{1,\ldots,d\}$.

If we sum and then apply the Cauchy–Schwarz inequality, we then obtain

$$\sum_{i=1}^d \|T_ix\|_A^2 + \sum_{i=1}^d \Re e(\alpha_i\bar{\beta}_i) \leq \sum_{i=1}^d |\alpha_i + \beta_i|\left|\langle T_ix, x\rangle_A\right|$$

$$\leq \left(\sum_{i=1}^d |\alpha_i + \beta_i|^2\right)^{\frac{1}{2}} \left(\sum_{i=1}^d \left|\langle T_ix, x\rangle_A\right|^2\right)^{\frac{1}{2}}.$$

By applying the famous arithmetic–geometric mean inequality, we observe that

$$2\left(\sum_{i=1}^d \|T_ix\|_A^2\right)^{\frac{1}{2}}\left(\sum_{i=1}^d \Re e(\alpha_i\bar{\beta}_i)\right)^{\frac{1}{2}} \leq \sum_{i=1}^d \|T_ix\|_A^2 + \sum_{i=1}^d \Re e(\alpha_i\bar{\beta}_i).$$

Therefore,

$$\left(\sum_{i=1}^d \|T_ix\|_A^2\right)^{\frac{1}{2}} \leq \frac{1}{2}\frac{\left(\sum_{i=1}^d |\alpha_i+\beta_i|^2\right)^{\frac{1}{2}}}{\left(\sum_{i=1}^d \Re e(\alpha_i\bar{\beta}_i)\right)^{\frac{1}{2}}}\left(\sum_{i=1}^d \left|\langle T_ix, x\rangle_A\right|^2\right)^{\frac{1}{2}}$$

and by taking the supremum over $x \in \mathbb{S}_A^1$, we obtain (38). □

Remark 6. *With the assumptions of Corollary 8, we can prove that*

$$\|T\|_A \leq \frac{1}{2}\frac{|\alpha + \beta|}{\sqrt{\Re e(\alpha\bar{\beta})}}\omega_A(T).$$

The following lemma plays a fundamental role in the proof of our next proposition.

Lemma 3 ([29] p. 26). *If $\sigma, \rho \in \mathbb{C}$ and $\zeta_j \in \mathbb{C}, j \in \{1,\ldots,d\}$ with the property that $\Re e(\rho\bar{\sigma}) > 0$ and*

$$\left|\zeta_j - \frac{\sigma + \rho}{2}\right| \leq \frac{1}{2}|\rho - \sigma|$$

for each $j \in \{1,\ldots,d\}$, then

$$\sum_{j=1}^d |\zeta_j|^2 \leq \frac{1}{4d}\frac{|\rho + \sigma|^2}{\Re e(\rho\bar{\sigma})}\left|\sum_{j=1}^d \zeta_j\right|^2. \tag{39}$$

By proceeding as in the proof of Theorem 4 and using Lemma 3, we state without proof the following result.

Proposition 3. *Let $T = (T_1, \ldots, T_d) \in \mathbb{B}_{A^{1/2}}(\mathscr{H})^d$, $\sigma, \rho \in \mathbb{C}$ with $\mathfrak{Re}(\rho\bar{\sigma}) > 0$. Suppose that (32) is satisfied. Then,*

$$\omega_A(T) \leq \frac{|\alpha + \beta|}{2d\sqrt{\mathfrak{Re}(\alpha\bar{\beta})}} \omega_A\left(\sum_{j=1}^{d} T_j\right).$$

The following result also holds.

Theorem 6. *Let $T \in \mathbb{B}_{A^{1/2}}(\mathscr{H})$ and $v \in \mathbb{C}\setminus\{0\}$, $r > 0$ with $|v| > r$. If*

$$\|T - vI\|_A \leq r, \tag{40}$$

then

$$\|T\|_A^2 \leq \omega_A^2(T) + \frac{2r^2}{|v| + \sqrt{|v|^2 - r^2}} \omega_A(T). \tag{41}$$

Proof. Let $x \in \mathbb{S}_A^1$. It follows from (40) that

$$\|Tx - vx\|_A \leq \|T - vI\|_A \leq r,$$

which yields that

$$\|Tx\|_A^2 + |v|^2 \leq 2\mathfrak{Re}\left[\bar{v}\langle Tx, x\rangle_A\right] + r^2. \tag{42}$$

By using (42), it can be seen that $|v|\left|\langle Tx, x\rangle_A\right| \neq 0$. So, by taking (42) into account, we obtain

$$\frac{\|Tx\|_A^2}{|v|\left|\langle Tx, x\rangle_A\right|} \leq \frac{2\mathfrak{Re}\left[\bar{v}\langle Tx, x\rangle_A\right]}{|v|\left|\langle Tx, x\rangle_A\right|} + \frac{r^2}{|v|\left|\langle Tx, x\rangle_A\right|} - \frac{|v|}{\left|\langle Tx, x\rangle_A\right|}.$$

Moreover, we see that

$$\frac{\|Tx\|_A^2}{|v|\left|\langle Tx, x\rangle_A\right|} - \frac{\left|\langle Tx, x\rangle_A\right|}{|v|}$$

$$\leq \frac{2\mathfrak{Re}\left[\bar{v}\langle Tx, x\rangle_A\right]}{|v|\left|\langle Tx, x\rangle_A\right|} + \frac{r^2}{|v|\left|\langle Tx, x\rangle_A\right|} - \frac{\left|\langle Tx, x\rangle_A\right|}{|v|} - \frac{|v|}{\left|\langle Tx, x\rangle_A\right|}$$

$$= \frac{2\mathfrak{Re}\left[\bar{v}\langle Tx, x\rangle_A\right]}{|v|\left|\langle Tx, x\rangle_A\right|} - \frac{|v|^2 - r^2}{|v|\left|\langle Tx, x\rangle_A\right|} - \frac{\left|\langle Tx, x\rangle_A\right|}{|v|}$$

$$= \frac{2\mathfrak{Re}\left[\bar{v}\langle Tx, x\rangle_A\right]}{|v|\left|\langle Tx, x\rangle_A\right|} - \left(\frac{\sqrt{|v|^2 - r^2}}{\sqrt{|v|\left|\langle Tx, x\rangle_A\right|}} - \frac{\sqrt{\left|\langle Tx, x\rangle_A\right|}}{\sqrt{|v|}}\right)^2 - 2\frac{\sqrt{|v|^2 - r^2}}{|v|}.$$

Since

$$\mathfrak{Re}\left[\bar{v}\langle Tx, x\rangle_A\right] \leq |v|\left|\langle Tx, x\rangle_A\right|$$

and

$$\left(\frac{\sqrt{|v|^2 - r^2}}{\sqrt{|v|\left|\langle Tx, x\rangle_A\right|}} - \frac{\sqrt{\left|\langle Tx, x\rangle_A\right|}}{\sqrt{|v|}}\right)^2 \geq 0,$$

then, we deduce that

$$\frac{\|Tx\|_A^2}{|v||\langle Tx, x\rangle_A|} - \frac{|\langle Tx, x\rangle_A|}{|v|} \leq \frac{2\left(|v| - \sqrt{|v|^2 - r^2}\right)}{|v|},$$

which gives the inequality

$$\|Tx\|_A^2 \leq \left|\langle Tx, x\rangle_A\right|^2 + 2\left|\langle Tx, x\rangle_A\right|\left(|v| - \sqrt{|v|^2 - r^2}\right). \tag{43}$$

By taking the supremum over $x \in \mathbb{S}_A^1$ in (43), we obtain

$$\|T\|_A^2 \leq \omega_A^2(T) + 2\omega_A(T)\left(|v| - \sqrt{|v|^2 - r^2}\right). \tag{44}$$

So, we immediately obtain (41). □

By making use of the inequalities (44) and (43), we are ready to establish the next two corollaries as applications of our previous result.

Corollary 9. *Let $\rho, \sigma \in \mathbb{C}$ be such that $\rho \neq \sigma$ and $\Re(\rho\bar{\sigma}) \geq 0$. Additionally, let $T \in \mathbb{B}_{A^{1/2}}(\mathscr{H})$ be such that either (4) or (5) holds. Then:*

$$\|T\|_A^2 \leq \omega_A^2(T) + \left[|\rho + \sigma| - 2\sqrt{\Re(\rho\bar{\sigma})}\right]\omega_A(T). \tag{45}$$

Proof. Set $v := \frac{\rho+\sigma}{2}$ and $r := \frac{|\rho-\sigma|}{2}$. Clearly, $|v| > r$. Moreover, since (5) holds, then so is (40). So, the desired result follows by applying (44) and then observing that

$$|v|^2 - r^2 = \left|\frac{\rho+\sigma}{2}\right|^2 - \left|\frac{\rho-\sigma}{2}\right|^2 = \Re(\rho\bar{\sigma}). \tag{46}$$

□

Remark 7. *Assume that $T \in \mathbb{B}_A(\mathscr{H})$. If $\theta \geq \mu > 0$ are such that either $(T^{\dagger_A} - \mu I)(\theta I - T)$ is A-accretive or*

$$\left(T^{\dagger_A} - \mu I\right)(\theta I - T) \geq_A 0$$

then, by applying (45), we infer that

$$\|T\|_A^2 \leq \omega_A^2(T) + \left(\sqrt{\theta} - \sqrt{\mu}\right)^2 \omega_A(T).$$

Corollary 10. *Let $\mathcal{T} = (T_1, \ldots, T_d) \in \mathbb{B}_{A^{1/2}}(\mathscr{H})^d$ and $\rho_i, \sigma_i \in \mathbb{C}$ with $\rho_i \neq \sigma_i$, $\Re(\rho_i\bar{\sigma_i}) \geq 0$ for $i \in \{1, \ldots, d\}$. Assume that*

$$\left\|T_i - \frac{\rho_i + \sigma_i}{2}I\right\|_A \leq \frac{1}{2}|\rho_i - \sigma_i|, \tag{47}$$

for all $i \in \{1, \ldots, d\}$. Then,

$$\|\mathcal{T}\|_A^2 \leq \omega_A^2(\mathcal{T})\left[\sum_{i=1}^d \left(|\rho_i + \sigma_i| - 2\sqrt{\Re(\rho_i\bar{\sigma_i})}\right)^2\right]^{\frac{1}{2}} \omega_A(\mathcal{T}).$$

Proof. Let $x \in \mathbb{S}_A^1$. Set $v_i := \frac{\rho_i + \sigma_i}{2}$ and $r_i = \frac{|\rho_i - \sigma_i|}{2}$ for all $i \in \{1, \ldots, d\}$. Clearly, we have $|v_i| > r_i$ and $\|T_i - v_i I\|_A \leq r_i$ for every i. Thus, an application of (43) shows that

$$\|T_i x\|_A^2 \leq \left|\langle T_i x, x \rangle_A\right|^2 + 2\left|\langle T_i x, x \rangle_A\right|\left(|v_i| - \sqrt{|v_i|^2 - r_i^2}\right).$$

This yields, through (46), that

$$\|T_i x\|_A^2 \leq \left|\langle T_i x, x \rangle_A\right|^2 + \left(|\rho_i + \sigma_i| - 2\sqrt{\mathfrak{Re}(\rho_i \overline{\sigma_i})}\right)\left|\langle T_i x, x \rangle_A\right|$$

for $i \in \{1, \ldots, d\}$.

If we sum and then apply the Cauchy–Schwarz inequality, we then obtain

$$\sum_{i=1}^d \|T_i x\|_A^2$$

$$\leq \sum_{i=1}^d \left|\langle T_i x, x \rangle_A\right|^2 + \sum_{i=1}^d \left(|\rho_i + \sigma_i| - 2\sqrt{\mathfrak{Re}(\rho_i \overline{\sigma_i})}\right)\left|\langle T_i x, x \rangle_A\right|$$

$$\leq \sum_{i=1}^d \left|\langle T_i x, x \rangle_A\right|^2 + \left[\sum_{i=1}^d \left(|\rho_i + \sigma_i| - 2\sqrt{\mathfrak{Re}(\rho_i \overline{\sigma_i})}\right)^2\right]^{\frac{1}{2}} \left(\sum_{i=1}^d \left|\langle T_i x, x \rangle_A\right|^2\right)^{\frac{1}{2}}.$$

By taking the supremum over this inequality, we derive the desired result. □

Another application of the inequality (45) provides an upper bound for the Euclidean operator A-seminorm of d-tuples of operators in $\mathbb{B}_{A^{1/2}}(\mathcal{H})^d$ and stated in the next proposition.

Proposition 4. Let $\mathcal{T} = (T_1, \ldots, T_d) \in \mathbb{B}_{A^{1/2}}(\mathcal{H})^d$. Let also $\rho, \sigma \in \mathbb{C}$ with $\rho \neq \sigma$ and $\mathfrak{Re}(\rho \overline{\sigma}) \geq 0$. Suppose that

$$\left\|T_i x - \frac{\rho + \sigma}{2} x\right\|_A \leq \frac{1}{2}|\rho - \sigma|, \qquad (48)$$

for any $x \in \mathbb{S}_A^1$ and all $i \in \{1, \ldots, d\}$. Then,

$$\|\mathcal{T}\|_{e,A}^2 \leq d \max_{k \in \{1, \ldots, d\}} \omega_A(T_k) \left\{\max_{k \in \{1, \ldots, d\}} \omega_A(T_k) + \left[|\rho + \sigma| - 2\sqrt{\mathfrak{Re}(\rho \overline{\sigma})}\right]\right\}.$$

Proof. From (45), we see that

$$\|T_i\|_A^2 \leq \omega_A^2(T_i) + \left[|\rho + \sigma| - 2\sqrt{\mathfrak{Re}(\rho \overline{\sigma})}\right]\omega_A(T_i)$$

for $i \in \{1, \ldots, d\}$.

Let $(v_1, \ldots, v_d) \in \overline{\mathcal{B}}_d$, multiply by $|v_i|^2$ and sum to obtain

$$\sum_{i=1}^d |v_i|^2 \|T_i\|_A^2 \leq \sum_{i=1}^d |v_i|^2 \omega_A^2(T_i) + \left[|\rho + \sigma| - 2\sqrt{\mathfrak{Re}(\rho \overline{\sigma})}\right] \sum_{i=1}^d |v_i|^2 \omega_A(T_i)$$

$$\leq \left(\sum_{i=1}^d |v_i|^2\right) \max_{k \in \{1, \ldots, d\}} \omega_A^2(T_k)$$

$$+ \left(\sum_{i=1}^d |v_i|^2\right) \max_{k \in \{1, \ldots, d\}} \omega_A(T_k) \left[|\rho + \sigma| - 2\sqrt{\mathfrak{Re}(\rho \overline{\sigma})}\right]$$

$$\leq \max_{k \in \{1, \ldots, d\}} \omega_A^2(T_k) + \left[|\rho + \sigma| - 2\sqrt{\mathfrak{Re}(\rho \overline{\sigma})}\right] \max_{k \in \{1, \ldots, d\}} \omega_A(T_k).$$

Moreover, since
$$\frac{1}{d}\left\|\sum_{i=1}^{d} v_i T_i\right\|_A^2 \leq \sum_{i=1}^{d} |v_i|^2 \|T_i\|_A^2,$$
hence
$$\frac{1}{d}\left\|\sum_{i=1}^{d} v_i T_i\right\|_A^2 \leq \max_{k\in\{1,\ldots,d\}} \omega_A^2(T_k) + \left[|\rho+\sigma| - 2\sqrt{\Re e(\rho\bar\sigma)}\right] \max_{k\in\{1,\ldots,d\}} \omega_A(T_k).$$

By taking the supremum over $(v_1,\ldots,v_d) \in \overline{\mathbb{B}}_d$ and using the representation (3), we obtain the desired result. □

The next lemma plays a crucial role in establishing our final result in this paper.

Lemma 4 ([30]). *If $\sigma, \rho, \zeta_j \in \mathbb{C}$ are such that $\Re e(\rho\bar\sigma) > 0$ and*
$$\left|\zeta_j - \frac{\sigma+\rho}{2}\right| \leq \frac{1}{2}|\rho - \sigma|$$
for each $j \in \{1,\ldots,d\}$, then we have
$$\sum_{j=1}^{d} |\zeta_j|^2 \leq \left(\frac{1}{d}\left|\sum_{j=1}^{d}\zeta_j\right| + |\rho+\sigma| - 2\sqrt{\Re e(\rho\bar\sigma)}\right)\left|\sum_{j=1}^{d}\zeta_j\right|.$$

Now, we are ready to state our final proposition.

Proposition 5. *Let $\mathcal{T} = (T_1,\ldots,T_d) \in \mathbb{B}_{A^{1/2}}(\mathcal{H})^d$ and let $\rho, \sigma \in \mathbb{C}$ be such that $\rho \neq \sigma$, $\Re e(\rho\bar\sigma) > 0$. Assume that the condition (16) is valid. Then,*
$$\omega_A^2(\mathcal{T}) \leq \left[\frac{1}{d}\omega_A\left(\sum_{j=1}^{d} T_j\right) + |\rho+\sigma| - 2\sqrt{\Re e(\rho\bar\sigma)}\right]\omega_A\left(\sum_{j=1}^{d} T_j\right).$$

Proof. The proof follows by proceeding as in the proof of Proposition 2 and then taking Lemma 4 into consideration. □

3. Conclusions

In this paper, we established several inequalities involving the generalized Euclidean operator radius of d-tuples of A-bounded linear operators acting on a complex Hilbert space $\mathcal{H}$. The obtained bounds lead to the special case of the classical A-numerical radius of semi-Hilbert space operators. We proved also some estimates related to the Euclidean operator A-seminorm of d-tuples of A-bounded operators. In addition, we stated, under appropriate conditions, several reverse inequalities for the A-numerical radius in single and multivariable setting.

These inequalities can be further utilized to provide reverse triangle inequalities for the operator A-seminorm and A-numerical radius of semi-Hilbert space operators that play an important role in the geometrical structure of the A-inner product space under consideration.

Additionally, the techniques and ideas of this article can be useful for future investigations in this area of research. In future papers, we aim to investigate the connections between the joint A-numerical radius and joint operator A-seminorm of some special classes of multivariable operators such that the class of jointly A-hyponormal operators in semi-Hilbert spaces.

Author Contributions: The work presented here was carried out in collaboration between all authors. All authors contributed equally and significantly in writing this article. All authors have contributed to the manuscript. All authors have read and agreed to the published version of the manuscript.

Funding: Distinguished Scientist Fellowship Program, King Saud University, Riyadh, Saudi Arabia, Researchers Supporting Project number (RSP2023R187).

Data Availability Statement: Data is contained within the article.

Acknowledgments: The authors wish to express their deepest gratitude to the editor and the anonymous referees for their useful comments. The first author extends her appreciation to the Distinguished Scientist Fellowship Program at King Saud University, Riyadh, Saudi Arabia, for funding this work through Researchers Supporting Project number (RSP2023R187).

Conflicts of Interest: The authors declare no conflict of interest.

References

1. Bhunia, P.; Dragomir, S.S.; Moslehian, M.S.; Paul, K. *Lectures on Numerical Radius Inequalities*; Infosys Science Foundation Series in Mathematical Sciences; Springer: Berlin/Heidelberg, Germany, 2022.
2. Baklouti, H.; Namouri, S. Spectral analysis of bounded operators on semi-Hilbertian spaces. *Banach J. Math. Anal.* **2022**, *16*, 12. [CrossRef]
3. Baklouti, H.; Namouri, S. Closed operators in semi-Hilbertian spaces. *Linear Multilinear Algebra* **2022**, *70*, 5847–5858. [CrossRef]
4. Bhunia, P.; Kittaneh, F.; Paul, K.; Sen, A. Anderson's theorem and A-spectral radius bounds for semi-Hilbertian space operators. *Linear Algebra Appl.* **2023**, *657*, 147–162. [CrossRef]
5. Kittaneh, F.; Zamani, A. Bounds for $\mathbb{A}$-numerical radius based on an extension of A-Buzano inequality. *J. Comput. Appl. Math.* **2023**, *426*, 115070. [CrossRef]
6. Kittaneh, F.; Zamani, A. A refinement of A-Buzano inequality and applications to A-numerical radius inequalities. *Linear Algebra Appl.* **2023**, in press. [CrossRef]
7. Arias, M.L.; Corach, G.; Gonzalez, M.C. Partial isometries in semi-Hilbertian spaces. *Linear Algebra Appl.* **2008**, *428*, 1460–1475. [CrossRef]
8. Douglas, R.G. On majorization, factorization and range inclusion of operators in Hilbert space. *Proc. Amer. Math. Soc.* **1966**, *17*, 413–416. [CrossRef]
9. Arias, M.L.; Corach, G.; Gonzalez, M.C. Metric properties of projections in semi-Hilbertian spaces. *Integral Equ. Oper. Theory* **2008**, *62*, 11–28. [CrossRef]
10. Arias, M.L.; Corach, G.; Gonzalez, M.C. Lifting properties in operator ranges. *Acta Sci. Math.* **2009**, *75*, 635–653.
11. Feki, K. Spectral radius of semi-Hilbertian space operators and its applications. *Ann. Funct. Anal.* **2020**, *11*, 929–946. [CrossRef]
12. Abu-Omar, A.; Kittaneh, F. A generalization of the numerical radius. *Linear Algebra Appl.* **2019**, *569*, 323–334. [CrossRef]
13. Moradi, H.R.; Sababheh, M. More accurate numerical radius inequalities (II). *Linear Multilinear Algebra* **2021**, *69*, 921–933. [CrossRef]
14. Moradi, H.R.; Sababheh, M. New estimates for the numerical radius. *Filomat* **2021**, *35*, 4957–4962. [CrossRef]
15. Sababheh, M.; Moradi, H.R. More accurate numerical radius inequalities (I). *Linear Multilinear Algebra* **2021**, *69*, 1964–1973. [CrossRef]
16. Sababheh, M. Heinz-type numerical radii inequalities. *Linear Multilinear Algebra* **2019**, *67*, 953–964. [CrossRef]
17. Omidvar, M.E.; Moradi, H.R. New estimates for the numerical radius of Hilbert space operators. *Linear Multilinear Algebra* **2021**, *69*, 946–956. [CrossRef]
18. Omidvar, M.E.; Moradi, H.R. Better bounds on the numerical radii of Hilbert space operators. *Linear Algebra Appl.* **2020**, *604*, 265–277. [CrossRef]
19. Sattari, M.; Moslehian, M.S.; Shebrawi, K. Extension of Euclidean operator radius inequalities. *Math. Scand.* **2017**, *20*, 129–144.
20. Sheybani, S.; Sababheh, M.; Moradi, H.R. Weighted inequalities for the numerical radius. *Vietnam J. Math.* **2023**, *51*, 363–377. [CrossRef]
21. Sheikhhosseini, A.; Khosravi, M.; Sababheh, M. The weighted numerical radius. *Ann. Funct. Anal.* **2022**, *13*, 3. [CrossRef]
22. Yamazaki, T. On upper and lower bounds of the numerical radius and an equality condition. *Studia Math.* **2007**, *178*, 83–89. [CrossRef]
23. Baklouti, H.; Feki, K.; Ahmed, O.A.M.S. Joint numerical ranges of operators in semi-Hilbertian spaces. *Linear Algebra Appl.* **2018**, *555*, 266–284. [CrossRef]
24. Chō, M.; Takaguchi, M. Boundary points of joint numerical ranges. *Pac. J. Math* **1981**, *95*, 27–35. [CrossRef]
25. Müller, V. On joint numerical radius. *Proc. Am. Math. Soc.* **2014**, *142*, 1371–1380. [CrossRef]
26. Drnovšek, R.; Müller, V. On joint numerical radius II. *Linear Multilinear Algebra* **2014**, *62*, 1197–1204. [CrossRef]
27. Popescu, G. Unitary invariants in multivariable operator theory. *Mem. Am. Math. Soc.* **2009**, *200*, vi+91. [CrossRef]
28. Altwaijry, N.; Feki, K.; Minculete, N. A new seminorm for d-tuples of A-bounded operators and its applications. *Mathematics* **2023**, *11*, 685. [CrossRef]

29. Dragomir, S.S. *Advances in Inequalities of the Schwarz, Grüss and Bessel Type in Inner Product Spaces*; Nova Science Publishers, Inc.: Hauppauge, NY, USA, 2005.
30. Dragomir, S.S. Reverses of the Schwarz inequality generalising the Klamkin-McLeneghan result. *Bull. Austral. Math. Soc.* **2006**, *73*, 69–78. [CrossRef]

Disclaimer/Publisher's Note: The statements, opinions and data contained in all publications are solely those of the individual author(s) and contributor(s) and not of MDPI and/or the editor(s). MDPI and/or the editor(s) disclaim responsibility for any injury to people or property resulting from any ideas, methods, instructions or products referred to in the content.

Article

Reinsurance Policy under Interest Force and Bankruptcy Prohibition

Yangmin Zhong [1] and Huaping Huang [2,*]

1   School of Law, Shanghai University of Finance and Economics, Shanghai 200433, China; zhongyangmin15@163.sufe.edu.cn
2   School of Mathematics and Statistics, Chongqing Three Gorges University, Wanzhou 404020, China
*   Correspondence: huaping@sanxiau.edu.cn

Abstract: In this paper, we solve an optimal reinsurance problem in the mathematical finance area. We assume that the surplus process of the insurance company follows a controlled diffusion process and the constant interest rate is involved in the financial model. During the whole optimization period, the company has a choice to buy reinsurance contract and decide the reinsurance retention level. Meanwhile, the bankruptcy at the terminal time is not allowed. The aim of the optimization problem is to minimize the distance between the terminal wealth and a given goal by controlling the reinsurance proportion. Using the stochastic control theory, we derive the Hamilton-Jacobi-Bellman equation for the optimization problem. Via adopting the technique of changing variable as well as the dual transformation, an explicit solution of the value function and the optimal policy are shown. Finally, several numerical examples are shown, from which we find several main factors that affect the optimal reinsurance policy.

Keywords: Hamilton-Jacobi-Bellman equation; stochastic optimal control; dynamic programming principle; dual transformation

MSC: 93E20; 91G30

Citation: Zhong, Y.; Huang, H. Reinsurance Policy under Interest Force and Bankruptcy Prohibition. *Axioms* **2023**, *12*, 378. https://doi.org/10.3390/axioms12040378

Academic Editor: Behzad Djafari-Rouhani

Received: 22 March 2023
Revised: 12 April 2023
Accepted: 13 April 2023
Published: 16 April 2023

Copyright: © 2023 by the authors. Licensee MDPI, Basel, Switzerland. This article is an open access article distributed under the terms and conditions of the Creative Commons Attribution (CC BY) license (https:// creativecommons.org/licenses/by/ 4.0/).

1. Introduction

The optimal reinsurance problem has a long history in the actuarial science. An insurance company has the option of transferring parts of premiums to a reinsurance company to reduce the payment of large claims. In the academic field, regarding the reinsurance problem, Ref. [1] studied the optimal dividend payout problem of the insurer by controlling the dividend as well as the risk exposure. Ref. [2] explored the optimal controlled reinsurance proportion and investment to maximize the expected utility at the terminal time in which the surplus is modelled by a perturbed classical risk process. Ref. [3] dealt with the non-proportional reinsurance schemes to minimize the ruin probability when the surplus follows a continuous diffusion model. For more past developments about reinsurance optimization, we refer interested readers to the excellent books [4,5].

In our model, we consider an insurance company that aims to reach a given goal at the terminal time. During the whole time period, the company has the choice to buy the reinsurance contract and decide the reinsurance retention level. Ref. [6] explored the optimal reinsurance problem while aiming to minimize the distance between the terminal wealth and a given goal. Unlike [6], besides a given goal, we also set up a bankruptcy prohibition for the insurance company, which means that the terminal wealth is not allowed to drop below 0. There are several works that concerns the ruin prohibition and control optimizations in the financial modelling area. As an example, Ref. [7] studied a mean-variance portfolio selection optimization problem where the surplus process is not allowed to drop below 0 at any time. Ref. [8] studied the optimal reinsurance and investment optimization with bankruptcy prohibition under the mean-variance criterion. Ref. [9] solved the optimal mean-risk portfolio problem aiming to minimize the expected payoff in a complete market.

There is an important element, that is, the interest rate, in the financial market. The government uses the interest rate as an instrument to control the geometry of the economy. In general, the interest rate will usually decrease if the central bank discovers that the current economic situation is weak. The capital market is very sensitive about the interest rate, which means that the money will gradually flow out of the bank to product with high investment returns or consumption, houses, cars, restaurants, and so on. Vice versa, when there is too much money in the market, which causes inflation, the central bank will raise the interest rate and the money from the stock market, funds, or real estate will slowly flow to banks. In our model, we assume that the interest rate is a constant, in other words, during the whole optimization phase the economy is steady. There is fruitful research about the constant interest rate in the area of actuarial science. As an example, Ref. [10] studied the ruin probability of the compound Poisson model in the finite time horizon under constant interest force. Ref. [11] studied the optimal dividend problem of an insurance company under constant interest force. One can also see [12–15] for more studies about the effect of interest rate in actuarial science. In our paper, although the interest rate is a constant, mathematical difficulty is still an issue. Affected by the interest rate, the target and the ruin prohibition are mathematically expressed as two curved boundaries, which cause the main difficulties in mathematical calculation.

We usually use stochastic optimal control theory to solve some optimization problems. By applying the stochastic control theory, the Hamilton-Jacobi-Bellman (for short, HJB) can be derived. By solving an explicit classical solution for the HJB equation, the corresponding optimal strategy and the optimal value function of the optimization problem can also be solved. As the mentioned above, in our model, due to the bankruptcy prohibition and the target of the terminal time, there are three boundary conditions (including two curved boundaries) in the HJB equation, which cause the main difficulty to solve the equation. We adopt the changing of the variable technique to simplify the curved boundary conditions. After the change of variable, the new HJB equation is a fully nonlinear partial differential equation (for short, PDE). To solve such a PDE, the dual transformation technique is used to convert the fully nonlinear PDE to a semilinear PDE. After calculating an explicit solution to the semilinear PDE, we can derive an explicit solution to the optimal policy.

The rest of the paper is constructed as follows. Section 2 introduces the surplus model and the optimization problem of the insurance company and then shows the HJB equation of the optimization problem. Section 3 presents the changing of the variable technique to simplify the original problem. We derive a new optimization problem and the corresponding HJB equation. In Section 4, the dual transformation is used and an explicit solution of the HJB equation is shown. A verification theorem is presented to prove that the solution to the HJB equation is indeed the value function of the optimization problem. Section 5 presents several numerical examples to depict the impacts of different parameters on the optimal strategy.

2. The Model

Denote $(\Omega, \mathscr{F}, \mathbb{P})$ as a complete probability space with filtration $\{\mathscr{F}_t\}_{t \geq 0}$. In the reality, the insurance company will receive premiums from individuals and then undertake possible loss for the insurant. Following the financial mathematical model of [16], we assume that the aggregate cumulative claims up to time t are written as follows:

$$C_t = mt - nB_t,$$

where $m > 0$ represents the expected loss in a unit time; $n > 0$ is the diffusion volatility rate; and B_t is a standard Brownian motion, which is adapted to the filtration $\{\mathscr{F}_t\}$. We assume that the insurance company sets the premium rate as $(1 + \xi)m$, where $\xi > 0$ is a constant representing the safety loading of the insurance contract. Denote i as the interest rate of the financial market, where $i > 0$ is a positive constant. Then, the dynamics of the surplus of the insurance company can be mathematically expressed as follows:

$$dY_t = iY_t dt + (1+\xi)mdt - (mdt - ndB_t).$$

Now, we add the feature of reinsurance in our model. We assume that the insurance company will transfer a proportion of claims to the reinsurance company. At the same time, parts of the premium will also be transferred to the reinsurance company. Mathematically speaking, at the time t, the retention level of the insurance company is denoted by q_t, where $q_t \geq 0$; the other proportion $1 - q_t$ of claims will be paid by the reinsurance company. Meanwhile, the parts of the premium rate $(1+\varrho)(1-q_t)m$ will be transferred to the reinsurance company from the insurance company, where $\varrho > 0$ is the safety loading of the reinsurance company. We assume that $\varrho > \xi$, which means that the reinsurance is non-cheap. Denote $Y(s;t,y,q(\cdot))$ as the surplus process of the insurance company with the initial data (t,y) and strategy $q(\cdot)$.

In what follows, denote $Y_t^q := Y(s;t,y,q(\cdot))$ for simplicity when there is no confusion. Then, the surplus process of the insurance company can be rewritten as

$$dY_t^q = iY_t^q dt + (\xi - \varrho + \varrho q_t)mdt + q_t n dB_t. \tag{1}$$

Let $T > 0$ be a finite time horizon. We assume that there is a non-bankruptcy constraint at the terminal time T for the insurance company. In other words, for any reinsurance strategy q, Y_T^q should be non-negative. To satisfy such a condition, at the time $t \in [0, T]$, if the surplus is

$$Y_t^q = \frac{\xi - \varrho}{i} m(e^{i(t-T)} - 1),$$

then for any time $s \in [t, T]$, the null strategy $q_s = 0$ should be invoked to make sure that $Y_T^q = 0$. Actually, when $Y_t^q = \frac{\xi - \varrho}{i} m(e^{i(t-T)} - 1)$, if there exists a time $s \in [t, T]$ such that $q_s \neq 0$, then there is always a positive probability that $Y_T^q < 0$ due to the Brownian motion in Equation (1).

On the other hand, if there exists a time $t \in [0, T]$ such that the wealth

$$Y_t^q < \frac{\xi - \varrho}{i} m(e^{i(t-T)} - 1),$$

then no matter which strategy is chosen, there is always a positive probability that the terminal wealth $Y_T^q < 0$. Eventually, the restriction of non-bankruptcy means that for any time $t \in [0, T]$, the surplus should satisfy

$$Y_t^q \geq \frac{(\xi - \varrho)m}{i}\left(e^{i(t-T)} - 1\right). \tag{2}$$

Now, we show a formal definition of the set of admissible strategies. For the initial time $t \in [0, T)$ and the initial wealth $y \in \left[\frac{(\xi-\varrho)m}{i}\left(e^{i(t-T)} - 1\right), +\infty\right)$, the set of admissible strategies is denoted by

$$\hat{D}_{t,y} := \Big\{ q(\cdot) \in L^2(\Omega \times [t, T]) | q(\cdot) \text{ is progressively measurable, } q(\cdot) \geq 0,$$
$$\forall s \in [t, T], Y(s; t, y, q(\cdot)) \geq \frac{\xi - \varrho}{i} m\left(e^{i(s-T)} - 1\right) \Big\}. \tag{3}$$

In the model presented in this paper, we assume that the insurance company with a certain scale aims to achieve a given goal G for the surplus at the terminal time T, where $G > 0$ is a constant. We define the loss function to measure the expected discounted distance between the final wealth and the goal:

$$\tilde{L}(t, y; q(\cdot)) = \mathbb{E}\left(e^{-\varepsilon T}(Y_T^q - G)^2\right), \tag{4}$$

where $\varepsilon > 0$ represents a discount factor to reflect the time value.

For any initial time $t \in [0, T]$ and initial wealth $y \geq \frac{(\xi-\varrho)m}{i}(e^{i(t-T)} - 1)$, the insurance company aims to minimize the loss function by choosing the optimal reinsurance policy. Now, we analyze more details about the constraints of surplus. If the initial wealth is

$$y = Ge^{i(t-T)} + \frac{(\xi-\varrho)m}{i}(e^{i(t-T)} - 1),$$

where t is the initial time, then the null strategy $q_t \equiv 0$ will be invoked so that $y_T^q = G$ and the loss function is minimized with value 0. If the initial wealth

$$y_t > Ge^{i(t-T)} + \frac{(\xi-\varrho)m}{i}(e^{i(t-T)} - 1),$$

this kind of situation is not in consideration since it is meaningless to reach the goal G when the initial value is large enough. Eventually, combining with Equation (2), we can narrow down the domain of the surplus to

$$\left[\frac{(\xi-\varrho)m}{i}(e^{i(t-T)} - 1), Ge^{i(t-T)} + \frac{(\xi-\varrho)m}{i}(e^{i(t-T)} - 1)\right].$$

Until now, the set of all admissible strategies $\hat{D}_{t,y}$ in (3) can be replaced by

$$\tilde{D}_{t,y} := \left\{ q(\cdot) \in L^2(\Omega \times [t,T]) | q(\cdot) \text{ is progressively measurable, } q(\cdot) \geq 0,\right.$$

$$\left. \forall s \in [t,T], \frac{\xi-\varrho}{i}m(e^{i(s-T)} - 1) \leq Y(s; t, y, q(\cdot)) \leq Ge^{i(s-T)} + \frac{(\xi-\varrho)m}{i}(e^{i(s-T)} - 1)\right\}.$$

Now, we define the value function as follows:

$$\tilde{S}(t, y) = \inf_{q \in \tilde{D}_{t,y}} \tilde{L}(t, y; q(\cdot)). \tag{5}$$

In what follows, for simplicity, denote

$$g_0(t) := \frac{(\xi-\varrho)m}{i}(e^{i(t-T)} - 1), \quad g_1(t) := Ge^{i(t-T)} + \frac{(\xi-\varrho)m}{i}(e^{i(t-T)} - 1), t \in [0, T].$$

By using the dynamic programming principle, the HJB equation of the optimization problem (5) is

$$\inf_{q \geq 0}\left\{\tilde{s}_t + \tilde{s}_y(iy + \xi - \varrho + \varrho q) + \frac{1}{2}\tilde{s}_{yy}m^2q^2\right\} = 0, \tag{6}$$

with the following boundary conditions:

$$\begin{cases} \tilde{s}(T, y) = e^{-\varepsilon T}(G - y)^2, & y \in [0, G], \\ \tilde{s}(t, g_1(t)) = 0, & t \in [0, T], \\ \tilde{s}(t, g_0(t)) = e^{-\varepsilon T}G^2, & t \in [0, T]. \end{cases} \tag{7}$$

From the theory of dynamic programming principle, as long as we find a continuously differentiable solution for (6) and (7), then such a solution $\tilde{s}$ equals the value function $\tilde{S}$, which is defined in (5). One can refer to [17] for the standard proof of such a conclusion.

Unfortunately, there are several complex boundaries in (7). Solving such an equation can be quite difficult. Thus, we seek the help of the changing variable that was used in [18] to simplify the boundary conditions in the next section.

3. Changing of Variable

Define the diffeomorphism $Q : [0,T] \times [0,G] \to \Psi$, where $\Psi := \{(t,y)|t \in [0,T], g_0(t) \le y \le g_1(t)\}$ and

$$(t,z) \to (t,y) = Q(t,z) = (t, Q_1(t,z)) =: \left(t, ze^{-i(T-t)} + \frac{(\xi-\varrho)m}{i}(e^{-i(T-t)} - 1)\right). \quad (8)$$

For any strategy $q(\cdot) \in \tilde{D}_{t,y}$, $Z(\cdot;t,z,q(\cdot)) := [Q_1(s,\cdot)]^{-1}(Y(\cdot;t,y,q(\cdot)))$, in which $z = Q_1^{-1}(t,y)$. We also denote $Z_s^q := Z(s;t,z,q(\cdot))$ for simplicity when there is no confusion. We can obtain that

$$Z_t^q := [Q_1(t,\cdot)]^{-1}(Y_t^q), t \in [0,T],$$

which leads to

$$Z_t^q = e^{i(T-t)}Y_t^q + \frac{(\xi-\varrho)m}{i}(e^{i(T-t)} - 1).$$

By some simple calculations, we see that

$$dZ_t^q = e^{i(T-t)}(\varrho q_t m dt + q_t n dB_t).$$

Moreover, for any given $s \in [0,T]$, if $Y_s^q = g_0(t)$, then $Z_s^q = 0$; if $Y_s^q = g_1(t)$, then $Z_s^q = G$. Regarding the new dynamics of Z_s^q, the set of all admissible strategies can be written as

$$D_{t,z} := \Big\{ q(\cdot) \in L^2(\Omega \times [t,T]) \big| q(\cdot) \text{ is progressively measurable, } q(\cdot) \ge 0,$$
$$\forall s \in [t,T], 0 \le Z(s;t,z,q(\cdot)) \le G \Big\}.$$

For any $(t,z) \in [0,T] \times [0,G]$, in terms of $Z(\cdot;t,z,q(\cdot))$, the original loss function (4) can be transformed to

$$L(t,z;q(\cdot)) = \mathbb{E}\big(e^{-\varepsilon T}(Z_T^q - G)^2\big).$$

The new value function is defined as

$$S(t,z) := \inf_{q(\cdot) \in D_{t,z}} L(t,z;q(\cdot)). \quad (9)$$

Now, we pay attention to solving the optimization problem (9). Again, by using the dynamic programming principle, the new version of the HJB equation is written by

$$\inf_{q \ge 0}\Big\{ s_t + e^{i(T-t)}\varrho q m s_z + \frac{1}{2}e^{2i(T-t)}q^2 n^2 s_{zz} \Big\} = 0, \quad \text{for all } (t,z) \in [0,T) \times (0,G), \quad (10)$$

with the boundary conditions:

$$\begin{cases} s(T,z) = e^{-\varepsilon T}(G-z)^2, & z \in [0,G], \\ s(t,G) = 0, & t \in [0,F], \\ s(t,0) = e^{-\varepsilon T}G^2, & t \in [0,T]. \end{cases} \quad (11)$$

As stated in Section 2, a continuously differentiable solution for (10) and (11) equals the value function defined in (9). Before solving Equations (10) and (11), we explore some properties of the value function.

Proposition 1. *The value function S defined in (9) is a decreasing function with regard to the variable z.*

We omit the proof since the conclusion is obvious.

Proposition 2. *The value function defined in (9) is convex on the variable z.*

Proof. For any $\beta > 0$, let $q^{\beta,z_1}, q^{\beta,z_2}$ be the β-optimal policies with initial data $(t, z_1), (t, z_2)$, respectively, i.e.,

$$L(t, z_1; q^{\beta,z_1}(\cdot)) \leq S(t, z_1) + \beta,$$
$$L(t, z_2; q^{\beta,z_2}(\cdot)) \leq S(t, z_2) + \beta.$$

Notice that
$$dZ_t^q = e^{i(T-t)}(\varrho q_t m dt + q_t n dB_t).$$

Denote $Z(s; t, z_1, q^{\beta,z_1}) =: Z_{1s}$, $Z(s; t, z_2, q^{\beta,z_2}) =: Z_{2s}$ for simplicity. For any fixed $\lambda \in (0,1)$, let $R_s := \lambda Z_{1s} + (1-\lambda) Z_{2s}$ and the corresponding reinsurance strategy of the surplus R_s be $q^{\beta,r} := \lambda q^{\beta,z_1} + (1-\lambda) q^{\beta,z_2}$, where $r = \lambda z_1 + (1-\lambda) z_2$. Then, we can obtain that

$$\lambda S(t, z_1) + (1-\lambda) S(t, z_2) \geq \lambda L(t, z_1; q^{\beta,z_1}) + (1-\lambda) L(t, z_2; q^{\beta,z_2}) - \beta$$
$$= \lambda \mathbb{E}\left(e^{-\varepsilon T}(Z_{1T} - G)^2\right) + (1-\lambda) \mathbb{E}\left(e^{-\varepsilon T}(Z_{2T} - G)^2\right) - \beta \quad (12)$$
$$\geq \mathbb{E}\left(e^{-\varepsilon T}(R_T - G)^2\right) - \beta,$$

where the last inequality is due to the convexity of the function $x \mapsto (x-G)^2$. Combining (12) with the fact that

$$\mathbb{E}\left(e^{-\varepsilon T}(R_T - G)^2\right) \geq S(t, r),$$

we obtain that

$$S(t, z_1) + (1-\lambda) S(t, z_2) \geq S(t, \lambda z_1 + (1-\lambda) z_2) - \beta.$$

Since $\beta > 0$ is arbitrary, the convexity of the value function on the variable z is proved. □

Remark 1. *By the definition of $\tilde{S}$ and S, i.e., Equations (5) and (9), for any $(t, y) \in [0, T] \times [0, G]$, it satisfies $S(t, z) = \tilde{S}(t, Q_1(t, z))$, where Q_1 is defined in (8). For any fixed time $t \in [0, T]$, the mapping $y \mapsto Q_1(t, y)$ is linear. Due to linearity, the convexity of $S(t, z)$ on z is equivalent to the convexity of $\tilde{S}(t, y)$ on the variable y. Proposition 2 implies that the value function $\tilde{S}(t, y)$ is also convex on y.*

In what follows, we attempt to solve a continuously differentiable convex solution for the HJB Equations (10) and (11).

4. Solving the HJB Equation

If there exists a continuously differentiable solution s for (10), then the minimizer of (10) is

$$q^* = -\frac{\varrho m s_z}{e^{i(T-t)} n^2 s_{zz}}. \quad (13)$$

Substitute (13) into (10) it gives

$$s_t = \frac{\varrho^2 m^2 s_z^2}{2n^2 s_{zz}}. \qquad (14)$$

Differentiate (14) with respect to z it leads to

$$s_{tz} = \frac{2\varrho^2 m^2 s_z s_{zz}^2 - \varrho^2 m^2 s_z^2 s_{zzz}}{2n^2 s_{zz}^2}. \qquad (15)$$

In this section, the dual transformation is used to transfer the above fully nonlinear PDE to a semilinear PDE. For each $(t, l) \in [0, T] \times (0, +\infty)$, define the mapping by

$$[0, G] \to \mathbb{R}^+, z \mapsto s(t, z) + zl,$$

where $\mathbb{R}^+$ denotes the set of positive real numbers. Assume that for any given (t, l), $\tau(t, l) \in (0, G)$ is the unique minimizer of $s(t, z) + zl$. If the function s is smooth enough, then the minimizer satisfies

$$s_z(t, \tau(t, l)) = -l. \qquad (16)$$

Differentiate (16) with respect to t, l it gives

$$s_{tz}(t, \tau(t, l)) + s_{zz}(t, \tau(t, l))\tau_t = 0, \qquad (17)$$
$$s_{zz}(t, \tau(t, l))\tau_l(t, l) = -1, \qquad (18)$$
$$s_{zzz}(t, \tau(t, l))\tau_l^2(t, l) + s_{zz}(t, \tau(t, l))\tau_{ll}(t, l) = 0. \qquad (19)$$

Substituting (16)–(19) into (15), we have

$$\tau_t(t, l) + hl\tau_l(t, l) + \frac{h}{2}l^2\tau_{ll}(t, l) = 0, \qquad (20)$$

where $h := \frac{\varrho^2 m^2}{n^2}$ is a positive constant. Combining with the boundary condition $s(T, z) = e^{-\varepsilon T}(G - z)^2$ of (11), we have

$$\tau(T, l) = (-\frac{l}{2}e^{\varepsilon T} + G) \vee 0. \qquad (21)$$

Following the similar analysis of [19], we can obtain the other two boundary conditions as follows:

$$\tau(t, 0) = G, \qquad \lim_{l \to +\infty} \tau(t, l) = 0.$$

Apparently, (20) admits a Kolmogorov probabilistic representation of

$$\tau(t, l) = \mathbb{E}[\tau(T, \Lambda(T; t, l))], \qquad (22)$$

where $\Lambda(\cdot; t, l)$ satisfies the following stochastic differential equation:

$$\begin{cases} d\Lambda(s) = h\Lambda(s)ds + \sqrt{h}\Lambda(s)d\tilde{B}_s, & s \in (t, T], \\ \Lambda(t) = l, \end{cases}$$

in which $\tilde{B}_s$ is a standard Brownian motion. Obviously, it is easy to see that

$$\Lambda(s; t, y) = \Lambda(t) \exp\left\{\frac{h}{2}(s - t) + \sqrt{h}(B_s - B_t)\right\}, s \geq t. \qquad (23)$$

Combining (22), (23) with (21) it leads to

$$\tau(t,l) = \mathbb{E}\left[\left(G - \frac{l\exp\{\frac{h}{2}(T-t) + \sqrt{h}(\tilde{B}_T - \tilde{B}_t) + \varepsilon T\}}{2}\right) \vee 0\right].$$

Using the fact that $\tilde{B}_T - \tilde{B}_t$ follows a normal distribution, we can directly calculate that

$$\begin{cases} \tau(t,l) = G\Phi\left(\frac{\ln(\frac{2G}{l}) - \frac{h(T-t)}{2} - \varepsilon T}{\sqrt{h(T-t)}}\right) \\ \quad - \frac{l\exp\{\varepsilon T + h(T-t)\}}{2}\Phi\left(\frac{\ln(\frac{2G}{l}) - \frac{h(T-t)}{2} - \varepsilon T}{\sqrt{h(T-t)}} - \sqrt{h(T-t)}\right), t \in [0,T), \\ \tau(T,l) = (G - \frac{l\exp\{\varepsilon T\}}{2}) \vee 0, \end{cases} \quad (24)$$

where Φ is the distribution function of standard normal distribution. Now, we are ready to show an expression of the solution to the HJB Equations (10) and (11).

Proposition 3. *Let τ be the function defined in (24), and define*

$$\begin{cases} s(t,z) = e^{-\varepsilon T}G^2 - \int_0^z [\tau(t,\cdot)]^{-1}(v)dv, & (t,z) \in [0,T) \times [0,G], \\ s(T,z) = e^{-\varepsilon T}(G-z)^2, \end{cases} \quad (25)$$

where $[\tau(t,\cdot)]^{-1}$ denotes the inverse function of τ. Then, $s(t,z)$ is a classical solution of (10) and (11).

This conclusion follows the direct calculations. Now, we show that the solution defined in Proposition 3 equals to the value function of the optimization problem (9), which is also called the verification theorem.

Theorem 1. *For any $(t,z) \in [0,T) \times [0,G]$, $s(t,z) = S(t,z)$, where $s(t,z)$ is defined in (25). Furthermore, the optimal strategy of optimization problem (9) is as follows:*

$$q^*(t,z) = \begin{cases} -\frac{\varrho m s_z}{e^{i(T-t)}n^2 s_{zz}}, & (t,z) \in [0,T) \times (0,G), \\ 0, & (t,z) \in [0,T) \times \{0,G\}. \end{cases} \quad (26)$$

Proof. We only prove the case of $(t,z) \in [0,T) \times (0,G)$ since the case of $[0,T) \times \{0,G\}$ is trivial.

For any admissible strategy $q \in D_{t,z}$ and initial state (t,z), denote Z_s^q as the corresponding surplus process under the strategy q. Define the stopping time

$$\gamma := T \wedge \gamma_0 \wedge \gamma_G,$$

where $\gamma_0 := \inf\{s|Z_s^q = 0, s \in [t,T]\}$ and $\gamma_G := \inf\{s|Z_s^q = G, s \in [s,T]\}$. Applying the Itô formula to $s(\gamma, Z_\gamma^q)$ and taking expectation on both sides of the Itô formula, we arrive at

$$\mathbb{E}\left(s(\gamma, Z_\gamma^q)\right)$$
$$= s(t,z) + \mathbb{E}\left[\int_t^\gamma \left(\frac{\partial s}{\partial t}(s, Z_s^q) + e^{i(T-t)}\varrho q_s m \frac{\partial s}{\partial z}(s, Z_s^q) + \frac{1}{2}e^{i(T-s)}q_s^2 n^2 \frac{\partial^2 s}{\partial z^2}(s, Z_s^q)\right)ds\right]. \quad (27)$$

Since the function s solves (10), we obtain that

$$\mathbb{E}\left[\int_t^\gamma \left(\frac{\partial s}{\partial t}(s, Z_s^q) + e^{i(T-t)}\varrho q_s m \frac{\partial s}{\partial z}(s, Z_s^q) + \frac{1}{2}e^{i(T-s)}q_s^2 n^2 \frac{\partial^2 s}{\partial z^2}(s, Z_s^q)\right)ds\right] \geq 0. \quad (28)$$

Substitute (28) into (27) it gives

$$\mathbb{E}\left(s(\gamma, Z_\gamma^q)\right) \geq s(t,z). \quad (29)$$

Combining (29) with the boundary conditions (11), we obtain that

$$s(t,z) \leq \mathbb{E}\big(e^{-\varepsilon T}(Z_T^q - G)^2\big) = L(t,z;q(\cdot)).$$

Take the infimum over the set, $D_{t,z}$, $s(s,z) \leq S(t,z)$ is proved.

On the other hand, using the standard verification arguments and combining the admissibility of q^* and the fact that s solves the HJB Equations (10) and (11), we can show that $L(t,z;q^*(\cdot)) = s(t,z)$, which implies that q^* is optimal. For more arguments about verification, one can refer to [17]. □

We have completely solved the optimal value function and the optimal policy for the optimization problem (9). In the following remark, we show the optimal policy for the original optimization problem (5) via Equation (8).

Remark 2. *For each $(t,y) \in [0,T) \times [g_0(t), g_1(t)]$, the policy defined by*

$$\begin{cases} q^* = -\dfrac{\varrho m s_z(t, Q_1^{-1}(t,y))}{e^{i(T-t)} n^2 s_{zz}(t, Q_1^{-1}(t,y))}, & (t,y) \in [0,T) \times (g_0(t), g_1(t)), \\ 0, & (t,y) \in [0,T) \times \{g_0(t), g_1(t)\}, \end{cases}$$

is the optimal policy of the initial optimization problem (5).

5. Numerical Example

Now we present several examples to vividly show the optimal policy and the value function.

Example 1. *We assume that the parameters are as follows. The goal of the terminal time $G = 10$; the interest rate $i = 0.15$; the discount factor $\varepsilon = 0.2$; and the safety loading parameters $\varrho = 0.4$, $\xi = 0.2$. The expected loss in unit time $m = 1$, and the diffusion volatility rate $n = 0.5$. The terminal time T is assumed to be 5.*

Figure 1 presents the value function of $s(1,z)$. Apparently, Figure 1 shows that the value function is decreasing and convex on the variable z, which verifies Propositions 1 and 2. Figure 2 shows the optimal policy of the different initial value z at time 1. As we can see, the reinsurance retention proportion will first increase and then decrease with respect to the wealth. This can explain that when the wealth is close to 0 or close to the target, the insurance company will prefer to transfer all of the risky claims to the reinsurance company and invest money on the risk-less asset.

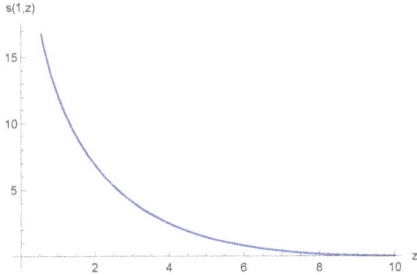

Figure 1. The optimal value function s with respect to z at time $t = 1$.

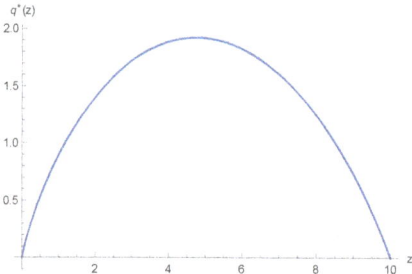

Figure 2. The optimal reinsurance policy with respect to z at time $t = 1$.

Example 2. *In this example, we use the same parameters as in Example 1, except that we change the time $t = 1, 2, 3$, respectively, and see the effect of the time variable on the optimal policy. Figure 3 shows the optimal reinsurance policy with respect to variable z at different times $t = 1, 2, 3$. As we can see, as time passes, the reinsurance retention proportion increases, which means that the insurance company would like to undertake more risks when the time is close to the deadline.*

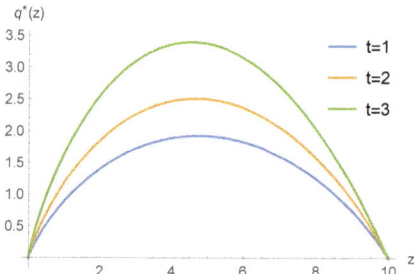

Figure 3. The optimal reinsurance policy with respect to z at time $t = 1, 2, 3$.

Example 3. *In this example, we use the same parameters as in Example 1, except that we change the interest rate $i = 0.5, 0.1, 0.15$, respectively. Figure 4 shows the effect of different interest rates on the optimal policy. As we can see, as the interest rate increases, the reinsurance retention proportion decreases, which means that the insurance company will prefer to invest more on the risk-less asset when the interest rate increases. This phenomenon is consistent with common sense because when the interest rates rise, investors are more inclined to keep their money in the bank.*

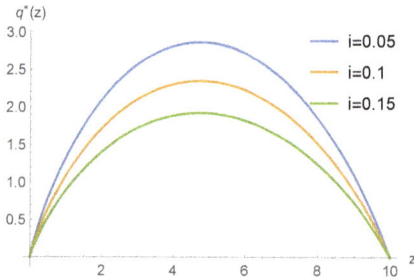

Figure 4. The optimal reinsurance policy with respect to z under different interest rates $i = 0.05, 0.1, 0.15$.

Example 4. *In this example, we use the same parameters as in Example 1 except that we change the diffusion volatility rate n. As n increases, the risk of large claims also increases. As shown in Figure 5, as n increases, the reinsurance retention level decreases. In other words, if the claim risk is* too high, the insurance company will prefer to transfer risks to the reinsurance company instead of keeping premiums.

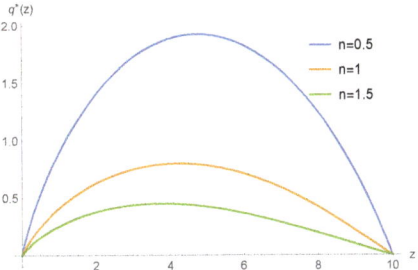

Figure 5. The optimal reinsurance policy with respect to z under different volatility rates $n = 0.5, 1, 1.5$.

Example 5. *In this example, we still use the same parameters as in Example 1 except the reinsurance safety loading ϱ. Figure 6 shows the optimal reinsurance retention level with different reinsurance safety loadings. The increasing of safety loading means that the reinsurance contract is more expensive. Thus, the optimal choice is to increase the reinsurance retention level so that the insurer can keep more premiums in the insurance company.*

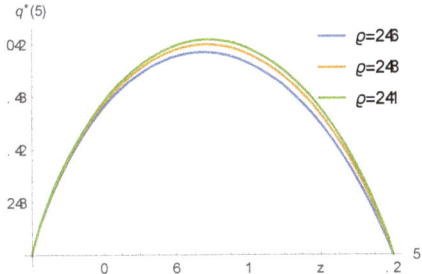

Figure 6. The optimal reinsurance policy with respect to z with different reinsurance safety loading $\varrho = 0.4, 0.5, 0.6$.

Example 6. *In this example, we still use the same parameters as in Example 1, except we change the expected loss in each unit time $m = 1, 1.5, 2$, respectively. Figure 7 shows that when m increases, the reinsurance retention level will also increase. This can be explained by the fact that when the parameter m increases, the insurance company obtains more premiums so that the optimal choice for the insurance company is to pull up the insurance retention level.*

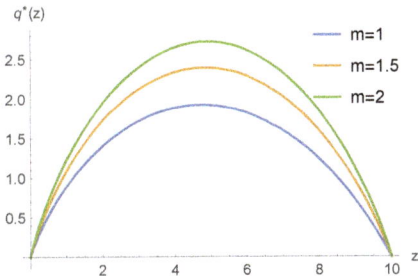

Figure 7. The optimal reinsurance policy under different expected losses in unit time $m = 1, 1.5, 2$.

6. Conclusions

As an application of probability, this paper explores a reinsurance optimization problem that has multiple curved boundaries. To simplify the optimization problem, the technique of changing variables is used. After changing variables, we adopt the dual transformation to solve the new HJB equation. Eventually, an explicit expression of the value function as well as the optimal policy is shown. With some numerical experiments, we list several important influential factors that affect the reinsurance retention level in Table 1. For simplicity, the notation ↑ means "increases" and ↓ means "decreases". Table 1 shows that the current time, the interest rate, the diffusion volatility rate, the reinsurance safety loading, and the expected loss in unit time will simultaneously affect the optimal reinsurance policy.

Table 1. Factors that affect reinsurance policy.

The Influence Factor	Insurance Retention Level
Time t ↑	↑
Interest rate i ↑	↓
Diffusion volatility rate n ↑	↓
Reinsurance safety loading ϱ ↑	↑
Expected loss in unit time m ↑	↑

Author Contributions: Y.Z. designed the research and wrote the paper. H.H. gave the methodology and the support of funding acquisition. All authors have read and agreed to the published version of the manuscript.

Funding: The work was sponsored by the Natural Science Foundation of Chongqing (cstc2020jcyj-msxmX0762, CSTB2022NSCQ-MSX0290) and the Talent Initial Funding for Scientific Research of Chongqing Three Gorges University (20190020).

Institutional Review Board Statement: Not applicable.

Informed Consent Statement: Not applicable.

Data Availability Statement: The data presented in this study are available upon request from the corresponding author.

Acknowledgments: The authors thank the editor and the referees for their valuable comments and suggestions, which improved greatly the quality of this paper.

Conflicts of Interest: The authors declare no conflict of interest.

References

1. Jøjgaard, B.H.; Taksar, M. Controlling risk exposure and dividends payout schemes: Insurance company example. *Math. Financ.* **1999**, *9*, 153–182. [CrossRef]
2. Irgens, C.; Paulsen, J. Optimal control of risk exposure, reinsurance and investments for insurance portfolios. *Insur. Math. Econ.* **2004**, *35*, 21–51. [CrossRef]
3. Hipp, C.; Taksar, M. Optimal non-proportional reinsurance control. *Insur. Math. Econ.* **2010**, *47*, 246–254. [CrossRef]
4. Azcue, P.; Muler, N. *Stochastic Optimization in Insurance: A Dynamic Programming Approach*; Springer: New York, NY, USA, 2014.
5. Schmidli, H. *Stochastic Control in Insurance*; Springer: London, UK, 2008.
6. Bäuerle, N. Benchmark and mean-variance problems for insurers. *Math. Meth. Oper. Res.* **2005**, *62*, 159–165. [CrossRef]
7. Bielecki, T.R.; Jin, H.; Pliska, S.R.; Zhou, X.Y. Continuous-time mean-variance portfolio selection with bankruptcy prohibition. *Math. Financ.* **2005**, *15*, 213–244. [CrossRef]
8. Bi, J.; Meng, Q.; Zhang, Y. Dynamic mean-variance and optimal reinsurance problems under the no-bankruptcy constraint for an insurer. *Ann. Oper. Res.* **2014**, *212*, 43–59. [CrossRef]
9. Wong, K.C.; Yam, S.C.P.; Zeng, J. Mean-risk portfolio management with bankruptcy prohibition. *Insur. Math. Econ.* **2019**, *85*, 153–172. [CrossRef]

10. Tang, Q. The finite-time ruin probability of the compound Poisson model with constant interest force. *J. Appl. Probab.* **2005**, *42*, 608–619. [CrossRef]
11. Albrecher, H.; Thonhauser, S. Optimal dividend strategies for a risk process under force of interest. *Insur. Math. Econ.* **2008**, *43*, 134–149. [CrossRef]
12. Gao, Q.; Zhuang, J.; Huang, Z. Asymptotics for a delay–claim risk model with diffusion, dependence structures and constant force of interest. *J. Comput. Appl. Math.* **2019**, *353*, 219–231. [CrossRef]
13. Chen, C.; Wang, S. Asymptotic ruin probability for a by–claim risk model with pTQAI claims and constant interest force. *Commun. Stat. Theory Methods* **2020**, *49*, 4367–4377. [CrossRef]
14. Geng, B.; Liu, Z.; Wang, S. On asymptotic finite–time ruin probabilities of a new bidimensional risk model with constant interest force and dependent claims. *Stoch. Models* **2021**, *37*, 608–626. [CrossRef]
15. Liu, X.; Gao, Q. Uniform asymptotics for the compound risk model with dependence structures and constant force of interest. *Stochastics* **2022**, *94*, 191–211. [CrossRef]
16. Liang, X.; Palmowski, Z. A note on optimal expected utility of dividend payments with proportional reinsurance. *Scand. Actuar. J.* **2018**, *4*, 275–293. [CrossRef]
17. Pham, H. *Continuous-Time Stochastic Control and Optimization with Financial Applications*; Springer: Berlin, Germany, 2009.
18. Dadashi, H. Optimal investment strategy post retirement without ruin possibility: A numerical algorithm. *J. Comput. Appl. Math.* **2020**, *363*, 325–336. [CrossRef]
19. Di Giacinto, M.; Federico, S.; Gozzi, F.; Vigna, E. *Constrained Portfolio Choices in the Decumulation Phase of a Pension Plan*; Carlo Alberto Notebooks, No. 155; 2010. Available online: http://ssrn.com/abstract=1600130 (accessed on 21 March 2023).

Disclaimer/Publisher's Note: The statements, opinions and data contained in all publications are solely those of the individual author(s) and contributor(s) and not of MDPI and/or the editor(s). MDPI and/or the editor(s) disclaim responsibility for any injury to people or property resulting from any ideas, methods, instructions or products referred to in the content.

Article

Self-Improving Properties of Continuous and Discrete Muckenhoupt Weights: A Unified Approach

Maryam M. Abuelwafa [1], Ravi P. Agarwal [2], Safi S. Rabie [1] and Samir H. Saker [1,*]

[1] Department of Mathematics, Faculty of Science, Mansoura University, Mansoura 35516, Egypt; room949@yahoo.com (M.M.A.)
[2] Department of Mathematics, Texas A & M University-Kingsville, Kingsville, TX 78363, USA; ravi.agarwal@tamuk.edu
* Correspondence: shsaker@mans.edu.eg

Abstract: In this paper, we develop a new technique on a time scale $\mathbb{T}$ to prove that the self-improving properties of the Muckenhoupt weights hold. The results contain the properties of the weights when $\mathbb{T} = \mathbb{R}$ and when $\mathbb{T} = \mathbb{N}$, and also can be extended to cover different spaces such as $\mathbb{T} = h\mathbb{N}$, $\mathbb{T} = q^{\mathbb{N}}$, etc. The results will be proved by employing some new refinements of Hardy's type dynamic inequalities with negative powers proven and designed for this purpose. The results give the exact value of the limit exponent as well as the new constants of the new classes.

Keywords: dynamic Hardy's type inequality; Muckenhoupt weights; self-improving properties; time scales

MSC: 26D07; 42B25; 42C10

1. Introduction

A weight u is a non-negative locally integrable function defined on a bounded interval $\hat{J}_0 \subset \mathbb{R}_+ = [0, \infty)$. We consider subintervals $\hat{J}$ of $\hat{J}_0$ of the form $[0, t]$, for $0 < t < \infty$ and denote by $|\hat{J}|$ the Lebesgue measure of $\hat{J}$. A weight u which satisfies

$$\frac{1}{|\hat{J}|}\int_{\hat{J}} u(t)dt \leq \mathcal{C} \operatorname*{ess\,inf}_{t \in \hat{J}} u(t), \text{ for all } t \in \hat{J}, \quad (1)$$

is called an $A^1(\mathcal{C})$– Muckenhoupt weight, where $\mathcal{C} > 1$. In [1], the author proved that if u is a monotonic weight that satisfies the condition (1), then there exists $p \in [1, \mathcal{C}/(\mathcal{C}-1)]$ such that

$$\frac{1}{|\hat{J}|}\int_{\hat{J}} u^p(t)dt \leq \frac{\mathcal{C}}{\mathcal{C} - p(\mathcal{C}-1)} \left(\frac{1}{|\hat{J}|}\int_{\hat{J}} u(t)dt\right)^p, \quad (2)$$

which is the reverse of Hölder's inequality. In [2], the authors improved the Muckenhoupt inequality (2) by establishing the best constant for any weight u, which is not necessarily monotonic. Their proof was obtained by using the rearrangement u^* of the function u over the interval $\hat{J}_0$. In particular, they proved that if u satisfies (1) with $\mathcal{C} > 1$, then

$$\frac{1}{|\hat{J}|}\int_{\hat{J}} u^p(t)dt \leq \frac{\mathcal{C}^{1-p}}{\mathcal{C} - p(\mathcal{C}-1)} \left(\frac{1}{|\hat{J}|}\int_{\hat{J}} u(t)dt\right)^p, \quad (3)$$

for $p < \mathcal{C}/(\mathcal{C}-1)$. A non-negative measurable weight u is called an $\mathcal{A}^p(\mathcal{C})$–Muckenhoupt weight for $p > 1$, if there exists a constant $\mathcal{C} > 1$, such that the inequality

$$\left(\frac{1}{|\hat{J}|}\int_J u(t)dt\right)\left(\frac{1}{|\hat{J}|}\int_J u^{-\frac{1}{p-1}}(t)dt\right)^{p-1} \leq C, \qquad (4)$$

holds for every subinterval $\hat{J} \subset \hat{J}_0$. The smallest constant C satisfying (1) or (4) is called the $\mathcal{A}^p$−norm of the weight u and is denoted by $[\mathcal{A}^p(u)]$. For a given fixed constant, $C > 1$ if the weight $u \in \mathcal{A}^p$ then $[\mathcal{A}^p(u)] \leq C$. In 1972, Muckenhoupt [1] introduced the full characterizations of $\mathcal{A}^p$−weights in connection with the boundedness of the Hardy and Littlewood maximal operator in the space $L_u^p(\mathbb{R}_+)$. In [3], the authors proved that if $u \in L^p(\mathbb{R}_+)$ and satisfies (4), then

$$\left(\frac{1}{|\hat{J}|}\int_J u(t)dt\right)\left(\frac{1}{|\hat{J}|}\int_J u^{-\frac{1}{q-1}}(t)dt\right)^{q-1} \leq C_1, \qquad (5)$$

for all $q < p$, where the constant $C_1 = C_1(q, C)$. In other words, Muckenhoupt's result for the *self-improving* property states that $u \in \mathcal{A}^p(C) \Rightarrow \exists\, \epsilon > 0$ such that $u \in \mathcal{A}^{p-\epsilon}(C_1)$, and then

$$\mathcal{A}^p(C) \subset \mathcal{A}^{p-\epsilon}(C_1). \qquad (6)$$

The properties of Muckenhoupt class have been deeply investigated, especially in one dimension, and the following aspects have been considered extensively:

(h_1). *Finding the exact value of the limit exponent q for which the self-improving property holds;*

(h_2). *Finding the best constants C_1 for which the improved $\mathcal{A}^q$− condition is satisfied.*

Some great work in the problems of finding the exact bounds of exponents for embedding (6) was achieved in many papers, see for example, [1,2,4–11]. Since it is impossible to give an exhaustive account of the results related to the problems under consideration, we shall dwell only on some of them, concerned with sharp results for a self-improving property given by Korenovskii [12]. In particular, Korenovskii found the sharp lower bound of the exponent (*self-improving property*), for which (6) holds and proved that the optimal integrability exponent q is the positive root of the equation

$$\frac{1}{x}\left(\frac{p-1}{p-x}\right)^{p-1} = C, \qquad (7)$$

and also found the explicit value of the constant of the new class. One of the most significant characteristics of the $\mathcal{A}^p$ Muckenhoupt weights is the extrapolation theorem that was announced, and a detailed proof was given, by Rubio de Francia in [13,14]. Many results related to this topic have been studied by several authors (see [15–22]).

Over the past few years, the interest in the area of discrete harmonic analysis has been renovated and it became an active field of research. This renovated interest began with an observation of M. Riesz in their work on the Hilbert transform in 1928, who proved that the Hilbert discrete operator

$$Hf(n) := \sum_{m\in\mathbb{Z}_+} \frac{f(n-m)}{m},$$

is bounded in ℓ^p−spaces if the operator

$$Hf(x) := p.v. \int_{\mathbb{R}} \left(\frac{f(x-t)}{t}\right) dt,$$

is bounded in L^p−spaces. In 1952, Alberto Calderón and Antoni Zygmund [23] extended the results to a more general class of singular integral operators with kernels. It is worth mentioning that the progress in the last years regarding discrete analogues of operators in harmonic analysis is related with Calderón–Zygmund analogues, discrete maximal operators and related problems with number theory, translation invariant fractional integral operators, translation invariant singular Radon transforms, quasi-translation invariant operators, spherical averages and discrete rough maximal functions; we suggest the reader to consider the paper [24] and the references cited therein.

As performed by Hughes (see [25] and the references therein), the discrete operators are nicely connected to critical problems in number theory. For example, Waring's problem, which questions whether each natural number k is associated with a positive integer s satisfying that every natural number is the sum of at most s natural numbers raised to the power k. This problem has been extended to find the the operator $G(k)$, which is defined to be the smallest positive integer s so that every sufficiently large integer (i.e., every integer greater than some constant) can be illustrated as a sum of no more than s positive integers to the power of k. Throughout the paper, we assume that $1 < p < \infty$ and assume that the discrete weights are positive sequences defined on $J \subset \mathbb{Z}_+ = \{1,2,3,\dots\}$, where J is of the form $\{1,2,\dots,N\}$. The notion X^d denotes the set of all nonincreasing and non-negative sequences of X. The discrete weight v is said to be in the discrete Muckenhoupt $\mathcal{A}_p$ class for $p > 1$, if there exists a constant $A > 1$ satisfying the inequality

$$\left(\frac{1}{n}\sum_{k=1}^n v(k)\right)\left(\frac{1}{n}\sum_{k=1}^n v^{\frac{-1}{p-1}}(k)\right)^{p-1} \leq A, \text{ for all } n \in J. \tag{8}$$

The discrete v is said to be in the discrete Ariño and Muckenhoupt $\mathcal{B}_p$ class for $p > 0$, if there exists a constant $A > 1$ such that the inequality

$$\sum_{k=n}^\infty \frac{v(k)}{k^p} \leq \frac{A}{n^p}\sum_{k=1}^n v(k), \text{ for all } n \in J. \tag{9}$$

The necessary and sufficient conditions for the boundedness of a series of discrete classical operators (Hardy–Littlewood maximal operator, Hardy's operator) in the weighted spaces $\ell^p(v)$ are the $\mathcal{A}_p$–Muckenhoupt condition, $\mathcal{B}_p$–condition on the weight v. In [26], the authors proved that the discrete Hardy–Littlewood maximal operator $\mathcal{M} : \ell^p(v)^d \to \ell^p(v)$, which is defined by

$$\mathcal{M}f(n) = \sup_{n \in J} \frac{1}{n}\sum_{k=1}^n f(k), \text{ for all } n \in J,$$

is bounded on $\ell^p(v)^d$ for $p > 1$ if and only if $v \in \mathcal{A}_p$. In [27], Heing and Kufner proved that the Hardy operator $\mathcal{H} : \ell^p(v)^d \to \ell^p(v)$, which is defined by

$$\mathcal{H}f(n) = \frac{1}{n}\sum_{k=1}^n f(k), \text{ for all } n \in J,$$

is bounded in $\ell^p(v)^d$ for $1 < p < \infty$ if and only if $v \in \mathcal{B}_p$ and $\lim_{n\to\infty}(v(n+1)/v(n)) = c$ for some constant $c > 0$ and $\sum_{n=1}^\infty v(n) = \infty$. In [28], Bennett and Gross-Erdmann improved the result of Heing and Kufner by excluding the conditions on v. In [29], the authors proved that the discrete Hardy operator is bounded in $\ell^p(v)^d$ for $p > 1$ if and only if $v \in \mathcal{A}_p$. The discrete weight v is said to be belong to the discrete Muckenhoupt $\mathcal{A}_1$–class if there exists a constant $A > 0$ such that the inequality $\mathcal{H}u(n) \leq A \inf_{n \in J} u(n)$, or equivalently $\mathcal{M}u(n) \leq Au(n)$, holds for all $n \in J$. In [29], the authors proved the self-improving property of the weighted discrete Muckenhoupt classes. They established also the exact values of the limit exponents as well as new constants of the new classes. These values correspond to the sharp values of the continuous case that has been obtained by Nikolidakis (see [7,8]). For more details of discrete results, we refer the reader to the papers [30–34].

In [28], the authors marked that the study of discrete inequalities is not a simple mission, and it is in fact more complicated to analyze than its integral counterparts. They discovered that the conditions do not coincide, in any natural way, with those that are obtained by discretization of the results of functions but the reverse is true. In other words, the results satisfied for sums holds, with the obvious modifications, for integrals which in fact proved the first part of basic principle of Hardy, Littlewood and Polya [35]. Obviously the proofs in the discrete form are transferred instantly and much more simpler, when applied to integrals.

The natural questions which arise now are as follows:

(Q_1). Is it possible to find a new approach to unify the proofs of the self-improving properties of continuous and discrete Muckenhoupt weights?

(Q_2). Is it possible to prove the self-improving properties of Ariño and Muckenhoupt B_p weights?

Our aim in this paper is to give an answer to the first question on time scales, which has received much attention and become a major field in pure and applied mathematics today. The second question will be considered later.

The general idea on time scales is to prove a result for dynamic inequality or dynamic equation, where the domain of the unknown function is a so-called time scale $\mathbb{T}$, which is an arbitrary nonempty closed subset of the real numbers $\mathbb{R}$. This idea has been created by Hilger [36] to unify the study of the continuous and the discrete results. He started the study of dynamic equations on time scales. The three most popular examples of calculus on time scales are differential calculus, difference calculus and quantum calculus, i.e., when $\mathbb{T} = \mathbb{R}$, $\mathbb{T} = \mathbb{N}$, $\mathbb{T} = h\mathbb{N}$, for $h > 0$ and $\mathbb{T} = q^{\mathbb{N}_0} = \{q^t : t \in \mathbb{N}_0\}$ where $q > 1$. The cases when the time scale is equal to the reals or to the integers represent the classical theories of integral and of discrete inequalities. In more precise terms, we can say that the study of dynamic inequalities or dynamic equations on time scales helps avoid proving results twice—once for differential inequality and once again for difference inequality. For more details we refer to the books [37,38] and the references they have cited. Very recently, the authors in [39–43] proved the time scale versions of the Muckenhoupt and Gehring inequalities and used them to prove some higher integrability results on time scales. This also motivated us to develop a new technique on time scales to prove some new results of inequalities with weights and use the new inequalities to formulate some conditions for the boundedness of the Hardy operator with negative powers on time scales and show the applications of the obtained results.

The paper is organized as follows: In Section 2, we prove some Hardy's type inequalities and new refinements of these inequalities with negative powers. In Section 3, we will employ some of these inequalities to prove the self-improving properties of the Muckenhoupt class on a time scale $\mathbb{T}$ for non-negative and nondecreasing weights. The main results give a solution on time scales of the problem of finding the exact value of the limit exponent $q < p$, for which the self-improving property holds and also for the problem of finding the best constants C_1 for which the improved A_q-condition satisfies (h_1) and (h_2) above.

2. Hardy's Type Inequalities with Negative Powers

In this section, we prove some Hardy's type inequalities and the new refinements of these inequalities with negative powers. First, we recall the following concepts related to the notions of time scales and for more details, we refer to the two books [44,45] which summarize and organize much of the time scale calculus. A function $f : \mathbb{T} \to \mathbb{R}$ is called right-dense continuous (rd-continuous) if f is continuous at left-dense points and right dense-points in $\mathbb{T}$, and left-side limits exist and are finite. The set $C_{rd}(\mathbb{T}) = C_{rd}(\mathbb{T}, \mathbb{R})$ denotes the set of all rd-continuous functions $f : \mathbb{T} \to \mathbb{R}$. The derivative of the product fg and the quotient f/g (where $gg^\sigma \neq 0$, here $g^\sigma = g \circ \sigma$) of two differentiable functions f and g are given by

$$(fg)^\Delta = fg^\Delta + f^\Delta g^\sigma = f^\Delta g + f^\sigma g^\Delta, \text{ and } \left(\frac{f}{g}\right)^\Delta = \frac{f^\Delta g - fg^\Delta}{gg^\sigma},$$

where $\sigma = \sigma(t) := \inf\{s \in \mathbb{T} : s > t\}$ is the forward jump operator on a time scale. Let $f : \mathbb{R} \to \mathbb{R}$ be continuously differentiable and suppose that $g : \mathbb{T} \to \mathbb{R}$ is delta differentiable. Then $f \circ g : \mathbb{T} \to \mathbb{R}$ is delta differentiable and the two chain rules that we will use in this paper are given in the next two formulas.

$$f^\Delta(g(t)) = f'(g(\xi))g^\Delta(t), \quad \text{for } \xi \in [t, \sigma(t)], \tag{10}$$

and

$$(f \circ g)^\Delta(t) = \left\{\int_0^1 f'\big(g(t) + h\mu(t)g^\Delta(t)\big)dh\right\}g^\Delta(t). \tag{11}$$

A special case of (11) is

$$\left[u^\lambda(t)\right]^\Delta = \lambda \int_0^1 [hu^\sigma + (1-h)u]^{\lambda-1} u^\Delta(t) dh. \tag{12}$$

In this paper, we will refer to the (delta) integral which, we can define as follows: If $G^\Delta(t) = g(t)$, then the Cauchy (delta) integral of g is defined by $\int_a^t g(x)\Delta x := G(t) - G(a)$. If $g \in C_{rd}(\mathbb{T})$, then the Cauchy integral $G(t) := \int_{t_0}^t g(x)\Delta x$ exists, $t_0 \in \mathbb{T}$, and satisfies $G^\Delta(t) = g(t)$, $t \in \mathbb{T}$. An infinite integral is defined as $\int_a^\infty f(x)\Delta x := \lim_{b \to \infty} \int_a^b f(x)\Delta x$. The integration on discrete time scales is defined by

$$\int_a^b g(t)\Delta t = \sum_{t \in [a,b)} \mu(t)g(t).$$

The integration by parts formula on time scale is given by

$$\int_a^\infty u^\Delta(t) v^\sigma(t)\,\Delta t = u(t)v(t)\big|_a^\infty - \int_a^\infty u(t)v^\Delta(t)\Delta t. \tag{13}$$

The Hölder inequality on the time scale is given by

$$\int_a^\infty f(t)g(t)\Delta t \le \left(\int_a^\infty f^\gamma(t)\Delta t\right)^{\frac{1}{\gamma}} \left(\int_a^\infty g^\nu(t)\Delta t\right)^{\frac{1}{\nu}}, \tag{14}$$

where $\gamma > 1$, $1/\gamma + 1/\nu = 1$ and $f, g \in C_{rd}([a, \infty)_\mathbb{T}, \mathbb{R}^+)$. The inequality (14) is reversed for $0 < \gamma < 1$. In the following, we will assume that $0 \in \mathbb{T}$ and $\mathbb{I} = [0, \infty)_\mathbb{T}$. Throughout this paper, we will assume that the functions in the statements of the theorems are rd-continuous functions and the integrals considered are assumed to exist and be finite. In addition, in our proofs, we will use the convention $0.\infty = 0$ and $0/0 = 0$. Throughout the paper, we assume that $1 < p < \infty$ and $\mathbb{I}$ is a fixed finite interval from $[0, \infty)_\mathbb{T}$. We define the time scale interval $[a, b]_\mathbb{T}$ by $[a, b]_\mathbb{T} := [a, b] \cap \mathbb{T}$. A weight ω defined on $\mathbb{T}$ is a Δ−integrable function of non-negative real numbers. We consider the norm on $L^p(\mathbb{T})$ of the form

$$\|\omega\|_{L^p(\mathbb{T})} := \left(\int_0^\infty |\omega(s)|^p \Delta s\right)^{1/p} < \infty.$$

A non-negative Δ−integrable function ω belongs to the Muckenhoupt class $\mathbb{A}^1(\mathcal{C})$ on the fixed interval $\mathbb{I} = [0, \infty)_\mathbb{T}$ if there exists a constant $\mathcal{C} > 1$ such that the inequality

$$\frac{1}{|\hat{\jmath}|}\int_{\hat{\jmath}} \omega(x)\Delta x \le \mathcal{A}\mathrm{ess}\inf_{x \in \hat{\jmath}} \omega(x), \quad \text{for all } x \in \hat{\jmath}, \tag{15}$$

holds for every subinterval $\hat{\jmath} \subset \mathbb{I}$. A non-negative Δ−integrable function ω belongs to the Muckenhoupt class $\mathbb{A}^p(\mathcal{C})$ for $p > 1$ if there exists a constant $\mathcal{C} > 1$ such that the inequality

$$\left(\frac{1}{|\hat{J}|}\int_{\hat{J}}\omega(x)\Delta x\right)\left(\frac{1}{|\hat{J}|}\int_{\hat{J}}\omega^{\frac{-1}{p-1}}(x)\Delta x\right)^{p-1} \leq C, \tag{16}$$

holds for every subinterval $\hat{J} \subset \mathbb{I}$. For a given exponent $p > 1$, we define the $\mathbb{A}^p$-norm of A non-negative Δ−integrable weight ω by the following quantity:

$$[\mathbb{A}^p(\omega)] := \sup_{\hat{J} \subset \hat{\mathbb{I}}}\left(\frac{1}{|\hat{J}|}\int_{\hat{J}}\omega(x)\Delta x\right)\left(\frac{1}{|\hat{J}|}\int_{\hat{J}}\omega^{\frac{-1}{p-1}}(x)\Delta x\right)^{p-1},$$

where the supremum is taken over all intervals $\hat{J} \subset \mathbb{I}$. Note that by Hölder's inequality $[\mathbb{A}^p(\omega)] \geq 1$ for all $1 < p < \infty$, and the following inclusion is true:

if $1 < p \leq q < \infty$, then $\mathbb{A}^1 \subset \mathbb{A}^p \subset \mathbb{A}^q$ and $[\mathbb{A}^q(\omega)] \leq [\mathbb{A}^p(\omega)]$.

For any function $f : \mathbb{I} \to \mathbb{R}^+$ which is non-negative, we define the operator $\mathcal{H}f : [0, \infty)_\mathbb{T} \to \mathbb{R}^+$ by

$$\mathcal{H}(t) = \frac{1}{t}\int_0^t f(s)\Delta s, \text{ for all } t \in \mathbb{I}. \tag{17}$$

From the definition of $\mathcal{H}$, we see that if f is nondecreasing, then

$$\mathcal{H}f(t) = \frac{1}{t}\int_0^t f(s)\Delta s \leq \frac{1}{t}\int_0^t f(t)\Delta s = f(t).$$

Additionally, we have determined by using the above inequality that

$$(\mathcal{H}f(t))^\Delta = \frac{1}{\sigma(t)}[f(t) - \mathcal{H}f(t)] \geq 0, \text{ for } t \in \mathbb{I}.$$

Furthermore, if f is nonincreasing, we have that

$$\mathcal{H}f(t) = \frac{1}{t}\int_0^t f(s)\Delta s \geq \frac{1}{t}\int_0^t f(t)\Delta s = f(t),$$

and

$$(\mathcal{H}f(t))^\Delta = \frac{1}{\sigma(t)}[f(t) - \mathcal{H}f(t)] \leq 0, \text{ for } t \in \mathbb{I}.$$

From these facts, we have the following properties of $\mathcal{H}f$.

Lemma 1.
(i). If f is nondecreasing, then $\mathcal{H}f(t) \leq f(t)$.
(ii). If f is nondecreasing, then so is $\mathcal{H}f$.

Lemma 2.
(i). If f is nonincreasing, then $\mathcal{H}f(t) \geq f(t)$.
(ii). If f is nonincreasing, then so is $\mathcal{H}f$.

Remark 1. As a consequence of Lemma 1, we notice that if f is non-negative, and nondecreasing, then $\mathcal{H}f^q \leq f^q$. We also notice from Lemma 1 that if f is non-negative, and nondecreasing, then $\mathcal{H}f^q$ is also non-negative and nondecreasing for $q > 1$.

Remark 2. As a consequence of Lemma 2, we notice that if f is non-negative, and nonincreasing, then $\mathcal{H}f^q \geq f^q$. We also notice from Lemma 2 that if f is non-negative, and nonincreasing, then $\mathcal{H}f^q$ is also non-negative and nonincreasing for $q > 1$.

In what follows, we will define f^σ, $\mathcal{H}^\sigma f$ and $\mathcal{H}[\mathcal{H}^\sigma f]^p$ where σ is the forward jump operator, by $f^\sigma(t) = (f \circ \sigma)(t)$,

$$\mathcal{H}^\sigma f(t) = \frac{1}{\sigma(t)} \int_0^{\sigma(t)} f(x) \Delta x, \text{ for } t \in \mathbb{I},$$

and

$$\mathcal{H}[\mathcal{H}^\sigma f]^p(t) = \frac{1}{t} \int_0^t \left(\frac{1}{\sigma(s)} \int_0^{\sigma(s)} f(x) \Delta x \right)^p \Delta s, \text{ for } t \in \mathbb{I}.$$

Theorem 1. *Assume that f is non-negative and nondecreasing on $\mathbb{I}$. If $s \geq r > 0$, then*

$$\int_0^{\sigma(t)} [f(x)]^{r/s} [\mathcal{H}^\sigma f(x)]^{-s-\frac{r}{s}} \Delta x \leq \left(\frac{s+1}{s} \right)^{r/s} \int_0^{\sigma(t)} [\mathcal{H}^\sigma f(x)]^{-s} \Delta x, \quad (18)$$

for any $t \in \mathbb{I}$.

Proof. First, we consider the case when $s = r$ and prove that

$$\int_0^{\sigma(t)} f(x) [\mathcal{H}^\sigma f(x)]^{-s-1} \Delta x \leq \left(\frac{s+1}{s} \right) \int_0^{\sigma(t)} [\mathcal{H}^\sigma f(x)]^{-s} \Delta x.$$

For brevity, we write $F = \mathcal{H} f$. By employing the integration by parts (13), with $u(t) = \sigma(t)$ and $v(t) = F^{-s}(t)$, we obtain

$$\int_0^{\sigma(t)} (F^\sigma(x))^{-s} \Delta x = u(x) F^{-s}(x) \big|_0^{\sigma(t)} - \int_0^{\sigma(t)} \sigma(x)(F^{-s}(x))^\Delta \Delta x$$

$$= u^\sigma(t)(F^\sigma(t))^{-s} - \int_0^{\sigma(t)} \sigma(x)(F^{-s}(x))^\Delta \Delta x \quad (19)$$

$$\geq -\int_0^{\sigma(t)} \sigma(x)(F^{-s}(x))^\Delta \Delta x. \quad (20)$$

By the chain rule (12), we see that

$$(F^{-s})^\Delta = -sF^\Delta \int_0^1 \frac{dh}{(hF^\sigma + (1-h)F)^{s+1}}$$

$$\leq -sF^\Delta \int_0^1 (hF^\sigma + (1-h)F^\sigma)^{-s-1} dh = -sF^\Delta (F^\sigma)^{-s-1}.$$

Substituting the last inequality into (20), we obtain

$$\int_0^{\sigma(t)} (F^\sigma(x))^{-s} \Delta x \geq s \int_0^{\sigma(t)} \sigma(x) F^\Delta(x) (F^\sigma(x))^{-s-1} \Delta x$$

$$\geq s \int_0^{\sigma(t)} x F^\Delta(x) (F^\sigma(x))^{-s-1} \Delta x. \quad (21)$$

Moreover, since

$$tF(t) = \int_0^t f(x) \Delta x,$$

the product rule gives

$$tF^\Delta(t) + F^\sigma(t) = f(t). \quad (22)$$

Substituting (22) into (21), we obtain

$$\int_0^{\sigma(t)} (F^\sigma(x))^{-s} \Delta x \geq s \int_0^{\sigma(t)} f(x)(F^\sigma(x))^{-s-1} \Delta x - s \int_0^{\sigma(t)} (F^\sigma(x))^{-s} \Delta x.$$

By combining like terms, we obtain

$$\int_0^{\sigma(t)} f(x)(F^\sigma(x))^{-s-1}\Delta x \leq \left(\frac{s+1}{s}\right) \int_0^{\sigma(t)} (F^\sigma(x))^{-s}\Delta x,$$

which proves the inequality (18) when $s = r$. Now, consider the case when $s \neq r$ and fix $r \in (0, s)$. Then by applying Hölder's inequality (14) with s/r and $s/(s-r)$, we obtain

$$\int_0^{\sigma(t)} [f(x)]^{r/s} (F^\sigma(x))^{-r-\frac{r}{s}} (F^\sigma(x))^{-s+r} \Delta x$$

$$\leq \left[\int_0^{\sigma(t)} f(x)(F^\sigma(x))^{-s-1}\Delta x\right]^{r/s} \left[\int_0^{\sigma(t)} (F^\sigma(x))^{-s}\Delta x\right]^{1-\frac{r}{s}}$$

$$\leq \left(\frac{s+1}{s}\right)^{r/s} \left[\int_0^{\sigma(t)} (F^\sigma(x))^{-s}\Delta x\right]^{r/s} \left[\int_0^{\sigma(t)} (F^\sigma(x))^{-s}\Delta x\right]^{1-\frac{r}{s}}$$

$$= \left(\frac{s+1}{s}\right)^{r/s} \int_0^{\sigma(t)} (F^\sigma(x))^{-s}\Delta x,$$

which is the desired inequality (18). The proof is complete. □

Theorem 2. *Assume that f is non-negative and nondecreasing on $\mathbb{I}$. If $s \geq r > 0$, then*

$$\int_0^{\sigma(t)} [\mathcal{H}^\sigma f(x)]^{-s}\Delta x \leq \left(\frac{s+1}{s}\right)^r \int_0^{\sigma(t)} f^{-r}(x)[\mathcal{H}^\sigma f(x)]^{-s+r}\Delta x. \quad (23)$$

Proof. From the elementary inequality (see Elliott [46]),

$$sy^{s+1} - (s+1)y^s \geq -1, \quad (24)$$

for every $y \geq 0$ and $s > 0$, we deduce by using $y = y_1/y_2$, where $y_1, y_2 > 0$, that

$$y_1^{-s} + sy_1 y_2^{-s-1} - (s+1)y_2^{-s} \geq 0. \quad (25)$$

Now, by defining

$$y_1 := \left(\frac{s}{s+1}\right)^{1+\frac{r}{s}} f^{r/s}(t)[\mathcal{H}^\sigma f(t)]^{1-\frac{r}{s}}, \text{ and } y_2 := \left(\frac{s}{s+1}\right) \mathcal{H}^\sigma f(t),$$

we obtain

$$y_1^{-s} := \left(\frac{s}{s+1}\right)^{-s-r} f^{-r}(t)[\mathcal{H}^\sigma f(t)]^{-s+r}, \text{ and } y_2^{-s} := \left(\frac{s}{s+1}\right)^{-s} [\mathcal{H}^\sigma f(t)]^{-s},$$

and then

$$y_1 y_2^{-s-1} := \left(\frac{s}{s+1}\right)^{-s+r/s} f^{r/s}(t)[\mathcal{H}^\sigma f(t)]^{-s-\frac{r}{s}}.$$

By using these values in (25), we have

$$\left(\frac{s}{s+1}\right)^{-s-r} f^{-r}(t)[\mathcal{H}^\sigma f(t)]^{-s+r} + s\left(\frac{s}{s+1}\right)^{-s+\frac{r}{s}} f^{r/s}(t)[\mathcal{H}^\sigma f(t)]^{-s-\frac{r}{s}}$$

$$\geq (s+1)\left(\frac{s}{s+1}\right)^{-s} [\mathcal{H}^\sigma f(t)]^{-s}. \quad (26)$$

By integrating (26) from 0 to $\sigma(t)$, we obtain

$$\left(\frac{s+1}{s}\right)^r \int_0^{\sigma(t)} f^{-r}(x)[\mathcal{H}^\sigma f(x)]^{-s+r} \Delta x$$
$$+s\left(\frac{s}{s+1}\right)^{\frac{r}{s}} \int_0^{\sigma(t)} f^{r/s}(x)[\mathcal{H}^\sigma f(x)]^{-s-\frac{r}{s}} \Delta x$$
$$\geq (s+1)\int_0^{\sigma(t)} [\mathcal{H}^\sigma f(x)]^{-s} \Delta x. \tag{27}$$

Now, by applying Theorem 1 on the term

$$\int_0^{\sigma(t)} f^{r/s}(x)[\mathcal{H}^\sigma f(x)]^{-s-\frac{r}{s}} \Delta x,$$

we obtain

$$\int_0^{\sigma(t)} f^{r/s}(x)[\mathcal{H}^\sigma f(x)]^{-s-\frac{r}{s}} \Delta x \leq \left(\frac{s+1}{s}\right)^{r/s} \int_0^{\sigma(t)} [\mathcal{H}^\sigma f(x)]^{-s} \Delta x. \tag{28}$$

Comparing (27) and (28), we have

$$\left(\frac{s+1}{s}\right)^r \int_0^{\sigma(t)} f^{-r}(x)[\mathcal{H}^\sigma f(x)]^{-s+r} \Delta x$$
$$+s\left(\frac{s}{s+1}\right)^{r/s}\left(\frac{s+1}{s}\right)^{r/s} \int_0^{\sigma(t)} [\mathcal{H}^\sigma f(x)]^{-s} \Delta x$$
$$\geq (s+1)\int_0^{\sigma(t)} [\mathcal{H}^\sigma f(x)]^{-s} \Delta x. \tag{29}$$

By combining like terms in the last inequality, we conclude that

$$\int_0^{\sigma(t)} [\mathcal{H}^\sigma f(x)]^{-s} \Delta x \leq \left(\frac{s+1}{s}\right)^r \int_0^{\sigma(t)} f^{-r}(x)[\mathcal{H}^\sigma f(x)]^{-s+r} \Delta x, \tag{30}$$

which is the desired inequality (18). The proof is complete. □

Theorem 3. *Assume that f is non-negative and nondecreasing on $\mathbb{I}$. If $0 < r_1 < r_2 < s$, then*

$$\int_0^{\sigma(t)} f^{-r_1}(x)[\mathcal{H}^\sigma f(x)]^{-s+r_1} \Delta x \leq \left(\frac{s+1}{s}\right)^{r_2-r_1} \int_0^{\sigma(t)} f^{-r_2}(x)[\mathcal{H}^\sigma f(x)]^{-s+r_2} \Delta x. \tag{31}$$

Proof. By applying Hölder's inequality (14) with r_2/r_1 and $r_2/(r_2-r_1)$ on the left-hand side of (31), we obtain

$$\int_0^{\sigma(t)} f^{-r_1}(x)[\mathcal{H}^\sigma f(x)]^{-s+r_1} \Delta x \leq \left(\int_0^{\sigma(t)} f^{-r_2}(x)[\mathcal{H}^\sigma f(x)]^{-s+r_2} \Delta x\right)^{\frac{r_1}{r_2}}$$
$$\times \left(\int_0^{\sigma(t)} [\mathcal{H}^\sigma f(x)]^{-s} \Delta x\right)^{1-\frac{r_1}{r_2}}. \tag{32}$$

Now, by replacing r with r_2 in (30), we obtain

$$\int_0^{\sigma(t)} [\mathcal{H}^\sigma f(t)]^{-s} \Delta x \leq \left(\frac{s+1}{s}\right)^{r_2} \int_0^{\sigma(t)} f^{-r_2}(x)[\mathcal{H}^\sigma f(x)]^{-s+r_2} \Delta x. \tag{33}$$

By combining (32) and (33), we see that

$$\int_0^{\sigma(t)} f^{-r_1}(x)[\mathcal{H}^\sigma f(x)]^{-s+r_1} \Delta x$$
$$\leq \left(\frac{s+1}{s}\right)^{r_2-r_1} \int_0^{\sigma(t)} f^{-r_2}(x)[\mathcal{H}^\sigma f(x)]^{-s+r_2} \Delta x,$$

which is the desired inequality (31). The proof is complete. □

Theorem 4. *Assume that f is non-negative and nondecreasing on $\mathbb{I}$. If $s \geq r > 0$, then*

$$\frac{1}{\sigma(t)} \int_0^{\sigma(t)} f^{r/s}(x)[\mathcal{H}^\sigma f(x)]^{-s-\frac{r}{s}} \Delta x \leq \left(\frac{s+1}{s}\right)^{r/s} \frac{1}{\sigma(t)} \int_0^{\sigma(t)} [\mathcal{H}^\sigma f(x)]^{-s} \Delta x$$
$$- \frac{r}{s^2}\left(\frac{s+1}{s}\right)^{r/s-1} [\mathcal{H}^\sigma f(t)]^{-s}. \quad (34)$$

Proof. We proceed as in the proof of Theorem 1 (without removing the term $\sigma^\sigma(t)(F^\sigma(t))^{-p}$) to obtain

$$\int_0^{\sigma(t)} (F^\sigma(x))^{-s} \Delta x = \sigma^\sigma(t)(F^\sigma(t))^{-s} - \int_0^{\sigma(t)} \sigma(x)(F^{-s}(x))^\Delta \Delta x$$
$$\geq \sigma(t)(F^\sigma(t))^{-s} - \int_0^{\sigma(t)} \sigma(x)(F^{-s}(x))^\Delta \Delta x$$
$$\geq \sigma(t)(F^\sigma(t))^{-s} + s \int_0^{\sigma(t)} \sigma(x)F^\Delta(x)(F^\sigma(x))^{-s-1} \Delta x$$
$$\geq \sigma(t)(F^\sigma(t))^{-s} + s \int_0^{\sigma(t)} xF^\Delta(x)(F^\sigma(x))^{-s-1} \Delta x$$
$$\geq \sigma(t)(F^\sigma(t))^{-s} + s \int_0^{\sigma(t)} f(x)(F^\sigma(x))^{-s-1} \Delta x - s \int_0^{\sigma(t)} (F^\sigma(x))^{-s} \Delta x.$$

By combining like terms, we obtain

$$\int_0^{\sigma(t)} f(x)(F^\sigma(x))^{-s-1} \Delta x \leq \left(\frac{s+1}{s}\right) \int_0^{\sigma(t)} (F^\sigma(x))^{-s} \Delta x - \frac{1}{s}\sigma(t)(F^\sigma(t))^{-s}. \quad (35)$$

If we fix $r \in (0,s)$ then by applying Hölder's inequality with s/r and $s/(s-r)$, we obtain

$$\int_0^{\sigma(t)} f^{r/s}(x)(F^\sigma(x))^{-r-r/s}(F^\sigma(x))^{-s+r} \Delta x$$
$$\leq \left[\int_0^{\sigma(t)} f(x)(F^\sigma(x))^{-s-1} \Delta x\right]^{r/s} \left[\int_0^{\sigma(t)} (F^\sigma(x))^{-s} \Delta x\right]^{1-\frac{r}{s}}$$
$$\leq \left[\left(\frac{s+1}{s}\right)\int_0^{\sigma(t)} (F^\sigma(x))^{-s}\Delta x - \frac{1}{s}\sigma(t)(F^\sigma(t))^{-s}\right]^{r/s}$$
$$\times \left[\int_0^{\sigma(t)} (F^\sigma(x))^{-s} \Delta x\right]^{1-\frac{r}{s}}. \quad (36)$$

Now, in order to complete the proof, we shall utilize the inequality

$$(u+v)^\gamma \leq u^\gamma + pu^{\gamma-1}v, \text{ where } 0 < \gamma < 1. \quad (37)$$

which is a variant of the well-known Bernoulli inequality. This inequality is valid for all $u \geq 0$ and $u+v \geq 0$ or $u > 0$ and $u+v > 0$ and equality holds if only if $v = 0$. Now, by employing (37) with $\gamma = r/s < 1$,

$$u := \left(\frac{s+1}{s}\right)\int_0^{\sigma(t)} (F^\sigma(x))^{-s}\Delta x, \text{ and } v := -\frac{1}{s}\sigma(t)(F^\sigma(t))^{-s},$$

and noting that

$$\left(\frac{s+1}{s}\right)\int_0^{\sigma(t)} (F^\sigma(x))^{-s}\Delta x - \frac{1}{s}\sigma(t)(F^\sigma(t))^{-s} > 0,$$

we obtain

$$\left[\left(\frac{s+1}{s}\right)\int_0^{\sigma(t)} (F^\sigma(x))^{-s}\Delta x - \frac{1}{s}\sigma(t)(F^\sigma(t))^{-s}\right]^{r/s}$$

$$\leq \left(\frac{s+1}{s}\right)^{r/s}\left[\int_0^{\sigma(t)} (F^\sigma(x))^{-s}\Delta x\right]^{r/s}$$

$$-\frac{r}{s}\left(\frac{s+1}{s}\right)^{r/s-1} \times \frac{1}{s}\sigma(t)(F^\sigma(t))^{-s}\left[\int_0^{\sigma(t)} (F^\sigma(x))^{-s}\Delta x\right]^{r/s-1}$$

$$= \left(\frac{s+1}{s}\right)^{r/s}\left[\int_0^{\sigma(t)} (F^\sigma(x))^{-s}\Delta x\right]^{r/s}$$

$$-\frac{r}{s^2}\left(\frac{s+1}{s}\right)^{r/s-1}\left[\int_0^{\sigma(t)} (F^\sigma(x))^{-s}\Delta x\right]^{r/s-1}\sigma(t)(F^\sigma(t))^{-s}.$$

Substituting the last inequality into (36), we obtain

$$\int_0^{\sigma(t)} f^{r/s}(x)(F^\sigma(x))^{-s-r/s}\Delta x$$

$$\leq \left(\int_0^{\sigma(t)} (F^\sigma(x))^{-s}\Delta x\right)^{1-\frac{r}{s}}\left[\left(\frac{s+1}{s}\right)^{r/s}\left(\int_0^{\sigma(t)} (F^\sigma(x))^{-s}\Delta x\right)^{r/s}\right.$$

$$\left.-\frac{r}{s^2}\left(\frac{s+1}{s}\right)^{r/s-1}\left[\int_0^{\sigma(t)} (F^\sigma(x))^{-s}\Delta x\right]^{r/s-1}\sigma(t)(F^\sigma(t))^{-s}\right]$$

$$= \left(\frac{s+1}{s}\right)^{r/s}\int_0^{\sigma(t)} (F^\sigma(x))^{-s}\Delta x - \frac{r}{s^2}\left(\frac{s+1}{s}\right)^{r/s-1}\sigma(t)(F^\sigma(t))^{-s},$$

which is the desired inequality (34). The proof is complete. □

Theorem 5. *Assume that f is non-negative and nondecreasing on $\mathbb{I}$. If $s \geq r > 0$, then*

$$\int_0^{\sigma(t)} [\mathcal{H}^\sigma f(x)]^{-s}\Delta x$$

$$\leq \left(\frac{s+1}{s}\right)^r \int_0^{\sigma(t)} f^{-r}(x)[\mathcal{H}^\sigma f(x)]^{-s+r}\Delta x - \frac{r}{s+1}\sigma(t)[\mathcal{H}^\sigma f(t)]^{-s}. \quad (38)$$

Proof. We proceed as in the proof of Theorem 2, so we have from (27) that

$$\left(\frac{s+1}{s}\right)^r \int_0^{\sigma(t)} f^{-r}(x)[\mathcal{H}^\sigma f(x)]^{-s+r}\Delta x$$

$$+s\left(\frac{s}{s+1}\right)^{\frac{r}{s}}\int_0^{\sigma(t)} f^{r/s}(x)[\mathcal{H}^\sigma f(x)]^{-s-\frac{r}{s}}\Delta x$$

$$\geq (s+1)\int_0^{\sigma(t)} [\mathcal{H}^\sigma f(x)]^{-s}\Delta x.$$

By applying Theorem 4, we obtain

$$\int_0^{\sigma(t)} f^{r/s}(x)[\mathcal{H}^\sigma f(x)]^{-s-\frac{r}{s}}\Delta x \le \left(\frac{s+1}{s}\right)^{r/s}\int_0^{\sigma(t)}[\mathcal{H}^\sigma f(x)]^{-s}\Delta x$$
$$-\frac{r}{s^2}\left(\frac{s+1}{s}\right)^{r/s-1}\sigma(t)[\mathcal{H}^\sigma f(t)]^{-s},$$

and then

$$\left(\frac{s+1}{s}\right)^r \int_0^{\sigma(t)} f^{-r}(x)[\mathcal{H}^\sigma f(x)]^{-s+r}\Delta x$$
$$+s\left(\frac{s}{s+1}\right)^{\frac{r}{s}}\left(\frac{s+1}{s}\right)^{r/s}\int_0^{\sigma(t)}[\mathcal{H}^\sigma f(x)]^{-s}\Delta x$$
$$-s\left(\frac{s}{s+1}\right)^{\frac{r}{s}}\frac{r}{s^2}\left(\frac{s+1}{s}\right)^{r/s-1}\sigma(t)[\mathcal{H}^\sigma f(t)]^{-s}$$
$$\ge (s+1)\int_0^{\sigma(t)}[\mathcal{H}^\sigma f(x)]^{-s}\Delta x.$$

By combining like terms, we obtain

$$\left(\frac{s+1}{s}\right)^r \int_0^{\sigma(t)} f^{-r}(x)[\mathcal{H}^\sigma f(x)]^{-s+r}\Delta x - \frac{r}{(s+1)}\sigma(t)[\mathcal{H}^\sigma f(t)]^{-s}$$
$$\ge \int_0^{\sigma(t)}[\mathcal{H}^\sigma f(x)]^{-s}\Delta x, \qquad (39)$$

which is the desired inequality (38). The proof is complete. □

Theorem 6. *Assume that f is non-negative and nondecreasing on $\mathbb{I}$. If $0 < r_1 < r_2 < s$, then*

$$\int_0^{\sigma(t)} f^{-r_1}(x)[\mathcal{H}^\sigma f(x)]^{-s+r_1}\Delta x + \frac{(r_2-r_1)s^{r_1}}{(s+1)^{1+r_1}}\sigma(t)[\mathcal{H}^\sigma f(t)]^{-s}$$
$$\le \left(\frac{s+1}{s}\right)^{r_2-r_1}\int_0^{\sigma(t)} f^{-r_2}(x)[\mathcal{H}^\sigma f(x)]^{-s+r_2}\Delta x. \qquad (40)$$

Proof. By applying Hölder's inequality with r_2/r_1 and $r_2/(r_2-r_1)$ on the left hand side of (40), we obtain

$$\int_0^{\sigma(t)} f^{-r_1}(x)[\mathcal{H}^\sigma f(x)]^{-s+r_1}\Delta x \le \left(\int_0^{\sigma(t)} f^{-r_2}(x)[\mathcal{H}^\sigma f(x)]^{-s+r_2}\Delta x\right)^{\frac{r_1}{r_2}}$$
$$\times \left(\int_0^{\sigma(t)}[\mathcal{H}^\sigma f(x)]^{-s}\Delta x\right)^{1-\frac{r_1}{r_2}}. \qquad (41)$$

Now, by replacing r with r_2 in (39), we obtain

$$\int_0^{\sigma(t)}[\mathcal{H}^\sigma f(x)]^{-s}\Delta x \le \left(\frac{s+1}{s}\right)^{r_2}\int_0^{\sigma(t)} f^{-r_2}(x)[\mathcal{H}^\sigma f(x)]^{-s+r_2}\Delta x$$
$$-\frac{r_2}{(s+1)}\sigma(t)[\mathcal{H}^\sigma f(t)]^{-s}. \qquad (42)$$

By combining (41) and (42), we obtain

$$\int_0^{\sigma(t)} f^{-r_1}(x)[\mathcal{H}^\sigma f(x)]^{-s+r_1} \Delta x \leq \left(\int_0^{\sigma(t)} f^{-r_2}(x)[\mathcal{H}^\sigma f(x)]^{-s+r_2} \Delta x \right)^{\frac{r_1}{r_2}} \times$$
$$\left[\left(\frac{s+1}{s} \right)^{r_2} \int_0^{\sigma(t)} f^{-r_2}(x)[\mathcal{H}^\sigma f(x)]^{-s+r_2} \Delta x \right.$$
$$\left. - \frac{r_2}{(s+1)} \sigma(t)[\mathcal{H}^\sigma f(t)]^{-s} \right]^{1-\frac{r_1}{r_2}}. \quad (43)$$

Now, by employing (37), with $\gamma = 1 - (r_1/r_2) < 1$,

$$u = \left(\frac{s+1}{s} \right)^{r_2} \int_0^{\sigma(t)} f^{-r_2}(x)[\mathcal{H}^\sigma f(x)]^{-s+r_2} \Delta x, \text{ and } v = -\frac{r_2}{(s+1)} \sigma(t)[\mathcal{H}^\sigma f(t)]^{-s},$$

we obtain

$$\left[\left(\frac{s+1}{s} \right)^{r_2} \int_0^{\sigma(t)} f^{-r_2}(x)[\mathcal{H}^\sigma f(x)]^{-s+r_2} \Delta x - \frac{r_2}{(s+1)} \sigma(t)[\mathcal{H}^\sigma f(t)]^{-s} \right]^{1-\frac{r_1}{r_2}}$$
$$\leq \left(\frac{s+1}{s} \right)^{r_2-r_1} \left[\int_0^{\sigma(t)} f^{-r_2}(x)[\mathcal{H}^\sigma f(x)]^{-s+r_2} \Delta x \right]^{1-\frac{r_1}{r_2}} - \frac{r_2-r_1}{r_2}$$
$$\times \left(\frac{s+1}{s} \right)^{-r_1} \left[\int_0^{\sigma(t)} f^{-r_2}(x)[\mathcal{H}^\sigma f(x)]^{-s+r_2} \Delta x \right]^{-\frac{r_1}{r_2}} \frac{r_2}{(s+1)} \sigma(t)[\mathcal{H}^\sigma f(t)]^{-s}$$
$$= \left(\frac{s+1}{s} \right)^{r_2-r_1} \left[\int_0^{\sigma(t)} f^{-r_2}(x)[\mathcal{H}^\sigma f(x)]^{-s+r_2} \Delta x \right]^{1-\frac{r_1}{r_2}}$$
$$- \frac{(r_2-r_1)s^{r_1}}{(s+1)^{1+r_1}} \left[\int_0^{\sigma(t)} f^{-r_2}(x)[\mathcal{H}^\sigma f(x)]^{-s+r_2} \Delta x \right]^{-\frac{r_1}{r_2}} \sigma(t)[\mathcal{H}^\sigma f(t)]^{-s}.$$

Substituting the last inequality into (43), we obtain

$$\int_0^{\sigma(t)} f^{-r_1}(x)[\mathcal{H}^\sigma f(x)]^{-s+r_1} \Delta x$$
$$\leq \left(\int_0^{\sigma(t)} f^{-r_2}(x)[\mathcal{H}^\sigma f(x)]^{-s+r_2} \Delta x \right)^{\frac{r_1}{r_2}}$$
$$\times \left[\left(\frac{s+1}{s} \right)^{r_2-r_1} \left[\int_0^{\sigma(t)} f^{-r_2}(x)[\mathcal{H}^\sigma f(x)]^{-s+r_2} \Delta x \right]^{1-\frac{r_1}{r_2}} \right.$$
$$\left. - \frac{(r_2-r_1)s^{r_1}}{(s+1)^{1+r_1}} \left[\int_0^{\sigma(t)} f^{-r_2}(x)[\mathcal{H}^\sigma f(x)]^{-s+r_2} \Delta x \right]^{-\frac{r_1}{r_2}} \sigma(t)[\mathcal{H}^\sigma f(t)]^{-s} \right]$$
$$= \left(\frac{s+1}{s} \right)^{r_2-r_1} \left(\int_0^{\sigma(t)} f^{-r_2}(x)[\mathcal{H}^\sigma f(x)]^{-s+r_2} \Delta x \right)$$
$$- \frac{(r_2-r_1)s^{r_1}}{(s+1)^{1+r_1}} \sigma(t)[\mathcal{H}^\sigma f(t)]^{-s},$$

which is the desired inequality (40). The proof is complete. □

Theorem 7. Assume that ω is non-negative and nondecreasing and $q > 1$. Then we have for every $t \in \mathbb{I}$ that

$$\frac{1}{\sigma(t)} \int_0^{\sigma(t)} \left[(\omega^\sigma(x))^{\frac{-1}{q-1}} \left[\mathcal{H}^\sigma \omega^{\frac{-1}{q-1}}(x) \right]^{\gamma-1} - \frac{(\gamma-1)}{\gamma} \left[\mathcal{H}^\sigma \omega^{\frac{-1}{q-1}}(x) \right]^\gamma \right] \Delta x$$

$$\leq \frac{1}{\gamma} \left[\mathcal{H}^\sigma \omega^{\frac{-1}{q-1}}(t) \right]^\gamma \qquad (44)$$

for any $\gamma \geq 1$.

Proof. Let $x \in \mathbb{I}$. Since $\omega^{\frac{-1}{q-1}}(x) = \left[x \mathcal{H} \omega^{\frac{-1}{q-1}}(x) \right]^\Delta$, it follows that

$$(\omega^\sigma(x))^{\frac{-1}{q-1}} \left[\mathcal{H}^\sigma \omega^{\frac{-1}{q-1}}(x) \right]^{\gamma-1} - \frac{(\gamma-1)}{\gamma} \left[\mathcal{H}^\sigma \omega^{\frac{-1}{q-1}}(x) \right]^\gamma$$

$$\leq \omega^{\frac{-1}{q-1}}(x) \left[\mathcal{H}^\sigma \omega^{\frac{-1}{q-1}}(x) \right]^{\gamma-1} - \frac{(\gamma-1)}{\gamma} \left[\mathcal{H}^\sigma \omega^{\frac{-1}{q-1}}(x) \right]^\gamma$$

$$= \left[x \mathcal{H} \omega^{\frac{-1}{q-1}}(x) \right]^\Delta \left[\mathcal{H}^\sigma \omega^{\frac{-1}{q-1}}(x) \right]^{\gamma-1} - \frac{(\gamma-1)}{\gamma} \left[\mathcal{H}^\sigma \omega^{\frac{-1}{q-1}}(x) \right]^\gamma. \qquad (45)$$

Moreover, utilizing the well-known product rule

$$(fg)^\Delta = fg^\Delta + f^\Delta g^\sigma,$$

for $f = x \mathcal{H} \omega^{\frac{-1}{q-1}}$ and $g^\sigma = \left[\mathcal{H}^\sigma \omega^{\frac{-1}{q-1}} \right]^{\gamma-1}$, we have that

$$\left[x \mathcal{H} \omega^{\frac{-1}{q-1}}(x) \right]^\Delta \left[\mathcal{H}^\sigma \omega^{\frac{-1}{q-1}}(x) \right]^{\gamma-1}$$

$$= \left[x \left(\mathcal{H} \omega^{\frac{-1}{q-1}}(x) \right)^\gamma \right]^\Delta - \left[x \mathcal{H} \omega^{\frac{-1}{q-1}}(x) \right] \left[\left(\mathcal{H} \omega^{\frac{-1}{q-1}}(x) \right)^{\gamma-1} \right]^\Delta, \qquad (46)$$

and for $f = x$ and $g^\sigma = \left[\mathcal{H}^\sigma \omega^{\frac{-1}{q-1}} \right]^\gamma$, we have that

$$\left[\mathcal{H}^\sigma \omega^{\frac{-1}{q-1}}(x) \right]^\gamma = \left[x \left(\mathcal{H} \omega^{\frac{-1}{q-1}}(x) \right)^\gamma \right]^\Delta - x \left[\left(\mathcal{H} \omega^{\frac{-1}{q-1}}(x) \right)^\gamma \right]^\Delta. \qquad (47)$$

By comparing (46) and (47) with (45), we obtain

$$(\omega^\sigma(x))^{\frac{-1}{q-1}} \left[\mathcal{H}^\sigma \omega^{\frac{-1}{q-1}}(x) \right]^{\gamma-1} - \frac{(\gamma-1)}{\gamma} \left[\mathcal{H}^\sigma \omega^{\frac{-1}{q-1}}(x) \right]^\gamma$$

$$\leq \left[x \left(\mathcal{H} \omega^{\frac{-1}{q-1}}(x) \right)^\gamma \right]^\Delta - \left[x \mathcal{H} \omega^{\frac{-1}{q-1}}(x) \right] \left[\left(\mathcal{H} \omega^{\frac{-1}{q-1}}(x) \right)^{\gamma-1} \right]^\Delta$$

$$- \frac{(\gamma-1)}{\gamma} \left[x \left(\mathcal{H} \omega^{\frac{-1}{q-1}}(x) \right)^\gamma \right]^\Delta + \frac{(\gamma-1)}{\gamma} x \left[\left(\mathcal{H} \omega^{\frac{-1}{q-1}}(x) \right)^\gamma \right]^\Delta$$

$$= \frac{1}{\gamma} \left[x \left(\mathcal{H} \omega^{\frac{-1}{q-1}}(x) \right)^\gamma \right]^\Delta \qquad (48)$$

$$- x \mathcal{H} \omega^{\frac{-1}{q-1}}(x) \left[\left(\mathcal{H} \omega^{\frac{-1}{q-1}}(x) \right)^{\gamma-1} \right]^\Delta + \frac{(\gamma-1)}{\gamma} x \left[\left(\mathcal{H} \omega^{\frac{-1}{q-1}}(x) \right)^\gamma \right]^\Delta.$$

On the other hand, since $\omega^{\frac{-1}{q-1}}$ is nonincreasing, then so is $\mathcal{H}\omega^{\frac{-1}{q-1}}(x)$, or equivalently, $\left[\mathcal{H}\omega^{\frac{-1}{q-1}}(x)\right]^{\Delta} < 0$, then we have

$$-x\mathcal{H}\omega^{\frac{-1}{q-1}}(x)\left[\left(\mathcal{H}\omega^{\frac{-1}{q-1}}(x)\right)^{\gamma-1}\right]^{\Delta} + \frac{(\gamma-1)}{\gamma}x\left[\left(\mathcal{H}\omega^{\frac{-1}{q-1}}(x)\right)^{\gamma}\right]^{\Delta} \quad (49)$$

$$\leq -x\mathcal{H}\omega^{\frac{-1}{q-1}}(x)\left[\left(\mathcal{H}\omega^{\frac{-1}{q-1}}(x)\right)^{\gamma-1}\right]^{\Delta} + x\left[\left(\mathcal{H}\omega^{\frac{-1}{q-1}}(x)\right)^{\gamma}\right]^{\Delta}.$$

Consequently, yet another application of the product rule, with $f = \mathcal{H}\omega^{\frac{-1}{q-1}}(x)$ and $g = \left[\mathcal{H}\omega^{\frac{-1}{q-1}}(x)\right]^{\gamma-1}$, yields that

$$\left[\left(\mathcal{H}\omega^{\frac{-1}{q-1}}(x)\right)^{\gamma}\right]^{\Delta} - \mathcal{H}\omega^{\frac{-1}{q-1}}(x)\left[\left(\mathcal{H}\omega^{\frac{-1}{q-1}}(x)\right)^{\gamma-1}\right]^{\Delta}$$

$$= \left(\mathcal{H}^{\sigma}\omega^{\frac{-1}{q-1}}(x)\right)^{\gamma-1}\left[\mathcal{H}\omega^{\frac{-1}{q-1}}(x)\right]^{\Delta},$$

by substituting the last equation in (49), we have

$$-x\mathcal{H}\omega^{\frac{-1}{q-1}}(x)\left[\left(\mathcal{H}\omega^{\frac{-1}{q-1}}(x)\right)^{\gamma-1}\right]^{\Delta} + \frac{(\gamma-1)}{\gamma}x\left[\left(\mathcal{H}\omega^{\frac{-1}{q-1}}(x)\right)^{\gamma}\right]^{\Delta}$$

$$\leq x\left(\mathcal{H}^{\sigma}\omega^{\frac{-1}{q-1}}(x)\right)^{\gamma-1}\left[\mathcal{H}\omega^{\frac{-1}{q-1}}(x)\right]^{\Delta} \leq 0. \quad (50)$$

Now, taking into account relations (48) and (50), we have that

$$(\omega^{\sigma}(x))^{\frac{-1}{q-1}}\left[\mathcal{H}^{\sigma}\omega^{\frac{-1}{q-1}}(x)\right]^{\gamma-1} - \frac{(\gamma-1)}{\gamma}\left[\mathcal{H}^{\sigma}\omega^{\frac{-1}{q-1}}(x)\right]^{\gamma}$$

$$\leq \frac{1}{\gamma}\left[x\left(\mathcal{H}\omega^{\frac{-1}{q-1}}(x)\right)^{\gamma}\right]^{\Delta}.$$

Finally, integrating the last inequality from 0 to $\sigma(t)$ and dividing by $\sigma(t)$, we obtain

$$\frac{1}{\sigma(t)}\int_0^{\sigma(t)}\left[(\omega^{\sigma}(x))^{\frac{-1}{q-1}}\left[\mathcal{H}^{\sigma}\omega^{\frac{-1}{q-1}}(x)\right]^{\gamma-1} - \frac{(\gamma-1)}{\gamma}\left[\mathcal{H}^{\sigma}\omega^{\frac{-1}{q-1}}(x)\right]^{\gamma}\right]\Delta x$$

$$\leq \frac{1}{\gamma}\left[\mathcal{H}^{\sigma}\omega^{\frac{-1}{q-1}}(t)\right]^{\gamma}.$$

The proof is complete. □

3. Self-Improving Properties of Muckenhoupt's Weights

In this section, we will prove the self-improving properties of the Muckenhoupt class on a time scale $\mathbb{T}$ for non-negative and nondecreasing weights.

Theorem 8. *Assume that ω is non-negative and nondecreasing on $\mathbb{I}$ and $q > 1$ such that $\omega \in \mathbb{A}^q(\mathcal{C})$. Then for any $\eta \geq 1$ satisfying that $\omega^{\sigma}(t) \leq \eta\omega(t)$, we have that $\omega \in \mathbb{A}^p(\mathcal{C}_1)$ for any $p \in (p_0, q]$ where p_0 is the unique root of the equation*

$$\frac{q-p_0}{q-1}(\mathcal{C}\eta p_0)^{\frac{1}{q-1}} = 1. \quad (51)$$

Furthermore, the constant C_1 is given by

$$C_1 := \left(\frac{p-1}{q-1}\frac{C^{\frac{1}{q-1}}}{\Psi^{q,p}(C)}\right)^{p-1}, \text{ where } \Psi^{q,p}(C) := \left(1 - \frac{q-p}{q-1}(C\eta p)^{\frac{1}{q-1}}\right)\eta^{\frac{-1}{p-1}} > 0.$$

Proof. By Lemma 7 with $\gamma = (q-1)/(p-1) > 1$ for $q > p > 1$, we obtain

$$\frac{q-1}{p-1}\int_0^{\sigma(t)}(\omega^\sigma(x))^{\frac{-1}{q-1}}\left[\mathcal{H}^\sigma\omega^{\frac{-1}{q-1}}(x)\right]^{\frac{q-p}{p-1}}\Delta x - \frac{q-p}{p-1}\int_0^{\sigma(t)}\left[\mathcal{H}^\sigma\omega^{\frac{-1}{q-1}}(x)\right]^{\frac{q-1}{p-1}}\Delta x \tag{52}$$

$$\leq \sigma(t)\left[\mathcal{H}^\sigma\omega^{\frac{-1}{q-1}}(t)\right]^{\frac{q-1}{p-1}}.$$

Since $\omega \in \mathbb{A}^q(C)$, we see that

$$\mathcal{H}^\sigma\omega(t)\left[\mathcal{H}^\sigma\omega^{\frac{-1}{q-1}}(t)\right]^{q-1} \leq C, \text{ for } C > 1. \tag{53}$$

Substituting the last inequality into (52), we obtain

$$\frac{q-1}{q-p}\int_0^{\sigma(t)}(\omega^\sigma(x))^{\frac{-1}{q-1}}\left[\mathcal{H}^\sigma\omega^{\frac{-1}{q-1}}(x)\right]^{\frac{q-p}{p-1}}\Delta x - \int_0^{\sigma(t)}\left[\mathcal{H}^\sigma\omega^{\frac{-1}{q-1}}(x)\right]^{\frac{q-1}{p-1}}\Delta x \tag{54}$$

$$\leq \frac{p-1}{q-p}C^{\frac{1}{p-1}}\sigma(t)[\mathcal{H}^\sigma\omega(t)]^{\frac{-1}{p-1}}.$$

Define

$$g_\xi(\rho) = \frac{q-1}{q-p}\xi\rho^{\frac{q-p}{p-1}} - \rho^{\frac{q-1}{p-1}},$$

with

$$\rho = \mathcal{H}^\sigma\omega^{\frac{-1}{q-1}} \text{ and } \xi = (\omega^\sigma)^{\frac{-1}{q-1}}.$$

Since ω^σ is nondecreasing, then we have $(\omega^\sigma)^{\frac{-1}{q-1}}$ is nonincreasing, then by Lemma 2, we have $(\omega^\sigma)^{\frac{-1}{q-1}} \leq \mathcal{H}^\sigma\omega^{\frac{-1}{q-1}}$, that is $\xi < \rho$. From the definition of $g_\xi(\rho)$, we see that

$$\frac{d}{d\rho}g_\xi(\rho) = \frac{q-1}{p-1}\xi\rho^{\frac{q-p}{p-1}-1} - \frac{q-1}{p-1}\rho^{\frac{q-p}{p-1}} = \frac{q-1}{p-1}\rho^{\frac{q-p}{p-1}-1}[\xi - \rho] < 0,$$

and so we can recognize that $g_\xi(\rho)$ is nonincreasing. By defining

$$\zeta = C^{\frac{1}{q-1}}[\mathcal{H}^\sigma\omega]^{\frac{-1}{q-1}},$$

and using $\rho \leq \zeta$, we have that

$$g_\xi(\rho) \geq g_\xi(\zeta),$$

and then we obtain

$$\frac{q-1}{q-p}\int_0^{\sigma(t)}(\omega^\sigma(x))^{\frac{-1}{q-1}}\left[\mathcal{H}^\sigma\omega^{\frac{-1}{q-1}}(x)\right]^{\frac{q-p}{p-1}}\Delta x - \int_0^{\sigma(t)}\left[\mathcal{H}^\sigma\omega^{\frac{-1}{q-1}}(x)\right]^{\frac{q-1}{p-1}}\Delta x$$

$$\geq \frac{q-1}{q-p}C^{\frac{q-p}{(p-1)(q-1)}}\int_0^{\sigma(t)}(\omega^\sigma(x))^{\frac{-1}{q-1}}[\mathcal{H}^\sigma\omega(x)]^{\frac{1}{q-1}-\frac{1}{p-1}}\Delta x$$

$$-C^{\frac{1}{p-1}}\int_0^{\sigma(t)}[\mathcal{H}^\sigma\omega]^{\frac{-1}{p-1}}\Delta x.$$

Compare last inequality and (54) we obtain

$$\frac{q-1}{q-p}C^{\frac{q-p}{(p-1)(q-1)}}\int_0^{\sigma(t)}(\omega^\sigma(x))^{\frac{-1}{q-1}}[\mathcal{H}^\sigma\omega(x)]^{\frac{1}{q-1}-\frac{1}{p-1}}\Delta x$$
$$\leq \frac{p-1}{q-p}C^{\frac{1}{p-1}}\sigma(t)[\mathcal{H}^\sigma\omega(t)]^{\frac{-1}{p-1}}+C^{\frac{1}{q-1}}\int_0^{\sigma(t)}[\mathcal{H}^\sigma\omega]^{\frac{-1}{p-1}}\Delta x.$$

Cancel a suitable power of C to obtain

$$\frac{q-1}{q-p}\int_0^{\sigma(t)}(\omega^\sigma(x))^{\frac{-1}{q-1}}[\mathcal{H}^\sigma\omega(x)]^{\frac{1}{q-1}-\frac{1}{p-1}}\Delta x$$
$$\leq \frac{p-1}{q-p}C^{\frac{1}{q-1}}\sigma(t)[\mathcal{H}^\sigma\omega(t)]^{\frac{-1}{p-1}}+C^{\frac{1}{q-1}}\int_0^{\sigma(t)}[\mathcal{H}^\sigma\omega]^{\frac{-1}{p-1}}\Delta x. \tag{55}$$

Replace s and r with $\frac{1}{p-1}$ and $\frac{1}{q-1}$ in the inequality (23), respectively, we obtain

$$\int_0^{\sigma(t)}[\mathcal{H}^\sigma\omega(x)]^{-\frac{1}{p-1}}\Delta x \leq p^{\frac{1}{q-1}}\int_0^{\sigma(t)}\omega^{\frac{-1}{q-1}}(x)[\mathcal{H}^\sigma\omega(x)]^{-\frac{1}{p-1}+\frac{1}{q-1}}\Delta x. \tag{56}$$

By combining (55) and (56), we see immediately that

$$\frac{q-1}{q-p}\int_0^{\sigma(t)}(\omega^\sigma(x))^{\frac{-1}{q-1}}[\mathcal{H}^\sigma\omega(x)]^{\frac{1}{q-1}-\frac{1}{p-1}}\Delta x$$
$$-(Cp)^{\frac{1}{q-1}}\int_0^{\sigma(t)}\omega^{\frac{-1}{q-1}}(x)[\mathcal{H}^\sigma\omega(x)]^{-\frac{1}{p-1}+\frac{1}{q-1}}\Delta x$$
$$\leq \frac{p-1}{q-p}C^{\frac{1}{q-1}}\sigma(t)[\mathcal{H}^\sigma\omega(t)]^{\frac{-1}{p-1}}. \tag{57}$$

Since $\omega^\sigma(t) \leq \eta\omega(t)$, so we can see that

$$\omega^{\frac{-1}{q-1}}(t) \leq \eta^{\frac{1}{q-1}}(\omega^\sigma(t))^{\frac{-1}{q-1}}.$$

Substituting the last inequality into (57) we see that

$$\frac{q-1}{q-p}\int_0^{\sigma(t)}(\omega^\sigma(x))^{\frac{-1}{q-1}}[\mathcal{H}^\sigma\omega(x)]^{\frac{1}{q-1}-\frac{1}{p-1}}\Delta x$$
$$-(C\eta p)^{\frac{1}{q-1}}\int_0^{\sigma(t)}(\omega^\sigma(x))^{\frac{-1}{q-1}}[\mathcal{H}^\sigma\omega(x)]^{-\frac{1}{p-1}+\frac{1}{q-1}}\Delta x$$
$$\leq \frac{p-1}{q-p}C^{\frac{1}{q-1}}\sigma(t)[\mathcal{H}^\sigma\omega(t)]^{\frac{-1}{p-1}},$$

which gives us that

$$\left[1-\frac{q-p}{q-1}(C\eta p)^{\frac{1}{q-1}}\right]\left(\frac{1}{\sigma(t)}\int_0^{\sigma(t)}(\omega^\sigma(x))^{\frac{-1}{q-1}}[\mathcal{H}^\sigma\omega(x)]^{\frac{1}{q-1}-\frac{1}{p-1}}\Delta x\right)$$
$$\leq \frac{p-1}{q-1}C^{\frac{1}{q-1}}[\mathcal{H}^\sigma\omega(t)]^{\frac{-1}{p-1}}. \tag{58}$$

The constant

$$K := 1 - \frac{q-p}{q-1}(C\eta p)^{\frac{1}{q-1}},$$

is positive for every $p \in (p_0, q]$, where p_0 is the unique positive root of the equation

$$\frac{q-p_0}{q-1}(C\eta p_0)^{\frac{1}{q-1}} = 1.$$

Since ω is nondecreasing then we obtain (from Lemma 1) that

$$\mathcal{H}^\sigma \omega(x) \leq \omega^\sigma(x).$$

This implies, since $p - 1 < q - 1$, that

$$[\mathcal{H}^\sigma \omega(x)]^{\frac{1}{q-1} - \frac{1}{p-1}} \geq (\omega^\sigma)^{\frac{1}{q-1} - \frac{1}{p-1}}(x). \tag{59}$$

which gives us

$$\left[1 - \frac{q-p}{q-1}(C\eta p)^{\frac{1}{q-1}}\right]\left(\frac{1}{\sigma(t)}\int_0^{\sigma(t)} (\omega^\sigma)^{\frac{-1}{p-1}}(x)\Delta x\right)$$
$$\leq \frac{p-1}{q-1}C^{\frac{1}{q-1}}[\mathcal{H}^\sigma \omega(t)]^{\frac{-1}{p-1}}. \tag{60}$$

Since $\omega^\sigma(t) \leq \eta \omega(t)$, so we can see that

$$(\omega^\sigma(t))^{\frac{-1}{p-1}} \geq (\eta \omega(t))^{\frac{-1}{p-1}}.$$

Substituting the last inequality into (60) we obtain

$$\left[1 - \frac{q-p}{q-1}(C\eta p)^{\frac{1}{q-1}}\right]\eta^{\frac{-1}{p-1}}\left(\frac{1}{\sigma(t)}\int_0^{\sigma(t)} \omega^{\frac{-1}{p-1}}(x)\Delta x\right)$$
$$\leq \frac{p-1}{q-1}C^{\frac{1}{q-1}}[\mathcal{H}^\sigma \omega(t)]^{\frac{-1}{p-1}}.$$

which implies that

$$(\mathcal{H}^\sigma \omega(t))\left(\mathcal{H}^\sigma \omega^{\frac{-1}{p-1}}(t)\right)^{p-1} \leq C_1,$$

where $C_1 = C_1(p, q, C, \eta)$ is positive constant. The proof is complete. □

Now, we will refine the result above by improving the constant that appears as following.

Theorem 9. *Assume that ω is non-negative and nondecreasing on $\mathbb{I}$ and $q > 1$ such that $\omega \in \mathbb{A}^q(C)$. Then $\omega \in \mathbb{A}^p(\tilde{C}_1)$ for any $p \in (p_0, q]$ where p_0 is the unique root of the equation*

$$\frac{q-p_0}{q-1}(C\eta p_0)^{\frac{1}{q-1}} = 1. \tag{61}$$

Furthermore the constant $\tilde{C}_1$ is given by

$$\tilde{C}_1 := \left(\frac{q}{p}\left(\frac{p-1}{q-1}\right)^2 \frac{C^{\frac{1}{q-1}}}{\Psi^{q,p}(C)}\right)^{p-1},$$

$$\Psi^{q,p}(C) := \left(1 - \frac{q-p}{q-1}(C\eta p)^{\frac{1}{q-1}}\right)\eta^{\frac{-1}{p-1}} > 0.$$

Proof. We will apply the same technique we use in Theorem 8 but we will replace s and r with $1/(p-1)$ and $1/(q-1)$ in (39), respectively to obtain

$$\int_0^{\sigma(t)} [\mathcal{H}^\sigma \omega(x)]^{-\frac{1}{p-1}}\Delta x \tag{62}$$
$$\leq p^{\frac{1}{q-1}}\int_0^{\sigma(t)} \omega^{\frac{-1}{q-1}}(x)[\mathcal{H}^\sigma \omega(x)]^{-\frac{1}{p-1}+\frac{1}{q-1}}\Delta x - \frac{p-1}{p(q-1)}\sigma(t)[\mathcal{H}^\sigma \omega(t)]^{-\frac{1}{p-1}}.$$

Now, combine (55) and (62), we see immediately that

$$\frac{q-1}{q-p}\int_0^{\sigma(t)}(\omega^\sigma(x))^{\frac{-1}{q-1}}[\mathcal{H}^\sigma\omega(x)]^{\frac{1}{q-1}-\frac{1}{p-1}}\Delta x$$
$$-(Cp)^{\frac{1}{q-1}}\int_0^{\sigma(t)}\omega^{\frac{-1}{q-1}}(x)[\mathcal{H}^\sigma\omega(x)]^{-\frac{1}{p-1}+\frac{1}{q-1}}\Delta x$$
$$\leq \frac{p-1}{q-p}C^{\frac{1}{q-1}}\sigma(t)[\mathcal{H}^\sigma\omega(t)]^{\frac{-1}{p-1}} - C^{\frac{1}{q-1}}\frac{p-1}{p(q-1)}\sigma(t)[\mathcal{H}^\sigma\omega(t)]^{-\frac{1}{p-1}}, \quad (63)$$

Since $\omega^\sigma(t) \leq \eta\omega(t)$, so we can see that
$$\omega^{\frac{-1}{q-1}}(t) \leq \eta^{\frac{1}{q-1}}(\omega^\sigma(t))^{\frac{-1}{q-1}}.$$

Substituting the last inequality into (63) we see that
$$\frac{q-1}{q-p}\int_0^{\sigma(t)}(\omega^\sigma(x))^{\frac{-1}{q-1}}[\mathcal{H}^\sigma\omega(x)]^{\frac{1}{q-1}-\frac{1}{p-1}}\Delta x$$
$$-(C\eta p)^{\frac{1}{q-1}}\int_0^{\sigma(t)}(\omega^\sigma(x))^{\frac{-1}{q-1}}[\mathcal{H}^\sigma\omega(x)]^{-\frac{1}{p-1}+\frac{1}{q-1}}\Delta x$$
$$\leq \frac{p-1}{q-p}C^{\frac{1}{q-1}}\sigma(t)[\mathcal{H}^\sigma\omega(t)]^{\frac{-1}{p-1}} - C^{\frac{1}{q-1}}\frac{p-1}{p(q-1)}\sigma(t)[\mathcal{H}^\sigma\omega(t)]^{-\frac{1}{p-1}},$$

which gives us
$$\left[1-\frac{q-p}{q-1}(C\eta p)^{\frac{1}{q-1}}\right]\left(\frac{1}{\sigma(t)}\int_0^{\sigma(t)}(\omega^\sigma(x))^{\frac{-1}{q-1}}[\mathcal{H}^\sigma\omega(x)]^{\frac{-1}{p-1}+\frac{1}{q-1}}\Delta x\right)$$
$$\leq \left[\frac{p-1}{q-1}-\frac{(q-p)(p-1)}{p(q-1)^2}\right]C^{\frac{1}{q-1}}[\mathcal{H}^\sigma\omega(t)]^{\frac{-1}{p-1}}$$
$$= \frac{q}{p}\left(\frac{p-1}{q-1}\right)^2 C^{\frac{1}{q-1}}[\mathcal{H}^\sigma\omega(t)]^{\frac{-1}{p-1}}. \quad (64)$$

Since ω is nondecreasing then we obtain (from Lemma 1) that
$$\mathcal{H}^\sigma\omega(x) \leq \omega^\sigma(x).$$

This implies, since $p-1 < q-1$, that
$$[\mathcal{H}^\sigma\omega(x)]^{\frac{1}{q-1}-\frac{1}{p-1}} \geq (\omega^\sigma)^{\frac{1}{q-1}-\frac{1}{p-1}}(x),$$

then, we obtain
$$\left[1-\frac{q-p}{q-1}(C\eta p)^{\frac{1}{q-1}}\right]\frac{1}{\sigma(t)}\int_0^{\sigma(t)}(\omega^\sigma(x))^{-\frac{1}{p-1}}\Delta x \leq \frac{q}{p}\left(\frac{p-1}{q-1}\right)^2 C^{\frac{1}{q-1}}[\mathcal{H}^\sigma\omega(t)]^{\frac{-1}{p-1}}. \quad (65)$$

Since $\omega^\sigma(x) \leq \eta\omega(x)$ so we can see that
$$[\omega^\sigma(x)]^{\frac{-1}{p-1}} \geq [\eta\omega(x)]^{\frac{-1}{p-1}},$$

Substituting the last inequality into (65) we obtain
$$\left[1-\frac{q-p}{q-1}(C\eta p)^{\frac{1}{q-1}}\right]\eta^{\frac{-1}{p-1}}\left(\frac{1}{\sigma(t)}\int_0^{\sigma(t)}\omega^{-\frac{1}{p-1}}(x)\Delta x\right) \leq \frac{q}{p}\left(\frac{p-1}{q-1}\right)^2 C^{\frac{1}{q-1}}[\mathcal{H}^\sigma\omega(t)]^{\frac{-1}{p-1}}.$$

which implies that
$$(\mathcal{H}^\sigma\omega(t))\left(\mathcal{H}^\sigma\omega^{\frac{-1}{p-1}}(t)\right)^{p-1} \leq \tilde{C}_1,$$

where $\tilde{\mathcal{C}}_1 = \tilde{\mathcal{C}}_1(q, p, \mathcal{C}, \eta)$ is positive constant, which proves that $\omega \in \mathbb{A}^p(\tilde{\mathcal{C}}_1)$. The proof is complete. □

Remark 3. *We note that Equation (61) can be written as*

$$\frac{1}{p_0}\left(\frac{q-1}{q-p_0}\right)^{q-1} = \mathcal{C}\eta. \tag{66}$$

When $\mathbb{T} = \mathbb{R}$, we see that $\eta = 1$ and then (66) becomes the Equation (7) which is given by

$$\frac{1}{p_0}\left(\frac{q-1}{q-p_0}\right)^{q-1} = \mathcal{C}. \tag{67}$$

When $\mathbb{T} = \mathbb{N}$, we can choose $\eta = 2$ and then (66) becomes

$$\frac{1}{p_0}\left(\frac{q-1}{q-p_0}\right)^{q-1} = 2\mathcal{C}, \tag{68}$$

for the discrete weights.

4. Conclusions

In this paper, we proved some Hardy's type inequalities on time scales and the new refinements of these inequalities with negative powers that are needed to prove the main results. Next, we used these inequalities to design and prove some new additional inequalities by using the Bernoulli inequality that will be also needed in the proof of the main results. These results are the self-improving results for the Muckenhoupt weights on time scales. The self-improving properties used in harmonic analysis to prove one of the important theorems, which is the extrapolation theorem. We also expect that the new theory on time scales will also play the same act in proving extrapolation theory on time scales via the $\mathbb{A}^q(\mathcal{C})$−Muckenhoupt weights. The results as special cases contain the results for the classical results obtained for integrals and the discrete results obtained for the discrete weights. The technique that we have applied in this paper give a unified approach in proving a general results and avoiding the proof of integrals and again for sums. The results in the discrete case that we have derived contain an additional constant which is different from the case in the integral forms, see (67) and (68). We have checked the results with some values and concluded that these equations has unique positive roots.

Author Contributions: All authors contributed equally to the manuscript. All authors have read and agreed to the published version of the manuscript.

Funding: This research received no external funding

Data Availability Statement: Not applicable

Conflicts of Interest: The authors declare no conflict of interest.

References

1. Muckenhoupt, B. Weighted norm inequalities for the Hardy maximal function. *Tran. Am. Math. Soc.* **1972**, *165*, 207–226. [CrossRef]
2. Bojarski, B.; Sbordone, C.; Wik, I. The Muckenhoupt class $A_1(\mathbb{R})$. *Studia Math.* **1992**, *101*, 155–163. [CrossRef]
3. Coifman, R.R.; Fefferman, C. Weighted norm inequalities for maximal functions and singular integrals. *Stud. Math.* **1974**, *51*, 241–250. [CrossRef]
4. Dindoš, M.; Wall, T. The sharp A^p constant for weights in a reverse Hölder class. *Rev. Mat. Iberoam.* **2009**, *25*, 559–594. [CrossRef]
5. Malaksiano, N.A. The exact inclusions of Gehring classes in Muckenhoupt classes. *Mat. Zametki* **2001**, *70*, 742–750. (In Russian)
6. Malaksiano, N.A. The precise embeddings of one-dimensional Muckenhoupt classes in Gehring classes. *Acta Sci. Math.* **2002**, *68*, 237–248.
7. Nikolidakis, E.N. A_1-weights on R: An alternative approach. *Ann. Acad. Sci. Fenn. Math.* **2015**, *40*, 949–955. [CrossRef]
8. Nikolidakis, E.N.; Stavropoulos, T. A refinement of a Hardy type inequality for negative exponents, and sharp applications to Muckenhoupt weights on R. *Colloq. Math.* **2019**, *157*, 295–308. [CrossRef]

9. Popoli, A. Optimal integrability in B_p^q classes. *Matematiche* **1997**, *52*, 159–170.
10. Popoli, A. Sharp integrability exponents and constants for Muckenhoupt and Gehring weights as solutions to a unique equation. *Ann. Acad. Sci. Fenn. Math.* **2018**, *43*, 785–805. [CrossRef]
11. Vasyuinin, V. The exact constant in the inverse Hölder inequality for Muckenhoupt weights. *Algebra Anal.* **2003**, *15*, 73–117. (In Russian)
12. Korenovskii, A.A. The exact continuation of a reverse Hölder inequality and Muckenhoupt's conditions. *Math. Notes* **1992**, *52*, 1192–1201. [CrossRef]
13. De Francia, J.L.R. Factorization and extrapolation of weights. *Bull. Am. Math. Soc.* **1982**, *7*, 393–395. [CrossRef]
14. De Francia, J.L.R. Factorization theory and A_p weights. *Am. Math. Soc.* **1984**, *106*, 533–547.
15. Cruz-Uribe, D.; Martell, J.M.; Pérez, C. Extrapolation from A_∞ weights and applications. *J. Funct. Anal.* **2004**, *213*, 412–439. [CrossRef]
16. Cruz-Uribe, D.; Pérez, C. Two weight extrapolation via the maximal operator. *J. Funct. Anal.* **2000**, *174*, 1–17. [CrossRef]
17. Cruz-Uribe, D.; Martell, J.M.; Pérez, C. *Weights, Extrapolation and the Theory of Rubio de Francia*; Operator Theory and Applications; Springer: Berlin/Heidelberg, Germany, 2011; Volume 125.
18. Dragičević, O.; Grafakos, L.; Pereyra, M.C.; Petermichl, S. Extrapolation and sharp norm estimates for classical operators on weighted Lebesgue spaces. *Publ. Mat.* **2005**, *49*, 73–91. [CrossRef]
19. Duoandikoetxea, J. Extrapolation of weights revisited: New proofs and sharp bounds. *J. Funct. Anal.* **2011**, *260*, 1886–1901. [CrossRef]
20. García-Cuerva, J. An extrapolation theorem in the theory of A_p weights. *Proc. Am. Math. Soc.* **1983**, *87*, 422–426.
21. García-Cuerva, J.; de Francia, J.L.R. *Weighted Norm Inequalities and Related Topics*; North-Holland Publishing Co.: Amsterdam, The Netherlands, 1985.
22. Grafakos, L. *Modern Fourier Analysis*, 2nd ed.; Graduate Texts in Mathematics, 250; Springer: New York, NY, USA, 2009.
23. Calderón, A.; Zygmund, A. On the existence of certain singular integrals. *Acta Math.* **1952**, *8*, 85–139. [CrossRef]
24. Cardona, D. Weak-type (1, 1) bounds for a class of operators with discrete kernel. *Rev. Integr.* **2015**, *33*, 51–60.
25. Hughes, K.J. Arithmetic Analogues in Harmonic Analysis: Results Related to Waring's Problem. Ph.D. Thesis, Princeton University, Princeton, NJ, USA, 2012.
26. Saker, S.H.; Mahmoud, R.R. Boundedness of both discrete Hardy and Hardy-Littlewood Maximal operators via Muckenhoupt weights. *Rocky Mount. J. Math.* **2021**, *51*, 733–746. [CrossRef]
27. Heing, H.P.; Kufner, A. Hardy operators of monotone functions and sequences in Orlicz spaces. *J. London Math. Soc.* **1996**, *53*, 256–270. [CrossRef]
28. Bennett, G.; Grosse-Erdmann, K.-G. Weighted Hardy inequalities for decreasing sequences and functions. *Math. Ann.* **2006**, *334*, 489–531. [CrossRef]
29. Saker, S.H.; Rabie, S.S.; Agarwal, R.P. On discrete weighted Hardy type inequalities and properties of weighted discrete Muckenhoupt classes. *J. Ineq. Appl.* **2021**, *168*, 1–19. [CrossRef]
30. Böttcher, A.; Spitkovsky, I. Wiener-Hopf integral operators with PC symbols on spaces with Muckenhoupt weight. *Rev. Mat. Iberoam.* **1993**, *9*, 257–279. [CrossRef]
31. Böttcher, A.; Seybold, M. *Wackelsatz and Stechkin's Inequality for Discrete Muckenhoupt Weights*; Preprint no. 99-7; TU Chemnitz: Chemnitz, Germany, 1999.
32. Böttcher, A.; Seybold, M. Discrete Wiener-Hopf operators on spaces with Muckenhoupt weight. *Studia Math.* **2000**, *143*, 121–144. [CrossRef]
33. Böttcher, A.; Seybold, M. Discrete one-dimensional zero-order pseudodifferential operators on spaces with Muckenhoupt weight. *Algebra i Analiz.* **2001**, *13*, 116–129.
34. Magyar, A.; Stein, E.M.; Wainger, S. Discrete analogues in harmonic analysis: Spherical averages. *Ann. Math.* **2002**, *155*, 189–208. [CrossRef]
35. Hardy, G.H.; Littlewood, J.E.; Polya, G. *Inequalities*, 2nd ed.; Cambridge University Press: Cambridge, UK, 1934.
36. Hilger, S. Analysis on measure chains-a unified approach to continuous and discrete calculus. *Results Math.* **1990**, *18*, 18–56. [CrossRef]
37. Agarwal, R.P.; O'Regan, D.; Saker, S.H. *Dynamic Inequalities on Time Scales*; Springer: Berlin/Heidelberg, Germany, 2014.
38. Agarwal, R.P.; O'Regan, D.; Saker, S.H. *Hardy Type Inequalities on Time Scales*; Springer: Cham, Switzerland, 2016.
39. Bohner, M.; Saker, S.H. Gehring inequalities on time scales. *J. Comp. Anal. Appl.* **2020**, *28*, 11–23.
40. Saker, S.H.; Kubiaczyk, I. Reverse dynamic inequalities and higher integrability theorems. *J. Math. Anal. Appl.* **2019**, *471*, 671–686. [CrossRef]
41. Saker, S.H.; Krnić, M.; Pečarić, J. Higher summability theorems from the weighted reverse discrete inequalities. *Appl. Anal. Discrete Math.* **2019**, *13*, 423–439. [CrossRef]
42. Saker, S.H.; Osman, M.M.; Krnić, M. Higher integrability theorems on time scales from reverse Hölder inequalities. *Appl. Anal. Discrete Math.* **2019**, *13*, 819–838. [CrossRef]
43. Saker, S.H.; O'Regan, D.; Agarwal, R.P. A higher integrability theorem from a reverse weighted inequality. *Bull. Lond. Math. Soc.* **2019**, *51*, 967–977. [CrossRef]
44. Bohner, M.; Peterson, A. *Dynamic Equations on Time Scales: An Introduction with Applications*; Birkhäuser: Basel, Switzerland, 2001.

15. Bohner, M.; Peterson, A. *Advances in Dynamic Equations on Time Scales*; Birkhäuser: Basel, Switzerland, 2003.
16. Elliott, E.B. A simple expansion of some recently proved facts as to convergency. *J. Lond. Math. Soc.* **1926**, *1*, 93–96. [CrossRef]

Disclaimer/Publisher's Note: The statements, opinions and data contained in all publications are solely those of the individual author(s) and contributor(s) and not of MDPI and/or the editor(s). MDPI and/or the editor(s) disclaim responsibility for any injury to people or property resulting from any ideas, methods, instructions or products referred to in the content.

Article

Inequalities for the Windowed Linear Canonical Transform of Complex Functions

Zhen-Wei Li [1,†] and Wen-Biao Gao [2,*,†]

[1] School of Computer Science and Artificial Intelligence, Wuhan Textile University, Wuhan 430073, China; lizhenweibit@163.com
[2] School of Mathematical Science, Yangzhou University, Yangzhou 225002, China
* Correspondence: wenbiaogao@163.com
† These authors contributed equally to this work.

Abstract: In this paper, we generalize the N-dimensional Heisenberg's inequalities for the windowed linear canonical transform (WLCT) of a complex function. Firstly, the definition for N-dimensional WLCT of a complex function is given. In addition, the N-dimensional Heisenberg's inequality for the linear canonical transform (LCT) is derived. It shows that the lower bound is related to the covariance and can be achieved by a complex chirp function with a Gaussian function. Finally, the N-dimensional Heisenberg's inequality for the WLCT is exploited. In special cases, its corollary can be obtained.

Keywords: Fourier transform; linear canonical transform; inequality; complex function

Citation: Li, Z.-W.; Gao, W.-B. Inequalities for the Windowed Linear Canonical Transform of Complex Functions. *Axioms* **2023**, *12*, 554. https://doi.org/10.3390/axioms12060554

Academic Editors: Wei-Shih Du, Ravi P. Agarwal, Erdal Karapinar, Marko Kostić and Jian Cao

Received: 26 April 2023
Revised: 29 May 2023
Accepted: 29 May 2023
Published: 4 June 2023

Copyright: © 2023 by the authors. Licensee MDPI, Basel, Switzerland. This article is an open access article distributed under the terms and conditions of the Creative Commons Attribution (CC BY) license (https://creativecommons.org/licenses/by/4.0/).

1. Introduction

Inequalities for the Fourier transform (FT) are widely used in mathematics, physics and engineering [1–6]. The classical N-dimensional Heisenberg's inequality of the FT is given by the following formula [7]:

$$\int_{\mathbb{R}^N} (\mathbf{t} - \mathbf{t^f})^2 \, |f(\mathbf{t})|^2 \, d\mathbf{t} \int_{\mathbb{R}^N} (\mathbf{u} - \mathbf{u^f})^2 \, |\hat{f}(\mathbf{u})|^2 \, d\mathbf{u} \geq \eth \|f\|^4_{L^2(\mathbb{R}^N)}, \tag{1}$$

where $\eth = (\frac{N}{4\pi})^2$, $\mathbf{t} = (t_1, t_2, \cdots, t_N)$, $\mathbf{u} = (u_1, u_2, \cdots, u_N)$. $\hat{f}(\mathbf{u})$ is the FT of any function $f \in L^2(\mathbb{R}^N)$,

$$\hat{f}(\mathbf{u}) = F\{f(\mathbf{t})\}(\mathbf{u}) = \frac{1}{\sqrt{2\pi}} \int_{\mathbb{R}^N} f(\mathbf{t}) e^{-i\mathbf{t}\mathbf{u}} d\mathbf{t}, \tag{2}$$

$$\mathbf{t^f} = \int_{\mathbb{R}^N} \mathbf{t} \, |f(\mathbf{t})|^2 \, d\mathbf{t}, \tag{3}$$

$$\mathbf{u^f} = \int_{\mathbb{R}^N} \mathbf{u} \, |\hat{f}(\mathbf{u})|^2 \, d\mathbf{u}, \tag{4}$$

$$\|f\|^2_{L^2(\mathbb{R}^N)} = \|f\|^2 = \int_{\mathbb{R}^N} |f(\mathbf{t})|^2 d\mathbf{t}, \tag{5}$$

Based on Formula (1), Zhang obtained the N-dimensional Heisenberg's inequality of the fractional Fourier transform (FRFT) [8].

The windowed linear canonical transform (WLCT) [9–11] is a generalized integral transform of the FT [12] and the FRFT [13]. In recent years, inequality of the WLCT has become a hot topic. Many scholars [14–17] have studied different types of inequalities for the WLCT.

The purpose of this paper is to obtain various kinds of N-dimensional inequalities associated with the WLCT.

2. Preliminary

Let any function $f(t) = f_1(t)e^{i\phi(t)} \in L^2(\mathbb{R}^N)$ and window function $0 \neq g(t) = g_1(t)e^{i\varphi(t)} \in L^2(\mathbb{R}^N)$.

Definition 1 ([18]). *Let $A = \begin{bmatrix} a & b \\ c & d \end{bmatrix}$ be a matrix parameter satisfying $a, b, c, d \in \mathbb{R}$ and $ad - bc = 1$. For any function $f(t)$, the linear canonical transform (LCT) of $f(t)$ is defined as*

$$L_A^f(u) = L_A[f(t)](u) = \begin{cases} \int_{\mathbb{R}^N} f(t) K_A(t, u) dt, & b \neq 0 \\ \sqrt{d} e^{i\frac{cd}{2}u^2} f(du), & b = 0 \end{cases} \tag{6}$$

where

$$K_A(t, u) = \frac{1}{\sqrt{i2\pi b}} e^{i\frac{a}{2b}t^2 - i\frac{1}{b}tu + i\frac{d}{2b}u^2}. \tag{7}$$

Additionally, the paper [19] presented the following properties:

$$K_A^*(t, u) = K_{A^{-1}}(u, t), \tag{8}$$

$$2\pi\delta(x) = \int_{\mathbb{R}^N} e^{\pm iux} du, \tag{9}$$

where $A^{-1} = \begin{bmatrix} d & -b \\ -c & a \end{bmatrix}$, $x = (x_1, x_2, \cdots, x_N)$.

If $b = 0$, then the LCT becomes a kind of scaling and chirp multiplication operations [20]. In this paper, we only consider $b \neq 0$.

The inverse formula of the LCT is given by [19]

$$f(t) = \int_{\mathbb{R}^N} L_A^f(u) K_{A^{-1}}(u, t) du. \tag{10}$$

Definition 2 ([9]). *Let $A = \begin{bmatrix} a & b \\ c & d \end{bmatrix}$ be a matrix parameter satisfying $a, b, c, d \in \mathbb{R}$ and $ad - bc = 1$. The WLCT of function f with respect to g is defined by*

$$\begin{aligned} W_g^A f(t, u) &= \int_{\mathbb{R}^N} f(y) g^*(y - t) K_A(y, u) dy \\ &= \int_{\mathbb{R}^N} f_t(y) K_A(y, u) dy, \end{aligned} \tag{11}$$

where $y = (y_1, y_2, \cdots, y_N)$ and $f_t(y) = f(y)g^*(y-t) = f_1(y)g_1^*(y-t)e^{i(\phi(y) - \varphi(y-t))}$.

Next, we will give a lemma.

Lemma 1. *For $f \in L^2(\mathbb{R}^N)$ and $g \in L^2(\mathbb{R}^N)$, we have*

$$W_g^A f(t, u) = \int_{\mathbb{R}^N} L_A^f(k) Q^*(k|u, t) dk, \tag{12}$$

where $A_1 = \begin{bmatrix} 0 & b' \\ -\frac{1}{b'} & d' \end{bmatrix}, 0 \neq b' = b \in \mathbb{R}$,

$$Q^*(\mathbf{k}|\mathbf{u},\mathbf{t}) = \sqrt{-i2\pi b} e^{i\frac{d'}{2b}(\mathbf{k}-\mathbf{u})^2} L_{A_1}^g(\mathbf{k}-\mathbf{u})^* K_A(\mathbf{t},\mathbf{u}) K_A^*(\mathbf{t},\mathbf{k}).$$

Proof. According to Definition 2 and Formula (10), we obtain

$$\begin{aligned} W_g^A f(\mathbf{t},\mathbf{u}) &= \int_{\mathbb{R}^N} f(\mathbf{y}) \overline{g(\mathbf{y}-\mathbf{t})} K_A(\mathbf{y},\mathbf{u}) d\mathbf{y} \\ &= \int_{\mathbb{R}^N} L_A^f(\mathbf{k}) \int_{\mathbb{R}^N} K_{A^{-1}}(\mathbf{k},\mathbf{y}) \overline{g(\mathbf{y}-\mathbf{t})} K_A(\mathbf{y},\mathbf{u}) d\mathbf{y} d\mathbf{k}. \end{aligned} \tag{13}$$

Assume that $Q^*(\mathbf{k}|\mathbf{u},\mathbf{t}) = \int_{\mathbb{R}^N} K_{A^{-1}}(\mathbf{k},\mathbf{y}) \overline{g(\mathbf{y}-\mathbf{t})} K_A(\mathbf{y},\mathbf{u}) d\mathbf{y}$ and $\mathbf{y}-\mathbf{t} = \mathbf{p}$, then

$$\begin{aligned} Q^*(\mathbf{k}|\mathbf{u},\mathbf{t}) &= \int_{\mathbb{R}^N} K_{A^{-1}}(\mathbf{k},\mathbf{y}) \overline{g(\mathbf{y}-\mathbf{t})} K_A(\mathbf{y},\mathbf{u}) d\mathbf{y} \\ &= \int_{\mathbb{R}^N} \overline{g(\mathbf{p})} \frac{1}{\sqrt{-i2\pi b}} \frac{1}{\sqrt{i2\pi b}} e^{-i\frac{(\mathbf{u}-\mathbf{k})}{b}(\mathbf{p}+\mathbf{t})+i\frac{d}{2b}(\mathbf{u}^2-\mathbf{k}^2)} d\mathbf{p} \\ &= \frac{1}{\sqrt{i2\pi b}} \int_{\mathbb{R}^N} \frac{1}{\sqrt{-i2\pi b}} \overline{g(\mathbf{p})} e^{i\frac{0}{-2b}\mathbf{p}^2 - i\frac{(\mathbf{k}-\mathbf{u})}{-b}\mathbf{p}+i\frac{d'}{-2b}(\mathbf{k}-\mathbf{u})^2} d\mathbf{p} \\ &\quad \times e^{i\frac{d'}{2b}(\mathbf{k}-\mathbf{u})^2+i\frac{d}{2b}(\mathbf{u}^2-\mathbf{k}^2)-i\frac{(\mathbf{u}-\mathbf{k})}{b}\mathbf{t}} \\ &= \frac{1}{\sqrt{i2\pi b}} e^{i\frac{d'}{2b}(\mathbf{k}-\mathbf{u})^2} L_{A_1}^g(\mathbf{k}-\mathbf{u})^* e^{-i\frac{\mathbf{u}\mathbf{t}}{b}+i\frac{d}{2b}\mathbf{u}^2} e^{i\frac{\mathbf{k}\mathbf{t}}{b}+i\frac{-d}{2b}\mathbf{k}^2} \\ &= \sqrt{-i2\pi b} e^{i\frac{d'}{2b}(\mathbf{k}-\mathbf{u})^2} L_{A_1}^g(\mathbf{k}-\mathbf{u})^* K_A(\mathbf{t},\mathbf{u}) K_A^*(\mathbf{t},\mathbf{k}). \end{aligned} \tag{14}$$

Hence the Formula (13) becomes (12). □

3. Inequalities Associated with the WLCT

The aim of this section is to obtain the new inequalities for the WLCT by the precise mathematical formulation.

Definition 3. *Let $f \in L^2(\mathbb{R}^N)$, then we can define* [21]

$$\mathbf{t^f} = \frac{1}{E} \int_{\mathbb{R}^N} \mathbf{t} \mid f(\mathbf{t}) \mid^2 d\mathbf{t}, \tag{15}$$

$$\mathbf{u^f} = \frac{1}{E} \int_{\mathbb{R}^N} \mathbf{u} \mid \widehat{f}(\mathbf{u}) \mid^2 d\mathbf{u}, \tag{16}$$

$$\mathbf{u_f^A} = \frac{1}{E} \int_{\mathbb{R}^N} \mathbf{u} \mid L_A^f(\mathbf{u}) \mid^2 d\mathbf{u}. \tag{17}$$

$$\Delta_f^2 = \frac{1}{E} \int_{\mathbb{R}^N} (\mathbf{t}-\mathbf{t^f})^2 \mid f(\mathbf{t}) \mid^2 d\mathbf{t}, \tag{18}$$

$$\Lambda_f^2 = \frac{1}{E} \int_{\mathbb{R}^N} (\mathbf{u}-\mathbf{u^f})^2 \mid \widehat{f}(\mathbf{u}) \mid^2 d\mathbf{u}, \tag{19}$$

$$\Lambda_{A,f}^2 = \frac{1}{E} \int_{\mathbb{R}^N} (\mathbf{u}-\mathbf{u_f^A})^2 \mid L_A^f(\mathbf{u}) \mid^2 d\mathbf{u}, \tag{20}$$

where

$$E = \int_{\mathbb{R}^N} \mid f(\mathbf{t}) \mid^2 d\mathbf{t} = \int_{\mathbb{R}^N} \mid L_A^f(\mathbf{u}) \mid^2 d\mathbf{u} = \int_{\mathbb{R}^N} \mid \widehat{f}(\mathbf{u}) \mid^2 d\mathbf{u}, \tag{21}$$

$$\mathbf{t^f} = (t_1^f, t_2^f, \cdots, t_N^f),\tag{22}$$

$$t_k^f = \frac{1}{E}\int_{\mathbb{R}^N} t_k \mid f(\mathbf{t}) \mid^2 d\mathbf{t},\tag{23}$$

$$\mathbf{u^f} = (u_1^f, u_2^f, \cdots, u_N^f),\tag{24}$$

$$u_k^f = \frac{1}{E}\int_{\mathbb{R}^N} u_k \mid \widehat{f}(\mathbf{u}) \mid^2 d\mathbf{u}.\tag{25}$$

Zhang [8] has generalized the N-dimensional Heisenberg's inequality of the FT for complex function. It can be restated as follows:

Lemma 2. *Let* $f(\mathbf{t}) = f_1(\mathbf{t})e^{i\phi(\mathbf{t})} \in L^2(\mathbb{R}^N)$, *for any* $1 \leq \varepsilon \leq N$, *the classical partial derivatives* $\frac{\partial f}{\partial t_\varepsilon}, \frac{\partial f_1}{\partial t_\varepsilon}, \frac{\partial \phi}{\partial t_\varepsilon}$ *exist at any point* $\mathbf{t} \in \mathbb{R}^N$, *then the inequality of the N-dimensional FT can be obtained:*

$$\Delta_f^2 \Lambda_f^2 \geq \frac{N^2}{16\pi^2}\|f\|^2 + COV_f^2,\tag{26}$$

where

$$COV_f = \int_{\mathbb{R}^N}|\mathbf{t} - \mathbf{t^f}|| \omega_t\phi - \mathbf{u^f}|f_1^2(\mathbf{t})d\mathbf{t},\tag{27}$$

and $\omega_t\phi = (\frac{\partial \phi}{\partial t_1}, \frac{\partial \phi}{\partial t_2}, \cdots, \frac{\partial \phi}{\partial t_N})$. *If* $\omega_t\phi$ *is continuous and* $f_1 \neq 0$, *then the equality holds if and only if* $f(\mathbf{t})$ *is a chirp function, the function is*

$$f(\mathbf{t}) = e^{-\frac{|\mathbf{t}-\mathbf{t^f}|^2}{2\varepsilon}} + \iota e^{2\pi i\left[\frac{1}{2\vartheta}\sum_{\kappa=1}^N \varrho(t_\kappa)|t_\kappa - t_\kappa^f|^2 + \mathbf{tu^f} + \iota\prod_{\sigma=1}^N \varrho(t_\sigma)\right]},\tag{28}$$

where $\varepsilon, \vartheta > 0$ *and* $\iota, \iota\prod_{\sigma=1}^N \varrho(t_\sigma) \in \mathbb{R}$,

$$\varrho(t_\sigma) = \begin{cases} 1, & \sigma \in \mathbf{z}_{1\tau} \\ -1, & \sigma \in \mathbf{z}_{2\tau} \\ sgn(t_\sigma - t_\sigma^f), & \sigma \in \mathbf{z}_{3\tau} \\ -sgn(t_\sigma - t_\sigma^f), & \sigma \in \mathbf{z}_{4\tau} \end{cases},\tag{29}$$

$$\mathbf{z}_{1\tau} = \{z_{11}, z_{12}, \cdots, z_{1\tau}\} = \left\{1 \leq s \leq N \mid \frac{\partial \phi}{\partial t_s} = \frac{1}{\vartheta}(t_s - t_s^f) + u_s^f\right\},\tag{30}$$

$$\mathbf{z}_{2\tau} = \{z_{21}, z_{22}, \cdots, z_{2\tau}\} = \left\{1 \leq s \leq N \mid \frac{\partial \phi}{\partial t_s} = -\frac{1}{\vartheta}(t_s - t_s^f) + u_s^f\right\},\tag{31}$$

$$\mathbf{z}_{3\tau} = \{z_{31}, z_{32}, \cdots, z_{3\tau}\} = \left\{1 \leq s \leq N \mid \frac{\partial \phi}{\partial t_s} = \begin{cases}\frac{1}{\vartheta}(t_s - t_s^f) + u_s^f, & t_s \geq t_s^f \\ -\frac{1}{\vartheta}(t_s - t_s^f) + u_s^f, & t_s < t_s^f\end{cases}\right\},\tag{32}$$

$$\mathbf{z}_{4\tau} = \{z_{41}, z_{42}, \cdots, z_{4\tau}\} = \left\{1 \leq s \leq N \mid \frac{\partial \phi}{\partial t_s} = \begin{cases}-\frac{1}{\vartheta}(t_s - t_s^f) + u_s^f, & t_s \geq t_s^f \\ \frac{1}{\vartheta}(t_s - t_s^f) + u_s^f, & t_s < t_s^f\end{cases}\right\},\tag{33}$$

and $\bigcup_{\rho=1}^{4} \mathbf{z}_{\rho\tau} = \{1, 2, \cdots, N\}$, $\mathbf{z}_{\rho'\tau} \cap \mathbf{z}_{\rho\tau} = \varnothing$ for $\rho \neq \rho'$.

Theorem 1. *Let* $f(\mathbf{t}) = f_1(\mathbf{t})e^{i\phi(\mathbf{t})} \in L^2(\mathbb{R}^N)$, $\mathbf{t}f(\mathbf{t}) \in L^2(\mathbb{R}^N)$, *for any* $1 \leq \varepsilon \leq N$ *the classical partial derivatives* $\frac{\partial f}{\partial t_\varepsilon}, \frac{\partial f_1}{\partial t_\varepsilon}, \frac{\partial \phi}{\partial t_\varepsilon}$ *exist at any point* $\mathbf{t} \in \mathbb{R}^N$, $E = 1$, *then inequality of the N-dimensional LCT can be obtained*

$$\Delta_f^2 \Lambda_{A,f}^2 \geq \frac{(bN)^2}{i16\pi^2}\|f\|^2 + COV_{f,A}^2, \tag{34}$$

where

$$COV_{f,A} = \int_{\mathbb{R}^N} |\mathbf{t} - \mathbf{t}^\mathbf{f}| |\omega_t \phi' - \mathbf{u}_f^A| f_1^2(\mathbf{t}) d\mathbf{t}, \tag{35}$$

$\phi'(\mathbf{t}) = \phi(\mathbf{t}) + \frac{a}{2b}\mathbf{t}^2$ *and* $\omega_t \phi' = (\frac{\partial \phi'}{\partial t_1}, \frac{\partial \phi'}{\partial t_2}, \cdots, \frac{\partial \phi'}{\partial t_N})$, *If* $\omega_t \phi$ *is continuous and* $f_1 \neq 0$, *then the equality holds if and only if* $f(\mathbf{t})$ *is a chirp function (28).*

Proof. According to the Formulas (2) and (6), we have

$$L_A[f(\mathbf{t})](\mathbf{u}) = \frac{1}{\sqrt{ib}} F\{f(\mathbf{t})e^{i\frac{a}{2b}\mathbf{t}^2}\}\left(\frac{\mathbf{u}}{b}\right)e^{i\frac{d}{2b}\mathbf{u}^2}, \tag{36}$$

let $\mathbf{u}' = \frac{\mathbf{u}}{b}$ and $f'(\mathbf{t}) = f(\mathbf{t})e^{i\frac{a}{2b}\mathbf{t}^2}$, then

$$\begin{aligned}
\Delta_f^2 \Lambda_{A,f}^2 &= \int_{\mathbb{R}^N} (\mathbf{t} - \mathbf{t}^\mathbf{f})^2 \mid f(\mathbf{t}) \mid^2 d\mathbf{t} \int_{\mathbb{R}^N} (\mathbf{u} - \mathbf{u}_f^A)^2 \mid L_A^f(\mathbf{u}) \mid^2 d\mathbf{u} \\
&= \frac{1}{ib} \int_{\mathbb{R}^N} (\mathbf{t} - \mathbf{t}^\mathbf{f})^2 \mid f'(\mathbf{t}) \mid^2 d\mathbf{t} \int_{\mathbb{R}^N} (\mathbf{u} - \mathbf{u}_f^A)^2 \mid F\{f'(\mathbf{t})\}\left(\frac{\mathbf{u}}{b}\right) \mid^2 d\mathbf{u} \\
&= \frac{b^2}{i} \int_{\mathbb{R}^N} (\mathbf{t} - \mathbf{t}^\mathbf{f})^2 \mid f'(\mathbf{t}) \mid^2 d\mathbf{t} \int_{\mathbb{R}^N} (\mathbf{u}' - \mathbf{u}_f'^A)^2 \mid F\{f'(\mathbf{t})\}(\mathbf{u}') \mid^2 d\mathbf{u}'.
\end{aligned} \tag{37}$$

By the Formula (26), we have

$$\Delta_f^2 \Lambda_{A,f}^2 \geq \frac{(bN)^2}{i16\pi^2}\|f\|^2 + COV_{f,A}^2. \tag{38}$$

□

Corollary 1. *When* $A = \begin{bmatrix} 0 & 1 \\ -1 & 0 \end{bmatrix}$, *the above theorem can become the Lemma 2.*

Corollary 2. *When* $A = \begin{bmatrix} \cos\alpha & \sin\alpha \\ -\sin\alpha & \cos\alpha \end{bmatrix}$, *the above theorem can reduce the N-dimensional Heisenberg's inequality of the FRFT for complex function [8].*

Definition 4. *Let* $f, g \in L^2(\mathbb{R}^N)$, *then we can give the definition [11]*

$$\mathbf{t}_A^W = \frac{1}{\|W_g^A f(\mathbf{t}, \mathbf{u})\|^2} \int_{\mathbb{R}^N} \int_{\mathbb{R}^N} \mathbf{t} \mid W_g^A f(\mathbf{t}, \mathbf{u}) \mid^2 d\mathbf{t}d\mathbf{u}, \tag{39}$$

$$\mathbf{u}_A^W = \frac{1}{\|W_g^A f(\mathbf{t}, \mathbf{u})\|^2} \int_{\mathbb{R}^N} \int_{\mathbb{R}^N} \mathbf{u} \mid W_g^A f(\mathbf{t}, \mathbf{u}) \mid^2 d\mathbf{t}d\mathbf{u}, \tag{40}$$

$$\Phi_{A,W}^2 = \frac{1}{\|W_g^A f(\mathbf{t},\mathbf{u})\|^2} \int_{\mathbb{R}^N} \int_{\mathbb{R}^N} (\mathbf{t} - \mathbf{t}_A^W)^2 \mid W_g^A f(\mathbf{t},\mathbf{u}) \mid^2 d\mathbf{t} d\mathbf{u}, \tag{41}$$

$$\Psi_{A,W}^2 = \frac{1}{\|W_g^A f(\mathbf{t},\mathbf{u})\|^2} \int_{\mathbb{R}^N} \int_{\mathbb{R}^N} (\mathbf{u} - \mathbf{u}_A^W)^2 \mid W_g^A f(\mathbf{t},\mathbf{u}) \mid^2 d\mathbf{t} d\mathbf{u}, \tag{42}$$

Next, the N-dimensional Heisenberg's inequality of the WLCT will be obtained.

Theorem 2. *Let $A = \begin{bmatrix} a & b \\ c & d \end{bmatrix}$ be a matrix parameter satisfying $a,b,c,d \in \mathbb{R}$ and $ad - bc = 1$. For $f(t) = f_1(t)e^{i\phi(t)} \in L^2(\mathbb{R}^N)$, $g(t) = g_1(t)e^{i\varphi(t)} \in L^2(\mathbb{R}^N)$, $tf(t) \in L^2(\mathbb{R}^N)$, we have*

$$\Phi_{A,W}^2 \Psi_{A,W}^2 \geq \frac{(bN)^2}{i16\pi^2}\|f\|^2 + COV_{f,A}^2 + \frac{(bN)^2}{i16\pi^2}\|g\|^2 + COV_{g,A_1}^2 \tag{43}$$

$$+ 2\left(\left(\frac{(bN)^2}{i16\pi^2}\|f\|^2 + COV_{f,A}^2\right)\left(\frac{(bN)^2}{i16\pi^2}\|g\|^2 + COV_{g,A_1}^2\right)\right)^{\frac{1}{2}}, \tag{44}$$

where $A_1 = \begin{bmatrix} 0 & b' \\ -\frac{1}{b'} & d' \end{bmatrix}$, $0 \neq b' = b \in \mathbb{R}$, the equality holds if and only if $f(t)$ is a chirp function (28).

Proof. On the one hand, according to Lemma 1 and the Formula (9), we obtain

$$\begin{aligned}
\|W_g^A f(\mathbf{t},\mathbf{u})\|^2 &= \int_{\mathbb{R}^N} \int_{\mathbb{R}^N} |W_g^A f(\mathbf{t},\mathbf{u})|^2 d\mathbf{t} d\mathbf{u} \\
&= \int_{\mathbb{R}^N} \int_{\mathbb{R}^N} \Big[\int_{\mathbb{R}^N} L_A^f(\mathbf{m}) \sqrt{-i2\pi b} e^{i\frac{d'}{2b}(\mathbf{m}-\mathbf{u})^2} \\
&\quad \times L_{A_1}^g(\mathbf{m}-\mathbf{u})^* K_A(\mathbf{t},\mathbf{u}) K_A^*(\mathbf{t},\mathbf{m}) d\mathbf{m} \Big] \\
&\quad \times \Big[\int_{\mathbb{R}^N} L_A^f(\mathbf{n}) \sqrt{-i2\pi b} e^{i\frac{d'}{2b}(\mathbf{n}-\mathbf{u})^2} \\
&\quad \times L_{A_1}^g(\mathbf{n}-\mathbf{u})^* K_A(\mathbf{t},\mathbf{u}) K_A^*(\mathbf{t},\mathbf{n}) d\mathbf{n} \Big]^* d\mathbf{t} d\mathbf{u} \\
&= \int_{\mathbb{R}^N} \int_{\mathbb{R}^N} |L_A^f(\mathbf{m})|^2 |L_{A_1}^g(\mathbf{m}-\mathbf{u})|^2 d\mathbf{m} d\mathbf{u}.
\end{aligned} \tag{45}$$

Let $\mathbf{m} - \mathbf{u} = \mathbf{v}$, then

$$\begin{aligned}
\|W_g^A f(\mathbf{t},\mathbf{u})\|^2 &= \int_{\mathbb{R}^N} \int_{\mathbb{R}^N} |L_A^f(\mathbf{m})|^2 |L_{A_1}^g(\mathbf{v})|^2 d\mathbf{m} d\mathbf{v} \\
&= \|L_A^f(\mathbf{m})\|^2 \|L_{A_1}^g(\mathbf{v})\|^2.
\end{aligned} \tag{46}$$

Moreover, we obtain

$$\begin{aligned}
\mathbf{t}_A^W &= \frac{1}{\|W_g^A f(\mathbf{t},\mathbf{u})\|^2} \int_{\mathbb{R}^N} \int_{\mathbb{R}^N} \mathbf{t} \mid W_g^A f(\mathbf{t},\mathbf{u}) \mid^2 d\mathbf{t} d\mathbf{u} \\
&= \frac{1}{\|L_A^f(\mathbf{m})\|^2 \|L_{A_1}^g(\mathbf{v})\|^2} \int_{\mathbb{R}^N} \int_{\mathbb{R}^N} \mathbf{t} \Big[\int_{\mathbb{R}^N} f(\mathbf{m}') \overline{g(\mathbf{m}'-\mathbf{t})} K_A(\mathbf{m}',\mathbf{u}) d\mathbf{m}' \Big] \\
&\quad \times \Big[\int_{\mathbb{R}^N} f(\mathbf{n}') \overline{g(\mathbf{n}'-\mathbf{t})} K_A(\mathbf{n}',\mathbf{u}) d\mathbf{n}' \Big]^* d\mathbf{t} d\mathbf{u} \\
&= \frac{1}{\|L_A^f(\mathbf{m})\|^2 \|L_{A_1}^g(\mathbf{v})\|^2} \int_{\mathbb{R}^N} \int_{\mathbb{R}^N} \mathbf{t}|f(\mathbf{m}')|^2 |g(\mathbf{m}'-\mathbf{t})|^2 d\mathbf{m}' d\mathbf{t}.
\end{aligned} \tag{47}$$

Let $m' - t = r$, then

$$t_A^W = \frac{1}{\|L_A^f(\mathbf{m})\|^2 \|L_{A_1}^g(\mathbf{v})\|^2} \int_{\mathbb{R}^N} \int_{\mathbb{R}^N} (\mathbf{m}' - \mathbf{r}) |f(\mathbf{m}')|^2 |g(\mathbf{r})|^2 d\mathbf{m}' d\mathbf{r}$$

$$= \frac{1}{\|L_A^f(\mathbf{m}')\|^2} \int_{\mathbb{R}^N} \mathbf{m}' |f(\mathbf{m}')|^2 d\mathbf{m}' - \frac{1}{\|L_{A_1}^g(\mathbf{v})\|^2} \int_{\mathbb{R}^N} \mathbf{r} |g(\mathbf{r})|^2 d\mathbf{r} \quad (48)$$

$$= \mathbf{t}^f - \mathbf{t}^g.$$

Using the same method, we can obtain

$$\mathbf{u}_A^W = \mathbf{u}_f^A - \mathbf{u}_g^{A_1}. \quad (49)$$

From the Formula (46), then

$$\Psi_{A,W}^2 = \frac{1}{\|W_g^A f(\mathbf{t}, \mathbf{u})\|^2} \int_{\mathbb{R}^N} \int_{\mathbb{R}^N} (\mathbf{u} - \mathbf{u}_A^W)^2 |W_g^A f(\mathbf{t}, \mathbf{u})|^2 d\mathbf{t} d\mathbf{u}$$

$$= \frac{1}{\|L_A^f(\mathbf{m})\|^2} \int_{\mathbb{R}^N} (\mathbf{m}' - \mathbf{u}_f^A)^2 |L_A^f(\mathbf{m}')|^2 d\mathbf{m}' + \frac{1}{\|L_{A_1}^g(\mathbf{v})\|^2}$$

$$\times \int_{\mathbb{R}^N} (\mathbf{v}' - \mathbf{u}_g^{A_1})^2 |L_{A_1}^g(\mathbf{v}')|^2 d\mathbf{v}' - 2 \frac{1}{\|L_A^f(\mathbf{m})\|^2} \quad (50)$$

$$\times \int_{\mathbb{R}^N} (\mathbf{m}' - \mathbf{u}_f^A) |L_A^f(\mathbf{m}')|^2 d\mathbf{m}' \frac{1}{\|L_{A_1}^g(\mathbf{v})\|^2}$$

$$\times \int_{\mathbb{R}^N} (\mathbf{v}' - \mathbf{u}_g^{A_1}) |L_{A_1}^g(\mathbf{v}')|^2 d\mathbf{v}'$$

$$= \Lambda_{A,f}^2 + \Lambda_{A_1,g}^2.$$

From the same method, we can obtain

$$\Phi_{A,W}^2 = \Delta_f^2 + \Delta_g^2, \quad (51)$$

On the other hand, using the Formulas (48)–(51), we can obtain

$$\Phi_{A,W}^2 \Psi_{A,W}^2 = (\Delta_f^2 + \Delta_g^2)(\Lambda_{A,f}^2 + \Lambda_{A_1,g}^2)$$
$$= \Delta_f^2 \Lambda_{A,f}^2 + \Delta_g^2 \Lambda_{A_1,g}^2 + \Delta_f^2 \Lambda_{A_1,g}^2 + \Delta_g^2 \Lambda_{A,f}^2. \quad (52)$$

According to the fact: $n^2 + m^2 \geq 2nm$, for $\forall n, m \in \mathbb{R}$, then

$$\Phi_{A,W}^2 \Psi_{A,W}^2 = \Delta_f^2 \Lambda_{A,f}^2 + \Delta_g^2 \Lambda_{A_1,g}^2 + \Delta_f^2 \Lambda_{A_1,g}^2 + \Delta_g^2 \Lambda_{A,f}^2$$
$$\geq \Delta_f^2 \Lambda_{A,f}^2 + \Delta_g^2 \Lambda_{A_1,g}^2 + 2\sqrt{\Delta_f^2 \Lambda_{A,f}^2 \Delta_g^2 \Lambda_{A_1,g}^2}. \quad (53)$$

From the Formula (34), we can obtain the result. □

Corollary 3. *When* $A = \begin{bmatrix} \cos \alpha & \sin \alpha \\ -\sin \alpha & \cos \alpha \end{bmatrix}$, *the N-dimensional Heisenberg's inequality of the windowed fractional Fourier transform (WFRFT)* [22] *for the complex function can be obtained:*

$$\Phi_{\alpha,W}^2 \Psi_{\alpha,W}^2 \geq \frac{(\sin \alpha N)^2}{i16\pi^2} \|f\|^2 + COV_{f,\alpha}^2 + \frac{(\sin \alpha N)^2}{i16\pi^2} \|g\|^2 + COV_{g,\alpha_1}^2 \quad (54)$$

$$+ 2\left(\left(\frac{(\sin \alpha N)^2}{i16\pi^2} \|f\|^2 + COV_{f,\alpha}^2\right)\left(\frac{(\sin \alpha N)^2}{i16\pi^2} \|g\|^2 + COV_{g,\alpha_1}^2\right)\right)^{\frac{1}{2}}, \quad (55)$$

where

$$\Phi_{\alpha,W}^2 = \frac{1}{\|W_g^\alpha f(\mathbf{t},\mathbf{u})\|^2} \int_{\mathbb{R}^N} \int_{\mathbb{R}^N} (\mathbf{t} - \mathbf{t}_\alpha^W)^2 \mid W_g^\alpha f(\mathbf{t},\mathbf{u})\mid^2 d\mathbf{t}d\mathbf{u}, \quad (56)$$

$$\Psi_{\alpha,W}^2 = \frac{1}{\|W_g^\alpha f(\mathbf{t},\mathbf{u})\|^2} \int_{\mathbb{R}^N} \int_{\mathbb{R}^N} (\mathbf{u} - \mathbf{u}_\alpha^W)^2 \mid W_g^\alpha f(\mathbf{t},\mathbf{u})\mid^2 d\mathbf{t}d\mathbf{u}, \quad (57)$$

$$\mathbf{t}_\alpha^W = \frac{1}{\|W_g^\alpha f(\mathbf{t},\mathbf{u})\|^2} \int_{\mathbb{R}^N} \int_{\mathbb{R}^N} \mathbf{t} \mid W_g^\alpha f(\mathbf{t},\mathbf{u})\mid^2 d\mathbf{t}d\mathbf{u}, \quad (58)$$

$$\mathbf{u}_\alpha^W = \frac{1}{\|W_g^\alpha f(\mathbf{t},\mathbf{u})\|^2} \int_{\mathbb{R}^N} \int_{\mathbb{R}^N} \mathbf{u} \mid W_g^\alpha f(\mathbf{t},\mathbf{u})\mid^2 d\mathbf{t}d\mathbf{u}, \quad (59)$$

$$COV_{f,\alpha} = \int_{\mathbb{R}^N} |\mathbf{t} - \mathbf{t}^f| |\omega_t \phi' - \mathbf{u}_{f,W}^\alpha| f_1^2(\mathbf{t})d\mathbf{t}, \quad (60)$$

$$COV_{g,\alpha'} = \int_{\mathbb{R}^N} |\mathbf{t} - \mathbf{t}^g| |\omega_t \phi' - \mathbf{u}_{g,W}^{\alpha'}| g_1^2(\mathbf{t})d\mathbf{t}, \quad (61)$$

$$\mathbf{u}_{f,W}^\alpha = \frac{1}{E} \int_{\mathbb{R}^N} \mathbf{u} \mid W_g^\alpha f(\mathbf{t},\mathbf{u})\mid^2 d\mathbf{u}, \quad (62)$$

$$\mathbf{u}_{g,W}^{\alpha'} = \frac{1}{E} \int_{\mathbb{R}^N} \mathbf{u} \mid W_g^\alpha f(\mathbf{t},\mathbf{u})\mid^2 d\mathbf{u}, \quad (63)$$

and $W_g^\alpha f(\mathbf{t},\mathbf{u})$ is the WFRFT of complex function

$$W_g^\alpha f(\mathbf{t},\mathbf{u}) = \begin{cases} \int_{\mathbb{R}^N} f(\mathbf{y}) g^*(\mathbf{y} - \mathbf{t}) K_\alpha(\mathbf{y},\mathbf{u}) d\mathbf{y}, & \alpha \neq n\pi \\ f(\mathbf{u}), & \alpha = 2n\pi \\ -f(\mathbf{u}), & \alpha = (2n+1)\pi \end{cases}, \quad (64)$$

and $K_\alpha(\mathbf{y},\mathbf{u}) = (1 - i\cot\alpha)^{\frac{N}{2}} e^{\pi i(|\mathbf{y}|^2 + |\mathbf{u}|^2)\cot\alpha - 2\pi i \mathbf{y}\mathbf{u}\csc\alpha}$.

Corollary 4. *When $A = \begin{bmatrix} 0 & 1 \\ -1 & 0 \end{bmatrix}$, the N-dimensional Heisenberg's inequality of the windowed Fourier transform (WFT) [23] for the complex function can be obtained:*

$$\Phi_W^2 \Psi_W^2 \geq \frac{N^2}{i16\pi^2}(\|f\|^2 + \|g\|^2) + COV_f^2 + COV_g^2 \quad (65)$$

$$+ 2\left(\left(\frac{N^2}{i16\pi^2}\|f\|^2 + COV_f^2\right)\left(\frac{N^2}{i16\pi^2}\|g\|^2 + COV_g^2\right)\right)^{\frac{1}{2}}, \quad (66)$$

where

$$\Phi_W^2 = \frac{1}{\|W_g f(\mathbf{t},\mathbf{u})\|^2} \int_{\mathbb{R}^N} \int_{\mathbb{R}^N} (\mathbf{t} - \mathbf{t}^W)^2 \mid W_g f(\mathbf{t},\mathbf{u})\mid^2 d\mathbf{t}d\mathbf{u}, \quad (67)$$

$$\Psi_W^2 = \frac{1}{\|W_g f(\mathbf{t},\mathbf{u})\|^2} \int_{\mathbb{R}^N} \int_{\mathbb{R}^N} (\mathbf{u} - \mathbf{u}^W)^2 \mid W_g f(\mathbf{t},\mathbf{u})\mid^2 d\mathbf{t}d\mathbf{u}, \quad (68)$$

$$t^W = \frac{1}{\|W_g f(\mathbf{t},\mathbf{u})\|^2} \int_{\mathbb{R}^N} \int_{\mathbb{R}^N} \mathbf{t} \mid W_g f(\mathbf{t},\mathbf{u}) \mid^2 d\mathbf{t} d\mathbf{u}, \qquad (69)$$

$$\mathbf{u}^W = \frac{1}{\|W_g f(\mathbf{t},\mathbf{u})\|^2} \int_{\mathbb{R}^N} \int_{\mathbb{R}^N} \mathbf{u} \mid W_g f(\mathbf{t},\mathbf{u}) \mid^2 d\mathbf{t} d\mathbf{u}, \qquad (70)$$

$$COV_f = \int_{\mathbb{R}^N} |\mathbf{t} - \mathbf{t}^f| |\omega_t \phi' - \mathbf{u}_{f,W}| f_1^2(\mathbf{t}) d\mathbf{t}, \qquad (71)$$

$$COV_g = \int_{\mathbb{R}^N} |\mathbf{t} - \mathbf{t}^g| |\omega_t \phi' - \mathbf{u}_{g,W}| g_1^2(\mathbf{t}) d\mathbf{t}, \qquad (72)$$

$$\mathbf{u}_{f,W} = \frac{1}{E} \int_{\mathbb{R}^N} \mathbf{u} \mid W_g f(\mathbf{t},\mathbf{u}) \mid^2 d\mathbf{u}, \qquad (73)$$

$$\mathbf{u}_{g,W} = \frac{1}{E} \int_{\mathbb{R}^N} \mathbf{u} \mid W_g f(\mathbf{t},\mathbf{u}) \mid^2 d\mathbf{u}, \qquad (74)$$

and $W_g f(\mathbf{t},\mathbf{u})$ is the WFT of the complex function

$$W_g f(\mathbf{t},\mathbf{u}) = \begin{cases} \int_{\mathbb{R}^N} f(\mathbf{y}) g^*(\mathbf{y}-\mathbf{t}) e^{-i\mathbf{y}\mathbf{u}} d\mathbf{y}, & \alpha \neq n\pi \\ f(\mathbf{u}), & \alpha = 2n\pi \\ -f(\mathbf{u}), & \alpha = (2n+1)\pi \end{cases}. \qquad (75)$$

4. Conclusions

In this paper, by the N-dimensional Heisenberg's inequality of the FT, the N-dimensional Heisenberg's inequalities for the WLCT of a complex function are generalized. Firstly, the definition for N-dimensional WLCT of a complex function is given. In addition, according to the second-order moment of the LCT, the N-dimensional Heisenberg's inequality for the linear canonical transform (LCT) is derived. It shows that the lower bound is related to the covariance and can be achieved by a complex chirp function with a Gaussian function. Finally, the second-order moment of the WLCT is given, the relationship between the LCT and WLCT is obtained, and the N-dimensional Heisenberg's inequality for the WLCT is exploited. In special cases, its corollaries can be obtained.

Author Contributions: Writing-original draft, Z.-W.L. and W.-B.G. All authors contributed equally to the writing of the manuscript and read and approved the final version of the manuscript.

Funding: This research received no external funding.

Data Availability Statement: Data are contained within the article.

Conflicts of Interest: The authors declare no conflict of interest.

References

1. Osipenko, K.Y. Inequalities for derivatives with the Fourier transform. *Appl. Comput. Harmonic. Anal.* **2021**, *53*, 132–150. [CrossRef]
2. Grunbaum, F.A. The Heisenberg inequality for the discrete Fourier transform. *Appl. Comput. Harmonic. Anal.* **2003**, *15*, 163–167. [CrossRef]
3. Lian, P. Sharp Hausdorff-Young inequalities for the quaternion Fourier transforms. *Proc. Am. Math. Soc.* **2020**, *148*, 697–703. [CrossRef]
4. De Carli, L.; Gorbachev, D.; Tikhonov, S. Pitt inequalities and restriction theorems for the Fourier transform. *Rev. Mat. Iberoam.* **2017**, *33*, 789–808. [CrossRef]
5. Nicola, F.; Tilli, P. The Faber-Krahn inequality for the short-time Fourier transform. *Invent. Math.* **2022**, *230*, 1–30. [CrossRef]

6. Johansen, T.R. Weighted inequalities and uncertainty principles for the (k, a)-generalized Fourier transform. *Int. J. Math.* **2016**, *27*, 1650019. [CrossRef]
7. Hardin, D.P.; Northington V, M.C.; Powell, A.M. A sharp balian-low uncertainty principle for shift-invariant spaces. *Appl. Comput. Harmonic. Anal.* **2018**, *44*, 294–311. [CrossRef]
8. Zhang, Z.C.; Han, Y.P.; Sun, Y.; Wu, A.Y.; Shi, X.Y.; Qiang, S.Z.; Jiang, X.; Wang, G.; Liu, L.B. Heisenberg's uncertainty principle for n-dimensional fractional fourier transform of complex-valued functions. *Optik* **2021**, *242*, 167052. [CrossRef]
9. Kou, K.I.; Xu, R.H. Windowed linear canonical transform and its applications. *Signal Process.* **2012**, *92*, 179–188. [CrossRef]
10. Wei, D.Y.; Hu, H.M. Theory and applications of short-time linear canonical transform. *Digit Signal Process.* **2021**, *118*, 103239. [CrossRef]
11. Gao, W.B.; Li, B.Z. Uncertainty principles for the short-time linear canonical transform of complex signals. *Digital Signal Process.* **2021**, *111*, 102953. [CrossRef]
12. Atanasova, S.; Maksimovic, S.; Pilipovic, S. Characterization of wave fronts of Ultradistributions using directional short-time Fourier transform. *Axioms* **2022**, *10*, 240. [CrossRef]
13. Tao, R.; Deng, B.; Wang, Y. *Fractional Fourier Transform and Its Applications*; Tsinghua University Press: Beijing, China, 2009.
14. Bahri, M.; Ashino, R. Some properties of windowed linear canonical transform and its logarithmic uncertainty principle. *Int. J. Wavelets Multiresolut. Inf. Process.* **2016**, *14*, 1650015. [CrossRef]
15. Huang, L.; Zhang, K.; Chai, Y.; Xu, S.Q. Computation of the short-time linear canonical transform with dual window. *Math. Probl. Eng.* **2017**, *2017*, 4127875. [CrossRef]
16. Kou, K.I.; Xu, R.H.; Zhang, Y.H. Paley-Wiener theorems and uncertainty principles for the windowed linear canonical transform. *Math. Methods Appl. Sci.* **2012**, *35*, 2122–2132. [CrossRef]
17. Gao, W.B.; Li, B.Z. Quaternion windowed linear canonical transform of two-dimensional signals. *Adv. Appl. Clifford Algebras* **2020**, *30*, 16. [CrossRef]
18. Kumar, M.; Pradhan, T. A framework of linear canonical transform on pseudo-differential operators and its application. *Math. Methods Appl. Sci.* **2021**, *44*, 11425–11443. [CrossRef]
19. Xu, T.Z.; Li, B.Z. *Linear Canonical Transform and Its Applications*; Science Press: Beijing, China, 2013.
20. Wolf, K.R. *Integral Transforms in Science and Engineering*; Plenum Press: New York, NY, USA, 1979.
21. Dang, P.; Deng, G.T.; Qian, T. A tighter uncertainty principle for linear canonical transform in terms of phase derivative. *IEEE Trans. Signal Process.* **2013**, *61*, 5153–5164. [CrossRef]
22. Gao, W.B.; Li, B.Z. Convolution theorem involving n-dimensional windowed fractional Fourier transform. *Sci. China Inf. Sci.* **2021**, *64*, 169302:1–169302:3. [CrossRef]
23. Gao, W.B.; Li, B.Z. Octonion short-time Fourier transform for time-frequency representation and its applications. *IEEE Trans. Signal Process.* **2021**, *69*, 6386–6398. [CrossRef]

Disclaimer/Publisher's Note: The statements, opinions and data contained in all publications are solely those of the individual author(s) and contributor(s) and not of MDPI and/or the editor(s). MDPI and/or the editor(s) disclaim responsibility for any injury to people or property resulting from any ideas, methods, instructions or products referred to in the content.

Article

Some New Estimates of Hermite–Hadamard Inequality with Application

Tao Zhang [1,*] and Alatancang Chen [2]

[1] College of Mathematics Science, Inner Mongolia Normal University, Hohhot 010022, China
[2] Center for Applied Mathematical Science, Inner Mongolia Normal University, Hohhot 010022, China; alatanca@imu.edu.cn
* Correspondence: zhangtaomath@imnu.edu.cn

Abstract: This paper establishes several new inequalities of Hermite–Hadamard type for $|f'|^q$ being convex for some fixed $q \in (0,1]$. As application, some error estimates on special means of real numbers are given.

Keywords: Hermite–Hardamard inequality; convex function; integral inequalities; special means

MSC: 26A51; 26D15

Citation: Zhang, T.; Chen, A. Some New Estimates of Hermite–Hadamard Inequality with Application. *Axioms* **2023**, *12*, 688. https://doi.org/10.3390/axioms12070688

Academic Editors: Wei-Shih Du, Ravi P. Agarwal, Erdal Karapinar, Marko Kostić and Jian Cao

Received: 5 June 2023
Revised: 8 July 2023
Accepted: 12 July 2023
Published: 14 July 2023

Copyright: © 2023 by the authors. Licensee MDPI, Basel, Switzerland. This article is an open access article distributed under the terms and conditions of the Creative Commons Attribution (CC BY) license (https://creativecommons.org/licenses/by/4.0/).

1. Introduction

For simplicity, in this paper we let $I \subseteq \mathbb{R} = (-\infty, +\infty)$ be an interval.

Definition 1. *A function $f : I \to \mathbb{R}$ is convex if*
$$f[t\alpha + (1-t)\beta] \leq tf(\alpha) + (1-t)f(\beta) \tag{1}$$
is true for any $\alpha, \beta \in I$ and $0 \leq t \leq 1$. The inequality (1) is reversed if f is concave on I.

Suppose that the function $f : I \to \mathbb{R}$ is convex on I, $\alpha, \beta \in I$ with $\alpha < \beta$, then
$$f\left(\frac{\alpha+\beta}{2}\right) \leq \frac{1}{\beta-\alpha}\int_\alpha^\beta f(x)\mathrm{d}x \leq \frac{f(\alpha)+f(\beta)}{2}. \tag{2}$$

It is well known in the literature as the Hermite–Hadamard inequality.

In [1], Dragomir and Agarwal obtained the following inequalities for the right part of (2).

Theorem 1 (Theorem 2.2 in [1]). *Suppose that $\alpha, \beta \in I^\circ$ and $\alpha < \beta$, the function $f : I^\circ \to \mathbb{R}$ is differentiable and $|f'|$ is convex on $[\alpha, \beta]$, then*
$$\left|\frac{f(\alpha)+f(\beta)}{2} - \frac{1}{\beta-\alpha}\int_\alpha^\beta f(x)\mathrm{d}x\right| \leq \frac{(\beta-\alpha)(|f'(\alpha)|+|f'(\beta)|)}{8}. \tag{3}$$

Theorem 2 (Theorem 2.3 in [1]). *Suppose that $\alpha, \beta \in I^\circ$, $\alpha < \beta$, and $p > 1$, the function $f : I^\circ \to \mathbb{R}$ is differentiable and $|f'|^{\frac{p}{p-1}}$ is convex on $[\alpha, \beta]$, then*
$$\left|\frac{f(\alpha)+f(\beta)}{2} - \frac{1}{\beta-\alpha}\int_\alpha^\beta f(x)\mathrm{d}x\right| \leq \frac{\beta-\alpha}{2(p+1)^{\frac{1}{p}}}\left(\frac{|f'(\alpha)|^{\frac{p}{p-1}}+|f'(\beta)|^{\frac{p}{p-1}}}{2}\right)^{\frac{p-1}{p}}. \tag{4}$$

In the literature, the extensions of the arithmetic, geometric, identric, logarithmic, and generalized logarithmic mean from two positive real numbers are, respectively, defined by

$$A(s,t) = \frac{s+t}{2}, \qquad s,t \in \mathbb{R},$$

$$G(s,t) = \sqrt{st}, \qquad s,t \in \mathbb{R}, \quad s,t > 0,$$

$$I(s,t) = \frac{1}{e}\left(\frac{t^t}{s^s}\right)^{\frac{1}{t-s}}, \qquad s,t > 0,$$

$$L(s,t) = \frac{t-s}{\ln|t| - \ln|s|}, \qquad |s| \neq |t|, \quad st \neq 0,$$

$$L_n(s,t) = \left[\frac{t^{n+1} - s^{n+1}}{(n+1)(t-s)}\right]^{\frac{1}{n}}, \qquad n \in \mathbb{Z}\setminus\{-1,0\}, \quad s,t \in \mathbb{R}, \quad s \neq t.$$

It is well known that $G(s,t) < L(s,t) < I(s,t) < A(s,t)$ for $s,t > 0$ with $s \neq t$, for example, see [2].

Dragomir and Agarwal used Theorem 1 and Theorem 2 to establish the following error estimates on special means:

Theorem 3 (Propositions 3.1–3.4 in [1]). *Suppose that $s,t \in I^\circ$, $s < t$, $n \in \mathbb{Z}$, then*

$$|A(s^n, t^n) - L_n(s,t)^n| \leq \frac{n(t-s)}{4} A\left(|s|^{n-1}, |t|^{n-1}\right), \qquad n \geq 2, \tag{5}$$

$$|A(s^n, t^n) - L_n(s,t)^n| \leq \frac{n(t-s)}{2(p+1)^{\frac{1}{p}}} \left[A\left(|s|^{\frac{(n-1)p}{p-1}}, |t|^{\frac{(n-1)p}{p-1}}\right)\right]^{\frac{p-1}{p}}, \qquad n \geq 2, \; p > 1, \tag{6}$$

$$|A\left(s^{-1}, t^{-1}\right) - L(s,t)^{-1}| \leq \frac{t-s}{4} A\left(|s|^{-2}, |t|^{-2}\right), \qquad 0 \notin [s,t], \tag{7}$$

$$|A\left(s^{-1}, t^{-1}\right) - L(s,t)^{-1}| \leq \frac{t-s}{2(p+1)^{\frac{1}{p}}} \left[A\left(|s|^{\frac{-2p}{p-1}}, |t|^{\frac{-2p}{p-1}}\right)\right]^{\frac{p-1}{p}}, \qquad 0 \notin [s,t], \; p > 1. \tag{8}$$

In [3], Pearce and Pečarić obtained a better upper bound for the inequality (4). Moreover, they obtained a similar inequality on the left part of (2).

Theorem 4 (Theorems 1 and 2 in [3]). *Suppose that $\alpha, \beta \in I^\circ$, $\alpha < \beta$ and $q \geq 1$, the function $f : I^\circ \to \mathbb{R}$ is differentiable and $|f'|^q$ is convex on $[\alpha, \beta]$, then*

$$\left|\frac{f(\alpha) + f(\beta)}{2} - \frac{1}{\beta - \alpha}\int_\alpha^\beta f(x)dx\right| \leq \frac{\beta - \alpha}{4}\left(\frac{|f'(\alpha)|^q + |f'(\beta)|^q}{2}\right)^{\frac{1}{q}} \tag{9}$$

and

$$\left|f\left(\frac{\alpha+\beta}{2}\right) - \frac{1}{\beta-\alpha}\int_\alpha^\beta f(x)dx\right| \leq \frac{\beta-\alpha}{4}\left(\frac{|f'(\alpha)|^q + |f'(\beta)|^q}{2}\right)^{\frac{1}{q}}. \tag{10}$$

By using Theorem 4, Pearce and Pečarić generalized and improved the error estimates (5)–(8) and obtained the following error estimates on special means:

Theorem 5 (Propositions 1 and 2 in [3]). *Suppose that $s,t \in \mathbb{R}$, $s < t$, $0 \notin [s,t]$, $n \in \mathbb{Z}$, $|n| \geq 2$, $q \geq 1$, then*

$$|A(s^n, t^n) - L_n(s, t)^n| \leq \frac{|n|(t-s)}{4}\left[A\left(|s|^{(n-1)q}, |t|^{(n-1)q}\right)\right]^{\frac{1}{q}}, \qquad (11)$$

$$|A(s, t)^n - L_n(s, t)^n| \leq \frac{|n|(t-s)}{4}\left[A\left(|s|^{(n-1)q}, |t|^{(n-1)q}\right)\right]^{\frac{1}{q}}, \qquad (12)$$

$$|A\left(s^{-1}, t^{-1}\right) - L(s, t)^{-1}| \leq \frac{t-s}{4}\left[A\left(|s|^{-2q}, |t|^{-2q}\right)\right]^{\frac{1}{q}}, \qquad (13)$$

$$|A(s, t)^{-1} - L(s, t)^{-1}| \leq \frac{t-s}{4}\left[A\left(|s|^{-2q}, |t|^{-2q}\right)\right]^{\frac{1}{q}}. \qquad (14)$$

However, using their method could not obtain the corresponding estimate for $q < 1$. In this paper, supposing that $|f'|^q$ is convex for some fixed $0 < q \leq 1$, we obtain some estimates of (2). Moreover, if $q = 1$, our results are the same as (9) and (10), respectively. As application, some error estimates on special means are given, then the inequalities (11)–(14) are improved.

2. Main Results

Theorem 6. Suppose that $\alpha, \beta \in I°$, $\alpha < \beta$ and $0 < q \leq 1$, the function $f : I° \to \mathbb{R}$ is differentiable and $|f'|^q$ is convex on $[\alpha, \beta]$.

(i) If $0 < q \leq \frac{1}{2}$, then

$$\left|\frac{f(\alpha) + f(\beta)}{2} - \frac{1}{\beta - \alpha}\int_\alpha^\beta f(x)dx\right| \leq \frac{q(\beta - \alpha)}{2(2q+1)}\left[\frac{q\left(q + 2^{\frac{1}{q}}\right)}{2(q+1)}(|f'(\alpha)| + |f'(\beta)|) \right.$$

$$\left. + (1-q)\sqrt{|f'(\alpha)f'(\beta)|}\right]. \qquad (15)$$

(ii) If $\frac{1}{2} < q \leq 1$, then

$$\left|\frac{f(\alpha) + f(\beta)}{2} - \frac{1}{\beta - \alpha}\int_\alpha^\beta f(x)dx\right| \leq \frac{q(\beta - \alpha)}{2(2q+1)}\left[\frac{1 + q \cdot 2^{-\frac{1}{q}}}{q+1}(|f'(\alpha)| + |f'(\beta)|) \right.$$

$$\left. + \left(1 - 2^{1-\frac{1}{q}}\right)\sqrt{|f'(\alpha)f'(\beta)|}\right]. \qquad (16)$$

Clearly, if $q = 1$, then (16) is the same as (9).

Corollary 1. Suppose that $\alpha, \beta \in I°$ and $\alpha < \beta$, the function $f : I° \to \mathbb{R}$ is differentiable and $|f'|^{\frac{1}{2}}$ is convex on $[\alpha, \beta]$, then for any $q \geq 1$, we have

$$\left|\frac{f(\alpha) + f(\beta)}{2} - \frac{1}{\beta - \alpha}\int_\alpha^\beta f(x)dx\right| \leq \frac{\beta - \alpha}{4}\left[\frac{3}{4}A(|f'(\alpha)|, |f'(\beta)|) + \frac{1}{4}G(|f'(\alpha)|, |f'(\beta)|)\right]$$

$$\leq \frac{\beta - \alpha}{4}A(|f'(\alpha)|, |f'(\beta)|)$$

$$\leq \frac{\beta - \alpha}{4}[A(|f'(\alpha)|^q, |f'(\beta)|^q)]^{\frac{1}{q}}. \qquad (17)$$

Proof. Let $q = \frac{1}{2}$ in the inequality (15) and we have the first inequality. Note that $\sqrt{|f'(\alpha)f'(\beta)|} \leq \frac{|f'(\alpha)| + |f'(\beta)|}{2}$, so the second inequality holds. By power–mean inequality, we can obtain the last inequality. □

Theorem 7. Suppose that $\alpha, \beta \in I°$, $\alpha < \beta$ and $0 < q \leq 1$, the function $f : I° \to \mathbb{R}$ is differentiable, and $|f'|^q$ is convex on $[\alpha, \beta]$.

(i) If $0 < q \leq \frac{1}{2}$, then

$$\left| f\left(\frac{\alpha+\beta}{2}\right) - \frac{1}{\beta-\alpha}\int_\alpha^\beta f(x)\mathrm{d}x \right| \leq \frac{q(\beta-\alpha)}{2(2q+1)}\left[\frac{q^2\left(2^{\frac{1}{q}+1}-1\right)}{2(q+1)}(|f'(\alpha)|+|f'(\beta)|) \right.$$

$$\left. +(1-q)\left(\left(\frac{1}{3}+\frac{1}{6q}\right)2^{\frac{1}{q}}-1\right)\sqrt{|f'(\alpha)f'(\beta)|}\right]. \tag{18}$$

(ii) If $\frac{1}{2} < q \leq 1$, then

$$\left| f\left(\frac{\alpha+\beta}{2}\right) - \frac{1}{\beta-\alpha}\int_\alpha^\beta f(x)\mathrm{d}x \right| \leq \frac{q(\beta-\alpha)}{2(2q+1)}\left[\frac{q\left(2-2^{-\frac{1}{q}}\right)}{q+1}(|f'(\alpha)|+|f'(\beta)|)\right.$$

$$\left. +\left(2^{\frac{1}{q}}-2\right)\left(\frac{1}{3}+\frac{1}{6q}-2^{-\frac{1}{q}}\right)\sqrt{|f'(\alpha)f'(\beta)|}\right]. \tag{19}$$

Clearly, if $q = 1$, then (19) is the same as (10). If we let $q = \frac{1}{2}$ in the inequality (18), then we have the following.

Corollary 2. *Suppose that $\alpha, \beta \in I^\circ$ and $\alpha < \beta$, the function $f : I^\circ \to \mathbb{R}$ is differentiable, and $|f'|^{\frac{1}{2}}$ is convex on $[\alpha, \beta]$, then for any $q \geq 1$, we have*

$$\left| f\left(\frac{\alpha+\beta}{2}\right) - \frac{1}{\beta-\alpha}\int_\alpha^\beta f(x)\mathrm{d}x \right| \leq \frac{\beta-\alpha}{4}\left[\frac{7}{12}A(|f'(\alpha)|,|f'(\beta)|) + \frac{5}{12}G(|f'(\alpha)|,|f'(\beta)|)\right]$$

$$\leq \frac{\beta-\alpha}{4}A(|f'(\alpha)|,|f'(\beta)|)$$

$$\leq \frac{\beta-\alpha}{4}[A(|f'(\alpha)|^q,|f'(\beta)|^q)]^{\frac{1}{q}}. \tag{20}$$

3. Lemmas

Lemma 1 (Lemma 2.1 in [1]). *Suppose that $\alpha, \beta \in I^\circ$ and $\alpha < \beta$, the function $f : I^\circ \to \mathbb{R}$ is differentiable, and $f' \in L[\alpha, \beta]$, then*

$$\frac{f(\alpha)+f(\beta)}{2} - \frac{1}{\beta-\alpha}\int_\alpha^\beta f(x)\mathrm{d}x = \frac{\beta-\alpha}{2}\int_0^1 (1-2t)f'[t\alpha+(1-t)\beta]\mathrm{d}t. \tag{21}$$

Lemma 2 (Lemma 2.1 in [4]). *Suppose that $\alpha, \beta \in I^\circ$ and $\alpha < \beta$, the function $f : I^\circ \to \mathbb{R}$ is differentiable, and $f' \in L[\alpha, \beta]$, then*

$$f\left(\frac{\alpha+\beta}{2}\right) - \frac{1}{\beta-\alpha}\int_\alpha^\beta f(x)\mathrm{d}x = (\beta-\alpha)\int_0^1 M(t)f'[t\alpha+(1-t)\beta]\mathrm{d}t, \tag{22}$$

where

$$M(t) = \begin{cases} -t, & t \in \left[0, \frac{1}{2}\right), \\ 1-t, & t \in \left[\frac{1}{2}, 1\right]. \end{cases}$$

The following result can be found in [5]. For the convenience of readers, we provide the proof below.

Lemma 3 (Lemma 2.1 in [5]). *Let $x, y > 0, r \in \mathbb{R} \setminus \{0\}$.*

(i) *If $r \geq 2$ or $0 < r \leq 1$, then*
$$x^r + (2^r - 2)x^{\frac{r}{2}}y^{\frac{r}{2}} + y^r \leq (x+y)^r \leq \frac{2^r}{2r}(x^r + (2r - 2)x^{\frac{r}{2}}y^{\frac{r}{2}} + y^r). \qquad (23)$$

(ii) *If $1 \leq r \leq 2$ or $r < 0$, then*
$$x^r + (2^r - 2)x^{\frac{r}{2}}y^{\frac{r}{2}} + y^r \geq (x+y)^r \geq \frac{2^r}{2r}(x^r + (2r - 2)x^{\frac{r}{2}}y^{\frac{r}{2}} + y^r). \qquad (24)$$

Each equality is true if and only if $r = 1, 2$ or $x = y$.

Proof. It is easy to see that every equality in (23) and (24) holds when $r = 1, 2$ or $x = y$, so we suppose that $r \neq 1, 2$, $y = 1$ and $x > 1$ in the following.

First, we prove that the left parts of the inequalities (23) and (24) hold, respectively. Let
$$f(x) = (x+1)^r - x^r - (2^r - 2)x^{\frac{r}{2}} - 1, \qquad x > 1,$$
$$g(t) = (1+t)^{r-1} - 1 - (2^{r-1} - 1)t^{\frac{r}{2}}, \qquad 0 < t < 1.$$

Then
$$f'(x) = rx^{r-1}g\left(\frac{1}{x}\right), \qquad x > 1,$$
$$g'(t) = (r-1)(1+t)^{r-2} - \frac{r}{2}(2^{r-1} - 1)t^{\frac{r}{2}-1}, \qquad 0 < t < 1.$$

The following proof is divided into four cases.

(1) If $r < 0$, then
$$g'(t) = -\left[(1-r)(1+t)^{r-2} - \frac{r}{2}(1 - 2^{r-1})t^{\frac{r}{2}-1}\right] < 0, \ 0 < t < 1.$$

Note that $g(1) = 0$, so $g(t) > 0$ ($0 < t < 1$). It follows that $f'(x) < 0$ ($x > 1$). Since $f(1) = 0$, we have $f(x) < 0$.

(2) If $0 < r < 1$, let
$$h_1(t) = -\left[\ln(1-r) + (r-2)\ln(1+t) - \ln\frac{r}{2} - \ln(1-2^{r-1}) - \left(\frac{r}{2} - 1\right)\ln t\right], \ 0 < t < 1,$$

then $h_1'(t) = -(\frac{r-2}{1+t} - \frac{r-2}{2t}) < 0$. It means that $h_1(t)$ is strictly decreasing on $(0, 1)$. Note that
$$h_1(0^+) = \ln\frac{r(1 - 2^{r-1})}{2(1-r)} + \frac{r-2}{2}\lim_{t \to 0^+}\ln t > 0,$$
$$h_1(1^-) = \ln\frac{r}{1-r} - \ln\frac{2^{r-1}}{1 - 2^{r-1}} < 0;$$

there exists $\xi_1 \in (0, 1)$, such that $h_1(t) > 0$ ($0 < t < \xi_1$) and $h_1(t) < 0$ ($\xi_1 < t < 1$). Since $g'(t)$ and $h_1(t)$ have the same sign, we obtain $g'(t) > 0$ ($0 < t < \xi_1$) and $g'(t) < 0$ ($\xi_1 < t < 1$). Note that $g(1) = g(0) = 0$, and we have $g(t) > 0$ ($0 < t < 1$). It follows that $f'(x) > 0$ ($x > 1$). Because $f(1) = 0$, we have $f(x) > 0$ ($x > 1$).

(3) If $1 < r < 2$, let
$$h_2(t) = \ln(r-1) + (r-2)\ln(1+t) - \ln\frac{r}{2} - \ln(2^{r-1} - 1) - \left(\frac{r}{2} - 1\right)\ln t,$$

then $h'_2(t) = \frac{r-2}{1+t} - \frac{r-2}{2t} > 0$. It means that $h_2(t)$ is strictly increasing on $(0,1)$. Note that

$$h_2(0^+) = \ln \frac{2(r-1)}{r(2^{r-1}-1)} - \frac{r-2}{2} \lim_{t \to 0^+} \ln t < 0,$$

$$h_2(1^-) = \ln \frac{r-1}{r} - \ln \frac{2^{r-1}-1}{2^{r-1}} > 0;$$

there exists $\xi_2 \in (0,1)$, such that $h_2(t) < 0$ $(0 < t < \xi_2)$ and $h_2(t) > 0$ $(\xi_2 < t < 1)$. Since $g'(t)$ and $h_2(t)$ have the same sign and $g(1) = g(0) = 0$, we have $g(t) < 0$ $(0 < t < 1)$. It follows that $f'(x) < 0$ $(x > 1)$. Note that $f(1) = 0$, and we have $f(x) < 0$ $(x > 1)$.

(4) If $r > 2$, then $h'_2(t) = \frac{r-2}{1+t} - \frac{r-2}{2t} < 0$. It means that $h_2(t)$ is strictly decreasing in $(0,1)$. Note that $h_2(0^+) > 0$, $h_2(1^-) < 0$, and there exists $\xi_3 \in (0,1)$, such that $h_2(t) > 0$ $(0 < t < \xi_3)$ and $h_2(t) < 0$ $(\xi_3 < t < 1)$. Since $g'(t)$ and $h_2(t)$ have the same sign and $g(1) = g(0) = 0$, we have $g(t) > 0$ $(0 < t < 1)$. It follows that $f'(x) > 0$ $(x > 1)$. Then by $f(1) = 0$, we have $f(x) > 0$ $(x > 1)$.

Next, we derive that the right parts of the inequalities (23) and (24) are true, respectively. Let

$$L(x) = (x+1)^r - \frac{2^r}{2r}(x^r + (2r-2)x^{\frac{r}{2}} + 1), \qquad x > 1,$$

$$l(t) = r(t+1)^{r-1} - 2^{r-1} - 2^{r-1}(r-1)t^{\frac{r}{2}}, \qquad 0 < t < 1.$$

Then

$$L'(x) = x^{r-1} l\left(\frac{1}{x}\right), \qquad x > 1,$$

$$l'(t) = 2^{r-2} r(r-1) t^{\frac{r}{2}-1}\left[\left(\frac{t+1}{2\sqrt{t}}\right)^{r-2} - 1\right], \qquad 0 < t < 1.$$

If $0 < r < 1$ or $r > 2$, then $l'(t) > 0$. Note that $l(1) = 0$, we have $l(t) < 0$ $(0 < t < 1)$, and $L'(x) < 0$ $(x > 1)$. Then by $L(1) = 0$, we have $L(x) < 0$ $(x > 1)$, so the right parts of the inequalities (23) holds.

If $r < 0$ or $1 < r < 2$, then $l'(t) < 0$. Note that $l(1) = 0$, we have $l(t) > 0$ $(0 < t < 1)$ and $L'(x) > 0$ $(x > 1)$. Then by $L(1) = 0$, we have $L(x) > 0$ $(x > 1)$, so the right parts of the inequalities (24) holds.

The proof is complete. □

Lemma 4. *Suppose that $\alpha, \beta \in I^\circ$, $\alpha < \beta$, $0 < q \leq 1$, $0 < t < 1$, the function $f : I \to [0,+\infty)$ is positive, and f^q is convex on $[\alpha,\beta]$.*

(i) *If $0 < q \leq \frac{1}{2}$, then*

$$f[t\alpha + (1-t)\beta] \leq q 2^{\frac{1}{q}-1}\left[t^{\frac{1}{q}} f(\alpha) + (1-t)^{\frac{1}{q}} f(\beta) + \left(\frac{2}{q} - 2\right)(t(1-t))^{\frac{1}{2q}} \sqrt{f(\alpha)f(\beta)}\right]. \tag{25}$$

(ii) *If $\frac{1}{2} \leq q \leq 1$, then*

$$f[t\alpha + (1-t)\beta] \leq t^{\frac{1}{q}} f(\alpha) + (1-t)^{\frac{1}{q}} f(\beta) + (2^{\frac{1}{q}} - 2)(t(1-t))^{\frac{1}{2q}} \sqrt{f(\alpha)f(\beta)}. \tag{26}$$

Proof. Since f^q is convex and $q > 0$, we have

$$f[t\alpha + (1-t)\beta] \leq [tf^q(\alpha) + (1-t)f^q(\beta)]^{\frac{1}{q}}.$$

If $0 < q \leq \frac{1}{2}$, then $\frac{1}{q} \geq 2$, by the right-hand side of the inequalities (23), then

$$[tf^q(\alpha)+(1-t)f^q(\beta)]^{\frac{1}{q}} \leq q 2^{\frac{1}{q}-1}\left[t^{\frac{1}{q}}f(\alpha)+(1-t)^{\frac{1}{q}}f(\beta)+\left(\frac{2}{q}-2\right)(t(1-t))^{\frac{1}{2q}}\sqrt{f(\alpha)f(\beta)}\right].$$

Thus, the inequality (25) is valid.

If $\frac{1}{2} \leq q \leq 1$, then $1 \leq \frac{1}{q} \leq 2$, by the left-hand side of the inequalities (24) we have

$$[tf^q(\alpha)+(1-t)f^q(\beta)]^{\frac{1}{q}} \leq t^{\frac{1}{q}}f(\alpha)+(1-t)^{\frac{1}{q}}f(\beta)+(2^{\frac{1}{q}}-2)(t(1-t))^{\frac{1}{2q}}\sqrt{f(\alpha)f(\beta)}.$$

Hence, the inequality (26) is valid.
□

4. Derivation of Theorem 6 and 7

The derivation of Theorem 6: (i) If $0 < q \leq \frac{1}{2}$, then by the inequalities (21) and (25), we can derive that

$$\left|\frac{f(\alpha)+f(\beta)}{2} - \frac{1}{\beta-\alpha}\int_\alpha^\beta f(x)dx\right|$$

$$\leq \frac{\beta-\alpha}{2}\int_0^1 |1-2t||f'[t\alpha+(1-t)\beta]|dt$$

$$\leq \frac{(\beta-\alpha)q 2^{\frac{1}{q}-1}}{2}\int_0^1 |1-2t|\left[t^{\frac{1}{q}}|f'(\alpha)|+(1-t)^{\frac{1}{q}}|f'(\beta)|+\left(\frac{2}{q}-2\right)(t(1-t))^{\frac{1}{2q}}\sqrt{|f'(\alpha)f'(\beta)|}\right]dt.$$

Note that

$$\int_0^1 |1-2t|(1-t)^{\frac{1}{q}}dt$$
$$= \int_0^1 |1-2t|t^{\frac{1}{q}}dt$$
$$= \int_0^{\frac{1}{2}} (1-2t)t^{\frac{1}{q}}dt - \int_{\frac{1}{2}}^1 (1-2t)t^{\frac{1}{q}}dt$$
$$= \frac{q(1+q\cdot 2^{\frac{-1}{q}})}{(q+1)(2q+1)},$$

and

$$\int_0^1 |1-2t|(t(1-t))^{\frac{1}{2q}}dt$$
$$= \int_0^{\frac{1}{2}} (1-2t)(t(1-t))^{\frac{1}{2q}}dt - \int_{\frac{1}{2}}^1 (1-2t)(t(1-t))^{\frac{1}{2q}}dt$$
$$= \frac{2q}{2q+1}(t(1-t))^{\frac{1}{2q}+1}\Big|_0^{\frac{1}{2}} - \frac{2q}{2q+1}(t(1-t))^{\frac{1}{2q}+1}\Big|_{\frac{1}{2}}^1$$
$$= \frac{q\cdot 2^{\frac{-1}{q}}}{2q+1},$$

so (15) is valid.

(ii) If $\frac{1}{2} < q \leq 1$, then by (21) and (26), we have

$$\left|\frac{f(\alpha)+f(\beta)}{2} - \frac{1}{\beta-\alpha}\int_\alpha^\beta f(x)dx\right|$$

$$\leq \frac{\beta-\alpha}{2}\int_0^1 |1-2t||f'[t\alpha+(1-t)\beta]|dt$$

$$\leq \frac{\beta-\alpha}{2}\int_0^1 |1-2t|\left[t^{\frac{1}{q}}|f(\alpha)|+(1-t)^{\frac{1}{q}}|f(\beta)|+(2^{\frac{1}{q}}-2)(t(1-t))^{\frac{1}{2q}}\sqrt{|f(\alpha)f(\beta)|}\right]dt$$

$$= \frac{q(\beta-\alpha)}{2(2q+1)}\left[\frac{1+q\cdot 2^{-\frac{1}{q}}}{q+1}(|f'(\alpha)|+|f'(\beta)|)+\left(1-2^{1-\frac{1}{q}}\right)\sqrt{|f'(\alpha)f'(\beta)|}\right].$$

so (16) is valid.

The derivation of Theorem 7: (i) If $0 < q \leq \frac{1}{2}$, then by (22) and (25) we can derive that

$$\left|f\left(\frac{\alpha+\beta}{2}\right) - \frac{1}{\beta-\alpha}\int_\alpha^\beta f(x)dx\right|$$

$$\leq (\beta-\alpha)\int_0^1 |M(t)||f'[t\alpha+(1-t)\beta]|dt$$

$$\leq (\beta-\alpha)q2^{\frac{1}{q}-1}\int_0^1 |M(t)|\left[t^{\frac{1}{q}}|f'(\alpha)|+(1-t)^{\frac{1}{q}}|f'(\beta)|+\left(\frac{2}{q}-2\right)(t(1-t))^{\frac{1}{2q}}\sqrt{|f'(\alpha)f'(\beta)|}\right]dt.$$

Note that

$$\int_0^1 |M(t)|(1-t)^{\frac{1}{q}}dt$$

$$= \int_0^1 |M(t)|t^{\frac{1}{q}}dt$$

$$= \int_0^{\frac{1}{2}} t^{\frac{1}{q}+1}dt + \int_{\frac{1}{2}}^1 (1-t)t^{\frac{1}{q}}dt$$

$$= \frac{q^2(1-2^{-\frac{1}{q}-1})}{(q+1)(2q+1)},$$

and

$$\int_0^1 |M(t)|(t(1-t))^{\frac{1}{2q}}dt$$

$$= \int_0^{\frac{1}{2}} t^{\frac{1}{2q}+1}(1-t)^{\frac{1}{2q}}dt + \int_{\frac{1}{2}}^1 t^{\frac{1}{2q}}(1-t)^{\frac{1}{2q}+1}dt$$

$$= -\frac{q\cdot 2^{-\frac{1}{q}-1}}{2q+1} + B\left(\frac{1}{2q}+1,\frac{1}{2q}+2\right)$$

where the beta function is

$$B(x,y) = \int_0^1 t^{x-1}(1-t)^{y-1}dt, \ x > 0, \ y > 0.$$

Clearly, $B(x,x)$ is decreasing on $(0,+\infty)$ and $\frac{1}{2q} \geq 1$, then

$$B\left(\frac{1}{2q}+1,\frac{1}{2q}+2\right) = \frac{1}{2}B\left(\frac{1}{2q}+1,\frac{1}{2q}+1\right) \leq \frac{1}{2}B(2,2) = \frac{1}{12}.$$

Thus, (18) is valid.

(ii) If $\frac{1}{2} < q \leq 1$, then by (22) and (26), we can induce that

$$\left| f\left(\frac{\alpha+\beta}{2}\right) - \frac{1}{\beta-\alpha}\int_\alpha^\beta f(x)dx \right|$$

$$\leq (\beta-\alpha)\int_0^1 |M(t)||f'[t\alpha+(1-t)\beta]|dt$$

$$\leq (\beta-\alpha)\int_0^1 |M(t)|\left[t^{\frac{1}{q}}|f(\alpha)| + (1-t)^{\frac{1}{q}}|f(\beta)| + (2^{\frac{1}{q}}-2)(t(1-t))^{\frac{1}{2q}}\sqrt{|f(\alpha)f(\beta)|}\right]dt$$

$$\leq \frac{q(\beta-\alpha)}{2(2q+1)}\left[\frac{q\left(2-2^{-\frac{1}{q}}\right)}{q+1}(|f'(\alpha)|+|f'(\beta)|) + \left(2^{\frac{1}{q}}-2\right)\left(\frac{1}{3}+\frac{1}{6q}-2^{-\frac{1}{q}}\right)\sqrt{|f'(\alpha)f'(\beta)|}\right].$$

Thus, (19) is valid.

5. Applications

In this section, we will use Corollary 1 and Corollary 2 to establish some error estimates on special means, then the inequalities (11)–(14) are improved.

Proposition 1. *Suppose that $s,t \in \mathbb{R}$, $s < t$, $0 \notin [s,t]$, $n \in \mathbb{Z}$, $n \geq 3$ or $n \leq -2$, then*

$$|A(s^n,t^n) - L_n(s,t)^n| \leq \frac{|n|(t-s)}{4}\left[\frac{3}{4}A\left(|s|^{n-1},|t|^{n-1}\right) + \frac{1}{4}G\left(|s|^{n-1},|t|^{n-1}\right)\right], \qquad (27)$$

$$|A(s,t)^n - L_n(s,t)^n| \leq \frac{|n|(t-s)}{4}\left[\frac{7}{12}A\left(|s|^{n-1},|t|^{n-1}\right) + \frac{5}{12}G\left(|s|^{n-1},|t|^{n-1}\right)\right]. \qquad (28)$$

Proof. Let $f(x) = x^n$, $x \in [s,t]$, $n \in \mathbb{Z}$, $n \geq 3$ or $n \leq -2$, then

$$\left(|f'(x)|^{\frac{1}{2}}\right)'' = \frac{\sqrt{|n|}(n-1)(n-3)}{4}|x|^{\frac{n-5}{2}} \geq 0.$$

Thus, $|f'(x)|^{\frac{1}{2}}$ is convex on $[s,t]$. It follows that (27) and (28) hold by using Corollary 1 and Corollary 2, respectively. □

Remark 1. *For any $q \geq 1$, by the inequalities (17) and (20), we have*

$$\frac{|n|(t-s)}{4}\left[\frac{3}{4}A\left(|s|^{n-1},|t|^{n-1}\right) + \frac{1}{4}G\left(|s|^{n-1},|t|^{n-1}\right)\right] \leq \frac{|n|(t-s)}{4}\left[A\left(|s|^{(n-1)q},|t|^{(n-1)q}\right)\right]^{\frac{1}{q}},$$

and

$$\frac{|n|(t-s)}{4}\left[\frac{7}{12}A\left(|s|^{n-1},|t|^{n-1}\right) + \frac{5}{12}G\left(|s|^{n-1},|t|^{n-1}\right)\right] \leq \frac{|n|(t-s)}{4}\left[A\left(|s|^{(n-1)q},|t|^{(n-1)q}\right)\right]^{\frac{1}{q}}.$$

Thus, for $n \geq 3$ or $n \leq -2$, we obtain an improvement of the inequalities (11) and (12), which is an improvement of the inequalities (5) and (6).

Proposition 2. *Suppose that $s,t \in \mathbb{R}$, $s < t$, $0 \notin [s,t]$, then*

$$|A\left(s^{-1},t^{-1}\right) - L(s,t)^{-1}| \leq \frac{t-s}{4}\left[\frac{3}{4}A\left(s^{-2},t^{-2}\right) + \frac{1}{4}G\left(s^{-2},t^{-2}\right)\right], \qquad (29)$$

$$|A(s,t)^{-1} - L(s,t)^{-1}| \leq \frac{t-s}{4}\left[\frac{7}{12}A\left(s^{-2}, t^{-2}\right) + \frac{5}{12}G\left(s^{-2}, t^{-2}\right)\right]. \quad (30)$$

Proof. Let $f(x) = \frac{1}{x}$, $x \in [s,t]$, then

$$\left(|f'(x)|^{\frac{1}{2}}\right)'' = \frac{2}{|x|^3} \geq 0.$$

Thus, $|f'(x)|^{\frac{1}{2}}$ is convex on $[s,t]$. It follows that (29) and (30) hold by using Corollary 1 and Corollary 2, respectively. □

Remark 2. For any $q \geq 1$, by the inequalities (17) and (20), we have

$$\frac{t-s}{4}\left[\frac{3}{4}A\left(s^{-2}, t^{-2}\right) + \frac{1}{4}G\left(s^{-2}, t^{-2}\right)\right] \leq \frac{t-s}{4}\left[A\left(|s|^{-2q}, |t|^{-2q}\right)\right]^{\frac{1}{q}},$$

and

$$\frac{t-s}{4}\left[\frac{7}{12}A\left(s^{-2}, t^{-2}\right) + \frac{5}{12}G\left(s^{-2}, t^{-2}\right)\right] \leq \frac{t-s}{4}\left[A\left(|s|^{-2q}, |t|^{-2q}\right)\right]^{\frac{1}{q}}.$$

Thus, we obtain an improvement of the inequalities (13) and (14), which is an improvement of the inequalities (7) and (8).

Proposition 3. Suppose that $t > s > 0$, then

$$\ln I(s,t) - \ln G(s,t) \leq \frac{t-s}{4}\left[\frac{3}{4}A\left(s^{-1}, t^{-1}\right) + \frac{1}{4}G\left(s^{-1}, t^{-1}\right)\right], \quad (31)$$

$$\ln A(s,t) - \ln I(s,t) \leq \frac{t-s}{4}\left[\frac{7}{12}A\left(s^{-1}, t^{-1}\right) + \frac{5}{12}G\left(s^{-1}, t^{-1}\right)\right]. \quad (32)$$

Proof. Let $f(x) = \ln x$, $x \in [s,t]$, then

$$\left(|f'(x)|^{\frac{1}{2}}\right)'' = \frac{3}{4}|x|^{-\frac{5}{2}} \geq 0.$$

Thus, $|f'(x)|^{\frac{1}{2}}$ is convex on $[s,t]$. It follows that (31) and (32) hold by using Corollary 1 and Corollary 2, respectively. □

Author Contributions: Conceptualization, T.Z. and A.C.; methodology, T.Z.; validation, T.Z.; formal analysis, T.Z. and A.C.; investigation, T.Z.; resources, T.Z.; writing—original draft preparation, T.Z.; funding acquisition, T.Z. and A.C. All authors have read and agreed to the published version of the manuscript.

Funding: This work was supported by the National Natural Science Foundation of China (No. 11761029, No. 62161044) and the Natural Science Foundation of Inner Mongolia (Grant No. 2021LHMS01008).

Data Availability Statement: Not applicable.

Conflicts of Interest: The authors declare no conflict of interest.

References

1. Dragomir, S.S.; Agarwal, R.P. Two inequalities for differentiable mappings and applications to special means of real numbers and to trapezoidal formula. *Appl. Math. Lett.* **1998**, *11*, 91–95. [CrossRef]
2. Dragomir, S.S.; Pearce, C.E.M. *Selected Topics on Hermite-Hadamard Inequalities and Applications*; RGMIA Monographs, Victoria University: Melbourne, Australia, 2000.
3. Pearce, C.E.M.; Pečarixcx, J. Inequalities for differentiable mappings with application to special means and quadrature formulae. *Appl. Math. Lett.* **2000**, *13*, 51–55. [CrossRef]
4. Kirmaci, U.S. Inequalities for differentiable mappings and applications to special means of real numbers and to midpoint formula. *Appl. Math. Comp.* **2004**, *147*, 137–146. [CrossRef]
5. Zhang, T.; Xi, B.Y.; Alatancang. Compared of generalized heronian means and power means. *Math. Pract. Theory* **2012**, *42*, 235–240. (In Chinese)

Disclaimer/Publisher's Note: The statements, opinions and data contained in all publications are solely those of the individual author(s) and contributor(s) and not of MDPI and/or the editor(s). MDPI and/or the editor(s) disclaim responsibility for any injury to people or property resulting from any ideas, methods, instructions or products referred to in the content.